Public Budgeting in African Nations

Public Budgeting in African Nations offers essential budgeting and fiscal policy management information to development practitioners interested in improving governance and the performance of government. It shares timely regional and cross-cultural experiences with international audiences and gives reflective attention to comparative budgeting and fiscal policy management.

This book adopts an interdisciplinary and pragmatic approach to analyzing research findings on public budgeting as a sustainable development tool, revealing that development practice benefits most from bottom-up, decentralized tactics of budgeting and fiscal policy, with the involvement of national, sub-national, and civil society institutions. The chapters in this volume together demonstrate that a balanced budget should draw from and reflect values and priorities across the full spectrum of social and political life.

Peter Fuseini Haruna is Professor of Public Administration at Texas A&M International University, USA and a 2010–2011 Fulbright Senior Scholar to Ghana.

Shikha Vyas-Doorgapersad is Professor of Public Management and Governance at the University of Johannesburg, South Africa.

Public Budgeting in African Nations

Fiscal Analysis in Development Management

Edited by
Peter Fuseini Haruna and
Shikha Vyas-Doorgapersad

Routledge
Taylor & Francis Group
NEW YORK AND LONDON

First published 2016
by Routledge
711 Third Avenue, New York, NY 10017

and by Routledge
2 Park Square, Milton Park, Abingdon, Oxon OX14 4RN

Routledge is an imprint of the Taylor & Francis Group, an informa business

Library of Congress Cataloging in Publication Data
Names: Haruna, Peter Fuseini, editor. | Vyas-Doorgapersad, Shikha, editor.
Title: Public budgeting in African nations : fiscal analysis in development management/edited by Peter Fuseini Haruna and Shikha Vyas-Doorgapersad.
Description: New York: Routledge, 2016. | Includes bibliographical references and index.
Identifiers: LCCN 2015036306| ISBN 9781498742139 (cloth: alk. paper) | ISBN 9781315637273 (ebook)
Subjects: LCSH: Finance, Public—Africa. | Budget—Africa. | Fiscal policy—Africa. | Public administration—Africa. | Economic development—Africa.
Classification: LCC HJ1441 .P83 2016 | DDC 352.4/8096—dc23LC record available at http://lccn.loc.gov/2015036306

ISBN: (hbk) 978-1-4987-4213-9
ISBN: (ebk) 978-1-315-63727-3

Typeset in Goudy
by Florence Production Ltd, Stoodleigh, Devon, UK

Contents

Figures and Tables

Figures

Tables

Foreword

There is a general consensus among economists that the budget is the meeting point between politics and reality. This is underscored by the tripartite role the budget is designed to play as a tool for enhancing macro-economic stability, communicating public policy, and translating government policies and programs into action. In the post-independence African context, in particular, the budget is expected to be the most important instrument through which government at all levels delivers the dividends of good governance such as reducing poverty and unemployment, and sustaining the pace of economic growth and development. The budget is the means by which governments provide public services and fulfill the goals and aspirations of their citizens. In a democracy, these goals and aspirations are often embodied in the election manifestos of the political parties that end up forming the governments; and are enacted by parliaments through annual appropriations. In authoritarian and non-democratic societies, budgets are enacted through decrees.

In an ideal world, public expenditure has to be *effective*—that is, it must achieve its purposes on time and with due regard to quality. This includes timely completion of infrastructure programs. Public expenditure has to be *efficient*. This includes completing projects and delivering services within the budget allocated—also called value for money. Public expenditure has to be *relevant*. This implies being directly related to its purpose, and not tangential. Public expenditure has to be *sustainable*. Sustainability implies the ability of government to incur the level of public expenditure that is approved or enacted by the legislatures, over a reasonable period. Such level of expenditure may be financed through taxation, external borrowing, and grants. Public expenditure has to involve *partnership* between the government and the public, as well as between the government and its development partners. The practice of public expenditure must include continuous *learning*. This means that lessons must be learned and shared—within the government and between practitioners and academicians. Learning must also be shared between advanced nations and developing nations—in part to avoid making the same mistakes over and over. Public expenditure must be *transparent* and *ethical* in order to help the various stakeholders feel confident that tax gathered is being used with due regard to safe-guarding the public interests. Finally, in order to be truly owned by the citizens, public expenditure decisions should ideally be formulated through a *participatory* process.

Unfortunately, in 2015 after many decades of independence, most African economies are yet to use the budget to harness their huge mineral and natural resource endowments to realize their economic potentials. This book does an impressive job of investigating this phenomenon in a scholarly fashion and provides a workable solution to the issue of how governments' budgets can best be adapted to foster inclusive growth and economic development in Africa. This compilation of the historical experiences in a sample of African countries will help enhance the understanding required to develop budgets that are sustainable, aligned with international best practice and most importantly, provide effective domestic economic development policy that takes into full consideration its socio-cultural environment.

The case studies drawn across many African economies are rich in content, academically robust, practical in context and intellectually engaging. The authors generally argue that development occurs in specific contexts and that in African nations, that context and landscape encompass historical legacies of slavery and colonialism, as well as unique economic, social, political, and cultural experiences. This fact is often ignored in economic policy blueprints in Africa, which in turn underpins most public financial management systems. Thus this kind of work is much needed as Africa grapples with the challenges of development and will go a long way to contribute towards the enhancing of knowledge and understanding of the use of public budgeting in accelerating socio-economic development in the African continent. This book makes significant contributions towards expanding our theoretical and empirical understanding of public expenditure formulation and management.

I commend the authors for this brilliant work. They can be assured that there will be many grateful readers who will have gained a broader perspective on the importance of fiscal sustainability in budgeting as a result of their efforts.

Joseph Makwata Wambia, MSC (Econ.)/MBA (Finance)
AECOM Technology Services Corporation

Preface

As Africa transitions steadily toward consolidating a democratic culture with emphasis on economic and political good governance, considerable attention must be directed to public budgeting, fiscal policy, and financial management to assure equity and sustainable development. There is no question that much effort has gone into reforming and improving fiscal policy and public financial management in that regard but much more remains to be done to achieve fiscal sustainability. This book captures and analyzes the essence of this reform effort in 11 African nations, while offering insights and research findings about how to move forward. The focus of the book is to highlight national experiences and present research findings within the framework of sustainable development that will be of interest to academics, policy-makers, and development practitioners. The detailed analyses of budgeting and fiscal policy management will expand and enrich the literature on African nations.

The book originated from our interest in contributing to the study and practice of public budgeting and fiscal policy in the context and culture of development management. Although budgeting and fiscal policy have been studied quite intensively in OECD member nations, this is not the case with African nations. Despite the research sponsored by the World Bank and International Monetary Fund, Africa remains relatively under-researched and ill-understood in terms of budgeting and fiscal policy management. While the existing studies have contributed valuable insights about the difficulties and challenges of budgeting and fiscal management systems, they often take an external perspective. Africa's own home-grown budget and fiscal policy initiatives are only just emerging. Focused research and scholarship from within that takes an internal perspective is lacking and sorely needed. This book is intended to fill that gap and provide essential reading for that purpose.

Our readers will find answers to questions, such as:

- How do African nations approach public budgeting and fiscal policy management?
- How has public budgeting and fiscal policy management changed in African nations?

- How can African nations create a culture of sustainable budgeting and fiscal policy?
- How can African nations achieve fiscal and financial sustainability?
- How do context and culture affect budgeting and fiscal policy in African nations?
- What challenges do public budgeting and fiscal policy face in African nations?
- What lessons have African nations learned about budgeting and fiscal policy?

In this research endeavor we focus on contributing new knowledge about how to cultivate a culture of sustainable budgeting, fiscal policy, and financial management that is relevant to and useful in African nations. It is essentially about knowledge and scholarship without delving into issues of a political nature. Our chapter contributors do not make statements about matters of national sovereignty but they do emphasize policy choices as being integral to budgeting and fiscal management. The term African nation is used in the book conservatively to refer to existing geographical areas and national boundaries in which formal budgetary, fiscal policy, and financial management processes are designed, implemented and maintained. In this respect, chapter authors with specific research and scholarly interests in African development were selected and specifically instructed to address national experiences with public budgeting and fiscal policy management while tying their analysis back to the common body of knowledge and scholarship defining the sub-field at a continental or global level as appropriate.

One of the motivations for the book is to provide budgeting, fiscal, and financial information to researchers and policy-makers interested in improving the quality of government performance. Peter Haruna starts off by analyzing the colonial heritage, examining socio-cultural experiences, and arguing for a sustainable approach to budgeting and fiscal policy management. In this sense, sustainable budgeting and fiscal policy should reflect the values and priorities across the spectrum of social and political life. Taolo Lucas and Theophilus Tshukudu trace the evolution of budgeting in Botswana from transitional through development planning to the current five-year strategies based on which projects are prioritized and resources allocated. Peter Ngwafu and Viviane Foyou analyze Cameroon and argue that it models budgeting and fiscal policy management after France, but also departs from it in terms of practice. Likewise, Lloyd Amoah offers a historical analysis of Ghana and argues that its budgeting and fiscal policy model minimizes rather than optimizes transformation. Building on this argument, Frank Ohemeng suggests in Chapter five that Ghana should move toward performance-based budgeting, a model that emphasizes results and outcomes. In Chapter six, Abel Meru and Rogers M'ariba affirm that Kenya's budget remains a development tool but that more coherence between planning and policy objectives is needed. Happy Kayuni contends that Malawi's budgeting system is a bureaucratic routine requiring reform to turn it into a vibrant tool for socio-economic development. Gerrit Waldt and Shikha Vyas-Doorgapersad examine South Africa, pointing out historical imbalances and challenges in public budgeting and also emphasizing the mechanisms for assuring accountability. Benon Basheka explores the theoretical foundation of budgeting and argues that much more needs to be done in Uganda to achieve development. On Zimbabwe, Gideon Zhou, Ricky Mukonza, and Hardlife Zvoushe analyze budgeting as the means for engineering sustainable development. Dominique Uwizeyimana's study of Rwanda captures the essence of the development strategy and connects it to the public financial management reform. Denis Kamugisha and John Kihamba emphasize the dominant role of the executive in budgeting and the consequences and implications for addressing citizens' preferences in Tanzania. In the concluding chapter, Peter Haruna and Shikha Vyas-Doorgapersad critique Africa's existing budget models and suggest reform with potential for achieving sustainable budgeting and fiscal policy management.

With the foregoing stimulating analyses and discussions, it is our aim that the book:

- blends experiential and theoretical generation of knowledge for development management;
- distils knowledge, skills, and abilities for implementing budgeting and fiscal policy;
- offers guidance to researchers, faculties, and students striving for updated and detailed understanding of public budgeting, fiscal policy, and financial management in Africa; and
- deals with emerging trends in public budgeting and fiscal policy management in Africa.

Finally, we would like to express our sincere gratitude to our publisher, Taylor and Francis, for providing us with the opportunity to share our insights with readers, and for supporting us. Their review processes and the advice provided to the editors and individual authors have greatly enhanced the quality of the final product. We also wish to thank individual experts who volunteered to review the chapters to improve their relevance and usefulness to development.

Peter Fuseini Haruna and
Shikha Vyas-Doorgapersad (Co-Editors)

Acknowledgments

An edited book volume can only be accomplished through the dedication and hard work of chapter contributors who share in its goal and purpose. These authors find fulfillment in the opportunity to tell their part of the unique story of public budgeting, fiscal policy, and financial management in Africa's emerging democracies. For our part as co-editors, we have had the honor of working with them conscientiously to bring the book to life. We wish to acknowledge the work and professionalism of the project coordinator, supervisor, and production staff at Taylor and Francis Publisher. Their guidance and reviews made this publication possible. As well, several people made it possible for us to work on this project through their support and cooperation. They include the leadership of our universities (Texas A&M International University and University of Johannesburg) and colleagues who have helped us beyond words. We deeply appreciate their support and contributions.

Peter Fuseini Haruna and
Shikha Vyas-Doorgapersad (Co-Editors)

About the Editors

Peter Fuseini Haruna is a 2010–2011 Fulbright Senior Scholar to Ghana and Professor of Public Administration in the Department of Social Sciences at Texas A&M International University, Laredo, Texas. He received his Ph.D. in Public Administration from The University of Akron, Akron, Ohio and his Post-Graduate Diploma in Public Management and Administration from the Ghana Institute of Management and Public Administration. He is a long-time member of the faculty of the Texas Certified Public Managers Chapter, who has taught undergraduate and graduate courses in public administration for 15 years. He has served as Associate Dean of the College of Arts & Sciences and played a leading role in both graduate and undergraduate programmatic assessment and quality control. His international experiences include serving as Director of Administration in the Ghana Civil Service and Director of Administration for the Scientific Instrumentation Center in Accra, Ghana, which is sponsored by the United Nations Development Programme. He also serves as an external examiner for the University of KwaZulu-Natal and the University of Zululand in South Africa. His current teaching, research, and outreach focus on international and comparative administration, public budgeting and finance, leadership, and governance structures, as well as public service education and training. His research and work have been presented at regional, national and international conferences and in books and journals. He is co-editor and author of *Public Administration Training in Africa: Competencies in Development Management* (Taylor & Francis, 2015). His peer-reviewed articles have appeared in *Public Administration Review*, *Public Integrity*, *Administrative Theory & Praxis*, *International Journal of Public Administration*, *Journal of Public Affairs Education*, and *African Studies Review*. His scholarly work has won awards and recognition including International Scholar of the Year (2010), University Honours Program Faculty of the Year (2011) and College of Arts & Sciences Scholar of the Year (2005). In addition to being a regular manuscript reviewer for several leading journals, he is also affiliated to professional associations including the American Society of Public Administration, the Public Administration Theory Network, and the Association for Research in Nonprofit Management.

Shikha Vyas-Doorgapersad is a Professor at University of Johannesburg, South Africa. She holds the degrees of M.A., M.Phil., and Ph.D. in Public Administration from the University of Rajasthan (India). She is involved in the Global Excellence and Stature Initiative at University of Johannesburg dealing with developing academic and research partnerships with universities (public management and public administration departments), world wide.

Her lecturing and research interests are in public policy, gender issues, and municipal governance. She has presented research findings at international conferences in India, South Africa, Namibia, Abu Dhabi, Mauritius, Brazil, Indonesia, Uganda, Botswana, Canada and Japan, and virtually in Greece and Italy. She has authored two books, edited two books, contributed chapters in books, and has published more than forty articles in national and international accredited and peer-reviewed journals. She serves as a guest editor, associate editor, and reviewer for South African and international journals including *Journal of Public Affairs*, USA; *International Journal of Interdisciplinary Social Sciences*, Australia; *International Journal of Environmental, Cultural, Economic and Social Sustainability*, Australia; and the South African journals *Journal for Trans-disciplinary Research in Southern Africa*, *Journal of Public Administration*, *Politeia*, *Administratio Publica*, *Agenda*, *New Contree*, and *Town and Regional Planning*. She is a member of international associations such as Africa Institute of South Africa; South African Association for Public Administration and Management; Association of Southern African Schools and Departments of Public Administration and Management; Indian Institute of Public Administration; Indian Society for Training and Development; The Centre for Administrative Change, and Public Relations Society of India. She has supervised sixteen master dissertations and promoted three doctorates. She serves as an external moderator or examiner for M.A.s and Ph.D.s for several universities in South Africa.

1 Public Budgeting and Fiscal Sustainability in African Nations: Opportunities and Challenges in Development Management

Peter Fuseini Haruna

Introduction

Fiscal sustainability is a challenge to governments, especially those of developing nations faced with fragile economies and poor resource management capacity. This is more so with African nations that seem to be trapped between fiscal opportunity and fiscal vulnerability (Africa Progress Panel, 2013, 2014, 2015; York & Zhan, 2009).[1] The Africa Progress Panel paints a rosy picture of fiscal opportunity in which Africa stands to gain from the use of its natural resource wealth to transform the quality of life. In fact, sub-Saharan Africa is forecast to remain one of the fastest growing regions with an estimated growth of 5.2 percent during 2015–2016 (World Bank, 2014). But the reports also raise concern about fiscal vulnerability and uncertainty surrounding the proper management of economic growth toward achieving fiscal sustainability. It is unclear how governments can restrict expansion in current spending that has resulted in a pandemic of fiscal imbalances. In short, there is a risk that opportunities presented by oil, gas, and mineral wealth can easily dissipate if adjustments are not made in budgeting and fiscal reform. The question of interest then is: how should African nations approach budgeting in a manner that fosters fiscal sustainability and thereby advance the course of good governance?

Equitable and inclusive growth is a running theme in the Africa Progress Panel (APP) reports. The 2013 APP report (p. 4) raises the concern that: "In many countries, for example, although much has been achieved, a decade of highly impressive growth has not brought comparable improvement in health, education, and nutrition." While acknowledging that there is evidence of encouraging developments, the 2014 Africa Progress Report (p. 14) is clear:

> Yet the progress in reducing poverty, improving people's lives and putting in place the foundations for more inclusive and sustainable growth has been less impressive. Governments have failed to convert the wealth created by economic growth into opportunities that all Africans can exploit to build a better future. The time has come to set the course towards more inclusive growths and fairer societies.

But how, then, can African nations begin the process of building "inclusive growths and fairer societies"? The 2014 Africa Progress Report continues with verve and clarity:

> Governments urgently need to make sure that economic growth doesn't just create wealth for some, but improves well-being for the majority. Above all, that means strengthening the focus on Africa's greatest and most productive assets, the region's farms and fisheries. This report calls for more effective protection, management and mobilization of the continent's vast ocean and forest resources. This protection is needed to support transformative growth.
>
> p. 14

This chapter contends that transformative growth requires reform in budgeting and fiscal management, one anchored in and by fiscal sustainability. Current budgeting approaches that are fixated on short-term fiscal objectives are unsustainable in the long run. As Stein argued long ago, "if something is unsustainable, it will stop" (Stein cited in Posner et al., 2013, p. 25). However, with the exception of a few studies (e.g., York & Zhan, 2009) that examine fiscal sustainability in oil-producing African nations, much of the contemporary discourse mostly addresses short-term budgeting and fiscal management. For example, the United Nations Human Settlements Programme and Municipal Development Partnership (2008) recommend participatory budgeting that has the potential to "improve transparency" and "strengthen social networks" while mediating "differences between elected leaders and civil society groups." Likewise, the Africa Parliamentary Strengthening Program for Budget Oversight (2010) exerts efforts on clarifying the "consultative process during budget preparation," emphasizing the need to strengthen the supervisory role of African legislatures in public budgeting and fiscal management. Of course, this kind of work is much needed and has contributed to the enhancement of knowledge and understanding of public budgeting in the context of development management. Nonetheless, on the question of public budgeting as the means of acquiring financial resources and allocating them judiciously among competing public purposes to serve both current and long-term interests of society, much more work needs to be done.

The perspective taken in this chapter is that fiscal sustainability—taking a long-term strategic view of the ability to finance both current and future public needs—presents continent-wide opportunities and challenges, but that this perspective has hardly gained the needed critical mass to translate it into coherent budgeting and fiscal administration policy. The theme of fiscal sustainability resonates well with and reinforces an emerging stream of public administration and policy theorizing that emphasizes a holistic, equitable, and far-sighted approach to decision-making (Zanetti & King, 2013; Cohen, 2011; Leuenberger & Bartle, 2009; Nelson, 1999). In a nutshell, a sustainability approach has the potential not only to alter the ways that humans relate to each other, but also how natural and human resources are nurtured, harnessed, and allocated for public interest purposes over time. Thus the theme of fiscal sustainability ought to foster knowledge, skill, and ability not just in short-term economic growth, but also in a deep sense of fiscal responsibility, interrelationships, civic environmentalism, and civic engagement.

This perspective should not deny the role of a macro-economic principle based on which current budgeting approaches are formulated. To be sure, sustainability budgeting should consider the question, "On what basis shall it be decided to allocate x dollars to activity A instead of activity B?" (Key, 1940, p. 1132). In Key's view, this question should be explored from the perspective of the economic theory of budgeting.[2] Although he raised this question in the context of US society several decades ago, it is of critical relevance to contemporary Africa where governments continue to face the basic challenge of just how to channel public resources into creating inclusive, equitable, and transformative growth.

Although the long-term development planning approach that characterized Africa's post-colonial experience has been abandoned, the short-term budgeting substitute now ingrained in Africa's public management culture is hardly helpful. The current budgeting approach has not only become an annual ritual, but also has been unable to grapple with the deep-seated hard-core poverty plaguing much of rural Africa. The adoption of the medium-term expenditure framework as a part of budgeting and public finance reform is a move in the right direction, but it is a critical piece of the "standardized international best practices thinking" that tends to ignore the contextual realities in Africa (Andrews, 2014; Savage, 2013; Beschel & Ahern, 2012).[3] As Savage (p. 894) points out, financial management reform should be customized to fit a specific "political, social, and economic context" and also take administrative capacity into account. The need for long-term, home-grown budgeting and fiscal policy reform considerations is even more urgent given Africa's fiscal pressures and its vulnerability to world commodity price volatility.

The purpose of the chapter, then, is to argue for budgeting reform, one that elucidates and is based in the need for fiscal sustainability in Africa. The chapter proceeds by synthesizing country case studies, as well as the literature on sustainable development, fiscal policy, and public management with the goal of raising the salience of fiscal sustainability. The first section lays out the context of public budgeting by summarizing conditions in, opportunities for, and challenges of Africa.[4] This section argues that public budgeting occurs neither in a political nor an economic vacuum: unique material conditions and socio-economic experience should be taken into account. The second section examines and critiques current budgeting approaches as a way of laying bare the basis for harnessing, allocating, and utilizing resources for development purposes. Because resources are scarce relative to public demands, the assumption is that returns from expenditures must be worth the costs. But budgeting should be more than business as usual because it is "where politics, policy and public management" meet (Purtell & Fossett, 2010).

The third section turns attention to and presents the building blocks for considering sustainable budgeting and fiscal management that advance the interest of development management. It argues for the notion of "sustainability budgeting," which has the potential to mitigate fiscal risks in the long run due to exhaustible mineral and oil wealth, as well as unstable non-oil budget balances. Unlike precipitous annual budgeting, the sustainability approach will serve as a proxy for Africa's development priorities by providing a systematic, clear, and transparent view of how public resources can be harnessed, allocated, and managed to address public interest purposes. This entails institutional change both within African nations and the donor community in spite of the deep-rooted "solutions-driven and international best practices development playbook" model now in vogue. The chapter concludes by analyzing the feasibility of sustainability budgeting and assessing Africa's preparedness. As African nations look ahead to the "post-2015 global development agenda and the UN's Sustainable Development Goals" and their own priorities in climate governance, the prospects bode well for sustainability budgeting reform.

Public Budgeting and Fiscal Sustainability in Context

Africa has come a long way since the attainment of political independence and self-governance, but it still has a long road to travel. There is evidence of slow but steady positive change in the conditions and lived experiences of the people.[5] In assessing progress toward achieving the Millennium Development Goals (MDGs), the UN Economic Commission for Africa (UNECA) has asserted that "when effort and initial conditions are factored in, African countries are among the top achievers of the MDGs" (UNECA, 2014, p. vii).[6] UNECA has also noted the rapid growth that African nations have experienced in the past decade. Concurring with this assessment, the APP has observed that poverty and child mortality rates have fallen "for the first time in over a generation." In spite of these changes, the panel has expressed concern that "economic recovery is less impressive" when viewed from the perspective of rural Africa. Panel Chair, Dr. Annan, raises two questions:

> Will we invest our natural resource revenue in people, generating jobs and opportunities for millions in present and future generations? Or will we squander this opportunity, allowing jobless growth and inequality to take root?

These are fiscal sustainability questions that go to the heart of this chapter. Because budgeting does not occur in a vacuum, a brief review of Africa's structural and environmental conditions is needed to facilitate the analysis of the continent's sustainable development effort.

Historical Conditions

Much of the analysis of Africa's material circumstances is devoted to its unique historical experiences—and rightly so: devastation of its valuable human resource during the infamous transatlantic and East African slave trade, as well as the exploitation of its natural resources and subjugation of its people during Western colonial rule.[7] In particular, the colonial legacy has been documented extensively elsewhere, especially by Afrocentric scholars and by scholars of the externalist school of thought (e.g., Ayittey, 1998; Ake, 1996; Mazrui, 1986; Davidson, 1966), so only a summary statement is necessary. This body of literature has sought to explain the cause and consequence of the human condition in Africa based in pre-colonial, colonial, and post-colonial experiences. In a nutshell, African nations inherited a predominantly extractive and a largely agriculture-dependent economy at the dawn of political independence. With an undeveloped infrastructure, low per capita incomes, low investible resources, and predominantly subsistence farming, Africa could hardly extricate itself from the cycle of poverty. Thus it is not surprising that early development economists concluded that poor nations are poor because they are poor. In other words, nations are undeveloped because they are undeveloped without digging into why and how a country is either developing or not developing.[8]

Ake (1996, p. 2) has perceptively observed the uniqueness of colonialism in Africa, arguing that it "was markedly different from the colonial experiences of the Americas, Europe, and Asia." It was, in his view, "unusually statist" and systematically created one of the world's poorest economic structures in Africa. The colonial governments "built roads, railways, and ports to facilitate the collection and export of commodities as well as the import of manufactured goods." In addition, they compelled their colonies to produce preferred cash crops such as cocoa in Ghana and coffee in Kenya. For example, by 1901 Ghana had become the leading producer and exporter of cocoa in the world, which subsequently created "a mono-cultural cocoa economy" in that country. Since then Ghana has virtually depended on and continuously struggled to extricate itself from being a primary producer to little or no avail.[9]

Moreover, colonial policies discouraged entrepreneurial and human resource development as a tactic for making "Africans available for wage labor" and thereby "keeping them from becoming independent producers." The low level of education and high illiteracy rate across the continent at independence was astounding. According to Ayittey (1998, p. 41), there were only 100 university graduates in Zambia and 16 in Tanzania in 1961. Guinea-Bissau not only had only 14 graduates in 1974, but also it had 267 miles of paved road and 97 percent illiteracy. With such low literacy rates, the future of Africa at independence was bleak. From the outset, then, economic development was hardly a part of the colonial agenda and the struggle to encourage it during the post-colonial period has followed a narrow path as will be argued later.

Social and Cultural Conditions

The historical legacy outlined above is incomplete without specifying the colonial perspective on African culture, a perspective that not only ignored it, but also sought to replace it with Western values and belief systems. Originating primarily from the now discredited modernization theories, this perspective presumed incorrectly that indigenous African cultural practices and institutions were dysfunctional and irrelevant to economic development and social progress (e.g., Wylie, 1999; Ake, 1996). Rooted in Western belief in money, science, and instrumental rationality, this theoretical approach assumed erroneously that African nations would progress through development stages along the lines that "developed" nations had experienced (e.g., White & Adams, 1994; Rostow, 1960, 1963). For example, French colonial rule aimed to eliminate indigenous structures and institutions and assimilate Africans into French society. In contrast, the British and Germans attempted to coopt indigenous socio-political structures in governing the colonies. Both approaches failed to deliver on their promises and several indigenous political institutions and social structures not only survived but also thrived long after the collapse of colonial rule (Wiarda, 1999; Ayittey, 1991; Wiarda, 1991).

The collapse of modernization theory and the regeneration of African culture have provided the intellectual firepower for Afrocentric scholars to examine the impact of colonial rule on indigenous institutions. Ake (1996) has pointed out that in discounting the cultural factor in development, colonial rule made "a costly error." The forces of African culture not only resisted change, but also thwarted efforts to implement policies. Such resistance often developed into open "hostility" that reinforced negative perceptions of African culture and Africans as being "conservative and suspicious of change, . . . irrational, unenterprising, superstitious, and too subjective and emotional in their attitudes." The apparent tensions and conflicts served neither the interests of colonial rule nor Africa because they tended to deflect attention away from the analysis of development processes and outcomes. Another, and perhaps more important consequence regarding development and social progress, was psychological: the fear of damaged self-worth and self-esteem. According to Ake, some Africans have "internalized a negative image of themselves" and "the superiority of developed societies," a mentality that in his view "cannot be conducive to development" (1996, p. 16).

Afrocentric scholars have also taken advantage of the collapse of modernization theory to recover the battered image of African culture and to advance the argument that no effective economic development policy can be divorced from its cultural milieu. Riding on the notion of alternatives to "developmentalism," they have contributed ideas about home-grown or indigenous models of development. Not only do such home-grown models and theories of development more closely align with local material conditions and lived experiences, but they also contribute to reassert Afrocentrism, cultural identity and unity.

Taken from a socialist perspective, Rodney (1981) has explained what he describes as the "uncontaminated" nature of African society and its complex social systems of family and kinship before the arrival of the Europeans. He has argued that Africans were indeed capable and continued to create their own history and development long before the arrival of Europeans in the continent. His central thesis is about "how Europe underdeveloped Africa," by using the capitalist system of economic exploitation. He has demonstrated that but for the denial of political power and subsequent disruption of the evolution of national solidarity and subsistence economies due to colonialism, Africa would have continued along the path of steady development in its own unique way. Although the socialist perspective on which he bases his argument has lost momentum, his analysis remains valid in the context of African development.

Similarly, Ayittey (1991) has provided a detailed description and analysis of African cultures, traditions, and institutions while contrasting them with pre-colonial, colonial, and post-colonial experiences. He has observed the decentralized and communal nature of African society and emphasized values and normative concerns that Africans cherish: tight kinship bonds and complex systems of rights and obligations shaping their daily living. For example, the institution of community serves as the organic unit of cultural, social, economic, and political organization and it is "the most powerful and effective force for unity and stability" (Ayittey, 1992, p. 38). Because these institutions compete for individual and group loyalty, as Busia (1967) has argued in the case of Ghana, and to the extent that the law recognizes them, they constitute both a threat to and an opportunity for rebuilding governance.

However, historical and socio-cultural experiences are not limited only to European colonialism. While it is reasonable to rationalize Africa's predicament on the basis of a narrowly structured economy, poorly developed infrastructure, and "Europeanization" at independence, the post-colonial legacy has been revealing as well. Sure, the top-down imposition of Westernized political and economic institutions and practices failed to reflect and address the local material conditions and realities. Much of the post-colonial period witnessed political violence and instability, economic mismanagement and incompetence, as well as social decay across the continent (Wylie, 1999; Ayittey, 1998; Ake, 1996). Both Ayittey and Ake argue that Africa has done little to prepare itself for the post-colonial development project. In particular, Ayittey has written eloquently but pessimistically about "Africa in chaos" and "Africa betrayed" to highlight the failures characterizing Africa's post-colonial experience. For his part, Ake states with despair that "political conditions in Africa are the greatest impediment to development" and concludes that development has never really been on the agenda.

Contemporary Conditions

Africa ushered in the millennium with a mixed bag of tragedy and despair on the one hand and hope and optimism on the other. The dominant discourse, foreshadowed by the blistering critiques of Ayittey (1992) and Ake (1996) crystalized around questions such as:

> Will the countries of Africa be overwhelmed by chaos and anarchy that are so prevalent in Rwanda and Central Africa today? Or, as in South Africa, will Western-style democracy and economic reforms be pushed forward, further challenging the social, political, and economic realities of indigenous Africa and possibly failing to take hold turning the inchoate multiparty democracies into de facto, corrupt, one party states? Or lastly will some combination of indigenous and Western elements as in Botswana pave the way for development in the twenty-first century?
>
> Wylie 1999, p. 97

In addressing these questions, Wylie posited that the future lay in Africa's ability to choose and tread the path of a hybrid model of development, one that adapts Western-style democracy to "African practices and culture." But even Wylie was ambivalent about the feasibility of the hybridized model because "not only is there little consensus on Western and imported institutions but there is no solid agreement on home-grown ones either." Given the economic crisis of the 1980s, food shortages, the HIV/AIDS pandemic, and high unemployment, the transition into the new millennium was certainly a challenge for Africa. In spite of varied and uneven national experiences, the UN Food and Agricultural Organization (FAO) assessed rightly that the 1980s was a lost decade for development that foreshadowed Africa's challenge in the millennium.[10]

However, political changes and neo-liberal economic reforms during the 1990s that continued into the millennium provided a ray of hope for African development (Moss, 2007; Gyimah-Boadi, 2004; Walle, 2004). The political changes included the transition from dictatorial regimes to multi-party democracies even if they failed to meet liberal ideals. Most notably, the emergence of Namibia (1989) and South Africa (1994) as multi-racial nation-states signaled a new era in Africa and fueled optimism about an "African renaissance" (Walle, 2004, p. 29). Along with the rebirth of the continental union and the formation of a home-grown development initiative—New Partnership for African Development (NEPAD)—Africa seemed poised to make a fresh start. So wide-ranging was the change that Moss (2007, p. 27) considered it worth classifying among political trends that tend to "sweep over the continent with remarkable uniformity" since colonialism. There was also optimism in terms of economic performance. Not only did the region record positive economic growth, but also growth spread across several countries in the late 1990s for the first time in over a generation. As a result, the International Monetary Fund had projected 1.3 percent growth in per capita gross domestic product.

Despite much reform effort, scholarly descriptions, evaluations, and predictions of governance quality and the human condition in Africa have been uninspiring, leading to speculation as to whether the millennium initiatives have made any difference. In one of the early assessments, Gyimah-Boadi and contributors (2004, p. 2) argued that "the pace and quality of current progress have varied across states and from sector to sector." Although the democratization project has gained momentum and civil society has blossomed, the overall governance climate is weak. In Diamond's (2004, p. 267) assessment, Africa has lagged behind economically because it has lagged behind in good governance. For example, 12 of the 17 African countries assessed in the 2003 global corruption report were among the most corrupt in the world. This has hardly changed in the 2013 report: 11 African countries (Cameroon, Ghana, Kenya, Liberia, Libya, Mozambique, Senegal, Sierra Leone, Tanzania, Uganda, and Zimbabwe) have recorded some of the highest bribery incidence in the world (Transparency International, 2013).[11] In fact, Diamond has estimated that by 2003:

> Only about two in every five of African governments are accountable to their people through the most minimal instrument of free, fair, and competitive national elections. And of these nineteen or so democracies (by the end of 2003), only about five can be said to be liberal, in terms of allowing extensive civil and political freedom. Certainly, freedom has improved and democracy has expanded dramatically in Africa since 1990, but the promise of a "second liberation" across the continent has stalled, and where political freedom is most abused so are economic and social development as well.

In addition to weak governance, progress on economic and institutional reform has been slow at best in many cases or has stagnated in what Walle (2004, p. 54) has described as a "partial reform syndrome." In his assessment, the economic reform that generated initial enthusiasm has been "partial, uneven, and rarely sustained," resulting in "unintended effects" with far-reaching implications for revitalized growth. While some achievements have been made in cutting fiscal deficits, improving exchange rates, and banking and credit infrastructure, other areas including fiscal adjustment, monetary and trade policy reforms have had the highest risk of implementation reversals.

> Of the unintended effects arising from partial reform, weakened state capacity has emerged as the most devastating. As a result of resource cutbacks, the capacity to formulate and implement policy has declined substantially. Although effort to rebuild capable states with adequate capacity for implementing policies and delivering services has received much attention, "capacity deficits continue to plague governance in Africa"
> (UNECA, 2009; 2011).

Thus Walle (2004, p. 57) has concluded by recommending that both governments and development partners:

> need to pay special attention to improving the professionalism and capacity of the civil service, to rehabilitate the public infrastructure, which has been allowed to atrophy for so long, and to reinforce the rule of law, notably through the strengthening of the judiciary.

In terms of economic liberalization policy under the World Bank's stabilization and structural adjustment programs, African nations have recorded much progress in pursuing deregulation and privatization measures but such measures have likewise suffered from partial or no sustained support.[11] It is correct that governments have removed price control and trade restrictions and also encouraged private participation and competition in the economy. It is equally correct that they have relaxed bank credit and interest rates regimes and divested state-owned enterprises. But as the cases of Senegal, Zambia, and Tanzania have indicated, skepticism about the government's commitment to liberalization has remained strong in the business community. In their study of business in Tanzania, Lofchie and Callaghy (1996) have laid out the progress that country has made by allowing the creation of a system of private currency exchange bureaus, private commercial banking systems, as well as investment by multinational corporations. But they have also argued that "Tanzania's business had remained one of high risk and great difficulty." They have specified business constraints, including bureaucratic red tape, corruption, poor infrastructure, and regime limitations hampering economic liberalization. Such barriers and constraints have been widespread rather than just a country-specific phenomenon.

Reform of the agricultural sector has been emblematic of the half-hearted approach to liberalization policy in African nations. On the one hand, government-controlled or guaranteed price-fixing for export crops such as cocoa in Cameroon and Ghana has hardly changed. Moreover, and as Walle (2004) has argued, prices of several export crops have not been liberalized. On the other hand, the sector has experienced some changes with the withdrawal of subsidies on agricultural supplies and inputs such as fertilizers and pesticides. Although the withdrawal of such subsidies has disproportionately hurt the poor and smallholder farmers, as Gibon, Harnerik, and Hernele (1993) have noted, little has been done to mitigate the negative impact of economic liberalization programs in African agriculture. Salami, Kamara, and Brixiova (2010, p. 1) found out that East African smallholder farmers suffered from poor infrastructure and limited access to market and credit that substantially constrained productivity. Not only have smallholder farmers occupied most of the land and owned most of the crops and livestock, but also they accounted for over 75 percent of agricultural production and over 75 percent of employment. It is from this unique economic environment that the APP (2014, p. 11) has focused on how to "boost our agriculture and fisheries," on which most Africans depend for their livelihoods.

In sum, the foregoing analysis demonstrates that: First, development occurs in a specific context. In African nations that context and landscape encompass historical legacies of slavery and colonialism, as well as unique economic, social, political, and cultural experiences. Initially conceptualized as narrowly based on economics, development has evolved into an all-embracing concept and its management has shifted from orthodox top-down approaches to a more open, delegated, and shared effort based on good governance. While some progress has been made in the overall quality of life, more work is needed to better align contemporary development policy and fiscal management with the material condition and lived experience of African society.

Second, development principle, policy, and practice from the perspective of leading international financial institutions and the acquiescence of African governments have focused mainly on short-term crisis management. But this approach has not served Africa well, and beyond that it has failed as a vehicle for transforming developing society from "traditional relations, traditional ways of thinking, traditional ways of dealing with health and education, traditional methods of production, to more 'modern' ways" (Stiglitz 1998, p. 3). This is not to deny the role of economics in development policy and management but to underscore the need for a holistic framework with more sensitivity to the material condition of African nations.

Finally, from the relatively prosperous north through the dense tropical rainforests to the well-endowed south, Africa presents a unique fiscal and economic environment that offers opportunities but poses challenges as well. Based mainly on enormous natural resources, the opportunities continue to attract investments and fuel growth but the APP (2013) cautions that care must be taken to manage them in a sustainable way. Of course, these resources remain as Africa's foremost attraction, but equally important is its human resource that has contributed knowledge, skills, and abilities to other societies abroad (Mazrui, 2008).[12] But the challenges are also daunting as the resources are not evenly distributed between regions and nations and within local populations. The question, then, is how does Africa harness and allocate these resources in a manner that fosters equitable, inclusive, and transformative growth? The next section explores budgeting and fiscal management approaches that have been applied to harness and judiciously allocate resources toward improving the human condition.

Public Budgeting and Fiscal Management Approaches

Africa faces an unprecedented budgeting and fiscal opportunity. The continent has averaged over 5 percent growth over the past decade in spite of the global economic downturn (2007–2008). According to the APP (2013), Cameroon, Ghana, Nigeria, and Zambia have moved from low-income to lower middle-income nations, while Angola, Botswana, Gabon, Namibia, and South Africa have joined the elite upper middle-income nations. Along with these developments, Africa has recorded improvements in the human development index rankings, which measure the quality of well-being. Nonetheless, poverty remains at high levels throughout the continent and has actually increased in Nigeria and Zambia. This contradictory picture raises the question of just how public budgeting is being conducted in Africa. This section explores the budgeting and fiscal management approaches that African nations have pursued and argues that if they continue on the path of collecting and spending in a piecemeal fashion, deficits and debts will pile up to unsustainable levels and crisis proportions.

Conceptualizing Public Budgeting

To a large extent, financial resources constitute the lifeblood of government and public administration, especially in times and places of fiscal scarcity and austerity. But human and material resources are equally important. According to the orthodox perspective on public administration and policy, a combination of financial, human, and material resources is necessary to accomplish public goals and objectives.[13] Governments and public administration then have to confront the hard reality that there are never enough resources to meet public need and demand. Based on this logic, often scholars conceptualize public budgeting broadly as the means of making decisions about how to acquire, allocate, use, and account for public resources (Lewis & Hildreth, 2013; Nice, 2002). Such a broad conceptualization affirms that "Budgets are not merely affairs of arithmetic, but in a thousand ways go to the root of prosperity for individuals, the relations of classes, and the strength of kingdom" (Gladstone quoted in Hyde, 1992, p. 1). As a result, a public budget performs several functions: aggregating interests, setting priorities, managing the economy, promoting efficiency and effectiveness, and ensuring accountability.

In that regard, the budget is not just a statement, but a plan of collective action that is inextricably linked to the human condition. This is more so in the context of developing societies such as those in Africa that are still struggling to find the most appropriate approach to harnessing and allocating their scarce resources toward improving the quality of life. As elsewhere, public budgeting and fiscal management are constitutionally and legally mandated. National constitutions create the governing institutions responsible for formulating budgeting and fiscal policy while statutes fill in the gaps by specifying the processes for approving and engaging in budgeting and fiscal management. Thus Ghana's budget derives its authority from the Constitution (1992: Articles 174–182) while the Financial Administration Act (2003) and other related Acts provide guidance for budgeting and fiscal management processes and procedures. Likewise, the authority of Benin's budget originates from its Constitution (1990: Articles 96–131) while its Organic Law (1986) specifies guidance for budgeting and fiscal management (Draman, 2010). The question, then, is how does Africa approach public budgeting? This is addressed along with the examination of budget reforms in the following sections.

Centralized Budgeting and Fiscal Management

The development of public budgeting and fiscal management is linked to colonial history, as well as reforms that have occurred within the African public sector over the last three decades. It is equally important to note how such reforms relate to the management of the public services and to other trends in the economy. Both history and public sector reform have contributed to define the contours of managerial and institutional arrangements surrounding budgeting systems in African nations. Historically, Anglophone Africa adopted the Anglo-American public budgeting and fiscal management model, which is based on British centralized government and managerialism. The model emphasizes the accountability of government to the public as well as efficiency in managing public resources. This is reflected in the constitutional provisions of Ghana, Kenya, Tanzania, Uganda, and Zambia, requiring that "money may not be withdrawn from the consolidated fund unless appropriated or provided by the law."[14] In contrast, Francophone Africa has adopted what Chan (2002, p. 9) has described as the "Latin" version of the Continental European model with a focus on "executive accountability to Parliament." Thus Benin, Cameroon, and Senegal, for example, have multiple organic laws modeled after French law that guide the budget processes and procedures (Draman, 2010).

The fact of the colonial heritage is deserving of further comment because of its impact on budget development and implementation in Africa. Regardless of the differences between the two colonial models, African nations have developed and consistently applied budgeting and fiscal management systems derived from their colonial heritage that do not necessarily align well with their unique geopolitical, economic, and cultural organizations. In examining the design and implementation of the financial management systems in Africa, Heidenhof, Gradvoinnet, Kianpour, and Rezaian (2002, p. 10) have noted the integration of budgeting and expenditure management systems and clarification of the roles and responsibilities of various actors. While integrating the different parts of the budgeting, accounting, and auditing systems into a common framework optimizes standardization and efficiency, it has created centralized and inflexible budgetary processes. The Survey of the Collaborative Africa Budget Reform Initiative (CABRI, 2008, p. x) found that African nations tended to have centralized budgets:

> The survey results show that the majority of countries have implemented some form of 'top-down' approach, which centralizes decision-making powers during the budget formulation stage to ensure fiscal discipline. Francophone countries are more numerous in this group. This might partly be due to the existence of clear fiscal rules stipulated as part of the West African Economic Monetary Union (WAEMU), which has adopted Maastricht-style limits on the levels of government debt and of fiscal deficits.

In addition, the CABRI survey results indicated that African countries with a "Westminster heritage tend to have weaker legislative bodies" with implications for institutional capacity for budgeting and financial scrutiny and oversight. The transposition of Western budgeting and fiscal management models to African nations has been hazardous. Although top-down approaches might contribute to "ensure fiscal discipline," it has also tended to tilt the power balance in favor of the executive but at the expense of legislative power and authority. The survey assessed the adequacy, transparency, and challenges of budget institutions and procedures in African nations, and results have suggested as much by reporting that no African country scored up to 0.5 on a scale of 0 (low) to 1 (high). Consequently, the concentration of executive budget authority and the weakened role of the legislature have reduced, if not substantially emasculated, the formal mechanisms for achieving accountability in the use of scarce public resources.

To address this challenge, the African Parliamentary Strengthening Program (APSP) for budget oversight has focused on increasing the capacity of African parliaments by researching and reporting on best practices in budgeting and fiscal management. The APSP has aimed to collect and analyze data, and to disseminate relevant budget information toward "promoting transparency, accountability, and efficient fiscal management by the executive." This aligns with changing trends of "assisting the legislature in recapturing some of its influence in the budget process" in the Organization for Economic Cooperation and Development countries—OECD (Posner & Park, 2007, p. 82). However, the APSP's efforts to enlarge the legislative role in budgeting and fiscal management have assumed that it would necessarily reinforce fiscal discipline by taking responsibility and serving as a countervailing force to executive budget authority. While no formal evaluation has been made to verify this assumption and to empirically determine the quality of performance, the APSP has highlighted the urgent need for reform in budgeting and fiscal management in general and legislative oversight much more specifically.

Decentralized Budgeting and Fiscal Management

It is fair to say that budgeting and fiscal management have evolved considerably since African nations adopted structural reforms in the 1980s to improve economic and political performance. As with other developing societies, the budgeting and fiscal management framework is not only weak, but it is also not well aligned with African society. In addition to liberalization reform, these nations have also pursued decentralization initiatives because of the failure of the top-down approach to achieve sustainable development in rural and dispersed clusters of communities. Decentralization—the process of devolving political power and administrative authority to sub-national units—aims to expand political participation, rationalize institutional and organizational functions, as well as strengthen budgeting and fiscal management capacity. The presumption is that a decentralized framework will create the needed space for effective governance by institutionalizing bottom-up planning and development. How have budgeting and fiscal management changed through decentralization? To what extent does the rhetoric of decentralization design match the reality of its implementation on the ground? This section summarizes national experiences, assesses the approach to fiscal decentralization, and argues that further reform is needed to improve development management.

There is no question that much work has been done to lay the foundation for formulating and implementing fiscal decentralization. Motivated by political and economic crisis, donor pressure for good governance, growing urbanization, and globalization, African nations have either de-concentrated or delegated their functions, or devolved political, economic, and fiscal responsibility (Dafflon & Madies, 2013; Olowu & Wunsch, 2004; Rondinelli & Cheema, 2003; Cheru, 2002). Noting declining resources, increasing indebtedness, and unsustainable fiscal imbalances, Olowu and Wunsch have observed a steady shift toward decentralization, involving the transfer of "important authority and resources from central governments to peripheral institutions." They have argued that as the pressure for reform mounted, especially from non-state actors such as civil society organizations (Mali) or grass-root resistance (Mozambique and Uganda), opportunities for "democratic decentralization" have developed across the continent.

Although African nations vary according to the degree of decentralization, the means for accomplishing it has been through constitutional provisions, legislative acts, and administrative procedures that empower and sustain sub-national units. Ghana's Constitution along with several pieces of legislation (e.g., District Assemblies Common Fund, Local Government Service, and Institute of Local Government Studies Acts) has created the institutional and administrative framework for implementing decentralized governance. Likewise, the South African Constitution (1996) stipulates the assignment of political and administrative powers and functions to sub-national governments. In addition, it requires the transfer of fiscal authority that ensures that "the provinces and municipalities are able to provide basic services and perform the functions allocated to them." As well, the Nigerian Constitution (1999) mandates statutory allocations from the federation account and also requires states to allocate 10 percent of their internally generated revenue to local jurisdictions (Haruna & Al-Ansar, 2013).

While these constitutional provisions and legal tools are essential, they are not enough to achieve decentralized governance (Dafflon & Madies, 2013; Olowu & Wunsch, 2004). It is true that they are needed to lay the institutional framework but as Dafflon and Madies have noted in their field studies of Burkina Faso, Ghana, Kenya, and Senegal, the degree and nature of decentralization depends on the trajectory and unique local conditions. They have demonstrated empirically that considerable discrepancies exist between the legislative frameworks in these countries and the implementation realities on the ground. Such discrepancies are attributable mainly due to political will, as well as local economic and fiscal capacity. Likewise, Olowu and Wunsch have emphasized unique local circumstances such as conflict and "local elite capture" that tend to shape the decentralization process and the realization of legislative intent.

However, appropriately conceptualized and applied, decentralization has the potential to enhance democracy by identifying and responding to local needs and priorities and by harnessing resources to deliver essential public services. In effect, decentralization can be a useful tool for including rural communities in decision-making and for realigning public finances toward achieving sustainable growth and development. To some extent, evidence of the effect of fiscal decentralization has been quite visible throughout the continent. In fact, on a country-by-country basis, there have been local spending increases consistent with what Steffensen and Trollegaard (2000, pp. 11–12) had earlier observed:

> Decentralization efforts in the African region are shifting much of the burden of infrastructure management and finance to sub-national levels . . . As part of their decentralization efforts, many African countries have begun to address democratic decentralization fiscal resource and mobilization. The countries in the sub-Saharan Africa are all at various stages in the decentralization process. Indeed, taken as a group, these six countries comprise a virtual continuum of the steps necessary to build strong municipal governance and infrastructure delivery systems.

From the above perspective, local units have increasingly been allocated wide jurisdictions, including responsibilities for social welfare, infrastructural development, environmental protection, and land management, to mention but a few. The constitutional principle of the fiscal autonomy of elected local jurisdictions has largely facilitated fiscal decentralization in several African nations. Based on expenditure decentralization (local government spending as a percentage of total government expenditure), revenue decentralization (local government revenue as a percentage of total government revenue), and financial autonomy (locally raised revenue as a percentage of total local expenditures), budgeting and fiscal management seem to have changed. Local government spending has reached as high as 40 percent in Nigeria, 30 percent in Ethiopia, 25 percent in Zimbabwe, and 21 percent in Uganda (Olowu & Wunsch, 2004, p. 54). The size of local manpower strength has also increased: 18.4 percent in Botswana, 16 percent in South Africa, 12.6 percent in Uganda, and 11.2 percent in Zimbabwe (International Labor Organization, 2001, p. 84). The case of Uganda is instructive because there has been a consistent effort to achieve devolution by transferring power vertically from the center to the district and horizontally from line agencies to civil society organizations (Ranis, 2012; Green, 2008). District councils have the authority to approve programs and budgets, as well as coordinate and monitor government functions. Between 2003 and 2008, local expenditure has remained stable at 30 percent although financial autonomy has been low at 10 percent (Ranis, 2012, pp. 10–11).

On the other hand, local government expenditures have remained relatively very low in countries such as Swaziland (2 percent), Zambia (3 percent), Senegal (7 percent), Zimbabwe (8 percent), and Ghana (8 percent) as Steffensen and Trollegaard (2001) have indicated. While these expenditures have increased over time in some countries, they have remained relatively low in others. As Ranis (2012) has reported, most of the local authority financing in Kenya comes from the central government with very limited discretion. Because local taxing power and fiscal capacity have been limited, financial autonomy as measured by locally generated revenue depends on mainly *ad valorem* or property tax. In assessing the future of decentralization in Kenya, Ranis has emphasized more county political empowerment and enhanced equity in revenue sharing.

Even in countries deemed to have made some advances in fiscal decentralization, central governments still retain much control over budgeting and fiscal management. Dafflon and Madies (2013, p. 270) have observed that in Burkina Faso and Senegal, local governments barely have taxing power while those in Ghana and Kenya have "slightly more flexibility on the tax front." Although Ghana has made steady progress, metropolitan, municipal, and district authorities depend heavily on external support to meet their total expenditures (Republic of Ghana: Annual Progress Report, 2009, pp. 190–191). Such external support, including contributions from the District Assembly Common Fund, Donor Grant, central government transfer, and Heavily Indebted Poor Country Fund provides the bulk of local government revenue (81 percent). As with all external support, these transfers come with restrictive discretion based on centrally predetermined and enforced guidelines. While internally generated revenue has seen modest increases over time, weak local economies, narrow tax bases, and low levels of horizontal decentralization have constrained local financial autonomy.

Consequently, spending in education and health with the potential to enhance local and rural development has been low and unstable since 2010 (Table 1.1). Although education spending has increased slightly in many cases (e.g., Burundi, Ghana, Malawi, and Mali), it has declined in others (e.g., Gambia, Niger, and South Africa). Similarly, spending on health has either increased modestly in the best case scenarios (e.g., Kenya, Swaziland, and

Table 1.1 Education and Health Spending as a Proportion of Government Expenditures in African Nations

Country	Education				Health			
	2010	2011	2012	2013	2010	2011	2012	2013
Burundi	16.6	15.0	16.3	–	62.3	63.0	60.1	54.7
Cameroon	18.8	14.9	15.2	–	30.1	31.7	32.4	34.7
Gambia	17.1	15.1	13.8	–	59.7	59.8	60.0	60.1
Ghana	21.2	33.4	–	–	71.8	74.4	68.3	60.6
Kenya	23.8	–	–	–	40.2	39.4	40.9	41.7
Malawi	11.6	14.9	–	–	60.3	55.5	56.1	50.0
Mali	18.8	19.3	–	–	41.1	44.2	38.8	39.7
Niger	18.1	21.2	19.2	–	34.4	36.6	33.1	36.7
Sierra Leone	12.8	12.4	14.1	–	22.5	22.8	17.9	14.3
South Africa	18.0	18.9	20.6	19.1	46.6	47.7	48.4	48.4
Swaziland	18.5	24.5	–	–	68.0	68.8	72.6	74.7
Rwanda	20.8	18.2	18.0	19.4	55.5	57.7	58.8	58.8
Uganda	13.5	13.3	14.0	–	48.6	45.5	43.0	44.4

Source for education expenditures: http://data.worldbank.org/indicators/SE.XPD.TOTL.GB.ZS/countries?display=default

Source for health expenditures: http://data.worldbank.org/indicators/SH.XPD.PUBL/countries?display=default

Uganda), remained flat (e.g., Gambia, Rwanda, and South Africa) or declined in the worst case scenarios (e.g., Burundi, Ghana, Malawi, and Sierra Leone). Thus the trend does not bode well not only for striving toward achieving the UN Millennium Development Goals (MDGs), but also for transitioning seamlessly into the era of the UN Sustainable Development Goals (SDGs).[15]

Medium-Term Expenditure Framework

In addition to the fiscal decentralization initiatives discussed above, African nations have implemented the medium-term expenditure framework (MTEF) with the goal of connecting policy, planning, and budgeting in a comprehensive fashion. Originating from the World Bank, the MTEF was developed mainly to overcome the inherent weakness of fragmentation in public budgeting and fiscal management. The World Bank (1998, p. 31) observed that in developing nations:

> Policy, planning, and budgeting take place independently of each other. Planning is often confined to investment activities, which in many developing countries refers to a series of donor-funded projects. Capital expenditures are already largely accounted for through the planning process, and a large portion of recurrent expenditures are pre-committed to the wage bill. For this reason, annual budgeting is reduced to allocating resources thinly across donor and domestically funded "investment" projects and to the nonwage portion of the recurrent budget. In addition line agencies tend to budget and spend on an ad hoc basis because even small discretionary allocations are rarely predictable.

The dominant view of public budgeting as being the control of public resources has exacerbated the problem of fragmentation because it has diverted attention away from "planning for the future allocation of resources and management of resources." The World Bank (1998, p. 11) has argued that:

> Ministries of Finance and central Banks (and the IMF) have been aggressive advocates of control of public resources. They have usually been supported by institutional arrangements whereby all revenues have to be paid into a central fund and only are drawn on by authority of the legislature. This helps explain why the line item budgeting has been so enduring. Support for the other two functions has been much more ephemeral.

Thus the rationale for the ubiquitous line-item budgeting technique was to reinforce the prevailing view by promoting accountability and safe-guarding against the misuse and abuse of public resources. However, in spite of its advantages, the technique has resulted in a short-term and a largely inflexible budgeting and fiscal management approach.

By integrating all aspects of budgeting and fiscal management in a logical framework, the MTEF not only addresses the inherent weaknesses entailed in traditional public expenditure management, but also fosters a performance orientation. In this approach, policy objectives drive public expenditure priorities over a period of time thereby promoting fiscal predictability and discipline. Specifically, the MTEF translates policy objectives into coherent expenditure programs within a three-year rolling plan. As the World Bank (1998, p. 33) argued, the MTEF focuses on enhancing "predictability of resource flows and the criteria by which funding decisions are made." To that extent, the MTEF addresses the central concern in African nations (disconnection between policy-making, planning, and budgetary processes) and also lays the foundation for building a culture of fiscal discipline, transparency, accountability, and sustainability.

In their assessment, Houerou and Taliercio (2002, p. 3) have emphasized the integration of the "top-down resource envelope with the bottom-up sector programs" as the MTEF's key contribution. They have described such integration as a "macro-economic model" that clarifies and specifies fiscal targets including national revenue sources and expenditure commitments. Also, they have observed that the model involves the analysis of policies and plans on a sector-by-sector basis "with an eye toward optimizing intra sector allocations." Nonetheless, the broad national expenditure framework reflecting policies and fiscal constraints makes room for the sectors to exercise discretion and manage progress toward achieving efficiency and effectiveness. Thus from a conceptual perspective, as they have pointed out, the MTEF has prospects to improve macro-economic balance, enhance budget allocation, and foster performance and accountability.

However, the MTEF reflects mainly an exercise in a comprehensive rational decision-making approach to budgeting and fiscal management with relatively little political and social sensitivity. The approach assumes that public budgeting should help Africa to make progress toward achieving important socio-economic goals such as poverty reduction and increased per capita incomes as welfare economists have argued.[16] As well, it assumes that effective budget reform requires precise information about whether and how well programs are working. Unfortunately, these assumptions are questionable in Africa where quality socio-economic data is hard to come by and where ethnic and cultural diversity make it hard to agree on goals and how to attain them.[17] Moreover, the approach tends to minimize budgeting as a human enterprise whereby actors and stakeholders have emotions as well as rational thinking inclinations. In short, policy-makers need to consider and factor in emotional consequences alongside rational analysis. As with previous reform approaches, the MTEF not only suffers from cultural insensitivity but also inadequate attention to historical experiences and material conditions (Houerou & Taliercio 2002, pp. 6–16).

Beyond these theoretical considerations, there are practical and operational concerns that cannot and should not be overlooked. In their review of the MTEF, Houerou and Taliercio (2002) have raised important operational constraints and obstacles that are worth calling attention to. They have noted divergence between the MTEF design and its operation in the context of African nations, which they attribute to the unique needs of "different countries to adapt the MTEF reform to their particular institutional and political circumstances." As they have observed, the MTEF is a prescriptive-conceptual model that does not address practical and operational questions as they apply to African nations, such as:

> What should be the sectoral scope of the MTEF? What information should sector expenditure frameworks include, and at what level of detail? What are the appropriate roles for the ministry of finance and the sector ministries? Where and how does the MTEF fit in with the existing budget process?
>
> Houerou & Taliercio 2002, pp. 5–6

In addressing these questions, they have provided insights about MTEF implementation challenges in several African nations, especially in respect of scope, i.e. whether the MTEF is government wide and whether it should include both recurrent and capital expenditures. These practical issues are relevant to Africa because they bear directly on the question of whether adequate capacity exists to implement comprehensive full-scale MTEF reform. As a result, and as Houerou and Taliercio have found out, MTEFs in many African nations deal mainly with central government and provide little to no "detailed organizational expenditure classification." By implication, sub-national jurisdictions are denied benefits accruing from MTEF reform. The overall preliminary evaluation of MTEFs' performance in African nations has yielded mixed results as well. Houerou and Taliercio have argued that with the exception of Uganda (1994–1995 and 1997–1998), there is little evidence to demonstrate the achievement of MTEF objectives, e.g., improved fiscal discipline, inter- and intra-sector resource reallocation, budget predictability, as well as political accountability and credibility.

In sum, traditional budgeting and fiscal management approaches have hardly served the interest of development management. They have been fragmented, centralized, annualized, and designed to ensure control and compliance. Such approaches have focused on and favored aggregate expenditure without much regard to the other basic budgetary functions of allocation and management. The annualized short-term approach has neither supported long-term policies nor promoted the analysis of the future cost implications of current spending. Coupled with narrow tax bases and weak tax administration systems, revenue forecasting and budget preparation have been unsatisfactory, to say the least. Consequently, and as the IMF has argued, African governments have tended to over-spend and in many cases underfunded debt servicing, utilities, and intergovernmental transfers (www.elibrary.imf.org/view/IMF002/06130–9781451800463/06130–9781451800463/0613).

Budgeting and fiscal management reforms that have occurred in African nations have sought to address long-standing public expenditure problems originating both from colonial and post-colonial experiences. Initial reforms have emphasized fiscal decentralization with the goal of devolving functional and fiscal responsibilities to sub-national jurisdictions to improve inclusion and equitable growth and development. However, fiscal decentralization has not delivered on its promise largely due to central government control, weak local economies, and the lack of financial autonomy. As with all unitary systems of government, tax organization lies within the purview of the state, thereby undermining the principles of devolution and local autonomy under decentralized governance. The adoption and implementation of a medium-term expenditure approach has sought to link policy, planning and budgeting and improve public expenditure management. Nonetheless, the approach poses conceptual and practical challenges that need to be sorted out to make it effective and more relevant to the African context.

Toward Sustainability Budgeting and Fiscal Management

The foregoing overview of budgeting and fiscal management approaches in Africa has highlighted interesting challenges and opportunities in development management. The key challenge is how to develop a model of budgeting and fiscal management that takes into account and engages the unique historicity and material condition of Africa. The purpose of such a model should be to spur inclusive, equitable, transformative and lasting growth, as the APP (2015) has envisioned. In short, the challenge is how to work toward creating a culture of sustainability in budgeting and fiscal management. Although each African nation is different in one way or the other, it can be argued that the challenge is transnational and cross cultural in nature along the lines described by and analyzed in various World Bank developing country studies. Together with country-specific case studies, reviews by international financial institutions have clarified the challenge and suggested broad outlines for addressing it.

On the other hand, the overview in this chapter has opened a window of opportunity for reframing budgeting and fiscal management in a manner that contextualizes and aligns them with reality and lived experience in Africa. Such reframing is opportune, given the accumulated literature on sustainable development (Picard & Lelei, 2015; Cohen, 2011; UN, 1992) and increasing scholarly attention to fiscal sustainability and responsibility (Rubin, 2015; Tang, Callahan, & Pisano, 2014; Palmer & Penner, 2012). Moreover, experience with successive reforms offers useful lessons for developing a sustainability approach to budgeting and fiscal management framework that fosters a paradigmatic shift toward a greater focus on the future. At its core, sustainable development concerns balancing present with future needs, as well as providing equity and opportunity. There has never been a better time in Africa than now to re-conceptualize budgeting and fiscal management based on sustainability, but how can it begin?

A Case for Sustainability Budgeting and Fiscal Management

In contrast to existing approaches that have been narrow and largely economistic and technocratic, the literature in multiple disciplinary areas provides insights and suggests ideas about how to approach budgeting and fiscal management from a broad sustainability perspective. The theory of budgeting is inextricably linked to the concept of development, which has expanded since the UN Conference on Environment and Development advocated more and better balance: an integration of the economic, social, and environmental dimensions (UN, 1992). Subsequent UN initiatives have generated energy and enthusiasm in support of a notion of sustainable development that incorporates all aspects of the human condition from health through economic to political well-being (UN, 2002). In recent times, UNECA has monitored and assessed the inter-relationships entailed in this approach in Africa (www.uncsd2012.org/content/documents/SDRA1%20managing%20land-based%20resources). Thus a principle of integration can be deduced as a critical piece of sustainability with important implications for budgeting and fiscal management reform.

Along these lines, the donor community and development partners have further elaborated on sustainability and focused on the human dimension, including quality-of-life measures: health, education, employment, and incomes. On its part, the World Bank (1989) has reinforced the idea of sustainable development, emphasizing environmental protection and the ability to meet present needs while providing opportunities for the future. Also, the World Bank has advocated a governance framework that promotes participation, inclusion, equity, and shared prosperity. To this end, the UN Millennium Declaration (2000) created a global partnership aimed at reducing poverty, improving education and health and promoting gender equality. Thus in addition to integration as identified above, the underlying principles that should inform budgeting and fiscal management include orientation toward the future and human development.

Concern for orientation toward the future and long-term fiscal sustainability has been a running theme in the mainstream fiscal policy analysis field since the global recession (2007–2008). In fact, US Government Accountability Office (2014) simulations demonstrate the increasing gap between expenditures and receipts in the long term, a fiscal sustainability challenge facing all government levels. Since the global recession, the journals *Public Budgeting & Finance* and *Public Administration Review* have featured articles that call attention to the urgency of fiscal sustainability and long-term fiscal challenges, drawing mainly on the US and European experiences (e.g., Tang, Callahan, & Pisano 2014; Aarle & Konings, 2013; Joyce, 2012; Palmer & Penner, 2012;). Palmer and Penner express concern over the US "unsustainable, long-term fiscal trajectory," analyze the increasing national debt that will "far outpace economic growth," and advocate "long-term deficit reduction." For their part, Tang, Callahan, and Pisano (2014) suggest the use of common-pool resource principles to address fiscal sustainability, while Aarle and Konings (2013) argue that it is important to gauge both short- and long-term consequences of macro-economic shocks.

In African nations, long-term budgeting and fiscal management reform is in the national, regional, and continent-wide interest for at least two reasons. First, a sustainability perspective serves as a motivation to identify appropriate national policies in the medium- to long-term. Such an approach foregrounds politics, enabling pluralistic interests to be addressed and resolved *a priori* along the lines that Wildavsky had theorized in his classic, *The Political Implications of Budget Reform* (1961). His theoretical insight is, as Rubin (2015, p. 25) puts it, "society is not a single entity with a single set of goals." Elaborating on this insight, Rubin posits an inherent "conflict orientation" in budgeting, including competition among groups, especially "power battles between the executive and legislative branches." This thought is relevant to Africa, where society is far from being homogeneous. On the contrary, African society is geographically and culturally fragmented. In light of this "conflict orientation," the APSP and CABRI initiatives (Africa Parliamentary Strengthening Program for Budget Oversight 2010, pp. 19–20) have the potential to make significant contributions to improving budgeting and fiscal management beginning with conflict resolution, appropriate policy identification, and prioritization of spending objectives through the political process.

The second reason for the sustainability approach concerns what UNECA describes as Land-based resources" or natural resource endowments that have contributed substantially to Africa's economic growth over the past decade. As UNECA argues, focusing on land-based resources is justifiable because African economies rely mostly on natural resources. As a matter of fact, Africa is well endowed in natural resources with considerable deposits of the world's precious natural resources: uranium, hydropower, oil, gas, and coal, to name but a few. As indicated in Table 1.2, uranium, which tops the list, is found in South Africa, Namibia, and Niger.

The APP (2013) considers twenty African countries as "resource rich" or "fiscally dependent" with over a quarter of domestic revenues derived from mineral export. It also estimates that 13 countries depend on natural resource exports for over half of their export revenues. In addition to the abundant mineral resources, the APP (2014) is optimistic about the potential of "Africa's Green and Blue Revolution," one based in improved smallholder production of grain and fish.

Although natural resources are not evenly distributed throughout the continent, the APP argues that resource wealth can strengthen economic growth and create opportunities to support human development overall. This is in line with the macro-economic theory of budgeting that posits that a growing economy

Table 1.2 Africa's Major Natural Resource Endowments

Natural Resource	*Deposit*	*% World Reserve*
Uranium	613.1 thousand metric tons	18.7%
Hydropower	1,917 TWh/year	12%
Oil Reserves	112.233 billion barrels	9.4%
Natural Gas Reserve	498.860 trillion cubic feet	7.84%
Coal Reserves	50.336 billion metric tons	5.5%

Source: www.uncsd2012.org/content/documents/SDRA1%20managing%20land-based%20 resources

will produce more revenues for service expansion. On the other hand, a declining economy forces reductions in spending while increasing borrowing to finance public services. However, and as York and Zhan (2009) found in a study of eight oil-producing sub-Saharan African countries, "management of oil wealth and improvement in fiscal policies in the region has not progressed much, so that there is a risk that opportunity has been lost." As they argue, these countries run the risk of fiscal vulnerability because oil price volatility and the lack of appropriate fiscal adjustment elevate the risk in African oil-producing countries. The risk is exacerbated due to boom-bust cycles and also to budgeting and fiscal management focused on short-term control measures and cash management. For this reason, the sustainability approach is needed to foster far-sightedness both by directing resources to present priority policy objectives and also by considering the implications of current policy for the ability to meet future needs.

Summary and Conclusion

To sum up, budgeting and fiscal management in African nations historically has been on an unsustainable path and largely continues to be so in spite of reform. By over-emphasizing short-term spending control and cash management, deficits and debts have accumulated to unsustainable levels that have resulted in dire fiscal conditions in many cases. The rule-of-thumb is to not spend more cash than the legislature has allocated. Reforms have entailed a concerted shift away from such a mind-set toward contributing to achieving outcomes of specified policy goals and objectives. Thus the long-term sustainability budgeting and fiscal management approach suggested here builds on the foundation that the fiscal decentralization and MTEF models have laid but with stronger emphasis on the setting out of policy goals and objectives.

The key argument of the chapter is supported by a theory of budgeting that foregrounds politics and conflict orientation (Rubin, 2015; Wildavsky, 1961). This theoretical perspective aligns well with the fragmented structure of African society, as well as its unique historicity and material conditions. It is also supported by calls even in the advanced nations for a "longer view of the budget to address the problem of its long-term sustainability" (Posner, Redburn, Joyce, & Meyers, 2013, p. 25). In a memo to the US government, Posner, Redburn, Joyce, and Meyers assert that "Fiscal sustainability, like price stability and full employment, should be an explicit goal of national fiscal policy and economic management." If fiscal sustainability is of such urgent concern in developed nations, it is even more so in developing nations.

MTEF implementation efforts in African nations have laid the groundwork for a multi-year and strategic view of budgeting and fiscal management. At the core is the integration of budgeting and fiscal management along with long-term fiscal targets. Figure 1.1 depicts the sustainability approach by integrating three functional areas of budgeting and fiscal management. Functional Area A involves clarification of the national vision and policy goals, as well as fiscal stocktaking in a multi-year fashion. This is consistent with the World Bank's

(1998) notion of "top-down resource envelope" and "bottom-up estimation of current and medium-term costs of existing policy." But unlike the World Bank's model, this phase factors in policy conflicts that lie within budgeting and fiscal management and must be addressed before a consensus around common concerns and interests can be developed. It overlaps with and must of necessity be carefully dovetailed into the other two intertwined fiscal functional areas B and C.

Functional Area B is where resource allocations are made, i.e., where the question of how to make hard fiscal choices is determined and where fiscal discipline is embedded. Functional Area C is just as important because it is where the financial management system kicks in to ensure judicious use of resources to achieve duly predetermined policy objectives. It is important because it induces fiscal accountability, responsibility, and transparency by providing timely information on how well fiscal targets are being met and how programs can be improved.

The question that remains is: how feasible is long-term sustainability budgeting and fiscal management in Africa, given its capacity limitations, political instability, and donor ideological commitment? It is true that a long-term budgeting and fiscal management perspective poses challenges ranging from structural and organizational to technical and practical considerations. In their critique of MTEFs in African nations, Houerou and Taliercio (2002) raise

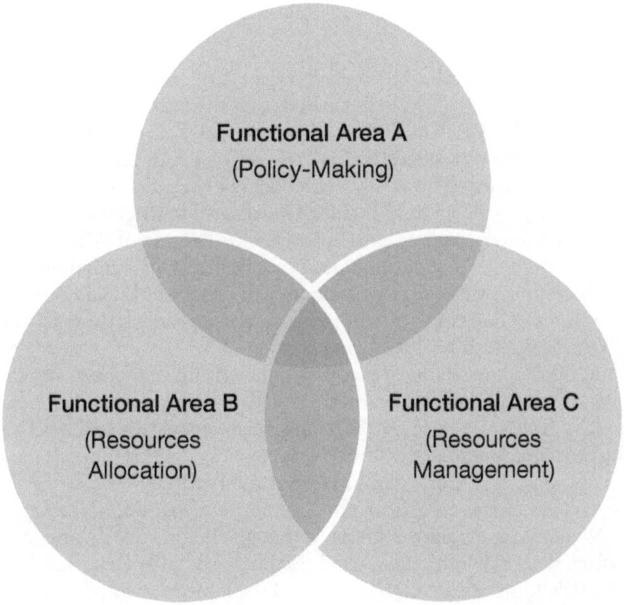

Figure 1.1 Conceptual scheme of sustainability budgeting and fiscal management based on three main functions of public budgeting

questions about operational difficulties, including capacity limitations, activity sequencing, and opposition to reform. They emphasize the fact that MTEFs are sound conceptually but flawed operationally. They assert that "MTEF is a multi-component reform in practice and most countries could not implement all reforms at once." There is no question but that capacity constraint is a concern; however considerable resources have been invested since the resurrection of the state as a key player in economic and political development (Grindle, 2010). Nonetheless, achieving long-term fiscal sustainability requires high-level expertise that is lacking in Africa, especially at sub-national levels. Even in countries such as Burkina Faso, Ghana, Kenya, and Senegal, where devolution has occurred, low fiscal capacity and political will substantially constrain effective performance.

Granted that sustainability budgeting and fiscal management as conceptualized here face potential challenges, a credible case can be made that momentum has been generated in its favor. A multi-year fiscal framework is emerging as an international standard and steadily creating a culture of long-term view and fiscal discipline. MTEFs have paved the way and provided useful lessons on which a longer term fiscal view can be built. The APP has advocated investment in human development, infrastructure, and the management of natural resources in a long-term framework. In launching the 2015 Sustainable Development Goals the APP offers a spur to move Africa forward in the direction of sustainability budgeting and fiscal management.[18]

Notes

1 The Africa Progress Report is prepared and published annually by the Africa Progress Panel (APP) consisting of 10 distinguished personalities from the private and public sectors. Chaired by Dr. Kofi Annan (former UN Secretary-General and Nobel Laureate), the Panel has issued reports and advocated for equitable and sustainable development in Africa. The 2014 report focused on how to boost agriculture and fisheries, which provide a livelihood for two-thirds of Africans.

2 This refers to micro-economic principles but in the case of Africa it is concerned specifically with the field of development economics, which enquires into why some countries including Africa remain economically backward while others are rich. It also addresses the questions of why poverty persists and how poor countries can become rich (e.g., Rostow, 1960, 1963).

3 The World Bank's concept of the medium-term expenditure framework (MTEF) aims at making sure that resources flow toward and align with policy and program priorities. MTEFs date back to the mid-1990s and have since gained currency in public expenditure management systems in the developing countries of Africa, Asia, Latin America and Eastern Europe (see Houerou and Taliercio, 2002).

4 Five sub-regions of the continent are commonly recognized: Northern, Southern, Eastern, Western, and Central Africa, although the broader distinction is between Black Africa (sub-Saharan Africa) and the predominantly Arab-speaking countries of North Africa, including Algeria, Egypt, Libya, Morocco, and Tunisia.

5 Several scholars and researchers have noted the presence of substantial numbers of people of African descent living around the world, including Versi (2003), Khan (2003), Emeagwali (2003), and Mazrui (2008). According to Ali Mazrui (2008),

there may be as many as 150 million Africans living outside of Africa, most of whom reside in the USA and Brazil.

6 The UN Millennial Declaration (2000) included concrete measurable objectives and Millennium Development Goals (MDGs), including goals related to maternal and childhood mortality, universal basic education, and gender equality, to mention but a few.

7 According to Ayittey (1998, p. 38), the East African slave trade, which was controlled by Arabs, caused much "suffering or death to at least 2 million black Africans in the nineteenth Century."

8 Development economics is assumed to have begun in the 1950s with the UN's *Measures for the Development of Underdeveloped Countries* (1951). Studies of poverty concluded that it is self-perpetuating and often associated with conditions that obstruct economic growth.

9 Cocoa continues to be one of Ghana's main export commodities along with minerals (e.g., gold, aluminum, and diamonds) as well as timber products. In recent years, crude oil export has gained considerable attention in the national budget but agriculture, which is mainly driven by cocoa exports, leads the growth of Ghana's economy (Republic of Ghana, 2015).

10 Against the background of famine and food shortages in Ethiopia, the Director-General of the UN FAO stated that the 1980s was a lost decade for development not only in Africa but also in Latin America.

11 Almost all African nations have adopted the World Bank and IMF stabilization and structural adjustment programs (SAPs) as conditions for accessing loan facilities. SAPs originated from the debt crisis that hit developing countries in the 1980s.

12 The East African Bribery Index indicates that the average bribe paid for land services in Kenya is more than USD 100 and the average bribe paid to the judiciary in Uganda is more than USD 200. See: www.transparency.org/gcb2013/report. Globally, corruption has impacted more than one in four people in the countries surveyed.

13 Luther Gulick and Lyndall Urwick pioneering public administration thinkers, identified executive functions as planning, organizing, directing, supervising, coordinating, and budgeting (PODSCORB) as a way of managing financial, human, and material resources back in the 1930s.

14 The Consolidated Fund or Consolidated Revenue Fund refers to the main bank account of governments in the Commonwealth nations. It is the account into which tax revenue is paid and from which withdrawals are made to meet legally authorized financial commitments.

15 Sub-Saharan Africa has lagged behind other regions and has not been forecast to meet the Millennium Development Goals in 2015 although much progress has been made in halving poverty, slowing the spread of HIV/AIDS, and increasing universal primary education. (Retrieved from: http://data.worldbank.org/products/wdi.)

16 Welfare economists and public choice theorists apply economic principles to analyze people's actions in collective decision-making such as taxation and spending. Briefly, they argue that people acting in the political market place—voters, politicians, lobbyists, and bureaucrats—tend to base their decisions on self-interest as they do in the individual market place.

17 It is common knowledge that African nations are racially homogeneous but ethnically heterogeneous and that ethnicity shapes how the political game is played and how public policy is formulated and implemented.

18 The Africa Progress Panel is planning to launch its 2015 Annual Report that highlights how Africa's engagement in climate change and environment policy is connected both to its energy independence and sustainability development (www.africaprogresspanel.org/publications/policy-papers/africa-progress-report-2015).

References

Aarle, B.V., & Konings, J. (2013). Budgetary sustainability in the presence of macroeconomic and financial market instability: An application to the case of Belgium. *Public Budgeting & Finance*, 33(1): 114–134.

Africa Parliamentary Strengthening Program for Budget Oversight (2010). The Budget Process in Africa: A Comparative Study of Seven Countries. [Online] Retrieved from: http://www.agora-parl.org/sites/default/files/the_budget_process_in_africa_2010_en.pdf

Africa Progress Panel. (2013). *Equity in Extractives: Stewarding Africa's natural resources for all*. [Online] Retrieved from: http://africaprogresspanel.org.

Africa Progress Panel. (2014). *Building on a Decade of Growth*. [Online] Retrieved from: www.africaprogresspanel.org/publications/policy-papers/2014.

Africa Progress Panel. (2015). *Why Climate Challenges are an Opportunity for Africa*. [Online] Retrieved from: http://africaprogresspanel.org/why-climate-challenges-are-an-opportunity-for-africa/.

Ake, C. (1996). *Democracy and Development in Africa*. Washington, DC: The Brookings Institution.

Andrews, M. (2014). *The Limits of Institutional Reform in Development: Changing rules in realistic solutions*. Cambridge: Cambridge University Press

Ayittey, G.B.N. (1991). *Indigenous African Institutions*. New York: Transnational.

Ayittey, G.B.N. (1992). *Africa Betrayed*. New York: St. Martin's Press.

Ayittey, G.B.N. (1998). *Africa in Chaos*. New York: St. Martin's Press

Beschel Jr., R.P., & Ahern, M. (2012). *Public Financial Management in the Middle East and North Africa: An overview of regional experience*. Washington, DC: The World Bank.

Busia, K.A. (1967). *Africa in Search of Democracy*. New York: Praeger.

Chan, J.L. (2002). Introduction. *OECD Journal of Budgeting*, 2(1): 9–10.

Cheru, F. (2002). *African Renaissance: Road maps to the challenges of globalization*. London: Zed Books.

Cohen, S. (2011). *Sustainability Management: Lessons from and for New York city, America, and the planet*. New York: Columbia University Press.

Collaborative Africa Budget Reform Initiative (CABRI). (2008). *Budget Practices and Procedures in Africa*. [Online] Retrieved from: www.afdb.org/fileadmin/uploads/afdb/Documents/Publications/CABRI%20AFDB%2-ENG.pdf.

Dafflon, B., & Madies, T. (2013). *The political economy of decentralization in Sub-Saharan Africa*. Washington, DC: World Bank.

Davidson, B. (1966). *Africa in History*. New York: Simon & Schuster.

Diamond, L. (2004). Promoting Real Reform in Africa. In E. Gyimah-Boadi (Ed.), *Democratic Reform in Africa: The quality of progress* (pp. 263–292). Boulder: Lynne Rienner Publishers.

Draman, R. (2010). *The Budget Process in Africa: A comparative study of seven countries*. [Online] Retrieved from: www.agora-parl.org/sites/default/files/the_budget_process_in_africa_2010_en.pdf.

The Economist. (2011) Africa's Impressive Growth. *The Economist Online*, June 6, 2011. [Online] Retrieved from: www.economist.com/blogs/dailychart/2011/01/daily_chart.

Emeagwali, P. (2003). *How do we reverse the brain drain?* [Online] Retrieved from: http//africanamericaspeakers.biz/speeches/brain-drain/to-brain-gain/reverse-brain-drain-from-africa.html.

Gibon, P., Havnevik, K.J., & Hermele, K. (1993). *A Blighted Harvest: The World Bank and African agriculture in the 1980s*. London: James Curry.

Green, E. D. (2008). Decentralization and growth in Uganda. *Conflict, Security, and Development*, 8(4): 427–450.

Grindle, M.S. (2010). Good governance: The inflation of an Idea. *HKS Faculty Research Working Paper Series, RWP 10–023*, Cambridge, MA: John F. Kennedy School of Government, Harvard University.

Gyimah-Boadi, E. (2004). Africa: The quality of political reform. In E. Gyimah-Boadi (Ed.) *Democratic Reform in Africa: The quality of progress*. Boulder, CO: Lynne Rienner.

Haruna, A.L., & Al-Ansar, G.U. (2013). *Nigerian Federalism and the Statutory Allocation of Funds: Analytical review of local government's third tier of government*. [Online] Retrieved from: www.academia.edu/4814577/Nigerian_Federalism_And_The_Statutory_Allocation_Of_Funds_Analytical_Review_Of_Local_Government_As_Third_Tier_Of_Government.

Heidenhof, G., Grandvoinnet, H., Kianpour, D., & Rezaian, B. (2002). *Design and Implementation of Financial Management Systems: An African perspective*. [Online] Retrieved fromwww.worldbank.org/afr/wps/index.htm.

Houerou, P. L., & Taliercio, R. (2002). *Medium Term Expenditure Frameworks: From concept to practice*. [Online] Retrieved from: www.worldbank.org.afr/wps/index.htm.

Hyde, A.C. (1992). *Government Budgeting: Theory, process, and politics*. Belmont, CA: Wadsworth.

International Labor Organization. (2001). *The Impact of Decentralization and Privatization on Municipal Services*. Geneva: ILO.

International Monetary Fund. (2006). *IMF Technical Assistance Evaluation: Public expenditure management reform*. [Online] Retrieved from: www.imf.org/external/pubs/ft/scr/2006/cr0667.pdf.

Joyce, P. (2012). The introduction to symposium: The crisis in federal budgeting. *Public Budgeting & Finance*, 32(3): 1–3.

Key, Jr. V.O. (1940). The lack of a budgetary theory. *American Political Science Review*, 34(1): 1137–1140.

Khan, F. (2003). Population: African union courts Africans in the diaspora. *Global Information Network* 1: 7–12.

Leuenberger, D.Z., & Bartle, J.R. (2009). *Sustainable Development for Public Administration*. New York: M. E. Sharpe.

Lewis, C.W., & Hildreth, W.B. (2013). *Budgeting: Politics & and Power*. New York: Oxford University Press.

Lofchie, M.F., & Callaghy, T. (1996). *Diversity in the Tanzanian Business Community: Its implication for economic growth*. [Online] Retrieved from: http://pdf.usaid.gov/pdf_docs/PNABY324.pdf.

Mazrui, A.A. (1986). *The Africans: A triple heritage*. London: BBC Publications.

Mazrui, A.A. (2008). The dual diaspora and the tensions of black liberation: From post-enslavement to post-coloniality. In K. Gyekye (Ed.) *Ghana @ 50 Anniversary Lectures* (pp. 211–237). Accra: G-Pak.

Moss, T. J. (2007). *African Development: Making Sense of the Issues and Actors*. Boulder: Lynne Rienner.

Nelson, L.S. (1999). Environment in the community, community in the environment. *Administrative Theory & Praxis*, 21(3): 354–361.

Nice, D. (2002). *Public Budgeting*. Belmont, CA: Wadsworth.

Olowu, D., & Wunsch, J. (2004). Introduction: local governance and democratic decentralization in Africa. In Dele Olowu & James Wunsch (Eds.) *Local Governance in Africa: The challenges of democratic decentralization* (pp. 1–27). Boulder, CO: Lynne Rienner.

Palmer, J.L., & Penner, R.G. (2012). The hard road to fiscal responsibility. *Public Budgeting & Finance*, 32(3): 4–31.

Picard, L.A., & Lelei, M.C. (2015). Achieving sustainable development in Africa: A governance perspective. In Louis Picard, Terry Buss, Taylor Seybolt, & Macrina Lelei (Eds.) *Sustainable Development and Human Security in Africa: Governance as the missing link* (pp. 3–19). Boca Raton, FL: Taylor & Francis.

Posner, P., & Park, C.K. (2007). Role of the legislature in the budget process: Recent trends and innovations. *OECD Journal on Budgeting*, 7(3): 78–102.

Posner, P., Redburn, S., Joyce, P., & Meyers, R. (2013). Budgeting for the long term, avoiding the real fiscal cliff. In Paul Posner, Allan Rosebaum, Antoinette Samuel, and Dan Blair (Eds.) *Memos to National Leaders* (pp. 25–29). Washington, DC: American Society for Public Administration.

Purtell, R.M., & Fossett, J.W. (2010). Beyond budgeting: Public service financial education in the 21st century. *Journal of Public Affairs Education*, 16(1): 95–110.

Ranis, G. (2012). *Vertical and Horizontal Decentralization and Ethnic Diversity in Sub-Saharan Africa*. New Haven: Yale University Economic Growth Center.

Republic of Ghana. (2009). *Implementation of the Growth and Poverty Reduction Strategy 2006–2009: 2008 Annual Progress Report*. Accra: National Development Planning Commission.

Republic of Ghana. (2015). *The Budget Speech of the Budget Statement and Economic Policy of the Government of Ghana for the 2015 Fiscal Year*. Accra: Government of Ghana.

Rodney, W. (1981). *How Europe Underdeveloped Africa*. Washington, DC: Howard University Press.

Rondinelli, D.A., & Cheema, S. (Eds.). (2003). *Reinventing Government for the Twenty-First Century: State capacity in a globalizing society*. Bloomfield, CT: Kumarian Press.

Rostow, W.W. (1960). *The States of Economic Growth*. Cambridge, MA: Cambridge University Press.

Rostow, W.W. (Ed.). (1963). *The Economics of Take-off into Sustained Growth*. London: Macmillan.

Rubin, I. (2015). Past and future budget classics: A research agenda. *Public Administration Review*, 75(1): 25–35.

Salami, A., Kamara, A.B., & Brixiova, Z. (2010). *Smallholder agriculture in East Africa: Trends, constraints, and opportunities*. [Online] Retrieved from: www.afdb.org/fileadmin/uploads/afdb/Documents/Publications/WORKING%20105%20%20PDF%20d.pdf.

Savage, J. D. (2013). The Development Dilemma: What's Going Wrong and What Can be Fixed? *Public Administration Review*, 73(6): 893–895.

Steffesen, J., & Trollegaard, S. (2000). *Fiscal Decentralization and Sub-National Government Finance in Relation to Infrastructure and Service Provision: Synthesis Report of 6 Sub-Saharan Country Studies*. Washington, DC: The World Bank.

Stiglitz, J.E. (1998). *Towards a New Paradigm for Development: Strategies, policies, and processes*. Prebisch Lecture at UNCTAD, Geneva.

Tanf, S.Y., Callahan, R.F., & Piscano, M. (2014). Using common pool resources principles to design local government fiscal sustainability. *Public Administration Review*, 74(6): 791–803.

Transparency International. (2013). *Global Corruption Barometer*. [Online] Retrieved from: www.transparency.org/gcb2013/report.

United Nations. (1992). *Sustainable Development: United Nations Conference on Environment & Development*. Rio de Janeiro, Brazil, June 3–14.

United Nations. (2002). *World Summit on Sustainable Development*. Johannesburg, South Africa, August 26–September 4, 2002.

United Nations Economic Commission for Africa. (2009). *African Governance Report 2005*. Addis Ababa: UNECA.

United Nations Economic Commission for Africa. (2011). *African Governance Report 2005*. Addis Ababa: UNECA.

United Nations Economic Commission for Africa. (2014). *Assessing Progress in Africa toward the Millennium Development Goals: Analysis of the common African position on the post-2015 development agenda*. Addis Ababa: UNECA.

United Nations General Assembly. (2000). *United Nations Millennium Declaration*. A/RES/55/2. 8th Plenary Meeting. September.

United Nations Human Settlements Programme and Municipal Development Partnership for Eastern and Southern Africa. 2008. *Participatory Budgeting in Africa—A Training Companion with cases from eastern and southern Africa*.[Online] Retrieved from: www.unpan1.un.org/intradoc/groups/public/documents/un-padmin/unpan042159.pdf.

United Nations Measures for the Development of Underdeveloped Countries (1951). World Economic Report 1949–1950. [Online] Retrieved from: http://www.un.org/en/development/desa/policy/wess/wess_archive/1949_1950_wer.pdf

United States Government Accountability Office. (2014). *State and Local Government Fiscal Outlook*. [Online] Retrieved from: www.gao.gov/fiscal_outlook/state_local_fiscal_model/overview#t=2.

Versi, A. (2003). Bring Home the Best and Brightest. *African Business* 286: 11–25.

Walle, N.V.D. (2004). Economic Reform: Patterns and Constraints. In E. Gyimah-Boadi (Ed.) *Democratic Reform in Africa: The quality of progress* (pp. 29–63). Boulder CO: Lynne Rienner.

White, J.D., & Adams, G.B. (1994). Making sense with diversity: The context of research, theory, and knowledge development in public administration. In J.D. White & G.B. Adams (Eds.) *Research in Public Administration: Reflections on Theory and Practice* (pp. 1–22). Thousand Oaks, CA: Sage Publications.

Wiarda, H.J. (1991). *New Directions in Comparative Politics*. Boulder, CO: Westview Press.

Wiarda, H.J. (1999). Introduction: The Western tradition and its export to the non-west. In H. J. Wiarda (Ed.) *Non-Western Theories of Development: Regional norms and global trends*. Fort Worth, TX: Harcourt Brace College.

Wildavsky, A. (1961). Political implications of budgetary reform. *Public Administration Review* (21): 183–190.

World Bank. (1989). *Sub-Saharan Africa: From Crisis to sustainable growth*. Washington, DC: World Bank.

World Bank. (1998). *Public Expenditure Management Handbook*. Washington, DC: World Bank.

World Bank. (2014). *Africa Overview*. [Online] Retrieved from: www.worldbank.org/en/region/afr/overview#1.

Wylie, L. (1999). Sub-Saharan Africa: Western influence and indigenous realities. In H. Wiarda (Ed.) *Non-Western Theories of Development: Regional norms and global trends*. Fort Worth, TX: Harcourt Brace College.

York, R., & Zhan, Z. 2009. *Fiscal Vulnerability and Sustainability in Oil Producing Sub-Saharan African Countries*. New York: International Monetary Fund.

Zanetti, L.A., & King, C.S. 2013. Transformational Public Service Revisited: Possibilities for changing the discipline? *Administrative Theory & Praxis* 35(1): 128–143.

2 Public Budgeting in Africa: The Case of Botswana

Taolo B. Lucas and Theophilus T. Tshukudu

Introduction

Public finance management and budgeting are at the heart of development management. It is through prudent use and management of public moneys that countries can achieve social and economic development objectives geared toward improving the quality of life of the majority of the people. In Botswana public finance and management are entrenched in the Constitution of the Republic in sections 117–124. To augment constitutional provisions on public finance, the Finance and Audit Act was passed by Parliament in 1970. It provides details on the use and management of public finances. In recent years the Finance Act was separated into two pieces of legislation, namely the Public Finance Management Act of 2011 and the Audit Act of 2012. The Minister of Finance has wide-ranging powers, according to the laws of Botswana pertaining to the use and management of public moneys. The minister through various structures in his or her ministry originates, prepares and presents the Budget Speech to the National Assembly. He or she has jurisdiction over different budget components and he or she participates in setting budget ceilings for line ministries through officers he or she seconds to them. He or she appoints accounting officers in different ministries and he or she is responsible for producing financial regulations and instructions on the use of public moneys. The Auditor-General is responsible for keeping Government books of accounts in check and he or she is empowered to audit any department of Government when he or she deems it necessary. The fundamentals of public finance management and budgeting are strong. The policies, laws, systems and processes are sound. However, there is still plenty of room for improvement. There is a need to empower oversight institutions such as Parliament and the Auditor-General to exercise authority over intransigent public bodies or persons. The budgeting process has to be transparent to allow for civil society and Parliament to take active part without undue constraints. It is also critical to reduce the dominance of the Executive and the Central Government in public budgeting according to Phirinyane (2009) and Tlhalefang (2013a). Parliament as well as Local Government structures must be given space in the preparation of the budget.

History of Planning and Budgeting

Botswana was a British colony from 1885 and it attained self-governance in 1965 when the first democratic elections were held. On the 30th September, 1966 Botswana became an independent state. During the 30 years of colonial rule, Botswana suffered benign neglect and no major socio-economic infrastructure was put in place. In administering the colony, the British employed the twin strategies of indirect rule and minimum expenditure. Indirect rule manifested itself through the use of the local tribal chiefs to administer the economy on behalf of the colonizers. Minimum expenditure entailed spending as little as possible in the colony, which was perceived to have no or very little economic or strategic value to British interests. Money for providing rudimentary services was largely derived from taxes levied on the local populations. To pay such taxes, many Botswana men, in the absence of opportunities for economic engagement locally, migrated to South African mines and used remittances from their employers (Parsons, 1980).

In the early 1960s as nationalistic fervour gripped most of Africa, it became clear that independence was imminent for Botswana. It was at this time that the British Government instituted some administrative measures that could be used to support an independent country. There was also an increase in the grants awarded to the colony to help put in place basic infrastructure and services. Independence finally came and at the time, Botswana was one of the poorest countries, not only in Africa, but in the world. The country was without basic infrastructure, illiteracy was high and health facilities were few and underdeveloped. The bulk of the country's recurrent and development costs were financed from the British Treasury and a few donors (Mwansa, Lucas & Osei-Hwedie, 1998).

It was at the time of independence that Botswana evolved a planning framework and a budgetary regime that informs development planning and process to this day. The Transitional Plan for Economic and Social Development was born in 1966 and ran up to 1968. The plan was a precursor to a system of five years then six-year National Development Plans (NDPs). The NDPs became blueprints for systematic development planning in Botswana. The NDPs are implemented through annual national budgets that have been formulated without interruption since independence. The regularity and predictability with which NDPs and the annual budgets are formulated in Botswana creates stability and certainty in both the planning and budget process. The question that could require further examination is whether or not implementation follows the letter of these two critical development instruments (Mwansa, Lucas & Osei-Hwedie, 1998; Madongo 2013).

Since independence, development planning in Botswana has been anchored on the national principles of democracy, development, self-reliance and unity. The national planning principles of rapid economic growth, social justice, economic independence and sustained development were a recurring theme in development discourse in Botswana for many years after independence. In 1996, the National Vision 2016 was adopted and together with the principles highlighted, defined the direction of development planning and resource allocation.

The strategy for development in Botswana has been to invest in massive mining exploration and exploitation with a view to raising adequate revenues to support social development. The discovery and mining of diamonds in Botswana in the early years of independence generated significant revenues for the Government and by 1973 the country had achieved budgetary self-sufficiency as per the second National Development Plan (Ministry of Finance and Development Planning, 2009). Since 1973 the country has managed to finance its recurrent and development budget with donor funds and grants only providing additional revenue to accelerate development. The dependency on mineral revenue and failure to meaningfully diversify the economy away from minerals has been a source of concern. The dependence on diamonds has made the economy vulnerable and susceptible to fluctuations in the price of diamonds in the international market. Fragility has become a feature of our economy despite relative success and positive economic indicators for the last five decades of independence (Malema 2014).

Public Finance Management and Budgeting: A Look at Critical Legislation

The Constitution

Public finance management and budgeting in Botswana is entrenched in the supreme law of the land—the Constitution of the Republic of Botswana. Sections 117–124 of the Constitution document the processes and procedures for handling public finances in Botswana. Section 119 in particular speaks to the preparation of the national budget. It states that:

> the minister for the time being responsible for finance shall cause to be prepared and laid before the National Assembly, before or not later than 30 days before the commencement of each final year, estimates of revenues and expenditure of Botswana for the year.

The Constitution also makes provision for the supplementary budget (section 118 (3)). Section 121 of the Constitution establishes the contingencies fund to cater for unforeseen expenditure. The Constitution also spells out the offices that are to be paid from the consolidated fund (section 122 (5)). Section 123 states that "there shall be charged on the consolidated fund all debt charges for which Botswana is liable."

The Public Finance Management Act

It is important to note that before the Minister fulfills the notable constitutional requirement of presenting the budget before the National Assembly a myriad of processes and activities must have occurred. The processes and activities have an express objective of prudent management and utilization of the country's financial, manpower and other resources. The critical players in public finance management and budget processes are the Ministry of Finance and Development Planning, the Minister of Finance and Development Planning, the National Assembly, the Auditor-General and accounting officers in line ministries. The work and functions of these institutions for many years were defined by the Finance and Audit Act of 1970, which was recently replaced by the Public Finance Management Act of 2011 and the Audit Act of 2012. The acts give a detailed account of the powers and functions of the Minister of Finance as articulated below.

The Minister of Finance: Powers, Functions and Duties

Developing and Implementing Macro-economic and Fiscal Policy Framework

Section 5 (2 of the Public Finance Management Act of 2011) outlines the Minister of Finance's functions as they relate to developing and implementing a macro-economic and fiscal policy framework consistent with the National Development Plan or other mid-term planning framework that may be adopted. The framework developed by the Minister covers the following critical areas:

a) broad strategic priorities by which government shall be guided in the preparation of the budget;
b) overarching policy goals that will guide the budget decisions;
c) policy areas that the government is to focus on;
d) accord between the budget of the year and the goals of the National Development Plan;
e) advice to Government on the total of public moneys which would be made available and the allocation of such moneys to individual programmes;
f) supervision and monitoring of public moneys; and
g) coordination of the international and intergovernmental financial and fiscal relations of Botswana.

The macro-economic fiscal policy objectives to be pursued by the minister are premised on the principles of fiscal management listed here under:

a) reduction of the total debt to prudent levels so as to provide protection against factors that may impact adversely on the level of total debt in the future;
b) maintenance of appropriate levels of debt that do not exceed the limitation on borrowing provided for in section 20 of the Stocks, Bonds and Treasury Bill Act;
c) prudent management of the fiscal risks facing the government; and

d) pursuit of policies that are consistent with a reasonable degree of predictability about the level and stability of tax rates for future years (section 5 (3)).

Appointment of Accounting Officers

The Minister of Finance and Development Planning as per the Public Finance Management Act is responsible for appointing or designating public officers to be accounting officers for Ministries and Departments as he or she deems appropriate. The functions of the appointed officers are as they appear in section 6 (4) of the act. They include:

a) the control of expenditure;
b) the collection of revenue and the payment thereof from the consolidated fund;
c) the procurement, control, custody, issue and use of all public supplies;
d) control, custody and use of public resources; and
e) such other matters as may be provided for in this act and the Financial Instructions.

Accounting responsibility for all ministries falls within the ambit of the appointed accounting officer.

Appointment of Government Audit Committee

Section 12 of the Public Finance Management Act of 2012 establishes a Government Audit Committee to be appointed by the Minister of Finance from the public and private sectors. The committee, as provided for in the Public Finance Management Act of 2012, section 12 (3), performs the following functions:

a) provision of an independent review and oversight of the government financial and other reporting activities;
b) reviewing of internal controls, risk management and governance processes;
c) monitoring and reviewing the effectiveness of the Government's internal audit function;
d) requiring the attendance of any public officer, including accounting officers, at its meetings to provide such information or answer such questions as the Government Audit Committee may require;
e) the creation and maintenance of the Audit Charter, which states the composition, powers and functions of the Government Audit Committee;
f) issuing of annual reports with respect to Government internal audit; and
g) such other powers and functions as the minister may prescribe.

The Government Audit Committee reports to the Minister of Finance, who shall exercise discretion that may include instituting surcharge proceedings against individuals; submission of a complaint to the Directorate of Corruption and Economic Crime; mobilizing disciplinary proceedings as provided in the Public Service Act or commencing court proceedings against alleged misconduct, misuse or misappropriation.

Presenting Budget Proposals to the National Assembly

As stated elsewhere in this chapter, the Minister of Finance is obligated by Section 119 of the Constitution to present budget proposals to the National Assembly on an annual basis. The presentation according to the Audit Act of 2012, section 5 (4) should include "a) current and projected state of the economy b) finances of Botswana and c) fiscal policy of the Government." Other useful information that should be a part of the Minister's presentation to the National Assembly includes recent trends and development indicators of the national economy; forecasts of economic indicators; and recent fiscal developments and forecasts in respect of revenues, recurrent and development expenditures, borrowing and debt servicing and contingent liabilities. The Minister's presentation to the National Assembly also incorporates information on the level of compliance by the Government with macro-economic objectives and the principles of fiscal management as they appear in the planning framework and as enunciated by the Minister in the budget preparation stages (Tlhalefang, 2013a; Mbekomize, 2014).

Establishment and Maintenance of Special Funds

Section 36 of the Public Finance Management Act empowers the Minister of Finance to establish a special fund by an order published in the Gazette stating the purpose of the Fund. Such a fund is established to meet a particular need that has risen and that requires special attention. The Minister then lays the same order before the National Assembly for approval. Some such fund orders that have previously been created include Public Debt Service Order; Revenue Stabilization Fund Order; Foreign Exchange Stabilization Reserve Fund Order; Sir Seretse Khama Memorial Fund Order for the Handicapped; Centre for Accounting Studies Special Fund Order and others. Special funds created are maintained until such time that they are dissolved.

Other Functions of the Minister

The Minister of Finance has jurisdiction over raising loans and borrowing money on behalf of the Government subject to ratification by the National Assembly (Public Finance Management Act, section 20). In so far as expenditure is concerned, there can be no withdrawal of money from the consolidated fund without the issue of a warrant by the Minister in accordance with section 118 of the Constitution of the Republic of Botswana (Public Finance Management Act, section 28). The Minister is also authorized by section 52 of the same act to come up with regulations, instructions and procedures for the good management of public moneys and supplies.

The President and Public Moneys

The President, who is the head of the Executive, is awarded some powers related to the management of public moneys but only under exceptional circumstances. The President features in situations where the Appropriation Act for whatever reason has been delayed. This act is an Act of Parliament passed by the Botswana government that allows the Bank of Botswana to issue funds out of the Consolidated Fund and also appropriates the funds—or allocates the funds disbursed the Consolidated Fund to individual government departments (Audit Act of Republic of Botswana, 2012). In that instance the President is empowered to issue a warrant to withdraw money from the consolidated fund from the beginning of the financial year and up to four months into that year. The situation is regularized once the Appropriation Act has been passed by the National Assembly. The President also comes into the picture where unforeseen circumstances requiring urgent attention arise. Section 32 (2) states that:

> if at any time the President is satisfied there has arisen an urgent and unforeseen need for the expenditure of public revenues for which no other provision exists and the circumstances are such that the expenditure cannot, without loss to the Government, be postponed until adequate provision is made by the National Assembly, the President may by warrant authorize advances from the Contingencies Fund in such amounts as from time to time be necessary to meet the need.

Clearly the President intervenes only in emergencies.

The Audit Act of 2012

In 1970 Parliament enacted the Finance and Audit Act, which cover the areas of public finance management and auditing. In recent years, with the expansion of the economy and increasing complexity of fiscal management, the need to separate finance and audit matters became urgent; hence the Public Finance Management Act and the Audit Act were created as separate pieces of legislation. The separate acts allow for comprehensive coverage of the two distinct yet related areas of development management. In its preamble, the Audit Act declares that it is:

> an act to provide for the Office of the Auditor-General established under section 124 of the Constitution; to provide for the appointment and tenure of the Office of the Auditor-General; to provide for the staff of the Office of the Auditor-General; to make further and better provision for

the audit of public accounts and the accounts of certain statutory corporations; to empower the Auditor-General with right of access to documents and information relevant to the performance of his or her functions and for matters connected or incidental thereof.

The Office of the Auditor-General

The Office of the Auditor-General is entrenched in the Constitution of the Republic of Botswana as an oversight body responsible for auditing all government or government-related financial transactions. The Auditor-General is appointed by the President but his or her office is expected to be independent and according to section 124 (5) of the Constitution "in the exercise of his or her functions the Auditor shall not be subject to the direction and control of any person or authority." The Audit Act of 2012 provides detail on the functions and operations of the Office of the Auditor-General and the Attorney General. The Act, which derives legitimacy from section 124 of the Constitution, stipulates under section 7 that in the discharge of his or her duties the Auditor-General should satisfy himself or herself of the following:

a) that all reasonable precautions are taken to safeguard the collection and custody of public moneys and that the laws,instructions and directions relating thereto have been duly observed;
b) that the disbursement of public moneys has taken place under proper authority and for the purposes intended by such authority;
c) that all reasonable precautions are taken to safeguard the receipt, custody, issue and proper use of public supplies, and that the instructions and directions relating thereto have been duly observed; and
d) that adequate instructions and directions exist for the guidance of officers responsible for the collection, custody, issue and disbursement of public moneys or the receipt, custody, issue and disbursement of public supplies.

Section 7 (2) of the Audit Act of 2012 empowers the Auditor-General where he or she deems it necessary to examine the economy, efficiency and effectiveness of public institutions and public officers in the discharge of their duties.

The Auditor-General submits his or her reports on public financial transactions to the Minister responsible for finance who in turn presents it to the National Assembly without alteration (Audit Act, section 20 (1)). Section 20 (2) provides the Auditor-General with an additional option in case the Minister does not comply. It states that:

> if the Minister responsible for finance fails to as required by subsection (1) lay any report mentioned in this section to the National Assembly, the Auditor-General shall send such report to the Speaker and the Speaker shall present the report to the National Assembly.

The Major Components of the Government Budget

The broad budgetary framework in Botswana is anchored on a system of five-year National Development Plans that define macro-economic and fiscal policy parameters and priorities. The National Development Plans set out manpower, recurrent and development budget growth rates as well as Government revenue forecasts for the plan period (Ministry of Finance and Development Planning, 2009). This becomes a basis for stabilizing Government spending. The administration of the budget in Botswana is primarily the work of the Ministry of Finance, Minister of Finance and line ministry accounting officers. In this exercise, the Development and Budget Division (DBD) in the Ministry of Finance and Development Planning takes the lead in the preparation of the budget assisted by staff they have seconded to line ministries. The DBD-seconded staff assist line ministries with budget requirements, consideration of ministerial budget estimates, supplementary budget estimates and such other advice as is necessary for budget preparation.

According to Ministry of Finance and Development Planning (2009), the Government budget has five major components, namely manpower budget, recurrent budget, development budget, consolidated fund revenue estimates and development fund revenue estimates. The manpower budget is prepared by the Manpower Sub-Committee of the Estimates Committee and it is chaired by the Director of the Directorate of Public Service Management. The sub-committee allocates new posts as per requests of ministries and departments. The manpower budgetary process yields the establishment register, which shows the number and level of personnel to be employed. The preparation of the recurrent budget is coordinated by the DBD. This budget comprises the cost of the establishment register as well as running costs for all line ministries. The development budget is moneys from the development fund as established under section 36 and 37 of the Public Finance and Management Act. The formulation of the Development Budget is coordinated by the Project Review Committee, which establishes the status of the different projects in line ministries and determines the moneys required for their completion. Shortfalls for financing development projects may be met from loans and grants. The development fund revenue estimates are derived from this exercise. The last component of the budget is the consolidated fund revenue estimates. In this component of the budget line ministries submit revenue to the DDB through finance officers seconded to them. The DDB then establishes trends from various sources to arrive at revenue estimates.

The Budget Ceilings

An important aspect of the budget process in Botswana is the determination of budget ceilings that guide ministries on the amount of money with which to budget. Ceilings are made in respect of manpower, recurrent and development budgets. The manpower ceiling gives guidance to the Manpower Sub-Committee referred to earlier on the budget parameters within which to operate in proposing new posts and upgrading existing ones. As for the recurrent budget, the base budget, which is the current year's budget, is adjusted for expected inflation, incremental creep of around 2 percent per annum and real growth arising from the introduction of new posts. Preliminary ceilings born out of adjustments are sent to ministries for comments and feedback on such issues as the necessity for increases given the introduction of new policies or changed circumstances. Following feedback, further adjustments are made as necessary. The development budget ceilings are arrived at through engagement between DDB and line ministries on the status of different projects in their purview. Firm ceilings are arrived at after the Project Review Committee has submitted its final report. Budget ceilings are then passed.

Final decisions on the allocation of manpower and financial resources to departments are made by the Estimates Committee, chaired by the Permanent Secretary of the Ministry of Finance and Development Planning (MFDP). Once the Estimates Committee has deliberated and discussed its agenda, it releases its report including recommendations made to the Minister of Finance and Development Planning. It is at this time that a draft cabinet memorandum on financial and manpower estimates, a draft estimates book and a revenue estimates book are produced and they inform the overall budget estimates. A cabinet memorandum is then produced that provides the basis for the cabinet to debate and discuss the estimates before they are submitted to the National Assembly. Cabinet may make adjustments if the President agrees with their arguments. The next stage is the presentation of the budget proposals to the National Assembly for debate before the Appropriation Act for the budget can be passed.

Execution of the Budget

The execution of the budget is carried out by ministries' or departments' executive branches. These include the minister responsible, permanent secretary and their deputies, or in the case of independent departments the budget is implemented by the accounting officers as appointed as per the provisions of the Public Finance Management Act. On receipt of a finance warrant from the Minister of the MFDP, the accounting officer issues sub-warrants to departments in their ministry. The departments in turn apportion their budgets according to their divisions and maintain commitment ledgers to monitor expenditure and revenue to measure how closely the organization is meeting its objectives. Carrying out budgets requires the discipline to spend using values close to those set at budget formation. This can become problematic when a government department is dealing with single suppliers who periodically review their prices and can lead to over-spending as well. The whole idea of budgeting is to avoid under- or over-spending. Over-spending should be a result of unforeseen circumstances. Keeping track of ministerial and departmental expenses is paramount for accountability's sake. The finance section should keep track of impress and advances. Since the introduction of the Government Accounting and Budgeting System, it has been relatively easy to produce imprest analyses and reports on advances on a monthly basis. Even though there has been a major improvement in government spending and accountability, the biggest challenges to most ministries and government departments have been failures to retire imprests and advances by some public officers.

Reporting

The internal auditor reviews the effectiveness of the internal controls as laid down by the financial instructions and procedures and other sources. The Auditor-General seeks to provide assurance that:

1. the form and content of accounts comply with the appropriate GAAPS;
2. all figures in the accounts are properly stated;
3. funds have been applied for the purposes intended by the legislature; and
4. payments and receipts are in accordance with relevant legislature.

He or she also examines how well public operations have been performed. The other role of the Auditor-General is to seek to apply the two basic rules of value for money, namely: effectiveness, which translates to realizing the policy goals or doing the right thing, and efficiency, which refers to doing the right thing economically. The Auditor-General also ensures that budgetary controls are put in place to monitor spending, i.e. to ensure that monthly or quarterly measures of spending compare with the budget.

Major Revenue Sources

Botswana's relative economic success has been built on a foundation of diamond mining, prudent fiscal policies, international financial and technical assistance, and a cautious foreign policy. Generally major Government revenue sources

Table 2.1 Major Revenue Sources During the Financial Year 2014/15

Serial	*Source of income*	*Amount in Billions of Pulas*	*Percentage of the TOTAL BUDGET*
1	Customs & Excise	15.97	31.8
2	Non-Mineral Revenues (Income Tax & VAT)	15.66	31.2
3	Minerals	15.24	30.12
4	Others		6.88
TOTALS		46.87	100

Source: Botlhale (2013a)

include customs and excise duties, income tax and VAT, and minerals (Botlhale 2013b). It is important to note that diamond mining in particular has been the dominant revenue earner for the Government for the past four decades. Diamonds have been so important that any fluctuations in their prices cause a major upset in the revenue base of the country.

The over-reliance on diamonds for revenue, the sluggish uptake of the diversification drive, the under-developed industrial sector, the incompetence of the manufacturing sector and heavy reliance on imports are but some of the structural deficiencies of Botswana's economy. The revenue though generally healthy remains prone to external influences. It is probably one of the reasons why Botswana has always kept extravagant levels of foreign reserves so that in case of significant drops in diamond prices, the reserves could cushion the impact.

Government Major Expenditure Items of Government

The major expenditure items of the Government should be a reflection of the macro-economic and fiscal policy objectives contained in the National Development Plans. Galebotswe (2014) presents useful information on both recurrent and development budgets which gives pointers on the pattern of expenditures for the Government. The budgets cover a seven-year period as depicted below (Table 2.2).

Recurrent Budget

Table 2.2 shows that expenditure on human capital (education and health) represents the largest allocation. In general, these kinds of allocations can ensure that the benefits of growth are widely shared across society. However, this depends on the incidence of such expenditures. The 2.6 percent at present allocated to the Ministry of Trade and Industry (MTI) is not consistent with inclusive growth. The Ministry has a critical role to play in helping the country transition from a factor-driven stage of competitive advantage. This requires budgetary resources to promote trade and investment, research, and innovation

Table 2.2 Recurrent Budget of Botswana for Selected Ministries from 2008/9–2014/15 Financial Years by Ministry (in billion pula)

Ministry	*2008/09*	*2009/10*	*2010/11*	*2011/12*	*2012/13*	*2013/14*	*2014/15*
Education and Skills Development	5	5	5		5	5.5	6
Transport and Communications	–	–	1	1	1.2	1.3	1.5
Health	2	1.8	2	2.5	3	3	3.5
Local Government	3	3	3	3	3	3	3.4
Defence Justice and Security	–	–	2	2.5	2.5	3	3

Source: Galebotswe (2014)
NB: a (–) signifies a very low budget in comparison to other ministries

programs, and support capability, and industrial infrastructure development, among others. Moreover, businesses, especially small and medium enterprises (SMEs), are struggling because the environment is not conducive for them to operate and grow. One would expect a pro-inclusive growth budget to allocate more resources to the MTI to enable it to address some of the challenges faced by these types of businesses. The other reason for expecting more allocation to MTI arises from the fact that most locally produced goods are sold in their raw form, thus depriving the nation of the incomes that would be derived from downstream processing (Galebotswe, 2014). According to Galebotswe, the current paradigm in economic development emphasizes the industrial cluster model of Michael Porter (2000) as a social organization of production that can deliver high skill and high value added, as well as combine economic efficiency and social equity. This model identifies clear roles for public policy intervention, and one would expect MTI to be adequately funded to enable the country to reach the benefits promised by this institutional arrangements. Allocations to Defence, Justice and Security ministries are significantly high throughout the years and that is difficult to rationalize given the pressing developmental challenges of Botswana.

Development Budget

The allocation to the Ministry of Minerals, Energy and Water Resource has been consistently high in the development budget. Transport and Communications has also had a significant share of the development budget allocations. These allocations provide good building blocks for rapid economic growth. These expenditures are also expected to generate short-term employment by increasing the demand for labor during construction stages, and also in the long term through improvements in the country's competitiveness and total factor production. However, these allocations have not transformed the employment landscape over the years. On the other hand, allocations to the Ministry of Local Government and Rural Development are substantial but they are

Table 2.3 Botswana's Development Budget for Selected Ministries for Financial Years 2008/9–2014/15 (in billion pula)

Ministry	*2008/ 09*	*2009/ 10*	*2010/ 11*	*2011/ 12*	*2012/ 13*	*2013/ 14*	*2014/ 15*
Minerals, Energy and Water Resources	2.2	1	2.4	2.3	3	3.9	3.5
Transport and Communications	–	–	1.5	1.6	1.3	1.6	1.7
Local Government	2	2.8	1.8	2.3	0.6	0.9	1.1
Health	1.6	1	0.7	0.8	0.5	0.6	1

Source: Galebotswe (2014)
NB: a (–) signifies a very low budget in comparison to other ministries

dominated by Ipelegeng (a poverty relief program), which accounts for 45.7 percent of the Ministry's expenditure. Ipelegeng provides temporary relief for the poor and the unemployed. It is not a productive investment and does not assist efforts toward sustainable economic development (Galebotswe 2014).

Budgetary Accountability and Control

As stated elsewhere budgetary accountability and control in Botswana is entrenched in the Constitution with Parliament and the Office of the Auditor-General having recognition as legitimate oversight institutions. Parliament debates the budget speech before the budget is passed as the enacted budget. The Office of the Auditor-General is empowered to audit all public bodies. Kaboyakgosi (2000) identifies eight budget documents that are useful in determining budget accountability, control and transparency in Botswana. They are:

- the pre-budget statement, which contains provisional budget detail and allocations;
- the executive budget proposal or budget speech, which contains budget proposals presented to Parliament;
- the enacted budget, which is the budget approved by Parliament;
- in-year reports, which report on budget effects during the fiscal year;
- the mid-term review, which details the effect of the budget at midpoint;
- the end of year report, which is the budget report for the financial year;
- the audit report, which explains how public moneys and supplies have been used in the year; and
- the citizens' budget, which is a simplified version of the budget for public consumption.

The documents of the budget keep track of the process and performance of the budget. However, accountability is compromised as documents such as the pre-budget statement, in-year reports and mid-term reviews are only available to the executive branch of Government and not to the National Assembly.

At execution or transactional level, accountability and control are necessary. In Botswana they are fostered through the Public Finance and Management Act and the roles played by Ministers as accounting officers, chief executive officers of public entities, permanent secretaries, accountant-general and internal auditors. At the audit level, the Auditor-General as established by the Audit Act ensures accountability. The financial regulations, instructions and procedures provide finer transactional details that ought to be followed by all concerned. It is at this level that different forms and materials have been produced to capture important accounting information.

A summary of the features that inform budgetary accountability and control in the public sector departments is presented in Figure 2.1. The schema presented

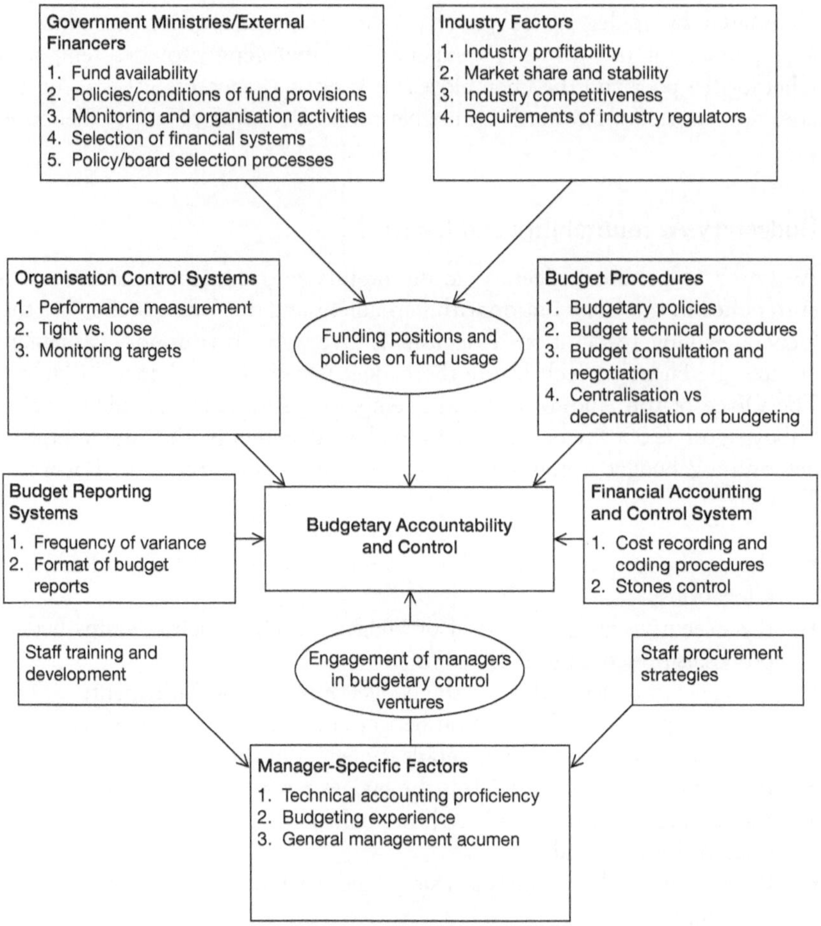

Figure 2.1 Determinants of budgetary accountability and control
Source: Phatshwane (2006, cited in Phatshwane and Baliyan, 2011)

by Phatshwane (2006, cited in Phatshwane & Baliyan, 2011) reveals that budgetary accountability and control is embedded in and influenced by an intricate matrix of factors that include broad policies, fund availability, organizational control systems, budgeting procedures, budgeting reporting systems, financial accounting and control systems, technical accounting proficiency, managerial experience and managerial acumen. The synergy that obtains between actors, policies and systems is one that ensures proper budgetary accountability and control. In Botswana, the policies, laws, processes, procedures, regulations, systems and actors are in place but implementation lapses are commonplace, resulting in losses that are regularly reported by the Auditor-General.

Botswana Budget Challenges

The Dominance of the Executive in Botswana's Budgeting Process

The executive arm of government in Botswana led by the Ministry of Finance and Development Planning is entirely responsible for the drafting of the country's most critical financial documents in the form of the national development plans and the annual budget speeches. The budget speech is an almost secret affair as both the recurrent and development budgets are compiled by this ministry and they can decide to halt certain projects or even to reduce the recurrent budget if they feel they have enough reason to do so (Molomo 1998). This therefore raises two important issues: Where is the transparency? Where is the citizen participation? To answer the first question, the budget process at draft level is a closed process and very little information is communicated to either the citizens or even members of Parliament. The budget is only available to the citizens and legislature as a completed product. There is very little that these actors can do to change what has been agreed by the executive and the bureaucrats. There is no direct contact with citizens to specifically discuss budgeting matters. Therefore it is only through the elected officials and the recently introduced budget pitsos (consultative forums) that citizens can provide their (minimal) input. The Executive excludes the legislature from involvement in pre-budget statements, in-year reports and mid-term reviews and this makes accountability very difficult (Kaboyakgosi, 2011; Botlhale, 2013b).

A Weak and Acquiescent Parliament

It is very clear from the above discussion that the legislature plays the most minimal of roles in the budget process. The legislature as a citizens' representative body comes at the very end of the process. It is expected to provide checks and balances on the Executive but because it is starved of relevant information on budgeting it is ineffective in this role. Parliament is thus ill-equipped to perform its oversight functions as it is given only limited time to peruse and debate a document that the Executive has taken a year to prepare. After presentation of the budget speech, Parliamentarians are given 48 hours to prepare for the debate. This means there is very little time for Parliamentarians to receive feedback from their constituents before starting the deliberations.

The dominance of the ruling party in Parliament and the fact that members of the Executive double also as MPs have relegated the role of Parliament to that of a rubber-stamping institution. The Parliamentary back-bench members are also obsessed with the possibility of being invited to join the Cabinet and as such they are unwilling to rock the boat. Robust debates are thus stifled. The Parliament in Botswana is for all intents and purposes treated as an extension of the Executive. Even the Parliament's agenda or business is controlled by the Executive. The Vice President and not the Speaker of the House is the Leader of Business in Parliament. In this respect, the Executive can easily frustrate budget debates in Parliament.

An Apathetic Civil Society

Civil society in other jurisdictions takes an active interest in budgetary matters and holds governments to account. The weak civil society that is evident in Botswana and many other African countries means that pressure groups, trade unions and others are either absent or too weak to engage the Government meaningfully. Other organs of civil society are heavily compromised because they benefit from the Government budget and any attempt to critically appraise the Government may lead to cuts in their funding in the future. Civil society has generally remained apathetic and indifferent to the budget in Botswana. BONCONGO—a coalition of non-governmental organizations (NGOs)—has in the past taken an interest in the budget and made presentations for an inclusive budget. Their contribution though commendable has always been weak and easily drowned by forces that support the Government.

Lack of Transparency and Absence of Information Accessibility Law

An informed citizenry is facilitated by the availability of information. It is therefore critical that in so far as the budget is concerned all information related to the budget should be made available to all the stakeholders including citizens (Laschinger, 2006). Budget preparation data—particularly information related to the amount of money available for the budget, the amount owed as a country and details of what informs allocation before it is made—is not readily available. The pre-budget statement is only for the Executive and the citizens and Parliament have no access to the statement. In Botswana, unfortunately, there is still no legislation that compels the public sector to make available information on any of its work and this is therefore a drawback in the fight for transparency and accountability in the budgetary process (Botlhale 2013b).

Ineffective Public Accounts Committee

One of the duties bestowed upon parliament in a democracy is to bring to the table all those entrusted with spending government funds and have them account for every pula that was allocated to them. This function in Botswana is the duty of the Public Accounts Committee, which consists of sitting members of Parliament. Despite the success of this committee in performing its oversight function and ensuring accountability, the problem still lies with the "what then," as after all its investigations its reports have to go through the Executive, which usually acts swiftly to protect some of its own by shelving the reports (Botlhale 2013b). In a nutshell, the Committee is toothless and to date has not been able to bring those who flaunt financial procedures to book. Until the Committee can not only summon miscreants but also institute disciplinary action, it cannot be considered effective. As it stands, it is just a celebrated talk show.

Centralization and the Problem of Reaching to the People

According to Botlhale (2011a), Botswana is a unitary state and this therefore implies that despite the two-tier government structure most of the powers lie with the central Government and this includes that of holding the purse-strings. The fact that local government bodies have little power to raise their own funds and rely on the central Government spells doom for the concept of citizen participation. This is so because citizen participation in the budget process is usually anchored by local government bodies as their closeness to the people allows them to easily take on board the contributions of the citizens. In Botswana, local authorities are not constitutionally entrenched and their existence has weak foundations hence the limited space for citizen engagement.

The Recommendations

The challenges that confront public finance management and budgeting in Botswana are numerous but surmountable. The fundamentals in terms of policy legislation, systems and process are relatively fine. There is however need for reform and improvement in critical areas. The recommendations for such are listed below:

1. The national development plan and budget preparation processes should be opened to give greater roles to the public and the legislature.
2. The macro-economic and fiscal policy framework informing the national development plans should truly reflect inclusive growth, social justice, human rights and sustainable development.
3. The status of Parliament as a legislature should be upgraded so that it becomes independent from the Executive and is empowered to perform its oversight functions without interference or hindrance from the Executive.
4. The Public Accounts Committee must be empowered to investigate cases of financial transgressions of public bodies and not only institute remedial action but disciplinary action as well.
5. Budget documents such as the pre-budget statements and periodic reports on the effect of the budget during the fiscal year should be made available to Parliament.
6. There should be regular and concerted follow-ups on all cases of financial impropriety and misuse of public funds reported by the Auditor-General.
7. An open democracy law otherwise known as a freedom of information law should be enacted to allow for ease of public access to information including budget information.
8. The scope and reach of Budget Pitsos should be broadened so that as many people as possible can have input into the pre-budget debate and discussions.
9. Local District Councils should be entrenched in the Constitution; their mandate should be broadened and they should be given leeway and space for revenue collection and budgeting for their programs.

10. The capacity to receive feedback from the public by Parliament and the Office of the Auditor-General on the budget must be expanded.

Conclusion

The search for best practices in public finance management and budgeting should continue. In Botswana, the issues of transparency and accountability in public budgeting loom large. The system that obtains now may have yielded positive results in the past but it is paramount that the two institutions that should provide budgeting oversight, namely Parliament and the Auditor-General, be accorded adequate scope and space to discharge their roles without undue constraints and hindrances. Parliament in particular must hold the Executive accountable right from conception, preparation, and presentation up to implementation of the budget. The Public Accounts Committee must be given more teeth to take action against transgressors. The Auditor-General should take action against all those who have flaunted financial procedures and processes and misused public finances. It is unacceptable that reports of the Auditor-General that document incidents of misuse and waste of public moneys continue to gather dust without any action being taken against perpetrators. Those who through corruption, negligence or reckless omission have caused loss of public money must be booked and charged. It is important that the public benefit from every thebe of its money.

References

Botlhale, E. (2011a). A quest to run the government by black ink in Botswana in 2012 and beyond. *Journal of Public Administration and Governance*. Vol. 1, No. 2, pp. 24–41.

Botlhale, E. (2011b). Gender responsive budget: The case of Botswana. *Development Southern Africa*. Vol. 28, No. 1, pp. 61–74.

Botlhale, E. (2013a). Privatization in Botswana: A case of firsts not happening first? *Research in Applied Economics*. Vol. 4., No. 1, pp. 17–30.

Botlhale, E. (2013b). Budgetary participation beyond budget pitsos in Botswana. *Development Policy Review*. Vol. 31, No. 6, pp. 717–735.

Galebotswe, O.B. (2014). A positive and pragmatic budget, but can it put Botswana onto a path of inclusive growth? *Stanbic Bank Quarterly Economic Growth Review*. No. 1 of 2014, pp. 4–5.

Kaboyakgosi, G. (2000). *Democracy Index for Botswana: A fine balance: Assessing the quality of governance in Botswana*. African Democracy Institute.

Kaboyakgosi, G. (2011). *Enhancing public budget transparency in Botswana. Why and How?* BIDPA Policy Brief No. 10. Gaborone.

Laschinger, K. (2006). Balancing the books. Economic trends and analysis. *Finweek*. Vol. 3, No. 7, pp. 56–67.

Madongo, A. R. (2013). *Accountability and roles of oversight bodies in the Botswana public budgeting process*. Unpublished research essay submitted for the requirements of Master Degree in Defence and Strategic Studies. Department of Political and Administrative Studies, University of Botswana.

Malema B.W. (2014). Public enterprises' performance is a significant function of government behavior. *Stanbic Bank Quarterly Economic Growth Review*. No. 1 of 2014, pp. 6–7.

Mbekomize, C.J. (2014). *Financial Budgeting in the Security Sector*: Paper presented at the Executive Course for Senior Officers and Officials in the Defence and Security Sector Management. Botswana Police Academy, Otse.

Molomo M. (1998). Democracy under siege: The presidency and executive powers in Botswana. *Pula: Journal of African Studies*. Vol. 14, No. 1, pp. 66–79.

Mwansa, L.K., Lucas, T., & Osei-Hwedie, K. (1998). The practice of social policy in Botswana. *Journal of Social Development in Africa*, Vol. 13, No. 2, pp. 55–74.

Parsons, J. (1980). *The Labor-Reserve in Historical Perspective: A political economy of the Bechuanaland protectorate*. Department of Political Science, College of Charleston, Charleston, USA.

Phatshwane, P., & Baliyan, P. S. (2011). Towards improved government budgeting, costing and accountability in the healthcare sector. The case of hospital and clinic services in Botswana. *International Journal of Economics and Business Studies*. Vol. 1, No. 2, pp. 14–25.

Phirinyane, M. (2009). *The State of Governance in Botswana*. United Nation Economic Commission for Africa, Gaborone.

Porter, M. (2000). *Competitiveness of African Nations*. Macmillan, London.

Republic of Botswana. (1966). *Constitution of Botswana*. Government Printer, Gaborone.

Republic of Botswana. (1970). *Finance and Audit Act*. Government Printer, Gaborone.

Republic of Botswana. (2011). *Public Finance Management Act, 2011* (Act, N.17 of 2011). Government Printer, Gaborone.

Republic of Botswana. (2012) *Audit Act*. Government Printer, Gaborone.

Tlhalefang, J.B. (2013a). The 2013 Botswana Budget. *Stanbic Bank Quarterly Economic Review*. No. 1 of 2013, pp. 48–60.

Tlhalefang, J.B. (2013b). The transparency and participation in budgeting process in Botswana. *Stanbic Bank Quarterly Economic Review*. No. 2 of 2013, pp. 28–31.

3 Public Budgeting in African Nations: The Case of Cameroon

Peter Ajongwa Ngwafu and Viviane E. Foyou

Introduction

A budget is an annual statement of all the revenues and expenditures of a state, and as such it is an important instrument of public policy-making. As Anderson (2015, p. 181) opines, budgeting is a means and a source of opportunities for shaping the direction, intensity and impact of public policies. Similarly, Milakovich and Gordon (2015, p. 327) argue that budgeting in the public sector is a process central to politics, especially administrative politics and the operation of government agencies and programs, because it is the major formal mechanism through which necessary resources are obtained, distributed, spent and monitored. As a result of these observations, it is important to note that national budgets, including those of African states, should be designed and implemented to provide mechanisms through which important public budgetary policies are translated into viable social, political, and economic outcomes. To that end, government decisions about how to allocate and spend financial resources have to be carefully formulated and implemented because they impact the viability of institutions and programs and the well-being of citizens in fundamental ways (CABRI, 2008).[1]

Against the background of the preceding discussion, this chapter will explore the historical background of Cameroon's budgeting system and its evolution from independence till now, review its approaches to budgeting and identify the key actors involved in the budgeting process, analyze its budget institutions, budget practices, major revenue sources and expenditure items and evaluate Cameroon's budget as a development tool. Finally, this chapter will focus on the lessons learned from a 54-year public budget or public financial management system in Cameroon, in an effort to address challenges and prospects for future improvement.

Historical Background of Cameroon's Budgetary System and its Evolution

As in other Sub-Saharan Francophone African countries, the public budgeting system in Cameroon is shaped and influenced by the French Public Expenditure

Management model (PEM) of the 1960s on which it was based. Bouley et al. (2003, p. 50), note that French legal and technical frameworks were extensively adopted to replace the treasury and budget systems that had been in place in Sub-Saharan Francophone Africa during the colonization period. Thus, following independence in 1960, Cameroon's budgeting system, like those of all independent francophone African countries of that era, was based on key public expenditure management features of the French reference model that was undergirded by the ordinance of 1959 on organic budget law and decree of 1962 on public accounting. The 1959 Organic Ordinance on Public Finance Acts, which was revised in 2001, describes the rules regarding the elaboration, approval and execution of the annual budget, and the 1962 Decree on the General Regulation of Public Accounting details the rules applicable to the public accounting framework (Bouley et al. 2003, p. 52).These two pieces of legislation constituted the legal framework of budgeting in France until 2001. Moussa (2004, p. 5) indicates that as specified by these two pieces of legislation, three types of budget are passed by the French Parliament: the initial budget law, which includes all government revenues and expenditures, the supplementary budget law, which modifies the initial law during its execution, and the budget review law, which reconciles the executed budget with the initial budget following the closing of the fiscal year.

The review law establishes, contrary to what happens in several Francophone African countries, that parliament has the first and last word regarding the use of public funds. However, the French constitution of 1958 also established the executive branch, which defines and conducts national policy, with the authority to bypass parliament on budget matters in specific exceptional circumstances (Moussa 2004, p. 25). It is apparent that, while Cameroon, as well as other Francophone African countries, has made several modifications to the French budgetary system from which it has borrowed extensively over the years, core features of the French model still remain, as in other Francophone African countries. In fact Moussa contends that Francophone nations in Sub-Saharan Africa share 57 to 74 percent of the PEM features of the French system. Figure 3.1 shows the overall similarity between the French PEM and those of Sub-Saharan Francophone African countries.

In order to understand the efficacy or lack thereof of the Cameroon budgeting system, it is appropriate to briefly examine two aspects of the French treasury system, the PEM process and the centralization of public funds, which have impacted the budgetary systems of Francophone African countries adversely and continue to do so. Bouley et al. (2003, p. 51) argue that the French Treasury system, which influences its expenditure or budget process, has always been highly regulated because it is driven by various controls. As a result, it is best suited to countries with effective financial management capacities. In the 1960s, the French system was overhauled thus rendering it more sophisticated and more demanding in terms of management capabilities. They maintain further, that Francophone African nations merely copied the new French system, even when it was obvious that it was not necessarily suited to their needs and management

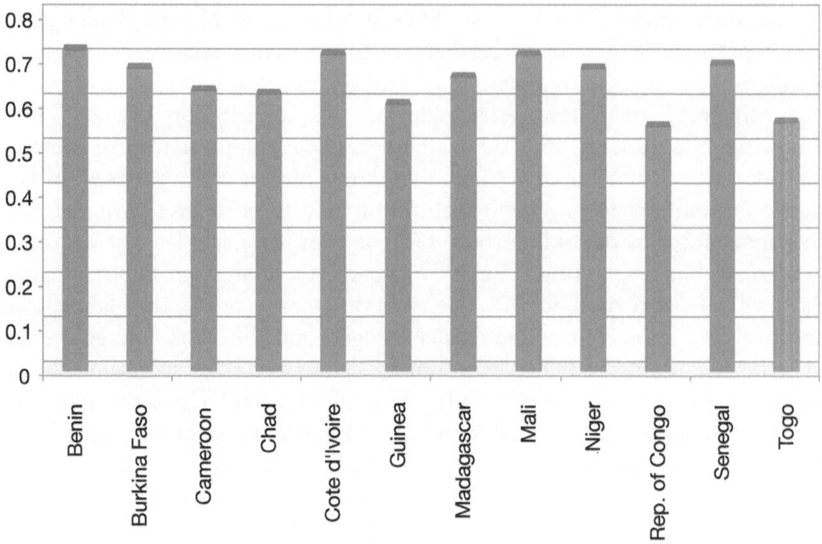

Figure 3.1 Overall similarity to France (at end of 2001)
Source: Moussa (2004)

capacities. Consequently, adverse conditions that currently prevail within budget systems in Sub-Saharan Francophone African countries, have been shaped by those two aspects or characteristics of the French system mentioned above.

The structure of the expenditure process, which calls for a clear distinction between the person who initiates the decision to spend (*l'ordonnateur*) and the person responsible for the payment itself (*le comptable*), is intended to reduce errors and irregularities through built-in checks. However, evidence exists indicating that the system has not only been abused but has also been complicated in Francophone Africa (Bouley et al. 2003, p. 51). The difference between the person who orders the payment and the person who executes it is important in the French public financial system. In that system, each line ministry initiates its own expenditure based on its budget allocations. To ensure transparency and avoid abuses and errors, the *ordonnateur* (the person who initiates the decision to spend) must be separated or dissociated from the *comptable* (the accountant who ultimately processes the payment). The accountant is protected by a specific statute that ensures his or her independence from the *ordonnateur*. The difference between the two officials extends also to tax collection. The French system distinguishes between the person who creates the tax base and the person who actually collects the money on behalf of the state. However, in Cameroon and other Francophone African countries the efficiency of the system suffers from the absence of the independence of the accountant, the impossibility of enforcing financial responsibility, the absence of treasury balances and the often poorly functioning legal system. As a result, the application of these principles in these countries turns out to be a very costly and ineffective financial management process (Bouley et al. 2003, p. 55). The centralization of funds, which requires public entities to deposit some or all of their money at the treasury, remains an important feature of the current system. Through this mechanism, the fiscal deficit can be offset by increased deposits by public banks, which substantially reduces the need for bank financing (Bouley et al. 2003, p. 51). In Cameroon and the other Francophone African nations, this feature has not functioned efficiently.

Just as in the French budgetary system, overall fiscal management in Cameroon is governed by a highly elaborate but complex framework set out in the February 7, 1962 *ordonnance* or finance law (similar to that of France) which is predicated on the principle of separation of functions between the payment authorizing officer (*ordonnateur*) and the government accounting officer (*comptable*) who is actually responsible for executing the payment. The different taxes and duties, including their collection mechanisms, are also provided for in the laws. Tax authorities are required to conduct their operations judiciously and methodically and exercise judgment with a view to preventing disputes (IMF 2000, p. 2). In essence, the 1962 ordinance regulates overall public financial management in Cameroon while the 1996 constitution defines the powers of the legislature regarding the adoption of the budget. The 1962 ordinance establishes the principles of resource and expenditure management and prescribes credit presentation per expenditure type. It also describes the rule of yearly budgeting of credits (with the exception of capital expenditure, which is budgeted on a multi-annual basis), the rule of budgeting by expenditure type, the rule of universality, which prohibits the underwriting of an item of revenue by an item of expenditure, and the rule of unity, which stipulates the budget in revenue and expenditure and calls for these items to be presented in a single document that excludes extra-budgetary funds. The ordinance also contains provisions for the execution of the budget. Decree 2003/011/PM of January 9, 2003 on budget nomenclature further explains the public finance legal framework in Cameroon (African Development Bank 2004, p. 8).[2]

The preceding discussion explains how Cameroon's budgetary system has borrowed extensively from the French. Unfortunately, however, Cameroon budget processes, practices and legal frameworks that were inspired by the French model have not functioned effectively and efficiently. For example, various revenue and expenditure items are in principle included in the budget law. However, in order to facilitate the financing of social sectors, administrative fees (*recettes de service*) collected by the organizations or institutions that oversee these sectors are directly earmarked to cover their operating costs. The management of these revenues remains weak and their collection and monitoring needs to be significantly improved (IMF 2000, p. 2). Furthermore, the most recent surveys by the IMF regarding Cameroon's observance of standards and codes or fiscal transparency show that public financial management in Cameroon is very poor and public access to financial information is scant if not non-existent.

This is due, in large part, to the fact that Cameroon's budget system is complex and is fraught with numerous administrative and political bottlenecks (Elangwe 2012, p. 5).

While core features of the French legal and technical frameworks continue to influence the budget systems of Cameroon and the other Francophone African nations, Cameroon has nonetheless modified a few aspects of the French model by enacting laws and statutes and instituting other reform measures, designed to improve its budget system and overall public financial management process. The 1996 constitution, previously discussed, defines the powers of the legislature regarding the adoption of the budget and the 1962 ordinance regulates public financial management in Cameroon. Also, Decree 2003/011/PM of January 9, 2003 on budget nomenclature or specifications further clarifies the public finance legal framework.

Because Cameroon's budget system is based on a model characterized by rigorous controls and therefore not suitable for its internal management capacities, it has sought to embrace more contemporary types of budgeting frameworks in an attempt to mitigate the adverse financial and economic conditions to which it has been subjected over the past four decades. Participatory budgeting and performance budgeting are two budget systems that Cameroon is currently experimenting with. Introduced in Africa at the special session on participatory budgeting at the Africities 3 Summit in Yaounde, Cameroon, in 2003, attended by more than 700 mayors and local government officials from across Africa, participatory budgeting (PB):

> involves local authorities and residents of a municipality or some other administrative unit, cooperating in determining the allocation of public money. Its primary objective is to provide an opportunity for citizens to influence decisions about the provision and location of services in the areas in which they live.
>
> Africa Research Institute 2012, p. 1

Although PB was initially implemented in Brazil in 1988, interest in this type of budgeting gained momentum in Africa in 2003, and by 2011, 162 municipalities in 23 African countries, with a total population of 23 million citizens, had adopted PB. In December 2012 an "African charter for citizen participation" was signed at Africities 6 in Yaounde, which was attended by 5,000 mayors, local government officials and representatives of civil society associations across Africa and international partners. A partnership agreement was also signed between Porto Alegre in Brazil, the birthplace of PB, and Yaounde V, a municipality that was embracing it for the first time. This agreement is reported to be the first of its kind between southern hemisphere municipalities (Africa Research Institute 2012, p. 7). With respect to PB in Cameroon, Jules Dumas Nguebou, coordinator of programs at *Associations des Amoureux du Livre* (ASSOAL), the leading civil society organization promoting the implementation of PB in Cameroon, states that its potential for improving the management of public finance in Cameroon is encouraging. He also argues that although PB in Cameroon is still in its infancy, it has provided Cameroonian citizens with the opportunity to participate in decision-making processes that affect their lives in fundamental ways. He further elaborates that while it has introduced tangible, albeit modest, improvements, PB can enhance collaboration between municipal authorities and the population thus allowing for important feedback about development projects and programs. He believes that in instances where it has been successful, PB has contributed to a reduction of corruption in public financial management. It is important to note here that PB outcomes vary from region to region given the array of variables that impact its effectiveness including the motives and objectives of the individuals and groups involved, the degree of participation and the extent to which it is genuinely collaborative, the scope of the projects or measures under discussion and the available resources (Africa Research Institute 2012, p. 3).[3]

Recently, Cameroon has also adopted performance budgeting as an additional type of public budgeting system. Broadly defined, performance budgeting refers to public sector funding mechanisms and processes designed to strengthen the linkage between funding and results (outputs and outcomes), through the systematic use of formal performance information, with the objective of improving the allocative and technical efficiency of public expenditure (Robinson., 2007, p. 1). Robinson maintains, further, that while the definition includes a general concept of performance budgeting that covers a wide range of performance budgeting systems across the world, it is compatible with the definition advanced by the OECD as a "form of budgeting that relates funds allocated to measurable results" or that of the US Government Accountability Office (GAO) as "the concept of linking performance information with the budget" (2007, p. 2). He also observes that in recent decades, performance budgeting has been adopted by nations as part of a comprehensive set of management and budgetary reforms aimed at improving the efficiency and effectiveness of the public sector so as to enhance the attainment of fiscal sustainability (2007, p. 3).

This type of budgeting falls into a variety generally referred to as managing for results. Performance budgeting, which was experimented with by a few African nations in 2000, was introduced in Cameroon and several other African countries in January 2013. According to the Collaborative African Budget Reform Initiative (CABRI, 2013), many African nations have adopted the global trend of introducing a performance orientation into annual budget processes as well as the planning of budgets over a multi-year period. Currently, over 80 percent of African countries are introducing or are committed to adopting some form of performance budgeting. The main objective of performance-driven budgeting is to link annual budget allocations to budget performance. In that regard, program performance is taken into consideration using systematic performance information during budget preparation. In Francophone Africa, performance budgeting has become the chosen model of budgeting (CABRI 2013, ix).[4] In the case of Cameroon, the Finance Minister, Alamine Ousmane, stated on July 9, 2013 during the second session of the Inter-ministerial Committee for the Examination of Budget Programs that Cameroon was one of the pioneer countries in Sub-Saharan Africa to implement results-oriented budgets known as performance budgets. The minister emphasized that the committee, created by Prime Ministerial Order 2011/2414/pm of August 17, 2011, was designed to ensure that all state projects proposed for funding were compatible with the "financial regime of the state adopted in 2007." Consequently, the minister reiterated that the July 9 meeting was aimed at evaluating the first half of the budget so as to ensure that the government submitted good budget documents for parliamentary scrutiny in 2014. He also stated that the implementation of this modern instrument seeks to enhance the management of government financial policies. In that context, he added, the drawing up and execution of the budget was undergoing total revolution in keeping with the growth and employment strategy of the state. Speaking on the intricacies of the newly introduced budget at the same meeting, the Director of the Budget in the Ministry of Finance, Antoine Félix Samba, indicated that the new programs were established to meet Cameroon's vision of becoming an emerging nation by 2035 (Yerima Kini Nsom on Cameroon Postline, posted July 16, 2013).

The Director indicated, as did the 2013 CABRI status report, that with respect to the successful implementation of program-based budget initiatives in Africa, various stakeholders in Cameroon encountered difficulties in their efforts to effectively implement components of the new budget programs. The historical background and evolution of Cameroon's budgetary system provides a useful overview of the legal framework and budgetary types that have shaped the nation's public financial management system for over four decades. A review of Cameroon's approaches to budgeting and identification of the key actors involved in the budget process should offer additional insights into the processes and procedures governing the allocation and expenditure of funds as well as the actors involved in those processes and procedures.

Cameroon's Approaches to Budgeting and Key Actors Involved in the Budgeting Process

Although Cameroon has just recently begun experimenting with modern budgeting approaches such as participatory and performance budgeting as discussed above, a review of the literature on public budgeting or in a broader sense, public expenditure management in Cameroon, has not produced evidence of the use of traditional approaches to budgeting similar to those used in more advanced nations such as the USA (including incremental budgeting, zero-based budgeting (ZBB), planning performance budgeting (PPB), performance-based budgeting (PBB), program budgeting (PB) and line-item budgeting. What existed in Cameroon in terms of approaches to budgeting, before the introduction of participatory and performance-based budgeting, was essentially a top-down approach to budgeting. Generally, this type of approach to budgeting is predicated on the view that directives for planning, creating, negotiating, approving and executing the annual budget come from a central office or central budget authority. This authority, which might operate under the supervision of the cabinet or council of ministers, is given the agenda role in relation to the other budget entities and is responsible for ensuring compliance with the budget laws and for enforcing control of budgetary expenditures. Under this approach, line ministries and other participants in the budget process have limited roles to play in the budget process (Dabla-Norris et al. 2010, p. 10).[5]

The budgeting process in Cameroon reflects the description of the top-down budgeting approach outlined above. Ideally, a national budget process falls into four stages, here described as it applies in the USA:

1. budget preparation and transmittal within the executive branch under the leadership of the Office of Management and Budgets with the assistance of executive departments and agencies;
2. congressional action on the budget and approval, which requires congress to review the President's budget, develop its budget resolution and approve spending and revenue bills;
3. budget execution, which calls on agency or program officials to execute the budget as enacted into law (Anderson 2015, p. 189); and
4. auditing, which assesses the accuracy and correct operation of agencies' accounting systems including validation of inventories and existing equipment, documentation of proper legal authority to carry out agency activities, adequacy of controls on fraud, waste and mismanagement and the effectiveness of agencies' programs (Smith & Lynch 2004, p. 393).

The American budgeting process adheres to a timeframe that clearly defines the roles of key actors as specified by the laws governing it. These actors play significant roles during the process as they draw on information and available data to make informed budgetary decisions following a transparent system that holds them accountable for their actions. While Cameroon's budget system has processes and procedures by which it is supposed to be executed, adherence to these mechanisms (specified in laws) is not often respected.

There are several characteristics of the PEM system of Francophone African countries that apply to approaches to budgeting as well as the budgeting process in Cameroon. Lienert (2003, p. 5) points out that in Francophone African countries there is always a legislative basis for budget preparation. She maintains that the constitutions of these countries typically include a statement that the annual budget law (*loi de finances*), determines the resources and expenses of the state. These constitutions, she argues further, also have provisions with respect to the timing of the presentation of the budget to parliament (often in October for a budget that begins on January 1) and actions to be taken by the executive branch if the annual budget is not adopted by parliament on time. Governments in Francophone Africa usually start executing the new budget on the basis of monthly authorizations. Within the France-based system prevalent in Cameroon and the other Francophone African countries, organic laws (adopted from the French in 1959) specify five key principles for budget preparation: annual basis, unity, universality, specificity, and equilibrium or balance. Organic laws define current and capital expenditures and loans/or advances, the broad categories of the economic classification of expenditures, the nature of documents to be submitted to parliament and procedures for preparing and adopting the annual budget law (Lienert 2003, p. 5). Also multi-year budget provisioning for capital expenditures is outlined in organic budget laws. Multi-year budget appropriations (*autorisations de programmes*) allow ministries to commit expenditures for capital projects for periods exceeding one year. These appropriations are accompanied by limits on annual payments (*crédits de paiements*), which are also included in the annual budget law. At the end of the budget year, all unspent appropriations are cancelled and re-appropriated in the next year's budget (Lienert, 2003, p. 6).

Budgets in Cameroon, as in other Francophone African countries, are traditionally prepared largely on a detailed line-item basis. hence the main budget document runs into hundreds of pages. Such detail complicates budgetary management. The budget is adopted by organizational classification such as ministry, administrative unit and province and by economic classification including salaries, current goods and services, transfers and capital spending. Adopted budgets in Francophone African countries are limited to central governments. Parliament approves central government transfers to lower levels of government. Estimates of the revenues of sub-national governments are usually not provided as background information, and revenues collected and retained by autonomous agencies such as hospitals, which depend on budget transfers for their main source of income, are often not shown transparently in the budget (Lienert 2003, p. 7). While the constitutions and organic budget laws of Francophone African countries clearly specify the dates for budget presentation and adoption by parliament, these are not always adhered to. Budgets in Francophone African countries are usually not discussed as extensively as in France or the USA, where budget commissions traditionally play important roles in reviewing the budget before its formal adoption by parliament. In Africa by contrast, there is a lack of capacity and inadequate attention to the role of parliament in the budget process. In terms of the key actors in the budget process in Cameroon as in other Francophone African countries, the ministry of finance as well as its various departments play all the important roles in the budget process. The key players include financial controllers (*contrôleurs financiers*), who are usually in the budget department of the ministry of finance, payment authorizing officers (*ordonnateurs*), who approve the issuance of payment orders to the treasury and public accountants (*comptables publics*) in the treasury.

Another characteristic of the French public expenditure management system found in the budget systems of Cameroon and other Francophone African countries is the separation of the payment authorizing officer and the treasury officer responsible for payment, previously discussed. Given that both of these functions are centralized in the ministry of finance, financial management in spending ministries is fuzzy or diluted. In Cameroon as in the other Francophone African states, the ministry of finance is the sole authorizing officer (*ordonnateur unique*) as well as the overseer of the functioning of the treasury and of public accounts. As a result, despite the principle of the separation of the authorizing officer and the accountant, the minister of finance is both the principal authorizing officer and head of all accountants (Lienert 2003, p. 12).

Key Actors in the Budget Process

Having discussed the characteristics of budget systems in Francophone African countries, it is important to assess Cameroon's budget process and its principal actors. Cameroon's budget process is dominated by its Ministry of Finance. It is the Department of Forecasts in the Ministry of Finance that prepares the budget, driven by macro-economic projections. These projections are essential in guiding the Department of Taxation and Customs to make its own projections on the level of fiscal and customs revenues. These forecasts are then centralized at the level of the Department of Forecasts, which validates the results and establishes ceilings for possible expenditures. Given these estimates, the Minister of Finance and the Budget recommends that the President of the Republic issue a budget orientation circular to the Prime Minister and all the members of government spelling out the revenue forecasts, policy choices and other measures to be taken for proper preparation of the budget (AfDB 2004, p. 8).

On the basis of this circular the spending ministers prepare their draft budgets and forward them to the Department of the Budget, which reviews them with the ministry in charge of investments, to determine aspects and the kinds of investment projects to be included in the list of projects to be financed. The Department of the Budget then submits a letter for the Prime Minister's signature addressed to ministries informing them of the final budget appropriations granted them, broken down into recurrent and investment credits. Upon receipt of these letters, the Department of the Budget holds a budget conference to assess the budget proposals of the ministries with their representatives as well as to finalize the ceilings, which were stated in the letters informing them of their final budget. While Cameroon's 1996 constitution defines the powers of the legislature regarding the adoption of the budget, the budget process described above fails to account for the role of the legislature. As a result, the Cameroon legislature has been reduced to simply rubber-stamping the budget that is often prepared solely by the finance ministry and its various departments and approved by the executive branch. Parliament does not have sufficient deliberative powers to examine the executive budget before it is signed into law.

The draft budget of Cameroon, presented in the form of overall ministerial budget estimates or projections, does not clearly delineate individual ministerial projects and programs to be funded nor does it describe the role of the legislature or national assembly in the budget process. To that end, it could be argued, as Elangwe (2012, p. 7) has done, that Cameroon's budget process does not allow for effective parliamentary control or oversight. He maintains that parliamentary budget oversight is a critical monitoring and control instrument in emerging economies for ensuring financial accountability and in gaining public trust in the government's policies and programs. Elangwe's observations about the critical role of parliament in the budgetary process are sustained by literature on the budget oversight responsibilities of parliaments. During the May 22–24, 2000 Inter-Parliamentary Union Seminar on Parliament and the Budgetary Process, held in Nairobi, Kenya, Mr. Colin Eglin, a Member of the Parliament of South Africa, remarked:

> Starting from the day the Minister of Finance makes his budget speech up till the day he tables the Appropriation Bill—until that proposal has gone through the various Parliamentary processes and is passed or rejected by Parliament—it remains the property of Parliament. In countries with parliamentary systems of government the national budget is a critically important instrument in ensuring transparency, accountability and good governance. The budget provides a regulating and disciplining framework in which Government departments must be managed and which services perform their functions. The issue of transparency, accountability and good governance hinges on the consequences of a well constructed budget in which Parliament has a significant role to play.
>
> IPU 2000

Ideally, that statement should hold true for all parliaments in terms of their budget oversight responsibilities. However, in Cameroon as in many Francophone (and even some Anglophone African) nations, the Ministry of Finance has monopolized the budgetary process, and given the fact that the Cameroon Parliament is not often given ample opportunity to deliberate on the budget, no amendments have been appended to the budget for several years. As a result, effective parliamentary oversight of the budget in Cameroon exists only in theory and not in practice.

Budget Institutions, Budget Practices, Major Revenue Sources and Expenditure Items

Much of the literature on public budgeting and public expenditure management systems stresses the importance of building legal, transparent and credible mechanisms within those systems in order to ensure that key actors are held accountable by the public in terms of how they spend the public's money and how processes are made transparent. These practices of good governance in the budget system can be strengthened through the implementation and enforcement of effective budget institutions because they determine, to a large extent, whether budget outcomes are ineffective or successful. Alesina and Perotti (1996, p. 3), consider budget institutions to include all the rules, regulations and procedures according to which budgets are drafted, approved and implemented. The authors also maintain that since most institutions are themselves endogenous, they can be changed as a result of unsatisfactory fiscal performance. Sophia Gollwitzer (2012, p. 1) views fiscal institutions as comprising the policies, rules and procedures of the public revenue and expenditure process thus representing the most important macro-economic commitment institutions for governments.

Despite minor differences in their definitions of budget institutions by these authors, they agree, nonetheless, that budget institutions constitute the legal framework upon which the budget processes of nations are based. Cameroon's budget institutions consist mostly of the decrees, laws and other protocols that impact the nation's budget process. As previously discussed, the first law that impacts Cameroon's budget process is its budgetary and accounting law, inspired by the French ordinance of 1959. Then there is the 1996 constitution which defines the legislature's powers concerning the adoption of the budget. The 1962 ordinance regulates public financial management in Cameroon, presents the principles of resource and expenditure management and prescribes credit presentation per expenditure type. Furthermore, the ordinance also outlines the rule of yearly budgeting of credits, the rule of budgeting by expenditure type, the rule of universality, which prohibits the underwriting of an item of revenue by an item of expenditure, and the rule of unity, which specifies that the budget, in revenue and expenditure, must be presented as a single document including extra-budgetary funds. The ordinance also includes provisions pertaining to budget execution. Decree 2003/011/PM of January 9, 2003 on budget nomenclature was designed to further clarify the public finance legal framework. Revolving around major state functions, sectors of activity, beneficiary services and expenditure type, the decree provides more detailed financial information on the finance law (AfDB 2004, p. 8).

Aside from the legal framework undergirding Cameroon's budget system, other procedures and control measures have been implemented over the years in an attempt to strengthen the overall public expenditure management system of the country. State accounts are handled by a network of 368 graded treasury stations whose responsibilities are to manage public expenditures and collect revenues. These stations include the central general treasury at the central level, 11 general treasuries in the different regions, 70 treasuries in the divisions and 286 sub-treasuries in subdivisions and districts. In addition to these stations located all over the nation, there are 36 diplomatic and consular treasury stations in countries where Cameroon has embassies. The centralization of operations is conducted as follows: sub-treasuries centralize their accounting operations every 10 days directly at the general treasury of their region, treasuries centralize their accounting operations every 10 days at the general treasury on which they depend, and general treasuries centralize their operations every 10 days, except the Yaounde and Douala general treasuries, whose operations are centralized on a daily basis (AfDB 2004, p. 10).The country's accounting plan, which was revised in 1997 and is modeled on the Union Douanière et Economique de l'Afrique Centrale (UDEAC) plan, is still ineffective in some respects.[6] Debt management is placed under the jurisdiction of the autonomous sinking fund, which is a public financial agency established in 1985 and governed by private law. However, law 99/16 of December 22, 1999, covering the general rules and regulations of public establishments and public and semi-public enterprises, provides that administrative establishments belonging to the state shall be managed in accordance with the rules provided for by the state financial system. The autonomous sinking fund has not functioned efficiently because of the contradictory dual role it performs. For example, it manages externally financed projects in liaison with the project officers and accountants as well as internal debt. The absence of a public accountant within this body has caused difficulties pertaining to the transfer of data to the treasury and the integration of such data into all state financial operations (AfDB 2004, p. 10).

Essentially, public expenditure auditing consists of internal and external auditing functions, including parliamentary and jurisdictional controls. Public expenditure is audited internally before payment of the expenditure (a priori control) and after payment of the expenditure (a posteriori control). The a priori control is conducted at the central level by the financial controller and the stores accountant and at the other levels by special controllers posted to all ministries, provinces, divisions, subdivisions and districts. In carrying out their control financial controllers refer to Decree 77/41 of February 3, 1977, which is not compatible with the more recent Decree 98/217 of September 9, 1998 passed to reorganize the Ministry of Finance. The lack of a manual of procedures for financial control is detrimental to accountability especially since workers appointed to this function do not receive initial training nor benefit from continuing training. (AfDB 2004, p. 11). Auditing by the Department of Stores and Accounting of the Ministry of Finance focuses on certification of services rendered as services provided to the state, public establishments and local authorities, and verification of the regularity of procurement operations and disposal of movable tangible property. The control carried out by this structure is ineffective because the workers have not had adequate professional training and maintain difficult relations with authorizing officers and vote-holders. African Development Bank assessments of this department indicate that it is not a useful link in the control chain and should have not been established in the first place. The assessments recommend that accounting services be established at the level of each administration to replace this inefficient department and to maintain joint orders of equipment at the level of the Ministry of Finance and Budget (AfDB 2004, p. 11).

A posteriori internal control is carried out first by the control services of the Ministry of Finance MOF and the Ministry in Charge of Investments and then by the Supreme State Audit. Five services carry out a posteriori control within the Ministry of Finance while the Ministry in Charge of Investments has its own inspectorate. The general inspectorates of the Ministry of Finance, which are responsible for a posteriori control, are concerned with administrative services, customs and taxation. These are reserved for cadres of the administration who are usually administrative officers with no specific training. Because the inspectorates have weak human and material capacities they are ineffective

(AfDB 2004, p. 12). The control brigades of the Ministry in Charge of Investments are yet another institution that impact the budget process. The duties of these brigades as defined by article 7 of Decree 98/70 of May 4, 1998, which was established to organize the Ministry in Charge of Investments, are to monitor the execution of the public investment budget, control the rate of consumption of credits and the preparation of periodic reports on the level of consumption of credits, permanently evaluate projects and project updates, consolidate data on the execution of domestic and external financing of the priority investment program and monitor public and private micro-projects benefiting from public financing. Article 29 of the decree stipulates that the sub-department of controls of the Ministry in Charge of Investments is responsible for the control of the physical outputs of programs and projects as well as for the a posteriori auditing and evaluation of public investment operations. Controls deal primarily with budget execution conditions and are designed to verify the physical realizations of investments by checking them against detailed descriptions in the order forms. While the Ministry in Charge of Investments brigades carry out non-repressive controls it sometimes occurs that a project is not physically implemented but the corresponding expenditure has already been made. According to African Development Bank analysis, the brigades lack manuals of procedures, the Department of Project and Program Control lacks staff and training of its human resources is inadequate. The internal controllers and general inspectorates send their reports to the Supreme State Audit which uses them to carry out further a posteriori controls (AfDB 2004, p. 12).

The Supreme State Audit, established in 1962, is currently governed by Decrees 97/47 and 97/48 of March 5, 1997. It is under the jurisdiction of the Minister of State, Secretary-General of the Presidency of the Republic. Generally, it is responsible for administrative, financial and accounts auditing, performance auditing and evaluation of the environmental impact of projects and programs. Its scope of operations is very wide and it covers different sectors. As a result it can carry out unexpected on-site and off-site audits at the level of all public services, local authorities, public enterprises, judiciary administration, the army, national security services and any other body benefiting from state subsidies or guarantees. Unfortunately, this crucial budget institution has been plagued by several problems over the years. First, this body does not guarantee efficiency nor accountability in its operations and does not meet the international norms of a Supreme Audit Institution given that its activities are confidential and the findings of its deliberations are not published. Second, its findings are intended for the President of the Republic, who decides what to do with them. Third, its annual program of work has not been adopted for many years and the auditors conduct very few missions—17 in 2003 for a staff of 60 state inspectors. Fourth, the Supreme State Audit acts as the permanent organ of the Budget and Finance Disciplinary Council. In the event that a serious management incident occurs or funds are misappropriated, the perpetrators are brought before the council, which could result in administrative or penal sanctions. Rarely are authorizing officers or other voting members brought before the disciplinary council. It has numerous sinecure positions filled with staff who have no professional sense of responsibility (AfDB 2004, p. 12).

The International Budget Partnership Open Budget Survey (Eoussa, 2010), notes that budget oversight provided by Cameroon's Supreme State Audit institution is weak because it is not fully independent from the executive. He argues that since the executive can remove the head of the institution without seeking final consent from the legislature or judiciary, it does not have complete discretion in the law as to what it chooses to audit, lacks adequate resources to meaningfully exercise its mandate, fails to issue timely audit reports on the final expenditure of national departments, has not established proper channels of communication with the public, and does not report on follow-up steps taken by the executive to address audit recommendations for remedial action, and legislative scrutiny of audits are insufficient (AfDB 2004, p. 12).

Two other budget institutions within Cameroon's budget system also deserve to be examined: parliamentary and jurisdictional controls. External control of public expenditure by parliament is based on the settlement law, which requires the assessment of the manner in which the estimates contained in the initial finance law were effectively executed. The audited budget act is prepared but it is not exhaustively presented with all the accounts of public accountants. On the contrary, it is presented in the form of overall amounts by ministerial department and does not outline the accounts by treasury station. Such a presentation does not make for effective control. Also, since it is submitted together with the finance law sufficient time is not devoted it; therefore parliamentary control is weakened. It is also worth noting that budget documents are generally deposited 15 days before the opening of the parliamentary session instead of the 30 days provided for by the constitution. This delay is due to administrative bottlenecks caused by the Department of the Budget, which is responsible for preparing the documents to be presented before parliament (AfDB 2004, p. 13).

Cameroon's budget process would be significantly improved and become more transparent if key budget documents were readily made available to the public, and a strong legislative body was put in place to provide effective budget oversight as well as provide greater opportunities for public engagement in the budget process. However, as the International Budget Partnership Open Budget Survey (Eoussa 2010, 2012) indicates, the budget oversight provided by Cameroon's legislature is inadequate because it does not have sufficient powers to amend the executive's budget proposal at the start of the year, or to approve any changes made to the budget over the course of the fiscal year. He also notes that the lack of legislative oversight does not provide opportunities for the public to testify during open budget discussions and approvals or to be present during legislative hearings when the executive testifies on its proposed budget. Cameroon's score on the open budget index was 2 out of 100 for 2008–2010 and 10 out of 100 in 2012, meaning that the government has provided almost no information on its budget and financial activities in four years. As a result, the unavailability of information to the public has made it impossible for the public to hold the government to account for its management of the public's money. Jurisdictional control of the budget is the responsibility of the audit bench, which was established by Law 2003/5 of April 21, 2003. The African Development Bank's assessment of this institution indicates that its creation was long delayed thus making it difficult for it to effectively audit the accounts of the public accountants. The delay in creating this institution left a gap in the proper management of public finance and called into question the issue of transparency in its operations. The fact that the audit bench is attached to the supreme court might rid the auditors of their independence in performing their duties. Additionally, the magistrates who are auditors may face a problem of competence if their initial and continuing training is not appropriately ensured. The duties of this institution should not be limited to the auditing of accounts. They should also include the evaluation of the manner in which expenditure is advised to be executed and the management of authorizing officers and voting members (AfDB 2004, p. 13).

It is impossible in this age of technology to prepare and execute a credible budget without using a reliable information management system. The African Development Bank's assessment of Cameroon's public financial management information system indicates that the management of public finance in Cameroon has for a long time been done by a network of computer applications that do not communicate with each other. According to its report, bank experts note that five computer systems, PAGPDE in the customs sector, ANTILOPE for salary management, IBIS-DM for state budget execution, PATRIOT for cash management and TRINITE for the tax sector are the key information systems used for public financial management in Cameroon. These systems are user specific because they are compartmentalized and therefore cannot be transformed into an integrated system. The lack of integration of these systems renders the coordination of financial and economic information impossible. In addition, these uncoordinated systems create bottlenecks and delays that are detrimental to access to information for decision-making. This grave weakness has forced the government to strive to put into place a new information system known as the Integrated Public Financial Management System. The main objectives of this new system include making overall management of public financial management in Cameroon more reliable, transparent and efficient. This integrated financial management system is expected to be accompanied by an economic and financial database called ECOFL, which will serve as the point of convergence of all economic and financial information, consolidated, integrated and updated to constitute an important decision-making tool (AfDB 2004, p. 22).

Budget Practices

Budget practices are generally understood as the techniques, methods and procedures that are used by states and organizations to prepare, approve, execute and audit or evaluate budgets so as to achieve desired outcomes. When properly conceived and implemented, budget practices can be effective and efficient standards or benchmarks for achieving the fiscal goals of an organization or nation. By contrast, when they are poorly conceived and executed, budget practices can become complicated, unreliable and ineffective thus making the attainment of desired outcomes impossible. The Collaborative Africa Budget Reform Initiative (CABRI) and the African Development Bank issued a report in 2008 about budget practices and procedures in Africa that prescribed a number of practices and procedures that have become the standard for assessing the budgets and public expenditure management systems of African nations. These recommended practices, which include timeliness of the budget, issues in budget formulation, the role of the legislature in the budget process, budget execution, fiscal transparency and debt management, will be used to assess Cameroon's budget practices and procedures. According to the Collaborative Africa Budget Reform Initiative (CABRI 2008, p. ix), budget timeliness refers to the duration and sequence of the budget process in individual countries, which reflect the different country-specific factors (such as administrative heritage and capacity, the balance of power between the different branches of government and the macro-economic context) that have the potential to impact budget outcomes. In terms of budget timeliness in Cameroon, the budget finance law of 2007, which governs the government financial system, established the conditions for preparing, presenting, executing and monitoring execution of the budget law. It, however, does not specify the budget calendar nor does it describe how long the fiscal year is. We can assume that Cameroon's fiscal year mirrors that of the French, which runs from January 1 to December 31. The budget law of 2007 also stipulates that the draft budget law must be submitted to parliament at least 15 days before the beginning of the budget session in November, and parliament has 20 days starting from the opening of the budget session to debate the draft budget law. There is no other formally articulated provision on the budget timetable. Also, the budget circular, which is signed by the President of the Republic, is published late and is of formal rather than practical value. Early in the year about April or May, the General Budget Directorate holds a seminar on preparing the budget law for the coming fiscal year and explains the major phases of the process followed by budget conferences in July, but this process is not formally established. The draft budget is usually approved on time before the start of the appropriate fiscal year (IMF 2010, p. 12).

The Collaborative Africa Budget Reform Initiative (CABRI) recommends that during budget formulation or preparation, governments ensure that there is consistency between the spending needs of line ministries and overall resource constraints while at the same time incorporating medium-term projections in budget frameworks so as allocate resources toward policy priorities. CABRI survey results of 2008 indicate that a majority of African countries (many of them Francophone African nations) have implemented some form of top-down budget approach to centralize decision-making powers during the budget formulation stage and ensure fiscal discipline (CABRI 2008, p. x). Given that the budget represents the most important vehicle for advancing economic growth and reducing poverty, budget preparation frameworks need to be aligned with the poverty reduction strategic paper (PRSP) initiated by the World Bank, to improve allocative efficiency. Cameroon has made improvements in this area. The budget preparation process now involves pre-budget and budget conferences to strengthen the involvement of line ministries, while sector strategies and medium-term expenditure frameworks (MTEFs) have been developed with World Bank support, to guide the allocation of inter-sectoral allocation of budgetary resources (Charlier & N'Cho-Oguie 2009, p. 77). The budget process, which has been driven by a top-down approach, is more comprehensive than it was before the implementation of poverty reduction measures. Charlier and N'Cho-Oguie also maintain that budget allocations to the priority sectors identified in the PRSP, especially health, education and infrastructure, have significantly increased since 2000. However, the introduction of technical instruments, political resolve, discipline and the implementation of a more participatory budget preparation process including line ministries, they argue, will be needed if the budget is to become an instrument of development (2009, pp. 73, 77).

As previously noted, the legislature has to play an important role in the budget process for it to be deemed credible and acceptable to the public. As CABRI (2008, p. 11) explains, the role of parliament in the budget process is one of the most distinguishing features of any public financial management system. The formal powers of the legislature, which generally include amendment powers as well as its organizational capacity, need to be assessed on a regular basis to ensure that its oversight role is effective. The legislature's role in the budget process in Cameroon has been inadequate because it lacks sufficient powers to amend the executive budget or approve any changes made to the budget over the course of the fiscal year. Also it does not have sufficient time to discuss and approve the budget given the short time that is allocated for its input between the presentation of the budget to the legislature and its approval. This situation could be significantly improved if mechanisms are put in place to strengthen the role of the legislature in the budget process as well as provide opportunities for the public to attend legislative hearings on the budget. Transparency in the budget process can also be improved through the dissemination of key budget documents (executive budget proposal, in-year reports, mid-year review, year-end report and audit report), via government websites that the government currently produces for internal use only (Essoua, 2010).

In its 2008 survey of budget practices and procedures in Africa, CABRI indicated that a major challenge faced by many African countries is to enhance the credibility of the budget by reducing the gap between planned and actual spending (2008, p. 16). Over the years, Cameroon has been plagued by budget execution problems caused by budget execution management shortcomings. For example, its budget information system was managed by a network of computer applications that were not designed to communicate with other. Charlier and N'Cho-Oguie (2008, p. 73), observe that the introduction of an integrated public finance information system has improved the tracking of the flow of resources through the budget execution chain, facilitated the preparation of budget execution reports and the regular reconciliation of payments and receipts, and improved the transparency of management. They also maintain that while an internal control system exists within the budget system, it remains weak in part, because of the lack of clarity of the mandates of the various control units, but also because of some difficulties resulting from the transition from manual to computerized information systems. However, the quality and timeliness of fiscal reporting have improved. Monthly fiscal data is now available within one month of the reporting period and are commitment- and cash-based. Since mid-2005, the Cameroon government has published monthly budget execution monitoring documents on a consistent basis (2008, p. 74).

Fiscal transparency and accountability in the budget processes of African nations have emerged as prime areas in need of improvement. According to CABRI, transparency in government finances implies "openness about policy intentions, formulation and implementation." Literature on budgeting systems across the world also subscribes to the view that fiscal transparency is associated with improved fiscal discipline, better credit ratings and reduced corruption. Citizens and taxpayers are entitled to full disclosure regarding the management of public money to ensure participation and accountability in public processes (CABRI 2008, p. 19). In describing what budget transparency is and why it is important, the World Bank-inspired Budget Transparency Initiative for Cameroon states:

> Budget transparency refers to the extent and ease with which citizens can access information about and provide feedback on government revenues, allocations and expenditures. Budgets are key documents reflecting how scarce resources are allocated across competing demands. They lay out a government's priorities in terms of policies and programs. Opening up budgets and democratizing the budget process, whether at the local or national level. allows citizens to have a say in policy formulation and resources allocation. Budget transparency, while not a goal in itself, is a prerequisite for public participation and government accountability. A budget that is not transparent, accessible and accurate cannot be properly analyzed. Its implementation cannot be thoroughly monitored nor its outcomes evaluated. Given the technical nature of budgets and the budget process, transparent budgets require that the information contained in them be actively disseminated to citizens in a timely manner and simplified form.
>
> Budget Transparency Initiative, Cameroon 2013, p. 1

According to the World Bank report, Cameroon's score in 2012 was only 45 out of 100, resulting in a ranking of 36 out of 52 countries. In the same year it was ranked 144th on Transparency International's corruption perception index. Over the past three years, Cameroon's open budget index score has failed to improve significantly. In 2012, Cameroon scored only 10 out of 100, far below the average score of 31 for Sub-Saharan African countries (Budget Transparency Initiative, Cameroon 2013, p. 3). In addition to the World Bank report cited above, Budget Transparency at the national level in Cameroon ranks low, constantly, on the Mo-Ibrahim governance index, compared to other countries.[7] As a result of these findings, the Cameroon government has been strongly criticized over the past several decades by regional and international organizations for a lack of transparency in its budget process. Dabla-Norris et al. (2010, p. 14) argue that:

> a transparent budget process which provides the public with all relevant information in a reliable, timely, understandable and internationally comparable manner is key for ensuring that public officials are held accountable for managing public resources.

Transparency through the entire budget process prevents hidden budgeting, another problem in many low-income countries, where the real budget is known only to a selected few, thus facilitating the misappropriation of funds and increasing the scope of misgovernment. Despite these negative findings, Cameroon has embraced some initiatives designed to introduce some modicum of transparency in its budget process. Legal provisions now exist in the country requiring the publication of budget documents. For example the government is required to publish all projects of the national investment budget at the beginning of the fiscal year in the *journal des projets*, which can be obtained in some government offices such as the regional delegations of the Ministry of Economy and Planning. Unfortunately, however, access to recurrent budget information is limited because there is no equivalent to the *journal des projects* in which it is included and the government's financial management systems make its extraction by lower levels of government technically difficult if not impossible. Also, access to information legislation about the nation's financial management systems has existed in Cameroon since 1999, but the law is vague and has no enforcement mechanisms. In fact, there are no sanctions for failing to provide information because the law stipulates that civil servants are allowed to disseminate information only after receiving clearance from their superiors. As a result, Global Integrity concluded that effective access to information about Cameroon's financial management systems is weak (Budget Transparency Initiative, Cameroon 2013, p. 3–4).

In terms of off-budget spending, several categories of budget expenditure exist in different countries that are often not subjected to routine budget procedures and thus are not included in budget documentation. According to CABRI (2008, p. xi), such practices reduce the degree of transparency of fiscal operations while creating liabilities that can undermine fiscal sustainability. It is therefore important that African nations that are facing such challenges initiate reform measures that would enable them to more effectively integrate off-budget expenditure into the budget process. In its 2010 report on Cameroon's observance of standards and codes according to the fiscal transparency model, the International Monetary Fund (2010, p. 15) observed that budget expenditure in Cameroon is occasionally executed without observance of normal procedures. The report notes that for various reasons that may include urgency and confidentiality of cash management, Cameroonian authorities sometimes ignore the normal expenditure procedures such as in cases where the state-owned oil company SNH makes payments on behalf of the government. Whereas SNH subtracts these payments from the oil revenues that it transfers to the government each month (according to the authorities), that expenditure is adjusted from a budgetary perspective, as the budget records the gross amount of the oil revenues as well as the outlay, initially as expenditure for adjustment and later in the budget categories deemed to correspond to the outlay in question. In essence, while all oil revenue collected by the government is shown in the budget documents, only a portion of that revenue is included in the definition of oil revenue used in those documents (IMF 2010, p. 38). This is not therefore a case of extra-budgetary expenditure, but rather one of expenditure executed without following the expenditure process. Since the expenditure does not go through the treasury, the treasury does not know of its execution or transaction until the SNH informs it during their monthly meetings on oil revenues (IMF 2010, p. 15).

Cameroon has to ensure that it reconciles differences in reporting oil sector revenues between the budget and the SNH. Under World Bank reforms, initiated under the auspices of its heavily indebted poor countries (HIPC) program, Cameroon has made significant progress in improving public financial management particularly in terms of budget formulation, execution and reporting. According to Charlier and N'Cho-Oguie (2009, p. 73), Cameroon's budget has become comprehensive because it now incorporates central government operations and integrates into the budget framework spending that used to be financed directly through SNH. Efforts should also be made to clearly show that revenue and expenditure allocated to entities outside the scope of the budget, such as SNH and other public administrative establishments are integrated into revenues and transfers on a consistent basis.

Debt Management

Debt management is an important component of budget formulation, execution and auditing for many nations. The International Monetary Fund (2001) defines debt management as a nation's ability to devise and execute a strategy for managing its debt such as raising the amount of required funding, achieving risk and cost objectives and meeting other debt management goals the nation may establish for itself. IMF experts also argue that governments should strive to ensure that both the level and rate of growth in their public debt should be fundamentally sustainable and can be serviced in a wide range of circumstances while meeting cost and risk objectives. Both debt managers and monetary policy advisors believe that public sector indebtedness should remain sustainable and that a credible strategy should be put in place to reduce excessive levels of debt. Concerns about the need to establish proper strategies for managing public debt are supported by the view that:

> poorly structured debt in terms of maturity, currency, or interest rate composition and large and unfunded contingent liabilities have been important factors in inducing or propagating economic crises in many countries throughout history.
>
> IMF 2001, p. 2

In its 2013 report reviewing Cameroon's economic development and other policies (part of an IMF Article IV Consultation), the IMF (2013, p. 5) stated that while Cameroon has maintained macro-economic stability, it remains vulnerable because its robust growth record has failed to meet Cameroonian authorities' ambitions for the nation to reach emerging economy status by 2015. The report also argued that since cancellation of Cameroon's debt under the HIPC initiative in 2006, the risk of debt distress has remained low and annual inflation has been contained. Nonetheless, per capita real GDP and most social indicators have stagnated despite an abundant and diversified natural resource base. The report further states that private-sector development has been impacted by poor financial management, a shallow financial sector and weak regional economic integration even within the Central African Economic and Monetary Community. Charlier and N'Cho-Oguie (2009, p. 102), also emphasize the need for Cameroon to maintain debt sustainability so as to attain macro-economic stability amid declining oil revenues. They caution that continued prudence in debt management is crucial if Cameroon is to consolidate its fiscal situation and allocate resources to finance growth and reduce poverty. In their view, although Cameroon has achieved relative success in managing its external debt following the devaluation of the franc, there were periods in the 1980s and 1990s when Cameroon's mounting external debt and debt servicing consumed a sizable part of government revenue. The debt increase reflected the economic depression and financial crisis of 1986–93. Cameroon reached five rescheduling agreements with the Paris club (a group of 19 creditor countries that meets regularly but informally in Paris to seek ways of helping debtor countries to manage their debts through coordinated rescheduling and other methods) between 1989 and 1997. Despite these agreements, external debt remained outstanding and unsustainable. As a result of continuing reforms and macro-economic stabilization, the debt situation began to improve in October 2000, when Cameroon reached a decision point under the enhanced HIPC initiative. Unfortunately, in 2004 Cameroon failed to meet its external debt service obligations, despite efforts to mobilize non-oil revenue and restrain expenditure. This situation led Cameroon to request a rescheduling of its bilateral and commercial debt obligations in 2005. Following successful structural reform efforts, Cameroon finally reached the HIPC completion point in 2006 and qualified for additional debt relief under the multilateral debt-relief initiative. The result has been a reduction in its external debt and debt servicing, reducing the net present value of external debt as a percentage of exports from 153 percent at the end of 2005 to 13 percent at the end of 2006 (Charlier & N'Cho-Oguie 2009, p. 103).

Also, in their 2014 African Economic Outlook, Richard Doffonsou of the African Development Bank (AfDB) and Lisa Singh of the United Nations Development Program (UNDP), explain in terms of Cameroon that in 2012, Cameroon's outstanding public and publicly guaranteed debt increased in nominal terms by 9.8 percent from an estimated XAF2.23 trillion (the XAF Central African CFA franc) to an estimated XAF2.45 trillion. However, its GDP fell by almost one percentage point from 18.5 percent to 17.8 percent. They maintain that public debt accounts for 88.7 percent of the total, while government guarantees account for the remaining 11.3 percent. The total amount of domestic and external finance commitments, in their view, was XAF1.01 trillion, 18 percent below the 2011 figure. The bulk of these commitments were for infrastructure, especially roads (45 percent), energy (19 percent) and telecommunications (10 percent) (Doffonsou & Singh 2014, p. 7). The report stresses that in 2013 the government continued to seek debt financing to support its huge program for building major infrastructure to maintain growth. The proportion of external borrowing was 50.7 percent and domestic borrowing was 49.3 percent. The aim is to reduce the proportion of outstanding external public debt from 64.5 percent at the end of 2012 to 63 percent by 2017. Following the cancellation of Cameroon's debt under the HIPC initiative in 2006, the nation's distress rating has been low. According to the debt sustainability initiative conducted jointly by the World Bank and the IMF, all external debt ratios remain below their thresholds. In addition to new borrowing, Cameroon's public debt-to-GDP ratio stood at 20.1 in 2013 (as reflected in Figure 3.2), making it very sustainable. This ratio could be 12.8 by 2017 with stronger growth. Considering the Economic and Monetary Community of Central Africa's critical debt-to-GDP ratio threshold of 70, Cameroon is poised to continue its development without running the risk of violating the convergence criteria. While a debt committee has been established to coordinate the country's debt policy and to ensure that it coheres with its development objectives, capacity building is necessary to improve the country's management of the loans increasingly being used to finance major infrastructure projects (Doffonsou & Singh, 2014, p. 8). See Figure 3.2 for a breakdown of Cameroon's debt from 2005 to 2012.

Revenues and Expenditures

Tabi et al. (2006, p. 3) contend that Cameroon derives most of its revenue from two main sources: oil and non-oil. Fiscal or tax revenue, which is a vital

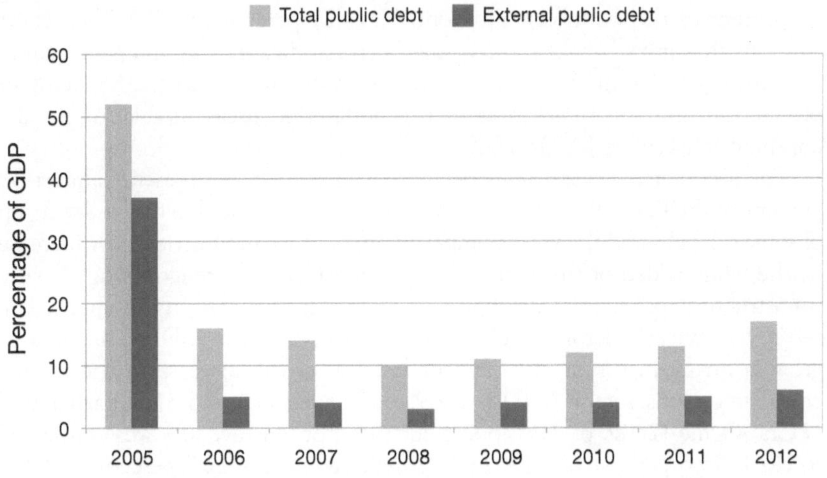

Figure 3.2 Cameroon: public debt, 2005–12
Source: IMF (2013)

component of the non-oil revenue, constitutes about 75 percent of total revenue and 11 percent of GDP. The types of taxes that account for the bulk of tax receipts are those on income and profits and indirect taxes such as taxes on goods and services and international trade. In terms of the contribution of each type of tax to national revenue, taxes from trade are the most important source of tax revenue. Import duties offer a more important source of total trade taxes than import taxes. Tabi et al. also state that while export tax as a share of total tax revenue ranged from 5 percent in the late 1960s to 0.3 percent in the early 1990s import taxes were as high as 30 percent in the early 1990s and as low as 1.5 percent in the early 1990s (2006, p. 3–4). In terms of the significance of the impact of indirect taxation on overall government revenue for the 1990s, in fiscal years 1990 to 2000, international trade taxes accounted for about 30 percent of total tax revenue. At a close second are taxes on goods and services such as turnover tax, value-added tax (VAT), excise taxes and tax on sales of petroleum products, which represented 20 percent of total tax receipts. Income tax, which ranks third, in terms of revenue, contributed less than 20 percent of total tax receipts over the same period (2006, p. 4).

The African Development Bank's 2010–2014 Country Strategy Paper on Cameroon notes that over the preceding five years, growth has been strongly driven by the activities of the oil and agricultural sectors. Revenues have been generated from wood or forestry products, banana, cocoa, coffee, cotton, and rubber and these revenues represent 50 percent and 25 percent of exports respectively. The report indicates further, that on the demand side, consumption has accounted for over 80 percent of GDP and investment 17 percent. On the supply side, the primary sector (agriculture), whose value added is rising, employs

60 percent of the workforce and contributes 21 percent of GDP. The report cautions that growth in this sector has been handicapped by the poor quality and inadequacy of rural infrastructure, constraints related to the financing of production and the remoteness of the population areas in relation to the consumption centers (AfDB 2009, p. 2).

The secondary sector (industry), whose value added represents almost 33 percent of GDP, is still characterized by a declining trend due to the drying up of some oil wells and the weak competitiveness of agro-industries. Any increase in the value added of this sector requires considerable strengthening of basic infrastructure and significant improvements in the business environment. The tertiary (services) sector, which represents 46 percent of GDP, continues to grow at an average rate of 6 percent because of the increase in the mobile communications sector (AfDB, 2009, p. 2) (see Figure 3.3). Charlier and N'Cho-Oguie (2009, p. 236), point out that non-oil revenues were projected to reach 13.6 percent of GDP by 2010, exceeding the 12.7 percent in 2006. This increase was expected to allow revenue to remain at 17.2 percent of GDP between 2006 and 2015, despite a decline in the oil sector's contribution to national revenue. Total spending was projected to be kept in check at 15.1 percent of GDP. The overall fiscal balance was expected to stabilize at about 1 percent of GDP between 2010 and 2015.

The key expenditure items for Cameroon between 2001 and 2015 included education, health, productive infrastructure and the rural sector. Charlier and N'cho-Oguie (2009, p. 239) maintain that total expenditures were expected to remain steady at 15.1 percent of GDP by 2010 with the increase in non-interest

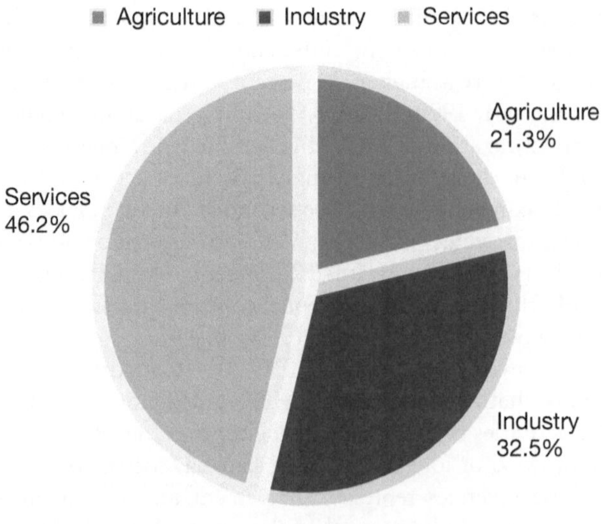

Figure 3.3 GDP by sector (2008)
Source: African Development Bank (2009)

spending absorbed by reduced debt services from debt relief. The increase in primary spending, they explain, is consistent with the PRSP priorities, with capital spending showing steady improvement between 2004 and 2007. PRSP priority sectors, which include education, health and productive infrastructure, will continue to be the main beneficiaries of the increase in capital spending. The PRSP projected increasing the education share of primary spending from 17.7 percent in 1995–2000 to 25.2 percent in 2007.The health sector's share of the primary budget was also expected to rise from 7.8 percent in 2003 to 9.7 percent in 2007. While the projected trends are impressive, they remain below what is required to achieve the millennium development goal targets. Productive infrastructure's share of the primary budget also increased substantially between 2001 and 2003, from 10.2 to 15.5 percent. The share of productive infrastructure is also projected to increase steadily over the next years to reach 17 percent of primary expenditure and 2.7 percent of GDP by 2015 (Charlier & N'Cho-Oguie, 2009, p. 239–242). Overall, Cameroon's revenue and expenditure outlook shows areas where improvements have occurred due to externally mandated reforms, as well as areas that need to be strengthened if Cameroon expects to maintain sustainability in its macro-economic growth.

Cameroon's Budget as a Development Tool

Ideally, when budget systems are properly formulated, executed and monitored, they can assist governments to manage public projects effectively, accountably and transparently and to enhance their capacities to accomplish planned developmental goals. Thus far, this study has examined the historical origins of Cameroon's budget system (public expenditure management system) as well as its budget process. From budget formulation or planning, to negotiation, execution and auditing or monitoring, we have found through abundant, diverse and well-substantiated sources that Cameroon has not fully embraced internationally accepted budget practices, nor has it enforced budget institutions or protocols that would otherwise enhance its capacity to use the budget as an effective tool of social, political and economic development. As a result, Cameroon has not been able to allocate resources toward the attainment of its own millennium development goals, which include eradicating extreme poverty and hunger, achieving universal primary education for its citizens, promoting gender equality and empowering women, reducing child mortality, improving maternal health, combating HIV/AIDS, malaria, and other diseases, ensuring environmental sustainability and developing a global partnership for development.[8] In order for Cameroon to use its budget as an effective development tool the government must strive to remove the constraints in the current budget system that make it difficult. First, the government must institute clarity, consistency and transparency in its budget process. Second, parliament must be given the opportunity to exercise its oversight role. Third, provisions must be established to allow for greater public participation in the budgetary process. Fourth, Cameroon must endeavor to adhere to internationally accepted protocols or institutions that reflect its capacity to embrace best practices in budgeting and public financial management in general.

Conclusions

This chapter has reviewed the budgeting system in Cameroon with a view to describing its historical background and evolution from independence until now. It has also examined its approaches to budgeting and identified the key actors involved in the budgeting process, analyzed its budget institutions, budget practices, major revenue sources and expenditure items and evaluated Cameroon's budget as a development tool. Despite the weakness and challenges that characterize Cameroon's budget process, the nation has nonetheless undertaken some reform initiatives to address some of these problems. For example, the legal framework for the management of public finances has been clarified and is now defined by laws and regulations, some of which are being amended to ensure their consistency with the constitution and with the law on the government financial system (IMF 2010, p. 8). Contrary to what existed before reforms were initiated, the 2007 law on the government financial system now establishes the conditions for preparing, presenting, executing and monitoring execution of the budget law. It also describes the structure and content of the budget law, defines the content and the process of presenting the budget review law in parliament, explains the principle of separation between the payment authorizing officer managing revenue or expenditure and the accountant, and defines the three categories of payment authorizing officers. The law also describes the types of accounting to be maintained by the government and the types of controls (administrative, parliamentary and jurisdictional) to be established over the public accounts. At the beginning of each fiscal year, a Minister of Finance circular specifies the procedures to be followed and gives detailed instructions to payment authorizing officers and accountants for execution and control of the government budget. The Decree of June 25, 1997, which established general regulations on public accounting, has been amended because several of its provisions are now inconsistent with the 2007 law (IMF 2010, p. 8).

The legislative basis for tax revenue collection has been strengthened and clarified. The International Monetary Fund (2010, p. 8), explains that all taxes and fees are now described in the General Tax Code and the Customs Code, and simplified manuals and prospectuses now exist. The structure of the tax legislation framework, the report asserts, is relatively stable and functions under a self-assessment system. Whereas the codes are generally precise, they leave in some cases some degree of administrative discretion. For example, the Director-General of Taxes or the Minister of Finance may authorize a total or partial reduction of penalties. Also, the granting of certain tax incentives is at the discretion of the authorities (IMF 2010, p. 8). In terms of tax administration, a legal and regulatory tax framework has been established and clearly defined. The administrative procedures of the General Tax Directorate are defined in the book of tax procedures and the administration is organized on a functional basis including legislation, disputes, audits and collection and by type of taxpayers. Specialized units cover large enterprises, professional firms, real estate firms and small taxpayers. While no code of conduct has been established for tax officers yet, they are required to maintain professional secrecy and other good practices specified in the book of tax procedures (IMF 2010, p. 9). There are also procedures manuals for some taxes, for the taxation of large enterprises and for all the tax functions and production structures. To enhance effective audits and collection, officers are entitled to request reports from third parties as specified in the book. Customs provisions are also similar. There is now a joint tax and customs unit that carries out audit missions in the field. Taxpayers now use single identification numbers for all taxes and tax units and reforms are being crafted to protect taxpayer identification numbers (IMF 2010, p. 9).

Reforms have also been initiated with respect to taxpayers' rights. These rights are currently well defined, and appeals against decisions on taxes and non-tax obligations are considered in a timely manner. In order to reduce tax disputes following decisions by government tax officials, taxpayers are now entitled to request early administrative decisions or advance tax rulings within 30 days of the tax consequences of any transaction or other act. In disputes taxpayers may appeal through a three-phase process that includes the regional directorate, the Director-General of Taxes and the the Minister of Finance. In all these phases, taxpayers are entitled to be represented by a third party in their relationships with the tax administration. The taxpayer also has the right to appeal to an independent court of law but that right is limited in practice because the appeal can only be heard at the administrative chamber of the Supreme Court in Yaounde. The provisions for custom duties are similar except that there is no mechanism for obtaining advance administrative decisions (IMF 2010, p. 9). In general, the government has implemented a new financial management system (strongly recommended by the World Bank, International Monetary Fund, and African Development Bank) that is designed to improve Cameroon's budget system and its overall management of other public expenditure items.

Recommendations

In the process of discussing and synthesizing the information that has shaped Cameroon's public financial management system since independence from the literature reviewed thus far, a number of lessons emerge. First, it is worth noting here that Cameroon's public expenditure management framework, like that of all Sub-Saharan Francophone African countries, was based on a French model that was not suited to Cameroon nor its other Francophone African counterparts. Moussa (2004, p. 25–26), observes that the French model was imported by Francophone African countries without the matching institutional, human and technical capacities necessary to sustain it. Second, a culture of transparency needs to be established by Cameroonian authorities to ensure that restrictive laws that prohibit public access to financial information are abolished. The issue of budget transparency is essential because transparency and oversight with respect to how resources are allocated and spent are powerful tools for dissuading officials from misusing or misappropriating funds and engaging in corruption. To that end, parliamentary scrutiny of the budget has to be strengthened in order to eliminate the potential for deviation from policy decisions and reversal of budget allocations as mentioned above.

Third, citizen participation in the budget process or participatory budgeting offers opportunities for citizens to provide feedback regarding the quality and adequacy of services and infrastructure provided. Quite often, public opinion is not sought concerning proposed laws, regulatory changes and broader policy changes. For example, annexes to the budget law are not confidential but are not systematically distributed or published (IMF 2010, p. 10). In describing the importance of budget transparency, the Cameroon Budget Inquirer, a collaborative initiative between the World Bank and the Open Knowledge Foundation, contends:

> Citizen feedback combined with reduced corruption results in more efficient use of resources. In many cases perceptions of high levels of corruption and the opaqueness of operations lie at the heart of citizens' distrust of their governments. Opening up their books of account is likely to lead to more trust in governments. Budget transparency can help generate higher revenues for governments since citizens are more likely to pay taxes if they trust that their money will be well spent.
>
> 2013, p. 2

Fourth, in terms of budget execution, accounting and reporting, the International Monetary Fund maintained in its 2010 report on the observance of standards and codes in Cameroon that the nation's accounting and internal control procedures are not entirely effective and the accounting system does not provide a basis for preparing reliable data on arrears (2010, p. 13). Also the lack of published information on expenditures for which payment orders have been issued but have not yet been paid makes any assessment of the fiscal situation difficult. The report explains that revenue is recorded mainly at the collections stage, and expenditure at the commitment, payment authorization, and payment stages for centralized services. Also most receipts occur through spontaneous deposits without giving rise to the issuance of receipt vouchers nor accounting entries. Only revenue for which receipt vouchers have been issued triggers accounting entries before actual collection. Consequently, knowing the full amount of accounts receivable is only possible for receipts for which vouchers have been issued. A computerized process that records all revenue at the collection stage would go a long way toward alleviating this problem.

Fifth, the government has to ensure that a legislative framework for debt management is established. The Minister of Finance is responsible for public debt. In that regard, all entities interested in loans have to obtain the authorization of the Ministry of Finance and the Ministry of Territorial Administration and Decentralization before they can take out a loan. The limits on central government debt are set within the framework of the budget law. Debt management by the autonomous amortization fund is limited to making long-term projections that cover only conforming commitments and take no account of possible liabilities. While the government prepared a debt strategy in 2010, it is not clear whether it has been approved (IMF 2010, p. 10).

Sixth, the weaknesses and challenges inherent in Cameroon's budget system, as articulated above, can be adequately addressed if the government clearly demonstrates a political commitment and ownership aimed at assuring the public that preparing, executing and monitoring a credible budget process is a national priority. Meaningful reforms should not be effected as a result of external conditional ties imposed by international organizations but rather as a national commitment to embrace sound budgeting practices so that the budget can become an effective tool of national development. Cameroon must therefore establish a strong governance framework that would enable it to rank higher on many of the human development indicators in which it has performed abysmally in the past several years. The Budget Transparency Initiative (BTI) indicated in its 2011 report that because of its weak governance capacity, Cameroon has consistently scored low on the Mo Ibrahim governance index (45 out of 100 in 2012), has obtained a low ranking on the 2012 corruption perception index (144), and in terms of budget transparency, it has scored only 10 out of 100 in the open budget index of 2012. The report further states that while budgets are public documents accessible to all citizens in principle, in practice, budget information is difficult to come by in Cameroon because of political, administrative, capacity, and logistical constraints and cost barriers at all levels of government. What has been implemented, the report concludes, is a governance partnership facility, for the dissemination of simplified budget information (BTI 2011, p. 1).

In sum, it is worth noting here that Cameroon is a nation endowed with vast potential in natural, agricultural and mineral resources. Revenues accruing from these sources can be used to support the budget as a tool of development so as to achieve strong and sustainable economic growth, if it can embrace the reform measures articulated above that have been recommended by multilateral and regional financial institutions. However, to accomplish this important task of national development the government must initiate and implement a credible public financial governance framework that clearly demonstrates its recognition of the budget as a national priority which should be transparent and open to public and parliamentary oversight and is undergirded by the law.

Notes

1 The Collaborative Africa Budget Reform Initiative (CABRI) is a pan-African network of senior budget officials in ministries of finance or planning created as a platform for its members to share experiences on budget reform programs and to contribute toward the efficacy of public financial management in Africa (CABRI 2008, ix).

2 For further discussion of the legal framework governing Cameroon's budgetary and accounting law, see the African Development Bank (African Development Fund) document Cameroon, Country Governance Profile (AfDB 2004) and D. Bouley, J. Fournel and L. Leruth (2003) How Do Treasury Systems Operate in Sub-Saharan Francophone Africa? *OECD Journal on Budgeting*, Vol. 2, No. 4.

3 For further information regarding the accomplishments and shortcomings of PB in Cameroon, see section two of the paper "The Book Lovers, The Mayors and the Citizens: Participatory Budgeting in Cameroon" which examines how the idea of Participatory Budgeting in Brazil has been adopted in Cameroon.

4 The Collaborative African Budget Reform Initiative (CABRI) 2013 status report offers a comprehensive discussion of the introduction, execution and performance of performance and program-based budgeting in Africa.

5 Top-down budget procedures or approaches clearly specify what role the central budget authority plays during each phase of the budget process from planning and negotiation, through to approval and implementation. For more information see Dabla-Norris et al. 2010, p. 10–12.

6 For details of Cameroon's accounting plan (modeled on the accounting plan of the Customs and Economics Union of Central Africa (UDEAC)) and its shortcomings, see the African Development Bank's 2004 Country Governance Profile on Cameroon's description of the key elements of the UDEAC accounting plan (AfDB, 2010, p. 10).

7 The Mo Ibrahim Foundation was established in 2006 with a focus on the critical importance of leadership and governance in Africa's leadership capacity and competence. By providing tools to support progress in leadership and governance, the foundation aims to promote meaningful change on the continent. As a non-grant making organization, the foundation focuses on defining, assessing and enhancing governance and leadership in Africa (www.moibrahimfoundation.org/). The International Budget Partnership launched the open budget survey and index in 2006 to compare the transparency budget level of countries' budgets and to assess their commitment to open and accountable governance (International Budget Partnership 2012 *Open Budget Survey for Cameroon*).

8 In 2000, member states of the UN, in partnership with many other international organizations, officially established the millennium development goals, a set of eight international development goals to be achieved by all 189 UN member states by 2015.

References

African Development Fund (AfDB). (2004). *African Development Fund: Cameroon, country governance profile*. Tunis: AfDB.

Africa Research Institute. (2012). *Participatory Budgeting in Yaounde, Cameroon*. London: Africa Research Institute.

Africa Research Institute. (2014). *The Book Lovers, the Mayors and the Citizens: Participatory Budgeting in Yaounde, Cameroon*. London: Africa Research Institute.

Alesina, A., & Perotti, R. (1996). *Budget Deficits and Budget Institutions*. Cambridge, MA: National Bureau of Economic Research.

Anderson, J. (2015). *Public Policy: An Introduction*, 8th ed. Stamford, CT: Cengage Learning.

Bouley, D., Fournel, L., & Leruth, L. (2003). How Do Treasury Systems Operate in Sub-Saharan Francophone Africa. International Monetary Fund. *OECD Journal on Budgeting*, 2(4):50.

Budget Transparency Initiative, Cameroon. (2011). *Simplifying and Disseminating Budget Information to Increase Citizen Feedback and Reduce Waste and Corruption*. Unpublished World Bank Report.

Budget Transparency Initiative, Cameroon. (2013). *A Local Transparency Index for Cameroon's Local Councils: Insights from a Benchmarking Exercise*. Washington, DC: World Bank.

Cameroon Budget Inquirer. (2013). *Why Budget Transparency? Transparency and Accountability*, Prepared by One. http://cameroon.openspending.org/en/why.html.

Charlier, F., & N'cho-Oguie, C. (2009). *Sustaining Reforms for Inclusive Growth in Cameroon: A development policy review*. Washington, DC:World Bank.

Collaborative Africa Budget Reform Initiative (CABRI). (2008). *Budget Practices and Procedures in Africa*. Waterkloof, Pretoria, South Africa: CABRI Secretariat.

Collaborative African Budget Reform Initiative (CABRI). (2013). *Performance and Programme Based Budgeting in Africa*. Waterkloof, Pretoria, South Africa: CABRI Secretariat.

Dabla-Norris, E., Allen, R., Zama, L., Prakash, T., Kvintradze, E., Lledo, V., Yakocovlev, Gollwitzer, I., & Gollwitzer, S. (2010). *Budget Institutions and Fiscal Performance in Low-Income Countries*. IMF Working Paper 10/80, Washington, DC: International Monetary Fund.

Doffonsou, R., & Singh L. (2014). *African Economic Outlook: Cameroon*. African Development Bank, Organisation for Economic Co-operation and Development and United Nations Development Program.

Elangwe, L. (2012). *The political economy of the budget process in Cameroon*. www.researchgate.net/publication/233981204_The_Political_Economy_of_Budget_Process_in_Cameroon.

Eoussa, L. (2010). *Open Budget Survey Index 2010*. Douala, Cameroon: Budget Information Center/International Budget Partnership.

Eoussa, L. (2012). *Open Budget Survey Index 2012*. Douala, Cameroon: Budget Information Center/International Budget Partnership.

Gollwitzer, S. (2012). *Budget Institutions and Fiscal Performance in Africa*. Centre for Research in Economic Development and International Trade, University of Nottingham, Nottingham, UK.

International Budget Partnership. (2012). *Open Budget Survey, Cameroon*. Washington, DC: International Budget Partnership.

International Monetary Fund. (2000). *Reports on Observance of Standards and Codes*. Cameroon and Washington, DC: International Monetary Fund.

International Monetary Fund. (2001). *Guidelines for Public Debt Management*. Washington, DC: International Monetary Fund and World Bank.

International Monetary Fund. (2010). *Cameroon: Report on the observance of standards and codes-fiscal transparency module*. IMF country report No. 10/264. Washington, DC: International Monetary Fund.

International Monetary Fund. (2013). *Cameroon 2013 Article IV Consultation*. IMF Country Report No. 13/279 9. Washington, DC: International Monetary Fund.

Inter-Parliamentary Union (IPU). (2000). *Parliament and the budgetary process including from a gender perspective*. New York: United Nations Development Program.

Lienert, I. (2003). *A comparison between two public expenditure management systems*. IMF Working Paper WP/03/2. Washington, DC: International Monetary Fund).

Milakovich M.E., & Gordon, G.J. (2015). *Public Administration in America*, 11th ed. Boston, MA: Wadsworth/Cengage Learning.

Moussa, Y. (2004). *Public Expenditure Management in Francophone Africa: A Cross Country Analysis*. Working Paper WP/04/42. Washington, DC: International Monetary Fund.
Robinson, M. (2007). *Performance Budgeting: Linking funding to results*. Washington, DC: IMF and Palgrave Macmillan.
Smith, R., & Lynch, T. (2004). *Public Budgeting in America*, 5th ed. Upper Saddle River, NJ: Pearson/Prentice Hall.
Tabi, A., Atabongawung, J., & Afeanyi, A. (2006). *The Distribution of Expenditure Tax Burden Before and After Tax Reform: The case of Cameroon*. Nairobi, Kenya: African Economic Research Consortium.

4 Economic Policy Formation in Ghana: is the Budgeting Process a Ritualized Anti-national Transformation Process?[1]

Lloyd G. Adu Amoah
Ashesi University, Berekuso, Ghana
and Strategy3, Accra, Ghana

> [. . .] *given the continued extreme reliance on cocoa and the continued deterioration of its soils and forests, the economic and therefore political prospects for Ghana are not favourable unless a means of breaking out of its present mold* can be found.
>
> John H. Dalton (1961, p. 563, emphasis mine)

> *How can we develop when the budget is not used as a planning tool but more like a decorative instrument?*
>
> Mary Aniwa (2015)

> *Too often statistical significance is confused with real world significance.*
>
> Philipp Bagus (2011, p. 542)

Introduction

On the Facebook page of noted Ghanaian columnist and writer Kwasi Gyan-Apenteng was this impassioned debate about the debilitating rationing and therefore unpredictable supply of power to homes and industry in Ghana, popularly christened "dumsor."[2] The debate had been triggered by Gyan-Apenteng's post titled "Dumsor Pain," quoted in full below, in which he sought to draw attention to the possible psychological toll this state of affairs could have on Ghanaians:

> The most painful part of the ongoing Dumsor frustration is the feeling of utter helplessness. It brings on grief knowing that there is nothing one can do except perhaps start your generator or inverter, light a candle; but of the core problem there is nothing one can do.
>
> Human beings are not supposed to live this way. We generate hope by actively confronting our problems with activities and ideas. That is how

> we keep hope alive and keep the human spirit alive with hope. Human beings are also able to tolerate adversity knowing that it will end, especially knowing *when* it will end.
>
> This Dumsor episode without a plan or timetable is creating a dangerous mental situation for the nation. We just don't know when it will end—*if it will end*. I am not a psychologist but I will be surprised if there are no mental health issues such as depression for many people.
>
> There has to be some kind of way out of this. This may sound like a cliché but we have to come together and work on this. Doing something constructive will help deaden the pain. But doing what? I'm afraid I don't have a clue!
>
> Gyan-Apenteng, Facebook, 2015

As Facebook goes this post was followed by comments as insightful as the original post was poignant. One from Mary Aniwa (Facebook, 2015) is worth quoting in full:

> it is the policy failure of successive governments that has brought us to this point. Because we fail to ask the questions "what, why, who, how and when" in our policy analysis, we get the solutions wrong! If we were planning properly, taking into consideration our population growth and projections we could have matched, to an extent, service delivery in energy, education, water, healthcare, housing etc. Not to mention the fact that most of the service sectors are starved of funds!! *How can we develop when the budget is not used as a planning tool but more like a decorative instrument, with the release of funds happening only in one quarter in some years!!* Heaven help us!! (italics mine).

Aniwa draws our attention to the old vexing question of the budget as a tool for responding effectively to the existential questions in a modern polity generally and more specifically in the post-colonial African state. Questions naturally arise from such a conception of the budget for Africa's transformation requirements of which Aniwa raises two salient ones:

1. Can and should the budget be used as a planning tool?
2. Has the budget become a mere "decorative instrument"?

I turn to trying to answer these questions in the following sections.

The Budget Globalized

Caiden (1978, p. 539) describes budgeting as "a universal and essential activity of governments" and adds further (1978, p. 540) that in its stylized (traditional) understanding or what she terms "pattern" the budget is about:[3,4,5]

> projections of public revenues and expenditures for a stipulated period (usually a year) whose provisions, which have the force of law, are

> implemented without unauthorized change in the period applicable. The pattern is a compelling one. It has been adopted with comparatively little variation in most, if not all, industrialized countries as a result of a roughly similar historical process.

Wildavsky (2006) and Caiden (1978) are unanimous in the view that the traditional budget in contemporary times is primarily concerned with accountability, control and efficiency regarding public funds. For our purposes Wildavsky (2006, p. 486) is illuminating and correct:

> In modern times, budgeting has also become an instrument of *economic management* and of *planning*. With the advent of Keynesian economics efforts have been made to vary the rate of spending so as to increase employment in slack times or to reduce inflation when prices are deemed to be rising too quickly . . . now as everyone knows, budgeting is not only an *economic but a political instrument*. (italics mine)

African countries such as Ghana have had to grapple in the post-colonial era with the economic and political Janus-face quality of the budget. The enormous tasks of urgent national transformation had to be a response to existential challenges of a decidedly economic and political nature and the traditional budget foisted (Amoah, p. 2011) on hitherto colonized territories was seen as an ideal instrument.

Dalton (1961, p. 558) recognized this duality in the case of Ghana in the period immediately following independence:

> Independence was found to have little that was liberating in itself, and the popular political elements aroused by the campaign for it constituted a latent threat, to which *material results* would have to be shown or *political leadership* discredited. The dynamism of the independence movement then ran into the recalcitrance of the colonial economy.[6] (italics mine)

With this dual nature in plain view I will argue that budgeting in Ghana has become inordinately narrowly politicized (a vital instrument of the cloistered self-serving calculus of the ruling elites) and in the event fundamentally abandoned the economic and by extension existential rationale. I employ a critical interpretivist paradigm (rooted in post-traditional public administration theory and practice, which is concerned with what Farmer (2005, p. 903) describes as the "quintet of alternative macro features" of public administration and policy), which engages with some key selected broad outcomes (empirics) of Ghana's budgets since 1992 and proffers explanations regarding why Ghana's budgets in the period have not furthered the national transformation agenda.[7,8] Such an approach provides a non-statistical perspective (which the literature scarcely displays) for understanding the difficult developmental trajectory of countries like Ghana in spite of efforts pecuniary and otherwise directed at such an undertaking.[9] On this I follow the advice of Huang and Gao (2015, p. 134), who argue that

> to understand human societies, we must not opt for just deterministic laws to the disregard of human choices, for the objective to the disregard of the subjective, for the necessary and predictable to the disregard of the contingent, and for the universal to the disregard of the particular.

In a sharp rebuttal of the deductivist tendencies that have come to dominate the social sciences Huang and Gao (2015, p. 131) are insightful in arguing for a research approach that takes as a starting premise:

> induction based on empirical evidence, thence to apply deduction to draw out the logical implications and hypothesis, and then return to the practical world to test the formulations, in an unending process, thereby to construct not universal and absolute theories, but theories and insights with delimited empirical conditions and boundaries.

The Budget and the Ghanaian Context

Understanding budgeting in Ghana requires an appreciation of the historical background from which it emerged. By a new Charter of July 24, 1874 the Gold Coast Colony was delinked from the Government of Sierra Leone and finally became a colony on its own by a Letters of Patent dated January 13, 1886. Jerven informs us that reliable economic data on Ghana covers "these two periods 1887–1938 and 1946–1989. There remains a significant gap in the data for most indicators for the years 1939–1945 and after 1989" (2012, p. 33). In other words a year after the Gold Coast become a full colony what could pass off as inchoate signs of the building of national accounts and therefore formal budgeting began in earnest. In the colonial era the Blue Books were the primary source of vital budgetary data (albeit with imperfections) on government revenue and expenditure; import and export volumes and values; infrastructure, health and education indicators; mineral extraction (on gold mining alone); wages and population.

It is vital at this juncture to return to Caiden (1978), who provides a convincing argument on the evolution of budgeting in modern times. Caiden identifies four patterns of budgeting pivoted around vital environmental factors that condition and constrain these patterns and therefore lend them their peculiar character. In this identification Caiden proffers three patterns as a counterpoise to the stylized, idealized traditional budget (referred to above) in order to show that vital environmental factors have a shaping force on budgeting:

> it [traditional budget] has proven capable of facilitating the considerable achievements of Twentieth century public authorities. This is the pattern upon which the "grand debates" about budgeting take place, but the *underlying conditions upon which it rests are ignored.*
>
> Caiden, 1978, p. 540

Caiden bristles about the traditional budget and the way it has been sold:

> discussions of public management of financial resources are concentrating upon a single pattern, either ignoring the possibility that other patterns may exist . . . Such an approach has in the past been responsible for the blanket perception of a single pattern as optimal, irrespective of *circumstances*.
>
> Caiden, 1978, pp. 539–540 (italics mine)

What are these *circumstances* then? What is that environment about which Caiden is clearly implacable?

> The need is to link budgeting and public finance with their *environment*, and to endeavor to promote meaningful hypotheses regarding mutual relationships between modes of handling financial resources and specific contextual features, between institutional constraints and possible budgetary outcomes.
>
> Caiden, 1978, p. 539 (italics mine)

She provides three environmental factors, namely resource mobilization, accountability, and administrative control, which interact and complement each other, are the product of historical evolution, and spawn the four patterns (Patterns I, II, III, and IV) of budgeting.[10] On resource mobilization the central point is the political capacity to tax, which not all governments possess and certainly not many governments in the developing world.[11] Without this the presence of a surfeit of wealth (paucity of wealth further undermines political capacity to tax by definition) does not mean much for generating revenue for budgeting purposes. Accountability is linked to the political capacity to tax and is essentially normative. Accountability must answer affirmatively the query about whether taxes raised will be used for the public good. Accountability is tied to the entire infrastructure of legislative and constitutional means by which close track and guardianship is kept of public expenditures via a verifiable information flow to citizens and sanctions applied in case of breaches. Administrative control refers to the bureaucratized system of officials, private or public, legally mandated through specific rules to organize public finances. There is a certain spatiality that administrative control must take into account: the larger the space the greater the questions of integrating various parts of a budget (given the greater number of budget units), information flow and the reach of budgetary policy.

Caiden (1978) places the budgeting process in developing countries into Pattern II. Budgeting in Pattern II is marked by low political capacity to tax, low accountability and low administrative control. The crucial feature of Pattern II budgets for our purposes here is what Caiden (1978, p. 543) calls "fictional budgets" or better still what I will call hyperreal budgets (a term derived from postmodern theory), which live a life of their own unrelated to the reality of pursuing especially long-term objectives for which they are put together.

Her analysis of budgeting as I have shown turns on the environment; she insists that the environment is the crucial variable which conditions and constrains the possibilities for budgeting. It is this environment, shot through with the sore absence of redundancy (following Landau, 1969), which has left its shaping influence on budgeting in developing countries such as Ghana, and which needs to be understood and analyzed.[12] Including history in the analysis points up the importance of path dependence for understanding from whence the lack of redundancy can be traced. In other words the lack of redundancy as the scourge of budgeting in developing countries has greater explanatory purchase when paired with the notion of path dependence, which posits that decisions to be made at any point in time:

> depend on past knowledge trajectory and decisions made, and are thus limited by the current competence base. In other words, *history matters for current decision-making situations and has a strong influence on strategic planning.* Competences that have been built in the past define the option range for today's moves.[13] (italics mine)

Budgeting in the Shadow of History in Ghana's Fourth Republic

My position in this chapter is that there is a historical environment exerting a powerful shaping influence on budgeting via path dependence in contemporary Ghana in the period under review. This historical environment sheds useful explanatory light on the lack of redundancy, which Caiden (1978, p. 2006) has been at pains to point out. I will attempt to show here the ways in which Ghana's economic record in especially the colonial era has provided the framings and continuities (and therefore hardly any disjunctures) within which contemporary budgeting has been set. In this enterprise I point to a distinction between the historical (and therefore remote) and the social (and therefore immediate) environments and consider budgeting in the Ghanaian case as an institutionalized undertaking impinged upon by historical and social forces. I utilize the insights of historical and sociological institutionalism in this analysis. While historical institutionalism concerns itself with "how institutions emerge from and are embedded in concrete temporal processes" (Thelen, 1999, p. 369) sociological institutionalism of the Dimaggio and Powell (1983) variant focuses on institutional change in terms of the mimetic, normative and coercive conduits through which ideas and practices flow and how all this is aided and abetted by the key roles of the professions, higher education and the media.[14, 15, 16] And here I proceed in my analysis on the enlightening advice of Huang and Gao (2015, p. 135) for understanding public policy formation in developing polities when they make a plea for "appropriate combining of particularistic narratives with more generalized social science analyses."

The colonial economic system was at worst exploitative and at best self-serving. Crafted to extract maximum material benefits from the colonies, its organizing and self-sustaining logic had no place for a future in which the colonized were in control of their own economic destiny.

Rodney underscores this view eloquently:

> the character of growth in Africa under colonialism was such that it did not constitute development, i.e., it did not enlarge the capacity of the society to deal with the natural environment, to adjudicate relations between members of the society, and to protect the population from external forces . . .
>
> In no African colony was there economic integration, or any provision for making the economy self-sustained and geared to its own local goals. Therefore, there was growth of the so-called 'enclave' import/export sector, but the only things which developed were dependency and under-development.

This position is reinforced in official records on colonial economies. In a 1944 memorandum the dominant view held by those who ran the economic machinery is revealed:

> Hardly any colonial government in the past has consciously planned the development of its territory. Law and administration have been the favorite sons, education and public health the not so favored daughters. [. . .] This approach to colonial administration belongs to an era that is passed.
>
> CEAC (44) 16 Appendix II, BLPES CEAC 4/7[17]

This brings us to the crucial historical framing influence on the Ghanaian economy which Dalton captures eloquently: British policy in the Gold Coast was to "maintain law and order, and a favorable climate for trade . . . Other activities, the provision of education and good works, were instrumental to these" (Dalton, 1961, p. 554). In other words for Dalton British administrative and economic objectives on the Gold Coast were sorely limited and limiting with regards to the political and economic interests of the indigenes. Dalton is worth quoting here again:

> Large scale investments in public facilities and a thorough transformation of agriculture were called for, and these were tasks which the British neglected and for which experience under British rule had *poorly prepared the new state*.
>
> Dalton, 1961, p. 564 (italics mine)

Contrary to the situation where the economic interests of the indigenes of the Gold Coast were constrained deliberately by British policy, Howard (1976) informs us that British economic and trade interests were allowed to flourish (with implicit and explicit official support) in the colony. In her insightful work Howard focused on:

> the mechanisms of the economic take-over of the Gold Coast, between approximately 1885 and 1939. Two aspects of the take-over are dealt with: the progressive oligopolization of trading, shipping and banking in the colony, and the influence which oligopolistic British firms exerted on government policy.
>
> Howard, 1976, p. 71

Howard understood this take-over as being responsible for stymieing the emergence of an African trading class and with it the potential rise of a formidable class with independent capital holdings to dominate and control the Ghanaian economy after independence. In addition to this Howard notes that "the pursuance of government policy dedicated to maintaining Ghana's role as a peripheral import-export economy resulted in the internal economic underdevelopment of the colony" (Howard, 1976, p. 72). The author shows the ways in which the banking, shipping and trade sectors under European control onshore (colonial economic and trade policy) and offshore (in the cities of Manchester, Liverpool, and London) colluded through interlocking directorates and made any independent African trade and economic undertaking excruciatingly difficult, if not impossible, and dependent on the European structure so constructed. The case of one Willian Ocansey, which she is at pains to point out, is poignant and instructive. In an attempt to avoid dependence on European shipping operations in the Gold Coast he attempted to buy a steam launch to be used on the Volta River. The European agent tasked to purchase the machine simply vanished with the money he was given (Howard, 1976 p. 489).

Essentially the picture that emerges is that of an economy deliberately constructed, structured and hardwired to be tied and dependent on the ebbs and flows of the world capitalist economy with scarcely room to maneuver (or at least requiring heroic effort to create room) in pursuit of the economic interests of the people of the Gold Coast.

> Between about 1880 and 1910 the Gold Coast entered the world capitalist system as a full-fledged peripheral nation producing raw materials for export to the rapacious factories and workers of the industrial West.
>
> Howard, 1976, p. 79

The logic of this colonial economy could only spawn deficiencies which both sustained and reproduced it. These historically generated deficiencies became evident as the Gold Coast transitioned into independence. The staffing of the bureaucracy with personnel possessing the required skills to run a new modern state was one of the initial key deficiencies that had to be grappled with (Amoah, 2014b; Adu, 1960; Agbodeka, 1972; Bentil, 2004; Greenstreet, 1972). On the economic and therefore budgeting front, the sore absence of statisticians was an early irritation. Data used by the colonial authorities was reportedly dubious (Serra, 2014, p. 11). Serra reports that it was not until 1948—62 years after the Gold Coast became a stand-alone colony—that the Office of the Government Statistician was set up.[18] (The first Gold Coast Government statistician was A.B. Reisz, a Hungarian). The creation of this office was actuated by the cocoa boom (inspired by the entrepreneurial vision of Nana John Kwame Ayew and his two brothers, Nana Adu-Ameyaw and Nana Asomani, of the Akyepere clan on the Akuapem Ridge) and the setting up of the World Bank and the International Monetary Fund (IMF), two bodies that have had arguably the greatest influence on economic policy formation of post-colonial African states. On the statistics problem Rimmer is uncharitably frank regarding his conceptual misgivings about national income accounting and more to the point the statistical basis for it in the Gold Coast in the 1950s:

> My difficulty became greater when I had the opportunity to observe the rough-and-ready methods by which national accounts were constructed in the Government Statistics Office in Accra. Much was guesswork. Much also was omitted . . . Also later I became conscious of the definitional and valuation problems that underlay the enumeration of economic output.
>
> Rimmer, 2003, p. 471

To all these crucially must be wedded with the conceptual and theoretical disquisitions (of the 1950s) on the application and practice of the science of economics in developing societies (which gave birth to development economics) in which the African indigenous intellectual input was all but absent.[19] Killick (2010) provides a fairly magisterial view of the discourses of the era and an account of the leading, mostly European, voices who dominated the conversation.[20] Ghana's first president Kwame Nkrumah relied heavily on the counsel of such economists, among them Albert Otto Hirschman, Dudley Seers, Nicholas Kaldor and Joszef Bognar, reflecting in many ways the long provenance of the externally oriented ideational focus that has marked economic policy thinking in Ghana. Essentially then my argument suggests the historicity of the ideational and concrete challenges that have marked Ghana's economic policy formation since independence, which budgeting in contemporary times most vividly reflects. I turn to the implications in the next section.

Anti-development Budgeting under Ghana's Fourth Republic

The early 1980s were difficult years for the Ghanaian economy and society. An insurrection led by junior army officers on June 4, 1979 (underlining the political instability that marked the post-Nkrumah years) resulted in the summary execution of three former heads of state. These bloody events however were to be followed on December 31, 1981 by a *coup d'état* against the democratically elected Dr. Hilla Limann's administration, sounding the death knell of the Third

Ghanaian Republic. The Provisional National Defense Council (PNDC) helmed by Jerry John Rawlings, a former junior fighter pilot in the Ghanaian air force, subsequently took the reins of power. The PNDC had barely settled when it was called upon to quell fires literally and figuratively. Key socio-economic indicators in the period were not encouraging. A lethal combination of bush fires and drought affected agricultural production, threatening famine. Inflation rose for example to 116.5 percent in 1981 (Aryeetey and Fosu, 2008). By 1983 the current account deficit had increased to USD294 million from USD2.75 million in 1975 (Aryeetey and Fosu, 2008). Basic necessities of life such as milk, soap, and sugar were in short supply, triggering the emergence of a black market in which these necessities were sold at exorbitant prices. Facing a restive population and the real threat of a revolt the PNDC (after internal wrangling in which its pragmatic wing prevailed over its radical leftist ideologues) turned to the World Bank and the IMF in 1983 after it had been spurned by the Soviet Union, which the leftist regime considered its natural ally.[21] In the 1980s neo-liberal economic orthodoxy had come back into vogue with the Thatcher and Reagan victories of 1979 and 1980. Peter Shore in a preface to collection of speeches of Nicholas Kaldor is lucid:

> The view that government intervention in economic activity, nationally and internationally, was integral and indispensable to modern government and indeed could be of enormous positive benefit became unfashionable in the difficult economic conditions of the 1970s.
>
> Peter Shore, cited in Kaldor, 1983, p. 1

As Kaldor notes, neo-liberal economics had faced bruising critiques all round (as far back as 1870 as well as in the early nineteenth century) including from the Tories and had in his words been "pronounced dead and buried." Kaldor added further, recoiling at the about-turn of Tories: "like true converts, the new Tories propound the creed with the fervour and vitality of a new religion, and in total oblivion of its dismal record."

Budget Reforms

Ghana thus adopted the Economic Recovery Programme/Structural Adjustment Programme (ERP/SAP) just when neo-liberal economics was ascendant. This development was to congeal in the New Public Management era of the 1990s (Amoah, 2012a and 2012b; Denhardt, 2000; Hood, 1991; Osborne and Gaebler, 1993) in which private-sector (and therefore market-derived) notions such as contracting out, management by objectives, and competition were believed almost with ecclesiastical conviction to hold the unmistakable key to unlocking the putative genetic inefficiency in the public sector worldwide. In Ghana, as in other developing countries under ERP/SAP, budgeting took on a managerialist posture and obsession with results anchored in "greater emphasis on output controls, resource allocation and rewards linked to measured performance"

(Hood, 1991, p. 4) and thus was born the voguish Performance-Based Budgeting (PBB) (Caiden, 2006).

Ghana's road to PBB can be traced to two public expenditure reviews undertaken by the Government of Ghana (GoG) in 1993 and 1994 under the auspices of the World Bank.[22] Confronted with a messy budgetary process and a culture marked by "incremental allocations process, frequent cutbacks and expenditure freezes affecting allocations, a cumbersome certification and payment procedure, and the predominance of unbudgeted expenditures" (Roberts & Andrews, 2005, p. 293), GoG introduced the Public Financial Management Reform Programme (PUFMARP) to tackle the problem.[23] Central to PUFMARP for our purposes was its focus on budget preparation and implementation, which obviously merited (given its criticality) an entire management system, the Budget and Public Expenditure Management System (BPEMS). This mélange of programs and systems captured under a potpourri of winding acronyms was to be ostensibly "implemented through the development of a Medium Term Expenditure Framework (MTEF)" (Roberts & Andrews, 2005, p. 293). Again it is important to emphasize here that if, as Roberts and Andrews (2005, p. 293) report, the MTEF "was intended to improve government's contribution to *development outcomes* and to facilitate greater stability in fiscal policy, improved resource allocation, and more efficient service delivery," the budget lay at its nexus. And to be sure, on account of this the budgeting process underwent a series of tinkering actions in the service of an ostensibly new focus on results (objectives) and therefore value for money.

In my view the re-engineering of the budget between 1990 and 2000 involved three key components: temporal measures, a more scientific approach and integration.[24] The temporal measures added two additional years to the active budget year to allow projection for taxing and spending plans. A more scientific approach meant the building of a macro-economic model, taking account of key variables such as inflation and GDP figures, to introduce certitude and exactitude regarding funding and revenue estimation. This replaced the traditional resource estimation model based on incremental projections. Integration focused on first strategically aligning the policies and programmes; the ministries, departments and agencies (MDAs) and second including the costs in the areas of personnel, service, administration and investments in the budget. The staff of the MDAs were retrained for this and expected to provide annual performance reports on it. While there was an initial triumphant view that the MTEF was producing the desired performance management results (tellingly and problematically this view was based on the MDAs having *lists* of mission statements, objectives, outputs and activities), almost a decade after the attempts at reform the failure of the MTEF was widely acknowledged by the GoG (Roberts & Andrews, 2005) and other interested parties. Budgeting in particular continued to show pre-MTEF weaknesses.

It is important to stress that the new Kufuor Administration had been in power for close to two years by 2002. Faced with these budgetary and financial management challenges it continued with earlier reforms for which a ministry to oversee public sector reforms was set up in May 2005 (Amoah, 2014b). In the Kufuor era the persistent challenges with the budget saw one key response. This response marked the beginnings of far-reaching and strident interference in the budget process by so-called donors in terms of inputs, targets and outcomes under the multi-donor budget support framework (MDBS). The Ghana Ministry of Finance (MOF) actually has a whole unit responsible for this.

The government's own description of the MDBS is instructive:

> Multi-Donor Budget Support (MDBS) is the name given to general budget support in Ghana. General Budget Support involves the transfer of financial aid from Development Partners (DPs) directly to a partner country's national budget . . . As a result, MDBS is the Ghana Government's preferred way of receiving aid.[25, 26]

The MDBS that was introduced in 2003 allowed, as never before in my view, the so-called DPs to directly control (to the point of derailing it if these funds were not released) the revenue stream of the Ghanaian budget (through aid) and also to determine the ideational principles and sectoral priorities of the GOG on a quid pro quo basis: Ghana had to demonstrate a commitment curiously certified by the DPs to poverty reduction, good governance and sound economic management.[27] The aid was supposed to plug the deeply contested "financing gap" thesis that has pitted development economists of the Kaldor, Hirschman, Seers, etc. persuasion against the marginalist neoclassical economists (Rimmer, 2003; Killick, 2010). Ultimately the MDBS via the budget according to GoG was aimed at improving the quality of life and social well-being of all Ghanaians:

> with particular focus on the poorest and most vulnerable. This includes investing in basic services, such as health, education, water and sanitation, as well as promoting shared and sustainable economic development.[28]

As per the GoG's own MDBS document utilized in this work (downloaded in May 2014) the MDBS has contributed approximately USD2.8 billion (USD300 million per year up to 2007 according to an ODI and CDD-Ghana Report, 2007)[29] to Ghana's budget in pursuit of the development objectives just alluded to.

The other key response occurred under the Atta-Mills administration. Here the framing idea was that the era of bits and bytes (Amoah, 2012) could help tackle the budgetary quandaries. In May 2009 the Ghana Integrated Financial Management Information System (GIFMIS) was launched. A World Bank document described GIFMIS as a system for "enhancing the accountability and transparency of government financial operations using ICT-based tools" (World Bank, 2010, p. 1). For GoG, the GIFMIS took off from where the BPEMS (1999–2008) had left off with all its unresolved complexities and problems regarding budgeting. GIFMIS served as the context within which PBB budgeting proper was being introduced.[29] It must be noted that GIFMIS was a new component added to an ongoing eGhana IT project (essentially an eGovernance project), which had taken off in 2006.

Explaining Ghana's Budget Strictures beyond the Recognition of Redundancy

The Ghanaian budgeting process can be safely understood as an institution to the extent that at stake is behavior modulation of the central actors on pain of sanctions from third parties (Thelen, 1999). In this case Ghanaian citizens through the legal, administrative and bureaucratic infrastructure of law, rules, and regulations, and, far more crucially, the DPs, constitute the third parties. In my view the DPs have become the most potent shaping influence on Ghana's budget, more potent than Ghanaian citizens themselves, reflecting the DPs' virtually unchallenged economic dominance; a process aided and abetted by Ghana's politicaland bureaucratic elites as I will demonstrate presently. The DPs' increasingly powerful (however cleverly disguised in the dialogic pretense couched in putatively democratic norms and narratives) and hegemonic role in Ghana's constantly changing budgeting approaches reflects rather sharply Dimaggio and Powell's (1983) claim that institutional change is brought about by the emergence of ideas and practices promoted by professional ties, higher education and the media.[31] These ideas and practices catalyze institutional change via mimicry, claims of normative superiority and, more importantly in Ghana's case, coercion. The text of Ghana's budget statements is a classic case. In the period under question these documents reflect uncannily the literary stamp of World Bank/IMF documents; the discourse and narratives of Ghana's economic policy-makers ooze with all the standard jargon (the obfuscated meaning of which one often struggles to decipher) of neo-liberal economic and social organization. Table 4.1 shows a word count of some of this jargon used in two randomly chosen documents. The count took into account the words and their cognates and the technical sense in which they had been used (for the "initiated" of course; the "uninitiated," the masses, for whom economic policy formation is about, will struggle to understand). In both documents one gets the impression that in some cases this jargon was simply thrown in for its fanciful effect rather than for any useful semiotic value. This jargon seems to have acquired omnibus meanings applicable to every policy context. Some examples will suffice:[32]

1. "Mr. Speaker, the NPRA will build a *robust* integrated pensions management and compliance system by acquiring ICT infrastructure for office automation . . . ." (GoG, 2015, p. 112).
2. "Mr. Speaker, the Ministry exist [sic] to achieve a *sustainable*, equitable economic growth and poverty reduction through citizen participation . . . ." (GoG, 2015, p. 65).
3. "GIFMIS will also support the development of *sustainable* human resource capacity in the MoFEP, MDAs, MMDAs . . ." (World Bank, 2010).

The career of Ghana's budgetary approaches to date as sketched demonstrates the impact of the historical and immediate social contexts. This is the position of Caiden (2006) and Roberts and Andrews (2005), which I share. Ghana's

Table 4.1 Lingo Isomorphism?

	Word Count	
Lingo	*Ghana Budget 2015*	*World Bank 2010 Report*
Consolidate	9	6
Sustainable	21	4
Robust	5	5
Sound	3	6

budget formation elites seem unwilling or incapable or both in responding to the historical path dependence (expressed in a contemporary lack of redundancy and therefore reflecting a duality of forces acting on the process) forces acting on the budget formation processes.

The Budgets and Data

Sixty-seven years after the Office of the Statistician was set up on the soil of Ghana, the nation's economic policy formation has been plagued by the same questions over reliable data already alluded to in this work. In the very first budget statement of the Kufuor administration presented to the Ghanaian Parliament in 2001 (PUFMARP had been in implementation phase for close to a decade), the Minister of Finance Yaw Osafo-Maafo (GoG, 2001, para 2) complained about the absence of reliable data on the Ghanaian economy, even though PUFMARP had been in implementation phase for close to a decade:[33]

> Mr. Speaker, the new administration has inherited economic and financial crises of serious dimensions. The actual order of magnitude still eludes us. There is a critical lack of adequate and reliable data on the state of the national economy. Public finances are in chaos.

The IMF will validate this with a press release dated February 4, 2002 reporting that Ghana's economic authorities had provided false data on its stock of reserve money. This had led to transfers totaling USD98.0 million to the Ghanaian treasury, which the country was not otherwise eligible for under the Poverty Reduction and Growth Facility (PGRF). The IMF wrote tellingly:

> These disbursements had been made in September 2000 and July 2001, respectively. In October 2001, the new Ghanaian authorities informed the Fund of an upward revision to data on the stock of reserve money, with the implication that the information available to the Fund at the time of approval of the September 2000 and July 2001 disbursements was incorrect.
>
> IMF, 2002

In 2015 economic statistical matters still hog the national discourse. In 2015 Dr. Mahamudu Bawumia, Oxford-trained economist and former deputy-governor of the Bank of Ghana, raised issues with Ghana's 2015 GDP figures of that year in a widely circulated speech. A whole section of the speech was dedicated to data issues, part of which is worth quoting:

> If your data is not credible, the anchor cannot hold. With make-believe data as the basis, the best you can achieve is make-believe results which will soon be exposed as we are witnessing currently. I would like to examine the two most critical pieces of data underlying the IMF program . . .
>
> Bawumia, 2015, p. 53

In the 2015 budget document the finance minister Seth Tekper reiterated the long years of public financial management reforms in pursuit of:

> *value for money* . . . Government has been *implementing* key Public Financial Management (PFM) reform initiatives. Notable among these initiatives are the Ghana Integrated Financial Management Information System (GIFMIS), Budget Reforms including the introduction of Programme-Based Budgeting (PBB) a new Budget Preparation and Management System . . . and Modernization of Revenue Management and Administration.
>
> GoG, 2015, p. 140 (italics mine)

If the public financial management system was to reflect its robustness after all the reform efforts, it should prove capable of limiting to a minimum the leaking of public funds into private pockets, and worryingly—as well sheer—wastage. Under the Fourth Republic mind-boggling amounts from the treasury have been lost to corruption reflecting for our purposes the persistence of the systemic problems that the lack of redundancy gives rise to in the budget and public finance system, in spite of the long years of reform. Two illustrative cases that captured national attention come to mind.

SADA, GYEEDA and the Taxpayer's Money

The Ghana Living Standard Survey 6 (2012/2013) indicates that the Northern Region of Ghana between 2005/2006 and 2012/2013 (a seven-year period) was the poorest in Ghana: the three Northern regions (i.e. Upper East, Upper West and Northern regions contribute more than a third to national poverty.[34] This was the stark background against which it was decided to set up the Savannah Accelerated Development Authority (SADA) under Act 805 to, among other things, "provide strategic planning guidance to government as regards the implementation and review of an *accelerated development strategy* for the Northern Savannah Ecological Zone" among other things (italics mine).[35] After receiving USD25 million seed money (the founding Act indicates that seed money is a key source of funds for the authority) initially provided by the Kufuor administration SADA by 2015 could not account in money for value terms for GHS 47,498,000.00 for two key projects on guinea fowl rearing and reafforestation.[36] SADA was mired in public controversy and deepening public mistrust regarding its capacity to pursue the objectives set for it: the board was reconstituted and a new chief executive officer appointed in 2014. Hence in that year the Ghanaian government allocated it a paltry GHS20 million (less than the half of the money wasted on the guinea fowl and reafforestation projects); for 2015 it had no allocation at all. Based on my calculation of total monies (including the figure for the reafforestation and guinea fowl projects) and based on the Auditor-General's 2013 records, SADA and by extension Ghana lost, through circumvention of financial procedures and shocking wastage of public funds, some of which went into private pockets, the amount of GHS51,526,760.00. In a country where the poorest households are headed by farmers, and 24.2 percent of the population, approximately 6.2 million Ghanaians cannot afford to spend GHS3.60 per day, it is confounding that SADA lost 714 bags of hybrid seeds valued at GHS165,000.00 because they were supplied late to the farmers. It is worthy of note that SADA reportedly did not have a contract register and an internal audit unit as required by Regulation 202 of the Financial Administration Regulations, 2004 (L.I. 1802) and section 16 (1) of the Internal Audit Agency Act, 2005 (Act 658). SADA's woes graphically reflect a golden opportunity, almost spurned, to correct a long-lasting 'wicked' policy problem that has left a sizeable chunk of Ghana's population in debilitating poverty and deprivation.

The Ghana Youth Employment and Entrepreneurial Development Agency (GYEEDA) was set up to respond to the potential social and political threat that pervasive, nation-wide youth unemployment could present to Ghana. It is important to recall that the West African coast had experienced some of its most violent civil wars in Liberia and Sierra Leone in 1990s. In both countries young people were among the central social actors in the lead up to the war and at the front lines. Ghana had to draw upon its diplomatic, military and political reserves to help respond to both wars, which threatened the whole of West Africa; its elites might have learned some lessons from these wars. GYEEDA began life as the National Youth Employment Program in 2006. By 2013 GYEEDA had received a total of approximately GHS950,000,000.00 from the Consolidated Fund and other statutory sources such as the Ghana Education Trust Fund, the National Health Insurance Scheme Fund, the Road Fund and the Communication Service Tax fund, all of which were underwritten by the Ghanaian taxpayer.[37] By 2013 massive corruption forced the Ghanaian government to institute investigations into the operations of GYEEDA. The Government's own report documents the rather shocking details of legislative, financial, administrative and political irresponsibility, which virtually put paid to a necessary policy intervention hinging on national stability and progress. I will be exhibiting prolixity if I go into the details of the report but one example should suffice in capturing the irresponsibility alluded to:

> The Committee found that the current CFO (or Deputy National Coordinator, Finance), the most senior finance person has no track record of a competent head of finance. Indeed, the officer himself admitted that he lacked the training and experience to operate effectively as head of finance.
>
> Government of Ghana, 2013a, p. 84

Table 4.2 Ghana–China HDI Comparison

Countries	*Year/HDI*	*Year/HDI*
Ghana	1980 0.423	2013 0.573
China	1980 0.423	2013 0.719

Here is a poignant example of the lack of redundancy seemingly hardwired into a state organization to guarantee its failure and with it the purloining and wastage of scarce national financial resources. These examples in the Ghanaian case raise questions about the failure of budgets as instruments of far-reaching national transformation in developing countries, which point up the explanatory limitations of focusing on the recognition of the absence of redundancy, however vital this is in making sense of the budget–national transformation nexus.

Again I must add that the Human Development Index, which according to the United Nations Development Programme is "a composite index measuring average *achievement* in three basic dimensions of human development—a long and healthy life, knowledge and decent standard of living" (italics mine), provides compelling evidence as to whether Ghana's budgeting and financial processes reformation in the last twenty odd years have aided the nation's transformation. A comparative analysis of HDI scores between Ghana and China should drive home the point. Ghana and China in 1980 had the same HDI score, as Table 4.2 shows. The year in question is critical for both developing countries. China had launched its opening up and reforms under Deng Xiaoping a year earlier; Ghana was two years away from turning fully to the World Bank for support. By 2013, China had shot into the high HDI bracket while Ghana remained stuck in the medium HDI league. China's public finances managers have clearly done a far better job than their Ghanaian counterparts.

The Budget and Their Truths

The budget documents yield their own truths about the economy and Ghana's development. In line with neo-liberal economic vision, the private sector has become the focus of economic policy. The idea has been that a private sector freed of constraints should provide the national economy with the needed drive. Under the Kufuor administration for example the private sector was strongly touted as the "engine of growth." The evidence of policy success should show in the performance over time of the manufacturing sector, which under the Fourth Republic was largely in private hands and has historically been central for developing polities attempting to transform. The 2015 budget records that the percentage growth of the manufacturing sector in 2012 was 2 percent; in 2014 the growth was negative at −0.8 percent. Over the three years from 2012 to 2014 industrial growth had more than halved from 11 percent in 2012 to

4.6 percent in 2014. The years are critical given that it is safe to assume that they should reflect the expected maturation (after two decades of reforms) in the industrial and manufacturing sectors if the budget was really playing its expected roles. The budgets from 2000 to 2015 show that real GDP growth rates, calculated by the author to be 6.5 percent on average over the period, have not been consistent enough to allow the Ghanaian economy to make the strides the tiger economies achieved; these economies grew consistently at between 8 percent and 10 percent over their transformation periods. From the foregoing I insist that the lack of redundancy regarding budgeting must be viewed as being the product of historical and social forces; but a pertinent question forces itself upon us: why has the lack of redundancy persisted in spite of all the apparent strenuous efforts to tackle it?

Explaining the Persistence of the Lack of Redundancy

First I think that there are ideational questions that have been neglected; ideational debates about conceptual, theoretical and practical questions have virtually been abandoned by those who have been handling Ghana's economy in the reform period. Ghana's economic managers have not dared to think beyond the orthodoxies of neo-liberal economics, which, as has been indicated, has been ascendant since the 1980s (Amoah, 2011). Essentially then familiarity

Table 4.3 Selected Ghana Budget Growth Rates in the Reform Period

Budget year	*Budget Theme*	*GDP Growth Rates (%)*
2000	N/A	3.7
2001	Economic Sanitization and Stabilization	4.2
2002	Towards Stability and Growth	4.5
2003	N/A	5.2
2004	Business Friendly Year	5.6
2005	Hope and Prosperity	5.9
2006	Good News	6.2
2007	Growth With Stability	6.5
2008	Bright Future	8.4
2009	Investing in a Better Ghana	4.0
2010	Growth and Stability	8.0
2011	Stimulating Growth for Development and Job Creation	15.0
2012	Infrastructural Development for Accelerated Growth and Job Creation	8.8
2013	Sustaining Confidence in the Future of the Ghanaian Economy	7.6
2014	Rising to the Challenge: Re-aligning the Budget to Meet Key National Priorities	6.9
2015	Transformational Agenda: Securing the Bright Medium Term Prospects of the Economy	3.9 (projected)

or mastery of the standard Washington Consensus policy tools, e.g. inflation targeting, pursuing low interest rates, privatizing every state asset, disdain for subsidies and so on, gives one a direct seat at the table of economic decision-making.[38] The net effect in my view is the abandonment of ideational independence critical for crafting economic policies derived and responsive to the concrete, historical and cultural specificities of a developing economy intent on quickly transforming. Such an intellectual posture has spawned an uncritical acceptance of World Bank/IMF prescriptions. Key economic decision-makers spend precious time attempting to master one new policy technique after another from without and in the process redirect vital intellectual and supervisory resources away from their surbordinates (and therefore from responding far more forcefully to the lack of redundancy problem) who must carry through policy decisions steadily if the desired outcomes are to be achieved. The thoughts of a senior Ghana Ministry of Finance official on a new macro-economic model interviewed for this work are instructive:

> It is called the Financial Programming and Policies (FFP) model. *We are just trying to master this tool* because it is really what the IMF uses in all its policy prescriptions for countries they have programmes with, i.e. support. Honestly *our existing models* complement this FPP model. (italics mine)

The acquiescent almost defeatist tone cannot be missed in the quote, and the readiness to jettison unique local direct experiences and insights derived from long years of work on the economy in response to WB/IMF fiat is evident. Roberts and Andrews report that there were attempts at macro-economic modeling as far back as 1999 (Roberts & Andrews 2005, p. 294). Those who work on the budget and national accounts cannot—nor do they indeed have the luxury of time—to keep learning continually. In this work economy of space does not allow me to discuss the ideational independence and creativity at the institutional, as they engaged with the WB/IMF, and theoretical level shown by the Chinese as they grappled with their own economic reforms; the path-breaking theoretical work of Justin Lin Yifu is a worthy example.[39]

This lack of ideational independence in my view deepens the power asymmetries between Ghana and the DPs and spawns in the process a veritable system of control in the Foucauldian sense: "the capillary function of power" (Foucault, 1991, p. 198). In other words this is a particular instantiation of the hegemonic character of the global political economy in which powerful nations and organizations dominate weaker ones; in this instance however the gain is mutual. My claim is that the prescriptions and solutions offered Ghana's economic bureaucrats have come to constitute a technology of power through which the DPs exert their control in a behavior-modulating ratchet-effect mode in which both parties are locked. For the DPs the gain (and reinforcement too for this has historical roots) is the sense of power, domination and control (derived in the main via pecuniary transfers; I might add material gains as well in the form of contracts for the supply of automobiles, for instance, or business openings for companies from the DP countries and other bodies involved) and the emotional reassurance that the old order does not change to give way to the new. For Ghana's economy bureaucrats and politicos they tick the prescription boxes (annual reports—tick; FPP model in place—tick; training seminars attended—tick; inflation targeting—tick; independent central bank—tick; subsidies removed—tick, and so on) and get the promised loans and grants or what Whitfield (2011, p. 6) calls "easy financing" (and there is bristling by these bureaucrats and politicos as of right when these do not get released on time). Budgeting is reified and essentially constructed from ticking boxes in return for goodies. A report on the MDBS (ODI & CDD-Ghana, 2007, p. 8) accurately captures in a rather diplomatic tone this sophisticated policy oware game in which interests collide:

> the use of the PAF both as a monitoring framework and as a conditionality mechanism has created contradictory incentives in which the government has sought to establish modest performance targets (so as to secure predictable levels of budget support) while MDBS partners have pushed for more ambitious targets.[40 41]

As the central interface with the DPs Ghana's economic elites seemed to have developed ideational hubris as well. The Finance Ministry has become the monarch of all that it surveys in Ghana's economic universe. Reflecting the neo-liberalism orthodoxy of its "pay masters" the ministry has abandoned the "planning" component of its name; it was initially known as the Ministry of Finance and Economic Planning, and the irony is that its website address still bears the "planning" stamp: *www.mofep.gov.gh*). And it has fashioned its objectives along unmistakably neo-liberal lines:

- to allocate and manage financial resources efficiently, effectively and rationally;
- to formulate and implement sound macro-economic policies;
- to reduce and restructure the domestic debt;
- to improve public expenditure management;
- to pursue prices and exchange rate stability;
- to account for all public finances properly;
- to improve the human resources and institutional management capacity;
- to improve fiscal resource mobilization; and
- to strengthen the private sector. [42]

One major implication of this ideational hubris is that important institutions that must work in tandem with the ministry in pursuit of national transformation have effectively been eclipsed, ignored, hampered or antagonized. The National Development and Planning Commission (NDPC) is one such organization. In interviews in 2007 with senior personnel they indicated their isolation and frustration given the finance ministry's overbearing posture. Roberts and Andrews correctly identify this lack of coordination between the NDPC and the ministry (2005, p. 296). Recently though, gestures have been made to incorporate the planning functions of the NDPC more intimately with the finance ministry's work, underscoring the challenge this has posed.[43] Under the Kufuor presidency, staff at the Policy Planning and Monitoring Unit (PPMU) at the seat of government (the Christiansborg's Castle) complained to this researcher about their angst over the finance ministry's royal contempt. The policy unit at the new seat of government, Flagstaff House, has virtually vanished from public discourse. It used to be active under senior policy advisor Dr. Sulley Gariba, who has since been made an ambassador, a far lower appointment in the executive infrastructure. One officer, Dr. Michael Whyte Kpessa, has been shunted off to the state's National Service Secretariat. Fights between the Bank of Ghana and Finance Ministry are documented (Thompson, 2003). One of the most symbolic reflections of the ministry's ideational hubris is the finance minister's yearly appearance in a halo of glory (bearing the whole Ghanaian "economy" in a briefcase) in parliament to present the budget statement. Ghana literally stops for the finance ministry. For four to five hours the minister speaks for all the MDAs in Ghana; essentially all policy is dubiously reduced to economic policy in this performance. It seems then that this high theatre of the reading of the budget is the essence of Ghana's budgeting process, for it captures the power game in images, texts and sounds. It is the climax of a chimeric performance along the budget chain in which all that is contemplated for the welfare of the people of Ghana remains just that; budgeting has become a soap opera enacted yearly to both tickle and deceive the senses, and the reading of the budget is the high point that most eloquently captures this. It is one big show in which the interests of the main protagonists rule; national development is not even an afterthought. The themes of the budget reflect the semantic show directed at both the external and internal audiences (see Table 4.3). The 2004 budget is for businesses; the theme disappears never to reappear. Job creation is mentioned in the themes for the 2011 and 2012 budgets (the only time in the sixteen fiscal years in the available data that some thematic consistency is shown) and then vanishes. In some of the years the themes are so general as to be comical. For example the 2005 budget speaks of hope and prosperity. How is this to be made sense of? By the figures in the budget document or by reading the theme? The 2013 budget's theme sounds like a motivational speaker's cultivated lines: the budget has been granted metaphysical powers to sustain confidence in a future that is yet to be. The themes of 2011–2015 are so unapologetically full of IMF/WB speak as to be almost meaningless. I argue that the DPs need to hear this jargon to demonstrate that their students are learning studiously according to plan; the economic elites know they need this semantic acrobatics to keep the aid coming. For Ghanaian citizens the themes have a decidedly political calculus about them spun by the economic policy elites. Jobs will be provided. The economy will grow. Roads will be built. Never mind if the words are backed by no or half-hearted action so long as the votes come in. It is all about the votes.

In this policy amensalism the welfare of Ghanaian citizens is inhibited, as the HDI figures show, but the economic policy elites gain as the acquirers and dispensers of state largesse (mostly material and financial resources acquired from DPs) to friends, relatives, schoolmates, party colleagues and those important in the vote-securing calculus (Whitfield, 2011).

In Conclusion: What Can be Done?

With the emergence in the 1980s of the neo-liberal conception of social and economic organization as the dominant and only pathway to development, Ghana's policy elites in the main have arguably ceased pondering alternative approaches. Margaret Thatcher had (in)famously quipped: there is no alternative. This has produced what I have described as ideational dependence, which is most vividly reflected in the budgeting process. If budgeting challenges have been identified as a matter of limited technical skills among Ghana's economic policy elites, as the lack of redundancy question theorizes, the response has been even more training related to the extant toolbox; fundamental ideational re-orientation has hardly been contemplated (reportedly or demonstrably). Thus canons such as privatization, limited state, antipathy to planning, low inflation at all cost, among others, have become immune to challenge because these are *universal truths* handed down from without and reinforced in policy prescriptions and training regimens. As the Ghana case has shown, ideational dependence produces a captive epistemic lock-in with devastating material consequences. A steady, deliberate conscious effort to escape. Fundamental ideational questions have not been raised regarding economic policy formation because the problems associated with the palpable absence of success with the extant policy tools have been cleverly rationalized as the product of implementation problems; Ghanaian officials repeat this line as if on cue at seminars, conferences and in their wider public statements. The upshot of this is that attempts at responding to the problem have been directed at technical skill-sets leaving aside any critical re-examination of ideational claims associated with neo-liberal dogma.

Curing this ideational dependence requires the training of bureaucrats who are thinkers (Amoah, 2014b). The ever insightful Korean economist Ha-Joon argues that the competencies required for the urgent tasks of development in countries such as Ghana "seems to be counter-intuitively, that of a generalist, rather than that of an economist (an least not of the mainstream kind)" and this is because what is most required for policy success is above all else good judgment on core issues and not specialist knowledge as such (Ha-Joon, 2010, p. 93), further adding:

> developing countries intent on developing a good economic bureaucracy should put more emphasis on recruiting people of generally high caliber

rather than looking for specialists in economics (more so experts in neo-liberal economics) and other related subjects. (parentheses mine)

Some philosophical contemplation has been exerted by Ghanaian (African) philosophers on the need for relativistic and therefore some culture-specific and historicized approaches to national transformation, as the examples of development in Asia demonstrate. In a fascinating work Ghanaian philosopher Kwabena Archampong (2013, p. 88) argues that Einstein's theory of relativity put into eternal doubt the universalizing (or better still transcendentalist) tendency of the "philosophical underpinnings of classical mechanics."[44] The point being made here is the need to develop the critical reflexes of our economic policy-makers to take local insights and contexts and approaches from the non-Western world into more serious account.

Broadly speaking the capabilities for pursuing the goals of a budget and raising ontological questions as discussed above are technical questions. Beyond the technical I think that realizing Ghana's developmental possibilities as they relate to the budget and public financial management is a moral matter and one also rooted in leadership. Amoah (2014b) argues that Ghana's public servants require training that has a strong ethical component, for those who run the economy the more so given their direct impact on the pecuniary and material fate of Ghana. Lee Kuan Yew (2000), the incomparable builder of modern Singapore, insisted that one of the key pillars upon which his People's Action Party approached the nation-building task was integrity. The party's choice of uniform and logo reflect this trenchant focus on integrity:

> The party's strong stand against corruption is reflected in its logo—the lightning symbol in red encircled by a blue ring against a white background . . . the white background symbolizes purity and integrity. The party uniform of white-on-white also signifies the purity and the incorruptibility of its members.[45]

The People's Action Party has become one of the most successful parties in the Global South and, in so doing, has demonstrated how crucial ethical questions must be for transforming a backward, dirt-poor post-colonial polity. To contemplate a Ghana completely transformed from what it is today and to actually build it must involve ethical choices. Leadership must be deeply bothered by inequality, poverty, bad social services, the rise of slums and all that underdevelopment brings, so that they want to respond to these and to appreciate that every public pesewa counts and must be accounted for (and to act on this). A strong moral compass is a vital foundation for the most advanced technical skills if such skills are not to be recruited in the service of the evil genius's artifices in the state bureaucracy. The finance ministry must begin to place equal value on training in public ethics and leadership for its officers and work harder in its efforts to recruit personnel with the required ethical outlook.

To reiterate, my argument is that the persistence of the absence of functional redundancy with respect to Ghanaian public budgeting must be understood as being central to the logic of a process directed at a sophisticated and cleverly disguised external and internal political economy of power and benefits involving national economic policy elites and the DPs. To understand the almost malignant failures of budgeting in a developing polity such as Ghana it is not enough to simply identify the lack of redundancy; today the crucial question should be why the absence of redundancy has persisted so long. In extending the focus on the lack of redundancy from identification to persistence I have attempted to provide responses to Aniwa's questions regarding why the Ghanaian budget has become a decorative instrument and whether it can yet become a planning tool. My view has been that understanding and unraveling the internal and external political economy of budgeting and public financial management in the reform periods should create the necessary conditions for making the budget an active document for pursuing national development goals. I have proffered my perspective.

Notes

1 Dedicated to Emmanuel Sithole, the Mozambique immigrant murdered violently in Johannesburg for simply wanting a better life.
2 In Akan, the most widely spoken language in Ghana, "dumsor" is a creative amalgamation of the word "dum," which in this context means "to turn off" and "sor," which means to " to turn on."
3 Caiden wrote a doctoral thesis on the evolution of the budget in the Western European context; France was the case study.
4 The term "traditional" is used to show that there have been attempts mainly within Western and particularly American public administration theory and practice to adopt different approaches to the original (and historically dominant) line-item budgeting that seek to cure its limitations and weaknesses. These counter approaches include planning-programming-budgeting (PPB) and zero-based budgetting. See Wildavsky 2006.
5 By pattern Caiden means " an observed configuration of variables which appears to recur in different contexts" (1978, p. 539).
6 Dalton (Belansky, 1959) had raised some of these questions in a 1959 public lecture titled "Problems of Economic Development in Africa," an account of which was given in the *Cornell Daily Sun* of January 14, 1959.
7 The quintet deals with the who (the kind of human being who makes public policy and is affected by it), the what (norms), the how (institutions), the where (symbols) and the why (ontology) questions. Post-traditional public administration presents counter-views to traditional (dominantly Euro-American) public administration understandings of the quintet, anchored as they are in economistic and positivistic foundations, and imagines new possibilities. The method is one of "imaginative play-playful hermeneutics"(Farmer, 2005, p. 908). And play here is "in the sense of unleashing the poetic imagination, the artistry of wonder, through openness to the play of events" (Farmer, 2005, p. 908). A special issue of the *International Journal of Public Administration*, 2005, p. 28 (11–12), engaged with these questions.
8 In this work I use the term "development" and "national transformation" interchangeably to mean (following Amoah, 2014a, p. 130) "the processes (material, intellectual and spiritual) by which a group of people as a collective attempt to

respond to their lived, concrete, historically and culturally mediated existential challenges." In this rendering I go beyond the classical economistic understanding of these notions in the literature.

9 See for example Jevern, 2012, who provides a typically statistical perspective.
10 See Caiden, 1978, p. 541–543.
11 In Ghana this was vividly brought home by the Kume Preko demonstrations, which rocked the entire nation and led to the death of a teenager in Accra from the shots of government-linked security operatives. The demonstrations had been called and organized by the Alliance for Change, a group made of leading politicians and activists such as Nana Addo Dankwa Akufo-Addo, Dr. Charles Wereko-Brobby, Kwaku Baako, Dr. Nyaho-Tamaklo, Mr. Akoto-Ampaw, among others, which was opposed to a new ad valorem tax imposed on Ghanaians in 1995.
12 For historical antecedents see Wildavsky and Caiden, 2006. In this work particularly in Chapter 2 the authors show how budgeting in the USA was shaped by the historical processes of the preceding colonial order, which had utilized the legislature as the chief check on expenditures. In the new republic the tussle over checks swung from the legislature to the executive (the Budgeting and Accounting Act of 1921) but the legislature still retains its oversight powers.
13 http://lexicon.ft.com/Term?term=path-dependence.
14 Here analytic concepts such as path dependence (already referred to), critical junctures and policy feedback are critical.
15 See also Katzenstein, 1996.
16 See for example Powell and Colyvas, 2008.
17 Quoted in Serra, 2014, p. 11.
18 The delay might be understandable in some sense given that in Britain itself the first modern national income accounts were compiled in 1920 by British economist Colin Clark (Speich, 2011).
19 The tussle between structuralism (encapsulated in development economics) and marginalism (represented in neo-liberal economics ascendant in the 1980s) has marked economic policy formation in developing countries such as Ghana till today.
20 See especially Chapter 2 of Killick, 2010.
21 See Yeebo, 1992.
22 The Ministry of Finance of Ghana either willfully obfuscates the issues or is oblivious of the processes by which progamme-based budgeting (PBB) or better still performance and programme-based budgeting (PPBB) (the two are used interchangeably in the literature) was set in motion in Ghana's budgeting universe (see for example Oduro, 2003 and CABRI, 2013) by indicating that it was using the activity-based budgeting approach introduced in 1998 and after some reforms adopted the PBB in 2010. We think Ghana was clearly locked into the PBB by the late 1990s given the general approach to budgeting. See www.mofep.gov.gh/divisions/pbb.
23 Roberts and Andrews, 2005, provides a detailed account of Ghana's budgetary reforms from 1992 to 2000, from which we draw liberally.
24 See Roberts and Andrews (2005, p. 293ff).
25 The DPs are African Development Bank, Canada, Denmark, European Union, France, Germany, Japan, Netherlands, Switzerland, United Kingdom and the World Bank. To this list we must add five additional agencies the IMF, JICA, UNDP, UNICEF and USAID, which participate as observers in MDBS meetings with the Government. It is instructive that China is not part of the MDBS. DP is a World Bank and IMF term.
26 www.mofep.gov.gh/mdbs.cfm.
27 Ibid.
28 Ibid.
29 Centre for Democratic Development-Ghana.

30 http://cagd.gov.gh/gifmis/index.php/implementation/implementation-status?showall=&start=1.
31 Hegemonic economic powers have always sought to influence the economic policy of weaker countries with whom they are tied in asymmetrical power relations. See for example Subramanian (2011) for an account of the tussle for economic supremacy between the USA and China.
32 The author plans to do more extensive work on this.
33 www.mofep.gov.gh/sites/default/files/budget/bud2001.pdf.
34 The Northern regions have been very poor historically.
35 The Savannah Ecological Zone consists of the three regions: Northern, Brong Ahafo and Volta.
36 The Report of the Auditor-General on the Public Accounts of Ghana (Public Boards, Corporations and other Statutory Institutions (2013)) indicates that the single-source procurement provisions of the Public Procurement Act, 2003 (Act 633) had been breached by SADA regarding the award of the reafforestation contract to one company with the express approval of the Public Procurement Authority. In the Auditor-General's view the nature of the contract in question did not meet the single-source procurement conditions under the Act.
37 See the GYEEDA Report, 2013.
38 See Frimpong-Ansah, 1996.
39 See Ferdinand and Wang, 2013 and Bottelier, 2007.
40 Oware is a traditional Akan board game grounded in fractals and involving many strategic moves.
41 PAF stands for Performance Assessment Framework.
42 www.mofep.gov.gh/?q=about/objectives.
43 The president of Ghana, John Mahama, swore into office in February 2015 the thirty-four member governing board of the NDPC and indicated that he wanted the schism bridged (https://www.ghanabusinessnews.com/2015/02/24/president-mahama-swears-in-ndpc-governing-board). Dr. Kwesi Botchwey, Ghana's longest reigning finance minister, is the head of the new board, signaling the weight the Ghanaian presidency may be attaching to this. This though has happened before under the Fourth Republic when J.H. Mensah, veteran bureaucrat instrumental in the drafting of Ghana's first development plan who advised Kwame Nkrumah and Busia on economic affairs, was appointed chairman of the NDPC under the Kufuor administration; no significant change occurred.
44 Here positivism.
45 www.pap.org.sg/news-and-commentaries/party-news/party-fashion.

References

Adu, A.L. 1960. Problems of Government in Emergent African States. *International Review of Administrative Sciences*, 26: 61–66.

Agbodeka, F. 1972. Sir Gordon Guggisberg's Contribution to the Development of the Gold Coast. *Transactions of the Historical Society of Ghana*, 13(1): 51–64.

Amoah, L.G.A. 2011. Public Policy Formation in Africa in the Wake of the Global Financial Meltdown: Building Blocks for a New Mind in a Multi-polar World. In T. Dietz, K. Havnevik, M. Kaag, & T. Oestigaard (Eds.) *African Engagements: Africa negotiating an emerging multipolar world*, Leiden and Boston, MA: Brill.

Amoah, L.G.A. 2012a. Constructing a New Public Administration in Africa: Reflections on Philosophical Clarity and the Process-Orientation Turn. *Administrative Theory & Praxis*, 34(3): 385–406.

Amoah, L.G.A. 2012b. Grey Hair, Grey Matter and ICT policy in the Global South: the Case of Ghana. In M.M. Islam & M. Ehsan (Eds.) *From Government to E. Governance: Public Administration in the Digital Age*, Hershey, PA: IGI Global.

Amoah, L.G.A. 2014a. The Rise of Telcos and Africa's Knowledge Society: What Have Telchambs Got to Do With It? In L.G.A Amoah (Ed.) *Impacts of the Knowledge Society on Economic and Social Growth in Africa*, Hershey, PA: IGI Global.

Amoah, L.G.A. 2014b. Training for Public Service in Ghana in an Evolving World: Some Suggestions for the Future. In P. F. Haruna & S. Vyas-Doorgapersad (Eds.) *Public Administration Training in Africa: Competencies in Development Management*, Boca Raton, London, New York: CRC Press.

Aniwa, M. 2015. *Response to "Dumsor Pain."* Facebook.

Archampong, C.B.K. 2013. The Philosophical Significance of Einstein's Relativity Theory. In M.S. Simpson, H.M. Majeed, K. Ackah, & E.I. Ani (Eds.) *Legon Readers: A Celebration of Philosophy and the Classics*, Banbury UK: Ayebia Clarke.

Aryeetey, E., & Fosu, A. 2008. Economic Growth in Ghana, 1960–2000. In R.J. Ndulu, S.A. O'Connel, J.-P. Azam,, R.H. Bates, A. Fosu, J.W. Gunning, & D. Njinku. (Eds.) *The Political Economy of Economic Growth in Africa, 1960–2000*, New York: Cambridge University Press.

Bagus, P. 2011. Morgenstern's Forgotten contribution to Economics: A Stab to the Heart of Modern Economics. *American Journal of Economics and Sociology*, 70(2): 540–562.

Bawumia, M. 2015. The IMF Bailout: Will the anchor hold? *Distinguished Speakers Series Lecture*. Central University College, Miotso, Ghana.

Belansky, E.R. 1959. Dalton shows African Need for Development. *The Cornell Daily Sun*, LXXV (71): 1.

Bentil, M.A. 2004. *50 years of Civil Service Reform Experience in Anglophone Africa: Reflections on the past to guide future efficiency in governance*. Accra: Design Solutions.

Bottelier, P. 2007. China and the World Bank: How a Partnership was Built. *Journal of Contemporary China*, 16(51): 239–258.

Butler, N. (Ed.). 1983. *The Economic Consequences of Margaret Thatcher: Speeches of Nicholas Kaldor (1979–1982)*. Fabian Tract 486. London: Fabian Society.

Caiden, N. n.d. *Patterns of Budgeting: The Experience of France 980–1830*. Unpublished doctoral thesis.

Caiden, N. 1978. Patterns of Budgeting. *American Society for Public Administration*, 38(6): 539–544.

Caiden, N. 2006. An Exploration into the Familiar and the New: Public Budgeting in Developing Countries. In E.E. Otenyo & N.S. Lind. (Eds.) *Comparative Public Administration: The Essential Readings*, Oxford, Amsterdam: Elsevier.

CEAC. 1944. Memorandum Referred to in Paragraph 24. Some Aspects of the Flow of Capital into British Colonies (44) 16 Appendix II. Quoted in Gerardo Serra. 2014. An uneven statistical topography: the political economy of household budget surveys in late colonial Ghana, 1951–1957. *Canadian Journal of Development Studies*, 35(1): 11.

Collaborative African Budget Reform Initiative (CABRI). 2013. *Performance and Programme-Based Budgeting in Africa: A Status Report*. Pretoria: CABRI.

Dalton, J.H. 1961. Colony and Metropolis: Some Aspects of British Rule in Gold Coast and Their Implications for Understanding Ghana Today. *The Journal of Economic History*, 21(4): 552–565.

Denhardt, R.B. 2000. *Theories of Public Organization*, 3rd ed. Orlando, FL: Harcourt Brace.

Dimaggio, P. J., & Powell, W.W. 1983. The Iron Cage Revisited: Institutional Isomorphism and Collective Rationality in Organizational Fields. *The American Sociological Review*, 48(2): 147–160.

Farmer, D.J. 2005. Quintet: Introduction to Post-Traditional Theory. *International Journal of Public Administration*, 28(11–12): 903–908.

Ferdinand, P., & Wang, J. 2013. China and the IMF: From mimicry towards pragmatic international pluralism. *International Affairs*, 89(4): 895–910.

Foucault, M. 1991. *Discipline and Punish: The Birth of the Prison*. London: Penguin.

Frimpong-Ansah, J.H. 1996. Flexibility and Responsiveness in the Ghana Economy: Reflections on Post-Decline Atrophy Syndrome. *The J.B. Danquah Memorial Lectures*. Accra: Ghana Academy of Arts and Sciences.

Government of Ghana. 2000. *Budget Statement*. Accra: Government of Ghana.

Government of Ghana. 2001. *Budget Statement*. Accra: Government of Ghana.

Government of Ghana. 2002. *Budget Statement*. Accra: Government of Ghana.

Government of Ghana. 2003. *Budget Statement*. Accra: Government of Ghana.

Government of Ghana. 2004. *Budget Statement*. Accra: Government of Ghana.

Government of Ghana. 2005. *Budget Statement*. Accra: Government of Ghana.

Government of Ghana. 2006. *Budget Statement*. Accra: Government of Ghana.

Government of Ghana. 2007. *Budget Statement*. Accra: Government of Ghana.

Government of Ghana. 2008. *Budget Statement*. Accra: Government of Ghana.

Government of Ghana. 2009. *Budget Statement*. Accra: Government of Ghana.

Government of Ghana. 2010. *Budget Statement*. Accra: Government of Ghana.

Government of Ghana. 2011. *Budget Statement*. Accra: Government of Ghana.

Government of Ghana. 2012. *Budget Statement*. Accra: Government of Ghana.

Government of Ghana. 2013a. GYEEDA *Report*. Accra: Government of Ghana.

Government of Ghana. 2013b. *The Auditor-General's Report on Public Boards, Corporations and other Statutory Institutions*. Accra: Government of Ghana.

Government of Ghana. 2013c. *Budget Statement*. Accra: Government of Ghana.

Government of Ghana. 2014. *Budget Statement*. Accra: Government of Ghana.

Government of Ghana. 2015. *Budget Statement*. Accra: Government of Ghana.

Greenstreet, D.K. 1972. An African Experiment: Public Administartion and Higher Education in Ghana: 1960/70. *International Review of Administrative Sciences*, 38: 12–20.

Gyan-Apenteng, K. 2015. *Dumsor Pain*. Facebook Post.

Ha-Joon Chang. 2010. How to "Do" a Development State: Political, Organizational and Human Resource Requirements for the Developmental State. In E. Omano. (Ed.) *Constructing a Democratic Developmental State in South Africa: Potentials and Challenges*, Cape Town: HRSC Press.

Hill, P. 1961. Migrant Cocoa farmers of Southern Ghana. *Africa: Journal of the International African Institute*, 31(3): 209–230.

Hood, C. 1991. Public Management for all Seasons? *Public Administration*, 69: 3–19.

Howard, R. 1976. Economic Imperialism and Oligopolization of Trade in the Gold Coast, 1886–1939. *Ufahamu: A Journal of African Studies*, 7(1): 71–92.

Huang, C.C.P., & Gao, Y. 2015. Should Social Science and Jurisprudence imitate Natural Science? *Modern China*, 41(2): 131–167.

International Monetary Fund (IMF). 2002. *IMF Executive Board Grants Waiver on Noncomplying Disbursement to Ghana*. Press Release No. 02/8. Washington, DC: IMF.

Jerven, M. 2012. Future challenges in measuring Africa's past: Lessons from estimating GDP for the Gold Coast, 1891–1954. *African Economic Working Paper Series* 3: 1–35.

Katzenstein, P. J. 1996. *Cultural Norms and National Security: Police and Military in Postwar Japan*. Ithaca, NY: Cornell.

Killick, T. 2010. *Development Economics in Action: A Study of Economic Policies in Ghana*. New York: Routledge.

Landau, M. 1969. Redundancy, Rationality, and the Problem of Duplication and Overlap. *Public Administration Review*, 29(4): 346–358.

Lee K.Y. 2000. *From Third World to First: The Singapore Story (1965–2000)*. Singapore: Times.

Oduro, K.N. 2003. *Results-Oriented Public Expenditure Management: Case Study of Ghana*. London: ODI.

Osborne, D., & Gaebler, T. 1993. *Reinventing Government: How the Entrepreneurial Spirit is Transforming the Public Sector*. New York: Plume.

Overseas Development Institute (ODI) and Centre for Democratic Development-Ghana (CDD-Ghana). 2007. *Joint Evaluation of Multi-Donor Support to Ghana: Final Report*. Accra, London: ODI/CDD-Ghana.

Powell, W.W., & Colyvas, J.A. 2008. Microfoundations of Institutional Theory. In R. Greenwood, C. Oliver, R. Suddaby, & K. Sahlin (Eds.) *The Sage Handbook of Organizational Institutionalism*, London: Sage Publications.

Rimmer, D. 2003. Learning about Economic Development from Africa. *African Affairs*, 102(408): 469–491.

Roberts, J., & Andrews, M. 2005. Something Funny Happened on the Way to Reform Success: The Case of Budget Reform Implementation in Ghana. *International Journal of Public Administration*, 28(3–4): 291–311.

Serra, G. 2014. An Uneven Statistical Topography: The Political Economy of Household Budget Surveys in Late Colonial Ghana, 51-57. *Canadian Journal of Development*, 35(1): 9–27.

Shore, P. 1983. Preface to *The Economic Consequences of Mrs Thatcher: Speeches of Nicholas Kaldor (1979–1982)*. Nick Butler (Ed.) *Fabian Tract 486*. London: Fabian Society.

Speich, D. 2011. The Use of Global Abstractions: National Income Accounting in the Era of Imperial Decline. *Journal of Global History*, 6(1): 7–28.

Subramanian, S. 2011. *Eclipse: Living in the Shadow of China's Economic Dominance*. Washington, D.C.: Pearson Institute for International Economics.

Thelen, K. 1999. Historical Institutionalism in Comparative Politics. *Annual Review of Political Science*, 2: 369–404.

Thompson, N.M. 2003. Financial Transition in an Emerging Democracy: The Ghanaian Experience and Lessons. *Paper Presented at the CDD-G/Ghana Academy of Arts and Sciences Seminar*. Accra, Ghana.

Whitfield, L. 2011. Competitive Clientelism, Easy Financing and Weak Capitalists: The Contemporary Political Settlement in Ghana. *Danish Institute for International Studies (DIIS) Working Paper*, 27: 1–43.

Wildavsky, A. 2006. A budget for all seasons? Why the traditional budget lasts. In J. Steven Ott & E.W. Russell (Eds.) *Introduction to Public Administration: A Book of Readings*, Beijing, China: Peking University Press.

Wildavsky, A., & Caiden, N. 2006. *The New Politics of the Budgetary Process*, Beijing, China: Peking University Press.

World Bank. 2010. Project Document on Additional Financing Credit. *Report No. 54603-GH*. Washington, DC: The World Bank.

Yeebo, Z. 1992. *Ghana, the Struggle for Popular Power: Rawlings, Savior or Demagogue*. London: New Beacon Books.

5 Reforming the Ghanaian Budget System from Activity-based Budgeting to Performance-based Budgeting: Eureka, or another Reform Illusion?

Frank L. Kwaku Ohemeng

Introduction

The New Public Management (NPM) ideas that have captivated and, perhaps, continue to captivate its proponents since the early 1980s culminated in a number of reforms of the public sector in many developed and developing countries. The greater goal was, and is still, stopping the so-called spilling effect of unrestrained spending in the public finance sector. One of the most extensive state reforms ever undertaken is the NPM-oriented budgetary reform effort under the general rubric of financial management reforms (World Bank, 1998). It emphasized transforming the existing norms, rules, process, and objectives of budgetary and financial management (Kelly & Wanna, 2000, p. 33).

Such reforms, according to their proponents, are necessary because:

> the traditional budget . . . contributed to ever increasing government expenditures by emphasizing planning rather than restraint and its reliance on incremental decision-making. Similarly, the control based financial management systems were designed to ensure probity in government spending and often hindered the pursuit of economy, efficiency, and effectiveness in service delivery.
>
> Kelly & Wanna, 2000, p. 40

Most notable among the weaknesses of past reform efforts has been the failure to address the relationships among: control; performance; the incentives for performance in the full range of formal and informal budgeting; decision-making; and management rules (restraints and flexibilities). Changes to budgetary systems that would contribute to better public sector performance, which continues to be at its lowest ebb, are therefore crucial.

Early budgetary reforms, especially those in the 1980s and 1990s, dealt with the introduction of various mechanisms, such as activity-based budgeting (ABB), the medium-term expenditure framework (MTEF), accrual accounting, and so on (Boothe, 2007; Fölscher, 2006; Schick, 2007). Unfortunately, implementing these systems or mechanisms has not yielded the desired results either, especially in developing countries (Foster et al., 2002; Simwaka, 2006). The main explanations offered involve the failure to link resource and performance indicators and the inability of government to monitor agencies' use of such resources (Joyce, 2003). In some African countries, too, the bottom-up approach used in these mechanisms and poor coordination of planning and budgeting functions have been blamed (Foster et al., 2002).

Thus the search for a better way to set budgets, especially in developing and transitional economies, continues. In most countries recently, performance-based budgeting (PBB) has prevailed (Pitsvada & LoStracco, 2002). Although not itself new, especially in the developed world (Joyce, 1999; OECD, 2007; Schick, 1966), it is the latest fashion in budgetary reforms in most developing countries.

Africa is no exception (CABRI, 2013; Robinson, 2013b). The adoption and implementation of PBB is growing faster there than anything except the human population (Fölscher, 2012; Vian & Bicknell, 2014). Ghana recently jumped onto the PBB bandwagon, moving from MTEF through to ABB, and so on. Performance-based budgeting was officially and formally introduced with the 2014 budget, after having been piloted through seven ministries, departments and agencies (MDAs) in 2010. (There was also a botched attempt in the late 1990s.)

The government believed that it would significantly improve its own efficiency, accountability, and performance, and be a complete departure from its ABB system, which it considered excessively centralized and impossible to monitor against objectives and indicators (See also Kwakye & Owuo, 2014). Adopting PBB, it is hoped, will help to simplify the budget preparation process, and allow MDAs to be more strategic in their approach to budget management by shifting the emphasis from input (activities) and output to outcomes, service delivery, and results. The government also thinks that ABB, which it has been using since the late 1990s, is too detailed, making budget preparation cumbersome, and contributing to excessively centralized control of implementation. Absence of performance indicators for MDA budgets was another major drawback (Killick, 2005; Kwakye & Owuo, 2014). In other words, in MDA budgets real strategic focus and connection between resource allocations and policy priorities have been insufficient. Additionally, PBB is part of the government's extreme preoccupation with using performance management to manage the public sector and as a way to build a democratic developmental public sector, which is part of its general goal of building a democratic developmental state (Ayee, 2015).

Not all, however, are enthusiastic about this new approach to budgeting in Ghana. Some members of parliament have argued that it will still not solve Ghana's myriad economic problems if those involved in implementation—whether politicians or technocrats—persist in acting corruptly. Opposition MP and ranking member of the parliamentary select committee on Finance,

Dr. Anthony Akoto Osei, denied that the new approach will mean significant change. He cautioned that the government should "not raise the expectations of Ghanaians so high, as if all of Ghana's problems are going to be over soon," and that with the new budget reforms the government has only changed from "first gear" to another "first gear" (is making slower than desirable progress).

The objective of this chapter is to critically examine the reasons for the adoption of PBB, and whether it will enable the government to achieve its stated objectives of introducing performance indicators, establishing clear lines for monitoring MDAs, and getting value for money for its programs. In the course of doing so we will also look at some of the capacity and institutional constraints that may affect PBB, and whether the government is prepared to deal with them. As argued by Robinson and Last (2009, p. 8):

> performance-based budgeting is not . . . an initiative that is appropriate for all countries. A decision about whether to introduce such a system in any specific country should be based on sober consideration of the governance conditions, the state of the basic public financial management (PFM) systems, and the available human and financial resources.

Nor is it the first time the PBB idea has been introduced as a budget mechanism in Ghana.

The chapter begins with a brief review of the literature on PBB, tracing its origin, definition, and characteristics. The discussion will then move to budgetary reforms in Ghana since the adoption of the Structural Adjustment Programme (SAP) in the early 1980s. This starting point is important, since the adoption of the SAP is considered a critical moment in the country's socio-economic development. Then follows a discussion of the adoption, implementation, and shortcomings of the MTEF and ABB, and another on the adoption of the PBB. We will analyze the foundational issues—which, if not addressed, may reduce good intentions to an illusion—and then conclude with some afterthoughts.

Dissecting the Performance-Based Budgeting Idea

Performance-based budgeting is believed to be a recent phenomenon, but in fact it has a long history (Diamond, 2003; Schick, 1966; 2014). It is only in recent years, though, that it has come to be seen as the cure for all budgetary ills (Berry, 2008; Joyce, 1999; Schick, 1966; 2014). Its recent extreme popularity has made it the subject of numerous contributions in the literature (de Lancer Julnes et al. 2008; Lu et al. 2015). Unfortunately, as is the case with many social science subjects, the abundance of writing on it has not yielded a single acceptable definition: it has, rather, generated some methodological difficulties in assessing the efficacy of the approach in budgetary reforms (Joyce, 1999; Lu et al., 2015; Mauro et al., 2015; Robinson & Brumby, 2005). Another issue compounding the definition problem is that PBB has been described in various terms. Concisely, such concepts as activity-based budgeting, performance budgeting, outcomes-based budgeting, results-based budgeting, and program budgeting have all been employed (KPMG, 2011; OECD, 2007; Robinson, 2011). According to Kong (2005), however, "while each term has its own nuance and appeal to its own customers, the differences are basically semantic." Whatever term is used, then, they are all concerned with introducing performance information into budget processes (OECD, 2007).

Existing definitions of PBB can be categorized as narrow or broad. Berry, taking the narrow view, thinks of it as consisting of "budget formats that link inputs with outputs, outcomes, or other measures of results" (2008, p. 288). Melkers and Willoughby (2001), who have written substantially on the subject, looking at cases in the USA, focus on management. They thus see it as requiring strategic planning regarding agency mission and objectives, and as a process that requires quantifiable data that will generate meaningful information about program outcomes. McNab and Melese have defined it as "a higher level of performance budgeting, with a focus on resource allocation, as any initiative or reform that attempts to quantify public sector outputs or outcomes and explicitly incorporates these outputs and outcomes in the budget process" (2003, p. 74).

Whereas the above definitions emphasize resource allocation, others examine the idea from a broader perspective. Such scholars include Joyce (2003, p. 17), who says it is "the use of performance information in all stages of the budget process including budget preparation, budget approval, budget execution and evaluation." Similarly, Kong (2005, p. 91) says that performance-based budgeting is concerned with "any reform that attempts to incorporate performance measures in the budget process." Consequently, to Joyce, "performance-based budgeting assumes that outcomes are considered in the process of allocating and managing government resources." (1999, p. 598). Smith (1999) defines it as the allocation of resources based on the achievement of specific, measurable outcomes. According to Moynihan, "this definition promises a rational, mechanistic link between performance measures and resource allocations, with the ability to state the level of outputs that can be achieved with an additional amount of resources" (2003, p. 1). In this chapter we adopt the definition of the OECD, which is that PBB is simply "a form of budgeting that relates funds allocated to measurable results" (OECD, 2003, p. 7).

Characteristics of Performance-Based Budgeting

In his extensive work on what he described as program budgeting—which, according to him, is the most widespread form of performance budgeting applied to the government budget as a whole—Robinson (2011) identifies four major characteristics of PBB, which we will use. First, in a PBB funds are allocated to results-based "programs." For example, the education ministry's budget allocates funds to a primary, a secondary, and a tertiary education program, while the environment ministry's budget includes a nature conservation program and an anti-pollution program. Second, "line item" controls—limits imposed by Parliament or the Ministry of Finance on what ministries can spend on specific types of inputs (such as office supplies, travel, and utilities)—are radically reduced, although certainly not entirely eliminated. Third, good performance information on programs is collected, and used in the budget preparation process to assist decision-makers in determining how much money should go to each program. Fourth is improved expenditure prioritization, which simply means that limited government resources are allocated to the programs that deliver the greatest benefits to the community for the money spent. By providing information on the costs and benefits of alternative programs, a program-budgeting system facilitates decisions about which areas of expenditure to cut back on and which to augment in order to best meet community needs. By contrast, a traditional budget, in which funds are mainly allocated by line item, is of limited value as a vehicle for choices about expenditure priorities. Expenditure prioritization is not, however, the only objective of program budgeting. By making program performance a systematically important factor in decisions on ministry budget allocations, program budgeting also aims to place significant pressure on ministries to improve the effectiveness and efficiency of their existing services (Robinson, 2013b).

Efficacy and Limitations of Performance-Based Budgeting

The literature on PBB is replete with discussions on its usefulness or otherwise to government (Brown, 2008; Curristine, 2007; Morgan et al. 2015; Moynihan, 2003). In this section we will briefly review some of these discussions. The debate on the efficacy of PBB is not yet over. Consequently, caution needs to be exercised in projecting it as the panacea for budgetary ills. What, then, are the pros and cons of PBB?

The popularity of PBB derives from the shortcomings of previous budget systems or models, particularly line-item, or what many refer to as input budgeting. It has been argued that PBB goes beyond inputs and line-item expenditures to ensure informed choices grounded in measurable progress. As conceded by Berry , "performance budgeting is built on the belief that budgeting can become a rationalized process in which decisions on resource allocation can be made on the basis of policy analysis and performance data" (2008, p. 292). Brown also says that "performance-based budgeting (PBB) links the results of program activities to budgeting and policy-making. It moves the budget process away from 'who gets how much' to 'what benefit is derived for how much'" (2008, p. 1469). Similarly, VanLandingham et al. state that "the theory behind performance-based program budgeting is clear: the amount of resources given to public programs should be influenced by their performance in achieving desired results" (2005, p. 234).

Managerial flexibility has also been noted as one important feature PBB adds to government (Curristine & Flynn, 2013). It denotes the relaxation of input controls in the areas of spending and staffing of managers (OECD, 2008). There is also an idea that it enables public organizations to identify organization goals and improve government capacity in organizational efficiency, effectiveness, and accountability (Wang, 2000). Furthermore, PBB may enhance the identification of direct and indirect costs in public sector dealings, which will encourage long-term planning and influence the allocation of resources, to some degree (Kluvers, 2001). McNab and Melese (2003) are also of the view that it can promote a shift in the focus of governmental functions from input control to outcome-oriented planning and management, while Willoughby (2004) believes that it can enhance communication, which in turn will inform budget decisions and improve agency management and operation. Smith (1999) also says that it can make managers more accountable for program decisions that may affect budget outcomes, as well as support better management by connecting budget results and budget performance measurement with program performance measurement in the process of monitoring, evaluating, and reporting results.

On the other hand, VanLandingham et al. (2005) have warned against embracing PBB as a solution for all budgetary problems. Smith (1999) even diagnoses it as a threat to governments. Curristine (2005), too, has identified what she sees as limitations to PBB. These include: how performance is measured, particularly the source of information; that not everything can be measured; and problems with cost, time, and capacity in the public sector when it comes to collecting performance information. She further identifies a number of challenges that governments may face in implementing PBB.

Lu et al. (2015) have also identified three limitations of PBB. First is the question surrounding the use of performance information in the budgetary process. They note how performance information may be distorted, which may affect the information needed for the budget and thus argue that "the question about the legitimate usage of performance information in budgeting still begs more careful consideration" (p. 433). A second challenge according to them, relates to performance budgeting at the operational level, that is what managers and budgeters should do with performance information, even if there is good political support and excellent performance information quality. They question "whether the government should cut a program's budget in light of high program performance, assuming it can do better with less, or increase its budget in light of low performance, assuming that more resource availability may improve performance" (p. 434). Finally, they identify the problem relating to "how human behaviour responds to financial incentives, particularly when the relevant dimensions of performance may be difficult to capture" (p. 444). They noted that some behaviors may change in response to performance measurement. Unfortunately, they continue, "behaviours may not change consistently across groups, or may change in any unexpected ways, there are concerns about incentive effectiveness and unintended consequences." Hence to them, it is necessary to "explore further how budget allocation should (or should not) be used as an incentive for performance in light of these complexities" (p. 444).

Trajectory of Budgetary Reforms in Ghana Since 1983

In Ghana budgetary reform is not a new phenomenon. It has preoccupied almost every government, military and civilian, since independence (Killick, 2005;

2010). In this section we will focus on budget reforms since the adoption of the SAP in 1983. The SAP was a milestone in getting government finances right. It also marked a turning point in the socio-economic and political governance of the country, as it led to the introduction of a number of neo-liberal state reforms (Hutchful, 2002; Ohemeng & Anebo, 2012).

Ghana and the now famous Asian Tiger countries achieved independence around the same time, yet Ghana was seen as more prosperous and better positioned for rapid socio-economic and political development, with vast economic resources and superior human resources to the Tigers. By the early 1980s, however, Ghana's economic situation had so deteriorated that it was on the brink of collapse. Herbst (1993) wrote that the country only existed then because the international community recognized it, as it was not a well-functioning state. It was in the context of this hopelessness that the Provincial National Defence Council (PNDC), a quasi-military government, assumed power in December 1981. The first two years of the regime saw further economic deterioration, causing it to turn for help to the Bretton Woods institutions, although it had denounced the activities of these same institutions, and even accused them of being among the causes of Ghana's socio-economic and political predicaments.

That approach led to the adoption of a structure adjustment program (SAP); in Ghana it was labelled the Economic Recovery Programme (ERP). Irrespective of what it is called, the assumed inherent purpose was correcting the finances of the state, and budgetary reform inevitably became a fundamental concern as a result of a number of problems (Kapur et al., 1991). For example, the rampant brain drain and the socio-economic and political decay that characterized the Ghanaian state in the 1970s and early 1980s adversely affected public sector financial management. Also, the proclivity of the government to distort the economy—in particular, through expenditure control—made public expenditure "overly centralized, directed almost exclusively at financial control as opposed to monitoring and evaluating program effectiveness" (Kapur et al., 1991, p. 35).

Consequently, when the PNDC decided to introduce the ERP, it emphasized enhancing the efficiency and effectiveness of the government expenditure programs, resulting in a number of initiatives: in particular, efforts to collect more detailed information on the composition of spending. This was not surprising in view of the theoretical foundations of the neo-liberal agenda of the ERP, which focused on curtailing the role of the state and enhancing the private sector as the engine of growth. An aspect of this reform was the rationalization of budgetary procedures with assistance from the IMF and the World Bank, and the pursuit of program evaluation and cost-effectiveness (Kapur et al., 1991, p. 35).

Since then various reforms have been introduced, all in the name of generating an optimal set of financial circumstances. It has been so because "fiscal discipline was poor prior to the introduction of the SAP in 1983. The government budget was in deficit during 1980–3, with an average share of GDP of −4.75%" (Antwi-Asare & Addison, 2000). Hence,

> The early restoration of fiscal discipline and the pursuit of a growth-oriented fiscal strategy [were made] integral to the adjustment program. Fiscal policy [was] directed at raising government savings and lowering the overall budget deficit, thus allowing, together with the increasing in-flows of net foreign financing, a sharp reduction in the government's recourse to domestic bank financing and, since 1987, sizable net repayments to the banking system.
>
> Kapur et al., 1991, p. 3

The financial sector reform involved institutional restructuring (budget restructuring), enhancement of the legal and regulatory framework for banking operations, and liberalizing interest rates (Sowa, 2002). The reform led government to achieve the first post-independence surplus budget, which continued until the early 1990s (Antwi-Asare & Addison, 2000; Sowa, 2002).

Although Ghana achieved significant success with the ERP, budgetary issues continued to constrain the government in its efforts to move the country to a middle-income status. The fact was more evident in the run-up to the first general elections under the Fourth Republic, where government expenditure went off course with an increase in the wages of public sector employees. Indeed, the evolution from authoritarian regime to liberal democracy drastically affected the budget situation, because of wage increases and other unplanned expenses, as the government attempted to win the election and secure its legitimacy. Depreciation of the Ghanaian currency was also accelerated beyond the norm, plunging the government back into high budget deficits (Dordunoo, 2000). These deficits "led to increasing interest rates on government debt reorienting credit away from the private sector to the government" (Antwi-Asare & Addison, 2000, p. 88). Kapur et al. (1991) believe that this out-of-control expenditure can be attributed to the way budgets were constructed at that time. They noted:

> The official budget of Ghana is constructed on a "narrow" basis, that is, excluding capital expenditure financed through external project aid, as well as the corresponding project grants and loans, but including foreign program grants. This has been done largely for reasons of administrative simplicity, but the calculation of the narrow budget can also be justified on the grounds that these capital outlays are financed by concessional foreign resources and have a large import content, and so have only a limited impact on aggregate domestic demand. Nonetheless, the narrow budget understates the impact of fiscal policy on economic activity and the balance of payments. To compensate for these limitations, a "broad" deficit has also been calculated, including capital expenditure financed through external project aid. It is envisaged that following improvements in data collection and budgetary procedures, the Government will soon begin to formulate the budget on a broad basis.
>
> Kapur et al., 1991, p. 37

The budget exhibited a number of weaknesses that needed to be addressed if the earlier success of the ERP and further growth were to be maintained. For example, the government focused on incremental budgeting without review and without knowing whether the funded activities should be continued. Further, the investment budget comprised a large number of projects, making it more difficult to connect the activities with the government's own priorities. In addition, the budget preparation process did not relate the achievement of objectives to the financial resources required. Other weaknesses included the general emphasis on the control of inputs, with less on improving performance of the sector through meeting its objectives and targets; the inability to cater for the cost implications of completed projects in subsequent recurrent estimates; the narrow perspective of the budget, concentrating solely on the domestic resource envelope; the inability of MDAs to assume ownership of their budgets and programs; and the lack of timely reporting from these agencies (Oku-Afari, n.d).

It was against this backdrop that in 1995 the newly elected National Democratic Congress government introduced another financial management reform, the Public Financial Management Reform Program (PUFMARP). The PUFMARP sought to develop an integrated financial management system in government when the government was seeking the means to enhance its budget and reduce poverty. It was also an important part of a wider transformational process of the public sector, undertaken by the government as part of its National Institutional Renewal Programme. The key budget objectives here were rationalization and modernization, including of public expenditure management, while simultaneously improving public sector efficiency and strengthening stakeholder participation and civic economic management.

As part of this reform an MTEF was introduced with a view to improving the links between policy-making and planning and budgeting systems; and, in 1996, the Budget and Public Expenditure Management System (BPEMS) was introduced (Short, 2003; World Bank, 2006b). The BPEMS was a comprehensive financial management system, developed to support the preparation of the budget in accordance with the priorities of the government beginning in 2000. It was expected to facilitate the production of a three-year rolling plan as the basis for the annual budget, based in turn on an MTEF process that has been operational since the budget year 1999. At the same time the BPEMS was also to provide for the effective control and monitoring of government expenditures, while permitting the classification, recording, and analysis of financial transactions in a timely and standardized manner.

The MTEF, Activity-Based Budgeting, and the Budgetary Process

As already noted, the government decided to introduce the MTEF to improve the contribution of the budget to sustainable development; also, and more importantly, to the realization of Vision 2020 in 1996, and as a component of a broader PUFMARP. Vision 2020 was the government's developmental strategy aimed at creating a stable macro-economic environment and implementing a decisive structural transformation to foster strong economic growth and a broad-based improvement of living standards. The MTEF has been described as a:

> framework designed specifically to link planning, which has a medium term outlook, with the annual budget, and, as a consequence, to link budgetary expenditures more systematically with socially desired outcomes, e.g. gender balance, slower population growth, higher literacy rates, [and] lower infant mortality rates. Its principal focus is on getting the government to allocate budgetary resources to programs, activities, and projects that promote the strategic priorities of the country.
>
> Campos & Walker, 2014, p. 1

The introduction of the MTEF followed from acknowledgment of the scope for improving links between, on one hand, policy-making and, on the other, planning and budgeting systems and processes at the regional, district, and sector levels, in central agencies, and at the political level. The larger objective was to improve the contribution that government makes to development outcomes. In terms of budget outcomes, the MTEF was intended to contribute to a more stable fiscal policy, improved allocation of resources to and spending on strategic priorities, and better delivery of services to citizens. The MTEF was thus seen as a tool for determining the available financial resources and the allocation of these resources in tandem with government priorities and macro-economic policies. The approach was based on the premise that financial resources are limited and unlikely to increase significantly in real terms in the medium term. It was, therefore, necessary to focus on "value for money" in the allocation of resources. The main feature of the MTEF budget structure is a broad-based resource envelope of central government activity, funded by both government and the donor community.

In spite of the support granted the government, the MTEF could not achieve the kind of success expected at its inception. It was not a holistically designed plan like the PUFMARP. Furthermore, it faced the same implementation problems as other public sector reform efforts: particularly, the macro-economic context, ownership and political support, the pace of reforms, the electoral cycle and change of government, the lack of organizational coherence and an integrated reform approach, incentives and organizational culture, a pervasive non-performance culture, and lack of accountability and capacity (Roberts & Andrews, 2005; Short, 2003)

As part of the MTEF approach the government further adopted an ABB, which continued until the recent introduction of the PBB (Roberts & Andrews, 2005). Hansen et al. (2003, p. 98) have described ABB as a budget approach that "focuses on generating a budget from an activity-based model of the organization, as opposed to the traditional product-market, responsibility center, or departmental focus." Shim et al. (2012) see the ABB as an activity-oriented budget that concentrates on the budgeted cost of activities required to produce and sell products and services, and emphasizes the planning and control purpose of cost management (p. 394). It focused on "understanding activities and their relationship to achieving strategic goals" (Brimson & Antos, 1999, p. 10).

In their study of ABB and costing, Brimson and Antos (1999) identified a number of advantages over the traditional budgeting system. These included: placing responsibility on and giving accountability to employees for managing their activities and reaching their performance targets; formulating a more realistic view of workloads, including the impact of service levels; giving actionable insights into causes of variation; cultivating the ability to understand how products and services create demand for specific activities that in turn drive the requirement for resources; embedding a process view to illustrate the interdependencies of departments; creating the ability to monitor and control at a more actionable level; and providing the visibility that makes it possible to manage both excess and insufficient capacity (p. 12).

A careful examination of these benefits, though, may lead to the conclusion that the ABB is not necessarily at variance with the PBB. Both focus on the management level, as well as on the links between resources, performance targets, and actions. They are thus interested in the outcomes of organizational actions that will lead to the justification of budgetary allocations. It has already been noted that ABB was introduced for the preparation of the National Budget in 1998, with a view to bringing a stronger performance focus to MDAs and linking strategic objectives to outputs and activities.

In spite of this, a recent review of the budget process and system has identified a number of limitations of the ABB (Maher, 2011; World Bank, 2006a; 2006b). It proved, for instance, overly detailed, making the budget cumbersome to prepare, and contributing to excessively centralized control over budget implementation (Maher, 2011). Furthermore, the lack of performance indicators of the MDAs' budgets, which was not the focus of the ABB, also made it hard to measure budget performance and outputs. There was also no real strategic focus in the MDAs' budgets, with limited linkage between resource allocations and policy priorities (MoFEP, 2013, p. 5). On this Maher notes that:

> while budgets have become more policy based in recent years, performance is held back by limited ability to cost strategies, the lack of effective wage-bill planning, and the absence of a transparent link between planned and executed budget activities.
>
> Maher, 2011, p. 29

Another issue undermining the budgetary process was transparency, which in turn damaged the budget's credibility. The opaque nature of the process enabled the government to shift resources without being found out and against certain established targets. A World Bank (2006a) review noted how the lack of transparency allowed the government to find expenditure money to foot some wage bills after the budget estimates had been voted on. In making room for these increases in spending the government reduced it in other areas, such as domestically financed capital spending. According to the bank, this action of the government raised "questions about the transparency of budgets, the planning and control of establishments and whether the budget has enough credibility for departments to plan and execute their work programs efficiently" (p. ix). Budget credibility, according to the World Bank (2006b, p. 9), "requires actual budgetary releases to be similar to voted budgets and requires appropriate fiscal discipline to be in place."

With these limitations on the MTEF and its budgetary components, and the continued implementation of the public financial management reforms through the introduction of the Ghana Integrated Financial Management System (GIFMIS), the government introduced a program-based budget for 2014 (Okudzeto et al., 2014, p. 10). It therefore intends to use the PBB to answer the criticisms of the budgetary process and budgetary allocations as raised by the World Bank in its review of the public financial management reforms.

The Approach to Performance-based Budgeting

Under PBB, the government expects expenditures to lead directly to clearly stipulated results, and to improved service delivery within the mandate of its organizations, particular MDAs. In this situation, it intended to shift from its ABB approach to one of outputs or outcomes, in service delivery and for results. The precise objectives it foresees are policy delivery, which means linking resource allocations to MDA functions and strategic policy objectives, and costing, which means identifying the inputs necessary to produce the core operations and projects needed to contribute to strategic objectives. These are then rolled up to determine sub-program and program costs. Budget users can then be aware of the cost of the government interventions designed to achieve each objective. There is now a framework against which to measure the performance of MDA expenditure programs. The program structure allows measurement of: the ability of the government to meet strategic objectives; the effectiveness and efficiency of the services produced under the program; the overall cost of addressing the objective; and management authority and responsibility. In this case, the PBB is expected to generate a management framework for the MDAs. In other words, program managers can be appointed and assigned human, physical, and financial resources, and the manager will be accountable for the outcome (MoFEP, 2013).

To ensure the success of the PBB the government undertook a pilot study while incrementally introducing the PBB approach to some selected MDAs. Through the Ministry of Finance in 2010 the government conducted an initial pilot with the Ministries of Tourism and Communication. They wanted to test the draft manual and guidelines prepared for the training programs. That program's success expanded the coverage to five additional MDAs, making a total of seven. A further roll out was made to 34 MDAs, which were, therefore, trained in the preparation of PBB, and were assisted to translate their 2012 ABB into programs and sub-programs.

In working with the MDAs the government encouraged them to identify their strategic objectives based on the Ghana Shared Growth and Development Agenda (GSGDA), and to cascade these objectives in up to seven programs. Each program could then be subdivided into up to five sub-programs. For each program and sub-program a series of strategic output performance indicators and targets was developed. The main areas covered were:

1. linking planning and budgeting—GSGDA policy objectives, MDA mission, core functions, MDA strategic objectives and policy outcomes and indicators;
2. developing programs and sub-programs; and
3. performance measurement—setting outputs, indicators and targets.

To deepen the processes and strengthen the performance management, monitoring, and evaluation systems in all MDAs, the ministry reviewed the key performance information in the PBBs of all MDAs. It engaged with key staff of all MDAs to discuss the key performance information, and measures to improve the quality of information, to enable them to review the performance indicators and targets and enhance their monitoring of the MDAs' performance (MoFEP, 2013).

Another area to which the government paid particular attention with a view to ensuring the success of the program was change management. This is not surprising, since previous attempts at instituting performance-based management systems had not yielded the results sought (Ohemeng, 2009; 2011). The government attributed that failure to the problem of change management (Annan-Prah & Ohemeng, 2015), which, therefore, seems to have become the mantra for a government that it is fair to say has become obsessed with performance management in the public sector (Annan-Prah & Ohemeng, 2015; Ohemeng & Ayee, 2015). Introducing the 2014 budget in Parliament, the Finance Minister confirmed this need for effective change management when he noted that it:

> requires significant change in roles played by all stakeholders. In line with this and to facilitate effective and efficient implementation of the budget reforms, a Change Management and Communication Strategy was developed to enhance the transition from ABB to PBB. As part of the implementation of the strategy, the Ministry trained Budget Officers in the MDAs, [and] engaged with Directors and Chief Directors of all MDAs on PBB to facilitate leadership commitment and participation in the budget reform process. In addition, other stakeholders including Development Partners and Civil Society Organisations, were also engaged on the implementation of PBB.

In addition, the Ministry conducted an assessment of the MDAs' performance in the preparation of PBB as part of the change management process, and developed strategies to further deepen the process.

Performance-Based Budgeting: The Panacea for Ghana's Budgetary Ills?

It has already been noted that Ghana's budgetary problems continue to affect its socio-economic development. The fact was clearly seen in the review by the World Bank in 2006a and 2006b. In a recent review Cole (2013), an international advisor working in Ghana, noted that the country's budget process was a façade in view of the extensive leaks in the system. He noted that the system was extremely "closed," with poor parliamentary oversight, large discretionary spending, and a very weak link to actual budget policy. Social accountability measures to address the shortfalls in the budgetary process under a new Social Public Expenditure and Financial Accountability (SPEFA) project are not working. Is PBB, therefore, the panacea for all budgetary ailments? In what follows we will identify what needs to happen to ensure that PBB does not descend to the same illusory status as other reform initiatives have done.

Spending so much on PBB means that the government believes it has, indeed, found the solution to Ghana's budgetary woes. To get the most from the program, though, the government needs to pay more attention to: both organizational and individual capacities; a change in organizational culture that enhances the adaptive capacity of organizations; education to ensure understanding of good governance and citizen participation; and transparency and access to government. It also needs to deal seriously with both corrupt public officials and unscrupulous citizens who may want to take advantage of the state.

ORGANIZATIONAL AND INDIVIDUAL CAPACITY PROBLEMS

The success of any administrative reforms or organizational transformation hinges on the capacities of individual employees and of the organization as a whole (Fukuyama, 2004; Nutt, 2007). Where both capacities are weak, reforms become a farce. Defining organizational capacity has become problematic, despite the word's ubiquitousness (Christensen & Gazley, 2008). For example, Yu-Lee (2002) describes it simply as the organization's "ability to perform work" (p. 1). This definition is broad, as it refers to every organization without distinction. In view of our focus on the public sector I will adopt the definition of Ingraham et al. (2003), according to which it is the "government's [*public organization's*] ability to marshal, develop, direct and control its financial, human, physical and information resources [*to undertake its assigned task*]" (p. 15, italics mine). The importance of organizational capacity stems from the notion that for governments to adapt to rapid changes, public organizations will need to continually question their purposes, reconsider their modes of operation, take responsibility for their performance, and reorient their roles (Caiden, 2010, p. 210).

On the other hand, individual capacity deals with cognitive skills used to analyze development needs, to design and implement strategies, policies, and programs to meet those needs, and to deliver public services. Such skills and mind-sets are required at all levels of an organization to innovate and implement programs successfully. The reason for concentrating on individual skills is that people are central to public sector innovation at every stage of its process.

> Thus innovations begin as ideas in the minds of citizens, public servants, managers and political leaders and are generated at the cross sections of human interaction. These ideas are inspired by the needs of citizens and are transformed from idea to practice through the commitment of public servants and leaders who anticipate these needs and respond to them.
>
> Daglio et al., 2015, p. 15

Both capacities are important in the introduction and implementation of PBB (Lee & Wang, 2009). Unfortunately, capacity issues continue to be a major stumbling block in Ghana despite years of capacity-building initiatives. Most MDAs and local government institutions that are expected to implement the program lack both capacities, as shown in the introduction of the MTEF and some of the problems it encountered (Roberts & Andrews, 2005). Resolving capacity problems, especially at the individual level, has focused more on training needs; and training, according to Thomas (2006, p. 1), although it almost always achieves the target numbers of people to be trained, is only part of the process of building human capacity. According to him, that emphasis neglects low salaries and poor working conditions, which often contribute to a voluminous outflow of trained staff. More important, the record is mixed when it comes to the effectiveness of organizations where the trained people are employed. Consequently, for PBB to work the government has to move beyond the surface dressing of capacity issues to build a more resilient organization. In short, donors should go beyond addressing human resource problems mainly by financing training of individuals, and include developing effective structures, meeting technological needs, and clarifying the organization's mission, and so on, that may affect overall capacity building to ensure the success of the program (Thomas, 2006, p. 1).

THE NECESSITY FOR A CHANGE IN ORGANIZATIONAL CULTURE

Changing the organizational culture is extremely important for the success of any reform. The classic work of Lewin (1951) tells us that it is important to understand that the existing culture of the organization may hinder performance and, hence, that it is always necessary to introduce a new culture, and then refreeze that culture, so that it becomes the dominant one in the organization. In a study on organizational performance Owusu (2012) noted that organizational culture affects the performance of public sector organizations in Ghana.

Organizational culture does not submit to a single acceptable definition (Watkins, 2013). It is made up of:

> Core values, behavioural norms, artefacts and behavioural patterns which govern the way people in an organisation interact with each other and invest their energy in their jobs and the organisation at large. It includes a web of basic assumptions that have proven to work in the past and are therefore accepted as common sense within the organisation. Organisational cultures are the unwritten rules and expectations based on the shared attitudes and values of individuals within an organisation.
>
> Daglio et al., 2015, p. 19

Irrespective of how the concept is defined, there is a general consensus that organizational culture affects both the individual and the general performance of the organization (Lim, 1995; Prajogo & McDermott, 2011).

Performance reform cannot occur in a culture that is not performance oriented. The old ways and habits must thus yield to new thinking and ways of doing things. The introduction of PBB should focus on addressing the existing organizational cultural dilemma from the "business as usual attitude to one of not business as usual," where performance is the key to success. This change in organizational culture must happen not only at the Ministry of Finance, but throughout the MDAs if the implementation of the PBB is to be successful. Without this, the PBB will become like its predecessors. We thus agree with Caiden who argues that:

> Budgetary reforms will need to be more than pretense on paper, and relate budgeting to management and to changes in organizational culture. But merely to pick out ideas or concepts is to miss the point: to write a 'next chapter,' one has to know and understand the chapters that have come before.
>
> Caiden, 2010, p. 210

LEGISLATIVE BACKING AS AN ESSENTIAL INGREDIENT

It has been well established that a successful PBB needs a strong legislative instrument or backing (Melkers & Willoughby, 1998). A study comparing the efficacy of PBB in the USA and South Korea by Lee and Wang (2009) concluded that the successful implementation of the system in the two countries could be well attributable to strong legislative backing. To this end, they wrote:

> passing a law and specifying how agencies should follow it provides public officials with a legal basis and responsibility for implementation. PBB legislation reinforces political urgency and underscores the importance of the reform, and it also provides legitimacy for requests and approvals of financial support for PBB, which is critical in PBB implementation and performance-based funding.
>
> Lee and Wang, 2009, S65

Russell-Einhorn (2007) also says that "appropriate legal and institutional frameworks can create significant participatory 'spaces' and opportunities—often grounded in individual and collective rights—for the public to exert such agency and make meaningful choices about service delivery quality, access, accountability, efficiency, and equity" (pp. 183–184).

In Ghana, it has also been established that for any reform to be successful, it needs such legislative backing stipulating what needs to be done and not to be done and at what time. Evidence is in the establishment of the Ghana Revenue Authority in 2010, after the failure of an earlier attempt (Ohemeng & Owusu, 2015). Unfortunately, a careful examination of the PBB indicates that such backing has not been provided, and there is no evidence of anything in the pipeline. We believe that government should have passed a law on the PBB detailing what it expects both politicians and civil servants to do in this regard. It would not necessarily mean using the stick (rather than the carrot) approach to managing the process, but a way to institutionalize it, as well as to secure the legitimacy needed for the reform. Furthermore, it could serve as an instrumental incentive for both politicians and civil servants to take the reform seriously.

EFFECTIVE STAKEHOLDER PARTICIPATION

Stakeholder participation in reform is considered one of the most powerful aids to success (Andrews, 2005; Lu et al. 2015; Russell-Einhorn, 2007). Stakeholder in this sense includes both civil servants and citizens. It has been amply noted that effective civil service participation is also essential if reforms are to succeed (Lee & Wang, 2009). According to Steger,

> broadly recognised, administration reforms can only survive if [*civil servants*] are respected or—even better—endorsed by those who do the day-to-day work within an administration. Otherwise, even reforms with a strong legal basis can run the risk of being paralyzed once in practice.
>
> Steger, 2010, p. 5

Similarly, Moynihan (2007) has also argued for effective citizen participation in reforms, and especially in budgetary reforms. He identified a number of benefits that may accrue. It has been acknowledged that citizen participation can bring transparency to government and further buy-in to reforms.

Unfortunately, in Ghana stakeholder participation in reforms has been extremely weak. Most reform initiatives have been top-down, with little involvement of civil servants (Ohemeng & Ayee, 2015). Similarly, although the new SPEFA project is promising, citizen participation in general remains feeble. Citizen partnerships in governance are constrained, primarily, by the weakness of mechanisms for them to participate in local planning and implementation and to hold local governments accountable. The lack of a systematic and coherent approach to fostering citizens' participation in public governance is an obstacle to realizing the full benefits of reforms.

Although the government piloted the new PBB reforms before their full implementation, there is thus no evidence that street-level bureaucrats were involved in thrashing out the reforms, as the initiative was restricted to a few ministries in Accra, excluding those in other regions and district levels. Nor is there evidence of citizen participation. So while the government might have involved a few non-governmental organizations (NGOs) and certain stakeholders, there is no reason to think this extended beyond those in Accra, or to the ordinary citizens, to enable them to understand what the reform is all about.

ENSURING TRANSPARENCY

One of the main reasons for the introduction of PBB is to ensure the transparency of budgets. According to Hawkesworth et al. (2011), the purpose of introducing PBB is to improve public finance management and strengthen allocative and operational efficiency, multi-year budgeting, and transparency and accountability. Governments must therefore ensure transparency in the budgetary process.

Transparency includes key indicators with published data showing the cost and impact of public services and departmental activities. Output and perhaps outcome measures are expected from public organizations. Crain and O'Roark (2004, p. 168) believe that:

> [such] tangible output measures are particularly appealing for public sector budgeting because a government agency's performance cannot be assessed on the basis of financial profits or losses, the standard alternative in private, for-profit enterprises. In the absence of a profit-loss performance yardstick, tangible output measures may provide a useful tool that enhances the transparency of agency strategic planning, monitoring, and evaluation.

The OECD (2002) also says that for budgetary transparency the draft budget should be submitted to the parliament far enough in advance to allow proper review. It should never be less than three months before the start of the fiscal year, before which that budget should also be approved by parliament (p. 8). It is thus believed that three months may be enough for thorough scrutiny of the budget not only by parliamentarians, but also by stakeholders and citizens in general.

This is not the case in Ghana. Parliamentarians see the budget after it has been presented, and then they are allowed to debate on it, which sometimes turns into a partisan exercise rather than a genuine attempt to create a national budget helpful for the development of the country. Second, in view of the time constraint, civil society groups, which usually lack the capacity to scrutinize the budget, are unable to do so. Organizational accountability, in terms of achieving targets set in the budget, is thus undermined.

PROMOTING EFFECTIVE OPEN ACCESS TO GOVERNMENT

Transparency and open access to government has become the mantra for modern-day governance. If performance budgeting is about measuring the work done by public agencies—and, for that matter, government in general—citizens must have access to government and agency documents, to be able to access their performance records. One way of doing so is by promoting open-access government. This can be done in a number of ways. With smartphones easily available, governments could put information such as budgets online. Furthermore, governments could pass freedom of information laws that would allow citizens to demand official and non-classified documents from government agencies.

In Ghana, although budgets can be found on the website of the Ministry of Finance, other documents on the performance of other organizations relating to the contents of the budget may be difficult to find. The government should therefore make it a priority to pass the promised freedom of information bill that will facilitate easy access to government documents. It would also compel bureaucrats to release such information, even though it exposes the weaknesses in their own performance.

ADEQUATELY DEALING WITH CORRUPTION

Corruption seems the bane of development in most developing nations. It has become a social cancer spreading and infecting people faster than biological diseases. In developing countries, governments use their budgets to transfer money to powerful constituencies that then allow them to maintain political power. According to Khan (2005; 2006), political power so secured and perpetuated prevents the use of transfers to organizations for development. Budgets must obviously be executed in accordance with appropriations and rules to prevent corruption and over-spending (Simson et al., 2011).

To achieve this, government must be prepared to prosecute public officials, as well as unscrupulous and opportunistic citizens. As already noted, if the government fails to do so, then the new PBB will simply dissipate as other reforms have done.

Conclusion

Budget reforms in Ghana were analyzed in this chapter. In particular, it focused on the adoption of PBB as the new way of developing and implementing budgets there. From the government's perspective the fundamental premise for introducing it is that it will help link organizational performance with set targets, which will in turn allow the government and citizens to hold such organizations more accountable. The underlying research question was whether the government has found the cure for the budgetary sickness of Ghana. It was argued that while PBB has become the most obvious candidate in terms of budgetary reforms, it will not turn out to be the sought panacea if steps are not taken to address certain institutional and capacity constraints that continue to afflict the public sector in Ghana.

A number of factors were identified that must be of maximum concern to the government if it is to benefit from PBB. Ghana's economy is at a crossroads, and while PBB promises change, that change will only occur if the government takes bold initiatives to address the fundamental concerns raised in this paper. Without that, at some point in the future we will say again that, "Something funny happened on the way to budgetary reforms in Ghana" (Roberts & Andrews, 2005).

References

Andrews, M. 2005. Performance-Based Budgeting Reform. In A. Shah (Ed.) *Fiscal Management, Public Sector Governance and Accountability* (pp. 31–70). Washington, DC: World Bank.

Annan-Prah, E., & Ohemeng, F.L.K. 2015. *Improving Productivity through Performance Management in Public Sector Organizations in Ghana: Is Change Management the Answer?* A paper prepared for the XVIII annual meeting of the International Research Society for Public Management (IRSPM), University of Birmingham, UK. March 30–April 1.

Antwi-Asare, T.O., & Addison, E.K.Y. 2000. *Financial Sector Reforms and Bank Performance in Ghana*. London UK: Overseas Development Institute.

Berry, S.F. 2008. Performance Budgeting Internationally: Assessing its Merits. In P. de Lancer Julnes, F.S. Berry, M.P. Aristigueta, & K. Yang (Eds.) *International Handbook of Practice-Based Performance Management* (pp. 285–297). Los Angeles: Sage.

Boothe, P. 2007. Accrual Accounting in the Public Sector: Lessons for Developing Countries. In A. Shah (Ed.) *Budgeting and Budgetary Institutions* (pp. 179–200). Washington, DC: World Bank.

Brimson, J.A., & Antos, J. 1999. *Driving Value using Activity-Based Budgeting*. New York: Wiley.

Brown, J.R. 2008. Performance-Based Budgeting. In E.M. Berman & J. Rabin, *Encyclopedia of Public Administration and Public Policy*, 2nd ed. (pp. 1462–1472). New York: Taylor & Francis.

Caiden, N. 2010. Challenges Confronting Contemporary Public Budgeting: Retrospectives/Prospective from Allen Schick. *Public Administration Review*, 70(2): 203–210.

Campos, J.E., & Walker, L. 2014. Linking planning and budgeting: the mediums term expenditure framework (MTEF), *The Governance Brief: African Development Bank (ADB)*. [Online] Retrieved from: http://elibrary.kiu.ac.ug:8080/xmlui/bitstream/handle/1/1158/linking_planning_budgeting_adb.pdf?sequence=1&isAllowed=y.

Christensen, R.K., & Gazley, B. 2008. Capacity for Public Administration: Analysis of Meaning and Measurement. *Public Administration and Development*, 28(4): 265–279.

Cole, N. 2013. The Practice of Budgeting: What Drives the Form and Functionality of Budget Systems? The 2013 CAPE Conference: Budgeting in the real world,

Conference report. [Online] Retrieved from: www.odi.org/sites/odi.org.uk/files/odi-assets/publications-opinion-files/8819.pdf.

Collaborative Africa Budget Reform Initiative (CABRI). 2013. *Performance and Programme-Based Budgeting in Africa: A Status Report*. Pretoria, South Africa: CABRI Secretariat.

Crain, W.M., & O'Roark, J.B. 2004. The Impact of Performance-Based Budgeting on State Fiscal Performance. *Economic Governance*, 5(2): 167–186.

Curristine, T. 2005. Government Performance: Lessons and Challenges. *OECD Journal of Budgeting*, 5(1): 127–151.

Curristine, T. (Ed.) 2007. *Performance Budgeting in OECD Countries*. OECD: Paris.

Curristine, T., & Flynn, S. 2013. In Search of Results: Strengthening Public Sector Performance. In M. Cangiano, T. Curristine, & M. Lazare (Eds.) *Public Financial Management and Its Emerging Architecture* (pp. 225–253). Washington, DC: IMF.

Daglio, M., Gerson, D., & Kitchen, H., 2015. Building Organisational Capacity for Public Sector Innovation. Background Paper prepared for the OECD Conference *Innovating the Public Sector: from Ideas to Impact*, Paris, November 12–13 2014.

de Lancer Julnes, P., Berry, F.S., P. Aristigueta, M.P., & K. Yang (Eds.) 2008. *International Handbook of Practice-Based Performance Management*. Los Angeles: Sage.

Diamond, J. 2003. *From Program Budgeting to Performance Budgeting: The Challenge for Emerging Market Economies*, IMF Working Paper WP/03/169.

Dordunoo, C. 2000. Fiscal Trends, 1970–1995. In E. Aryeetey, J. Harrigan, & M. Nissanke (Eds.) *Economic Reforms in Ghana: The Miracle and the Mirage*. Oxford, UK: James Currey.

Fölscher, A. 2006. African Experience With Budget Reform: Introduction. *OECD Journal on Budgeting*, 6/2. [Online] Retrieved from: http://dx.doi.org/10.1787/budget-v6-art6-en.

Fölscher, A. 2012. Achieving Effective Programme and Performance-Based Budgeting: Lessons from Africa and Elsewhere. In A. Fölscher (Ed.) *Budgeting for Results: Moving Towards Performance Budgeting* (pp. 2–7). Pretoria, South Africa: CABRI Secretariat.

Foster, M., Fozzard, A. Naschold, F., & Conway, T. 2002. *How, When and Why Does Poverty Get Budget Priority? Poverty Reduction Strategy and Public Expenditure Reform in Five African Countries, Synthesis Paper*, Working Paper 168. London: Overseas Development Institute.

Fukuyama, F. 2004. *State-Building: Governance and World Order in the Twenty-First Century*. London: Profile Books.

Hansen, S.C., Otley, D.T., & Van der Stede, W.A. 2003. Practice Developments in Budgeting: An Overview and Research Perspective. *Journal of Management Accounting Research*, 15: 95–116.

Hawkesworth, I., Trapp, L.V., & Nielsen, D.F. 2011. Performance Budgeting in Poland: An OECD review. *OECD Journal on Budgeting*, 11(1), pp. 7–57.

Herbst, J. 1993. *The Politics of Reform in Ghana, 1982–1991*. Berkeley: University of California Press.

Hutchful, E. 2002. *Ghana's Adjustment Experience: The Paradox of Reform*. Oxford: James Currey.

Ingraham, P. W., Joyce, P. G., & Donahue, A.K. 2003. *Government Performance: Why Management Matters*. Baltimore, MD: Johns Hopkins University Press.

Joyce, P. G. 1999. Performance-Based Budgeting. In R.T. Meyers (Ed.) *Handbook of Government Budgeting* (pp. 597–619). San Francisco, CA: Jossey-Bass.

Joyce, P. G. 2003. Linking Performance and Budgeting: Opportunities in the Federal Budget Process. In *Managing for Performance and Results Series* (October). IBM Center for The Business of Government.

Kapur, I., Hadjimichael, M. T., P. Hilbers, P.L.C., Schiff, J.A., & Szymczak, P. 1991. *Ghana: Adjustment and Growth (1983–91)*. Washington, DC: International Monetary Fund.

Kelly, J., & Wanna, J. 2000. New Public Management and the Politics of Government Budgeting. *International Public Management Review*, 1(1): 33–55.

Khan, M.H. 2005. Markets, States and Democracy: Patron-Client Networks and the Case for Democracy in Developing Countries. *Democratization*, 12(5): 705–725.

Khan, M.H. 2006. Determinants of Corruption in Developing Countries: The Limits of Conventional Economic Analysis. In S. Rose-Ackerman (Ed.) *International Handbook on the Economics of Corruption* (pp. 216–246). Cheltenham UK: Edward Elgar.

Killick, T. 2005. *The Politics of Ghana's Budgetary System*. CDD/ODI Policy Brief No. 2.

Killick, T. 2010. *Development Economics in Action: A Study of Economic Policies in Ghana*. New York: Routledge.

Kluvers, R. 2001. An Analysis of Introducing Program Budgeting in Local Government. *Public Budgeting and Finance*, 21(2): 29–45.

Kong, D. 2005. Performance-Based Budgeting: The U.S. Experience. *Public Organization Review*, 5(2): 91–107.

KPMG. 2011. *Making the Transition: Outcome-Based Budgeting: A Six Nation Study*. KPMG International Cooperative. [Online] Retrieved from: www.kpmg.com/MY/en/IssuesAndInsights/ArticlesPublications/Documents/2011/making-the-transition.pdf.

Kwakye, J.K., & Owuo, N. 2014. *Righting the Ills of Budget Preparation, Implementation and Oversight in Ghana*, IEA Monograph 39: Accra, Ghana: Institute of Economic Affairs.

Lee, J.Y., & Wang, X. 2009. Assessing the Impact of Performance-Based Budgeting: A Comparative Analysis across the United States, Taiwan and China. *Public Administration Review*, 69(1): S60–S66.

Lewin, K. 1951. Frontiers in group dynamics. In D. Cartwright (Ed.) *Field Theory in Social Science: Some Selected Papers* (pp. 188–237). New York: Harper.

Lim, B. 1995. Examining the Organizational Culture and Organizational Performance Link. *Leadership and Organization Development Journal*, 16(5): 16–21.

Lu, Y.E., Mohr, Z, & Ho, A.T. 2015. Taking Stock: Assessing and Improving Performance Budgeting Theory and Practice. *Public Performance & Management Review*, 38(3): 426–458.

McNab, R.M., & Melese, F. 2003. Implementing the GPRA: Exploring the Prospects for Performance Budgeting in the Federal Government. *Public Budgeting and Finance*, 23(Spring): 73–95.

Maher, C.S. 2011. The Republic of Ghana: A Success Story? In C.E. Menifield (Ed.) *Comparative Public Budgeting: A Global Perspective* (pp. 21–41). Sudbury, MA: Jones and Bartlett Learning.

Mauro, S.G., Cinquini, L., & Grossi, G. 2015. *Insights Into Performance-Based Budgeting: A Literature Review and a Research Agenda*. A paper prepared for the XVIII annual meeting of the International Research Society for Public Management (IRSPM), University of Birmingham, UK. March 30–April 1.

Melkers, J.E., & Willoughby, K.G. 1998. The State of the States: Performance-Based Budgeting Requirements in 47 out of 50. *Public Administration Review*, 58(1): 66–75.

Melkers, J.E., & Willoughby, K.G. 2001. Budgeters' Views of State Performance-Budgeting Systems: Distinctions across Branches. *Public Administration Review*, 61 (Jan/Feb): 54–64.

Ministry of Finance and Economic Planning (MoFEP). 2013. *Programme Based Budgeting Guidelines: Concept and Specification*. Accra, Ghana: Ministry of Finance.

Morgan, D., Robinson, K.S., Strachota, D., & Hough, J.A. 2015. *Budgeting for Local Governments and Communities*. New York: Routledge.

Moynihan, D.P. 2003. Performance-Based Budgeting: Beyond Rhetoric. *The World Bank Poverty Reduction and Economic Management Notes*, 78: 1–4.

Moynihan, D.P. 2007. Citizen Participation in Budgeting: Prospects for Developing Countries. In A. Shah (Ed.) *Participatory Budgeting* (pp. 55–87). Washington, DC: World Bank.

Nutt, P. C. 2007. Strategically Repositioning and Transforming Public Organizations. *Research in Organizational Change and Development*, 16: 253–288.

OECD. 2002. OECD Best Practices for Budget Transparency. *OECD Journal on Budgeting*, 1(3): 7–14.

OECD. 2003. *Public Sector Modernization: Governing for Performance*. Paris: GOV/PUMA.

OECD. 2007. *Performance Budgeting in OECD Countries*. Paris: OECD Publishing.

OECD. 2008. *Sequencing and Pacing of Performance Budgeting Reforms*, Summary of the 5th annual meeting of SBO network on performance and results, October 27–28. [Online] Retrieved from: www.oecd.org/gov/budgeting/42188165.pdf.

Ohemeng, F.L.K. 2009. Constraints in the Implementation of Performance Management Systems in Developing Countries: The Ghanaian Case. *International Journal of Cross Cultural Management*, 9(1): 109–132.

Ohemeng, F.L.K. 2011. Institutionalizing the Performance Management System in Public Organizations in Ghana: Chasing a Mirage? *Public Performance & Management Review*, 34(4): 467–488.

Ohemeng, F.L.K., & Anebo F.K. 2012. The Politics of Administrative Reforms in Ghana: Perspectives from Path Dependency and Punctuated Equilibrium Theory. *International Journal of Public Administration*, 35(3): 161–176.

Ohemeng F.L.K., & Ayee, J.R.A. 2015. *The "New Approach" to Public Sector Reforms in Ghana: A Case of Politics as Usual or a Genuine Attempt at Reforms?* A paper prepared for the XVII annual meeting of the International Research Society for Public Management (IRSPM), Ottawa, Ontario, April 9–11.

Ohemeng, F.L.K., & Owusu, F.Y. 2015. Implementing a Revenue Authority Model of Tax Administration in Ghana: An Organizational Perspective. *American Review of Public Administration*, 45(3): 343–364.

Oku-Afari, K. B. n.d. *Overview of the Budgetary Process: Government of Ghana Budget Cycle*, A Presentation CEPA Seminar series on macro-economic modelling and public accounts management, Accra, Ghana.

Okudzeto, E., Mariki, W.A., Paepe, G.D., & Sedegah, K. 2014. Ghana 2014. African Economic Outlook. [Online] Retrieved from: www.africaneconomicoutlook.org/fileadmin/uploads/aeo/2014/PDF/CN_Long_EN/Ghana_ENG.pdf .

Owusu, F.Y. 2012. Organizational Culture and Public Sector Reforms in a Post-Washington Consensus Era: Lessons from Ghana's Good Reformers. *Progress in Development Studies*, 12(2–3): 135–151.

Pitsvada, B., & LoStracco F. 2002. Performance Budgeting—The Next Budgetary Answer. But what is the Question? *Journal of Public Budgeting, Accounting and Financial Management*, 14(1): 53–73.

Prajogo, D.I., & McDermott, C.M. 2011. The Relationship between Multidimensional Organizational Culture and Performance. *International Journal of Operations and Production Management*, 31(7): 712–735.

Roberts, J., & Andrews, M. 2005. Something Funny Happened on the Way to Reform Success: The Case of Budget Reform Implementation in Ghana. *International Journal of Public Administration*, 28(3–4): 291–311.

Robinson, M. 2011. *Performance-Based Budgeting*, Washington, DC: CLEAR/World Bank.

Robinson, M. 2013a. *Program Classification for Performance-Based Budgeting: How to Structure Budgets to Enable the Use of Evidence*, IEG Evaluation Capacity Development Series, Washington, DC.

Robinson, M. 2013b. Performance Budgeting. In R. Allen, B. Potter and R. Hemming (Eds.), *International Handbook of Public Financial Management* (pp. 237–258). New York: Palgrave Macmillan.

Robinson, M., & Brumby, J. 2005. Does Performance Budgeting Work? An Analytical Review of the Empirical Literature. *IMF Working Paper*, WP/05/210.

Robinson, M., & Last, D. 2009. *A Basic Model of Performance-Based Budgeting*. Washington, DC: IMF.

Russell-Einhorn, M. 2007. Legal and Institutional Frameworks Supporting Accountability in Budgeting and Service Delivery Performance. In A. Shah (Ed.) *Performance Accountability and Combating Corruption* (pp. 183–232). Washington, DC: World Bank.

Schick, A. 1966. The Road to PPPB: The Stages of Budget Reform. *Public Administration Review*, 26(4): 243–258.

Schick, A. 2007. Performance Budgeting and Accrual Budgeting: Decision Rules or Analytic Tools? *OECD Journal on Budgeting*, 7(2): 109–138.

Schick, A. 2014. The Metamorphoses of Performance Budgeting. *OECD Journal on Budgeting*, 13(2): 49–79.

Shim, J.K., Siegel, J.G., & Shim, A.I. 2012. *Budgeting Basics and Beyond*, 4th ed. Hoboken, NJ: Wiley.

Short, J. 2003. *Country Case Study 4: Assessment of the MTEF in Ghana*. London: Overseas Development Institute.

Simson, R., Sharma, N., & Aziz, I. 2011. A Guide to Public Financial Management Literature for Practitioners in Developing Countries. [Online] Retrieved from: www.who.int/pmnch/media/events/2013/pfm_literature.pdf.

Simwaka, C. 2006. Malawi: Lessons Learnt from First Reforms Lead to New Approach. *OECD Journal on Budgeting*, 6(2): 1–22.

Smith, F.J. 1999. The Benefits and Threats of PBB: An Assessment of Modern Reform. *Public Budgeting and Finance*, 19(3): 3–15.

Sowa, N.K. 2002. *Financial Sector Reform Policies and Poverty Reduction*. Accra, Ghana: Center for Policy Analysis.

Steger, G. 2010. Austria's Budget Reform: How to Create Consensus for a Decisive Change of Fiscal Rules. *OECD Journal on Budgeting*, 10: 1–14.

Thomas, V. 2006. *Linking Individual, Organizational and Institutional Capacity Building to Results*, Development Briefs, World Bank Institute.

VanLandingham, G, Wellman, M., & Andrews, M. 2005. Useful, but not a Panacea: Performance-Based Program Budgeting in Florida. *International Journal of Public Administration*, 28(3–4): 233–253.

Vian, T., & Bicknell, W.J. 2014. Good Governance and Budget Reform in Lesotho Public Hospitals: Performance, Root Causes and Reality. *Health Policy Planning*, 29(6): 673–684.

Wang, X. 2000. Performance Measurement in Budgeting: A Study of County Governments. *Public Budgeting and Finance*, 20(Fall): 102–118.
Watkins, M. 2013. What is Organizational Culture? And Why Should We Care? *Harvard Business Review*. [Online] Retrieved from: https://hbr.org/2013/05/what-is-organizational-culture.
Willoughby, K.G. 2004. Performance Measurement and Budget Balancing: State Government Perspective. *Public Budgeting and Finance*, 24(2): 21–39.
World Bank. 1998. *Public Expenditure Management Handbook*, Washington, DC: World Bank.
World Bank. 2006a. *Ghana 2006: External Review of Public Financial Management*, Vol. I, Washington, DC: World Bank.
World Bank. 2006b. *Public Finance Management Performance Report and Performance Indicators*, Public Expenditure Review (PER), Washington, DC: World Bank.
Yu-Lee, R.T. 2002. *Essentials of Capacity Management*, New York: John Wiley & Sons.

6 Public Budgeting in African Nations: The Case of Kenya

Abel Kinoti Meru and
Rogers Kinoti M'ariba

Introduction

The public budgeting system in Kenya has been very dynamic with a long history albeit slow with rich transformation. Over the last five decades a wide range of budgeting systems have been deployed within a very strong legal framework initially borrowed from Westminster, UK, but later became part of Kenyan law. Since the mid-1950s the budgeting system has evolved to become more integrative, collaborative and consultative with Parliament playing an oversight role in budget planning, execution, and control process, while the then Ministry of Finance [MOF] played a key role in facilitating the budgeting process. However, after the promulgation of the Constitution of Kenya, 2010, and the formation of national and county governments in 2013 the National Treasury and county treasuries shouldered the budgeting responsibilities, but still with Parliament and now county assemblies having oversight responsibilities.

This chapter explores the public budgeting systems and reforms over the last fifty years in Kenya. The first section examines the evolution of the budgeting system starting with the pre-colonial period to the present. The second section presents the budget framework from a legal perspective, while the third section identifies the key actors in the budgeting process. The fourth section outlines the key budget institutions, followed by analysis of revenue and expenditure items. Finally, the chapter provides an evaluation of the budgeting process and recommendations for policy implication and practice.

Evolution of Budgeting Systems in Kenya

The development of budgeting systems in Kenya can be categorized into two distinct epochs; pre-independence (1895–1963) and independence (1963 to the present), incorporating the budgeting systems before and after the promulgation of the Constitution of Kenya, 2010, that led to the formation of a devolved governing system, made up of national and county governments.

Pre-Independence (1895–1963)

The British Colonial Government ushered in a budgeting process in Kenya from 1895 to 1963, under the leadership of a governor. There is little literature available on budget planning, execution and control procedures then, but the Exchequer and Audit Act, 1955 confirms that there was public financial management. Upon attaining independence from the British Government in 1963, the management of public affairs was handed over to the Government of the Republic of Kenya.

Independence Period (1963 to the Present)

Since independence we have witnessed an array of budgeting tools all geared toward enhancing efficiency, consistency and inclusiveness in revenue collection and allocation aimed at improving citizens' quality of life. At the outset it is imperative to note that the budgeting systems used across diverse countries share similarities on account of historical background, political interest, regional consideration and the influence of the donor community.

Some of the budgeting systems adopted over the years include incremental budgeting, line budgeting, zero-based budgeting (ZBB), performance budgeting, program-based budgets, performance review and forward budgeting (PRFB), budget rationalization program (BRP), public investment program (PIP) and medium-term expenditure framework (MTEF). The later four, namely PRFB, BRP, PIP, and MTEF represent key budgetary reform measures adopted over the years. Interestingly, the approaches are dependent on each other and elements of a proper budget may rely on one or more of these budgeting systems.

Incremental Budgeting

Incremental budgeting though widely used today by governmental agencies and non-state institutions was prevalent in Kenya until the beginning of the third millennium. Incremental budgeting is normative, relying more on micro-budgeting, drawn from sub-parts, instead of being an integral approach (macro-budgetary) utilizing a bottom-up process of allowing insignificant adjustments to annual estimates (LeLoup, 2002). The emphasis is purely on the need for initial funding for new activities or additional funding for ongoing activities, meaning that unless there are affirmative measures, activities are funded at no less than their current level (Granof & Khumawala, 2011).

Before the year 2000, budgets were an outcome of a delicate balancing process between key state operators and a few others drawn from the private sector, resulting in a closely guarded secret. However, the shared adjustments and negotiating process used rarely translated to any meaningful budgeting outcomes (LeLoup, 2002). Citizens zealously waited to listen to budget speeches, since the outcomes had effects commencing at midnight of the same day.

Traders used to hoard products hoping to cash in on shortages and price adjustments once the budget was read in Parliament.

Besides, in Africa, due to reliance on foreign donors to finance budgets, the process was weighty, since government technocrats had to dance to the master's tune. This meant the process was very much an inward-looking approach, with limited outcomes, bent on perpetuating the status quo. No wonder that toward the end of the last millennium, most Africa economies had stagnated or nearly collapsed.

Line Budgeting

Line budgeting was born out of the late nineteenth and early twentieth century budgetary reforms in the USA aimed at encouraging accountability over comprehensive use of public resources, which advocated the listing of the next year's public expenditures against elaborate line items with predetermined budget allocation ceilings (World Bank, 1998). Line budgeting also known as the line-item, object-of-expenditure or traditional classification approach focuses more on expenditure control (Freeman et al. 2011) enforced through strict expenditure authorization. Surprisingly, this happens at the expense of government development plans and visible measurable results.

The 1963 Independence Constitution of Kenya (GoK, 1963) ingrained the public budgeting process as a centralized function undertaken by the Ministry of Finance, which eventually adopted the line budgeting method. Line budgeting was the preferred budgeting approach since resources were allocated as prioritized in development plans. The budgets covered one year with no provisions for any development expenditure overlaps for multi-year projects. The annual budget was seen as a tool for commanding and controlling the economy. The focus was more on input control without due consideration for the outputs. GOK (2011a, p. 3) summarizes the focus as follows: "Line budgeting is associated with an input-oriented budget preparation process with detailed ex-ante controls and well defined appropriation rules, such as rules regulating or forbidding transfers between line items."

By their very nature line-object classification budgets discourage planning and encourage bottom-up line-itemized budgeting not based on inputs and measurable outcomes (Granof & Khumawala, 2011). However, it is imperative to note that an object-of-expenditure budget may also be a performance, program, zero-based budget or any other type under consideration, simply due to changing budgeting terminologies. As a result of this lopsided pattern based on cutting back inputs without optimizing outputs, many countries later on adopted performance-based budgets. GOK (2011b) asserts that line-item budgeting does not link government objectives to deliverables, is not results-oriented, ignores linkage with government policy and furthermore, the line-item budget and its equal counterpart line-item control permit modest room for flexibility.

Zero-Based Budgeting

Zero-based budgeting (ZBB) is a variant of program-based budgets (Granof and Khumawala, 2011), which was introduced in Kenya in the late 1970s to counter the drawbacks of merely incremental budgeting (GOK, 2011b). ZBB annually examines each program or activities from a clean slate, meaning budgets are developed from a zero base. Under ZBB both current and proposed activities are commonly reviewed and ranked on a priority basis, and budget request made in the form of a decision package made up of expressed objectives, alternative means of achievement, repercussions of not undertaking the activity, and inputs, outputs and outcomes (Granof & Khumawala, 2011).

In Kenya the ZBB approach has been used for occasional expenditure reviews but not per se in the preparation of yearly budgets, since the process is complicated (GOK, 2011b). Furthermore the GOK manual observes that the preparation of ZBB budgets requires more time, training and it is difficult to define and justify decision units and packages.

Performance Budgets

According to Granof and Khumawala (2011), performance budgets focus on predetermined measurable elements of efforts, services and achievements, unambiguously linking expenditures to operational objectives. Performance budgeting is not based on incremental budgeting but on the division of proposed expenditures into activities against a set of a workload measures pertaining to that activity performed to cost, thus, the emphasis is on work to be done (World Bank, 1998).

Performance budgets have been used instead of or to complement traditional line-item-object classification budgets (Granof & Khumawala, 2011). Performance budgeting is based on program budgeting but utilizes performance criteria as the basis for preparing the budget (GOK, 2011b). Overall, performance budgets have been found to be inefficient, as they delink the annual budget cycle from future plans, and do not account for the effectiveness of the expenditures. This led to a change of focus to program-based budgets (World Bank, 1998).

Program-Based Budgets

The most common type of performance budget is the program-based budget, which identifies resources and results as activities rather than line items (Granof and Khumawala, 2011). Program-based budgets seek to balance budgetary choices among competing policies. Program-based budgeting uses objectives as variables, delinking program costs from the program outcomes (World Bank, 1998). The line-item principle of allocation does not disappear, but item classification is less detailed, allowing for flexibility between budget votes (expenditure dockets), hence enabling the government to prioritize and enhance decision-making (GOK, 2011b).

Program-based budgeting (PBB) seeks to enhance the prioritization of budgeting expenditure and assist government ministries in Kenya to deliver services efficiently and effectively (GOK, 2011b). Crucial to program-based budgets is the program, which comprises a set of interrelated activities working toward a common purpose (GOK, 2011b), in other words, a public policy objective with necessary steps to accomplish it on a multi-year basis which is measurable (World Bank, 1998).

Program Review and Forward Budgeting

Before the introduction of program review and forward budgeting (PRFB) in the early 1990s, the first key reform in the budgeting process, the Government prepared two budget estimates, one for recurrent and the other for development purposes, with the MOF providing the ceilings for both estimates to line ministries (GOK, 2011a). The GOK manual further expounds that all other ministries thereafter would prepare itemized budgets and forward them to the Treasury for appraisal, endorsement and compilation. The rationale for introducing PRFB was to link the annual budgets to the development plan, thus tying planning to the budget (GOK, 2011b).

The output of PRFB was an annual document providing rolling estimates for a three-year period with detailed indicative resource allocations (Kiringai & West, 2002). The key challenges of PRFB were that Parliament had no oversight authority over the three-year estimates, economic planning was hampered by lack of data and a skilled workforce, there was over-reliance on foreign experts and little consultation, if any. As a result, the public budget was less effective as a planning tool compared to later periods (GOK, 2011a). The Institute of Economic Affairs (IEA, 2007) confirms that the forward budget approach became of little significance with the introduction of MTEF, explained later.

Budget Rationalization Program

A budget rationalization program was adopted due to endemic weaknesses in channeling resources to key areas and the need to justify the development plan priorities. This budget approach required a clear justification before allocation of any resources. The main objective was to reduce wastage and improve productivity of scarce public resources through prioritization and rationalized channeling (GOK, 2011a). Other related objectives were to improve centralized planning and budgeting at the Treasury, increase the contributions of resources from user fees (cost-sharing) and rationalize the structure of external financial assistance (IEA, 2007).

The Bretton Woods institutions, the World Bank and the International Monetary Fund, insisted on accountability and waste reduction and thus provided oversight over this approach. The budget rationalization approach was participatory in nature as all budget vote-holders and program managers were required to justify resource needs to the Treasury before an allocation was made.

The performance of budgets was also closely monitored to ensure that resource use was in line with the justification for the allocation. As more emphasis continued to be laid on the channeling of resources to priority areas, it emerged that public investment project performance needed closer scrutiny. Despite the adoption of a budget rationalization program, revenue generation did not increase as anticipated, and donors never provided additional funds to support government initiatives as envisaged (GOK, 2011a). Besides, the political will to curb wastage and align expenditure to real priorities proved to be a challenge, and the coveted rationalization program never translated into meaningful results, leading to the adoption of a Public Investment Program (PIP).

Public Investment Program

The Public Investment Program involved the evaluation and ranking of public investments, the development of links between program priorities, and the concentration of resources on core investments. This approach helped control project choices based on priorities and improved implementation success (Kiringai & West, 2002). According to GOK (2011a) the justification for PIP was to support the use of a more elaborate tool for planning and prioritization of expenditures. It was hoped that PIP would strengthen project cycles, help scrutinize public-sector capital-creation targets, assist in coordinating donor funds, realign public expenditure management (PEM) to departmental priorities, help with project scheduling, oversee state enterprises and provide fair forecasting of future recurrent expenditure (GOK, 2011a). PIP categorizes projects as core, high priority or others. After the introduction of the MTEF in mid-2000, the Government discarded PIP since, under MTEF, budgets focus on priority areas (IEA, 2007).

The Medium-Term Expenditure Framework

A key determinant of how utilization of public resources is geared toward realization of the common good is the functioning of the public expenditure management (PEM) system (Khainga et al., 2007) since it fosters fiscal discipline, priorities and operational efficiency. To assess the functioning of the PEM system in 1997, the Kenyan Government undertook a critical public expenditure review (PER) to unearth expenditure patterns against sustainability, growth and equity policy as envisaged over the years (Khainga et al., 2007). The review found significant mismatches between public expenditure trends and economic growth, equity and budget implementation (Khainga et al., 2007) and recommended the strengthening of PEM system.

However, the recommendations were not adopted until the 2000/01 fiscal year, when the MTEF budget process was introduced to enhance fiscal discipline, expenditure prioritization and operational efficiency. GOK (2011a) defines

MTEF as "a transparent planning and budget formulation process that attempts to improve the decision-making process so as to link Government policies, priorities and requirements within limited resource constraints."

In Kenya as a result of problems experienced in ensuring that line ministries and implementing agencies remained within their expenditure ceilings, there was a need to create a structured framework for setting ceilings and monitoring compliance through consultation and realignment of the planning process. Thus, MTEF sought to address the three critical issues of comprehensive financial discipline (absolute control of revenue and expenditure), efficient allocation of resources in line with set priorities and program objectives) and technical efficiency in provision of public services (GOK, 2011a). Hence, the MTEF model places Kenyan government policies and priorities at the heart of the budget planning as shown in Figure 6.1.

From Figure 6.1 it is evident that the key units in the MTEF budget cycle are policy development, the MTEF budget process, budget implementation, accounting and monitoring, and evaluation and audit (GOK, 2011a). MTEF ushered in a consultative and collaborative process that brought more players on board. However, the responsibility for the direction and control of the budget process remained within the Treasury.

To foster planning, in 2003 the new government regime introduced radical socio-economic development measures to reduce poverty and foster economic development. The economic recovery strategy (ERS) for wealth and employment creation 2003–2007 paper (GOK, 2003) was geared toward growing the economy, improving infrastructure, reducing poverty and promoting good governance. Fundamental to economic development was a raft of budgetary and public expenditure reforms aimed at trimming down government expenditure relative to GDP and redeploying expenditure toward development areas and critical sectors among others.

ERS was replaced in 2008 by the Kenya Vision 2030, a long-term development plan aimed at bringing the macro-economic stability needed to transform the country into a middle-income economy by 2030 (GOK, 2008a). The implementation of Vision 2030 was centered on five-year medium-term plans (MTPs). The first MTP ran from 2008 to 2012, while the second MTP runs from 2013 to 2017.

After the promulgation of the Constitution of Kenya on August 27, 2010, a devolved governing structure comprising national and county governments was endorsed, paving way for the establishment of national and county governments in year 2013. As a result, the budgeting process changed from being a centralized to a devolved system. This notwithstanding, the economic planning perspective remained the same, mirrored on a long-term plan (Vision 2030), medium-term plans (MTPs) and on short-term forecasts (annual budgets). The Constitution of Kenya, 2010, sections 215–219 and 220–224 outlines the general principles and framework of public finance, and further states that revenue collected nationally shall be equitably distributed among the national and county governments.

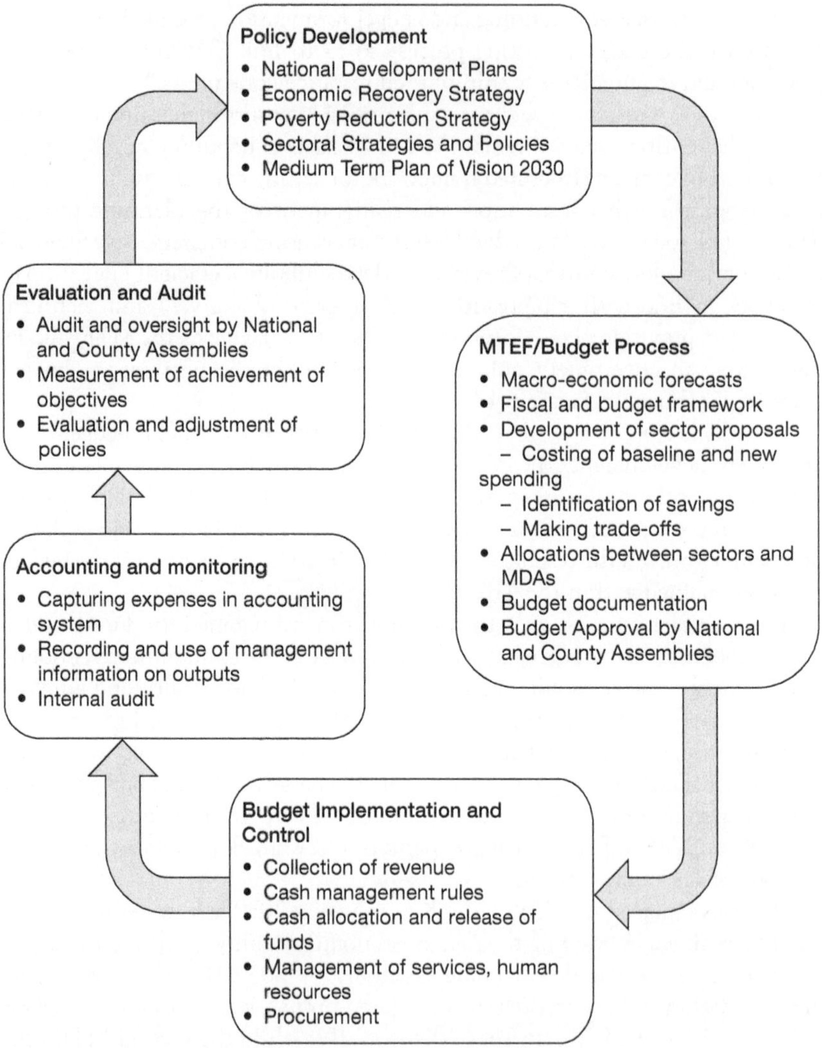

Figure 6.1 MTEF budget framework
Source: Adapted from GOK (2011a)

With the decentralization of government and the creation of 47 county governments new requirements for preparation and approval of national and county budgets came into being. The budget-making process is spelled out in the Public Finance Management Act, 2012, section 35 for the national and section 125 for the county governments, together with the County Government Act, 2012 section 91 (C), taking cognizance of subsequent amendments. The National Treasury is tasked with the responsibility of preparing the national

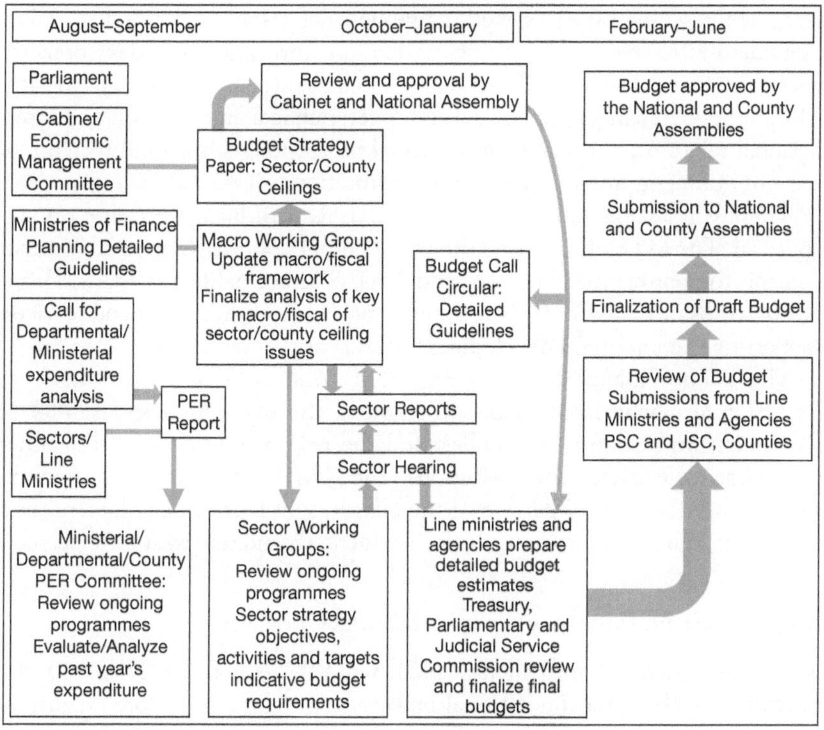

Figure 6.2 The MTEF process in Kenya
Source: Adapted from GOK (2011a)

budget while county treasuries are charged with formulating county budgets. The process follows the MTEF model.

It is imperative to note that the MTEF budget process consists of three milestones and timelines, namely; macro planning (August–September), analyzing sectoral priorities (October–January), and preparation and approval of budgets (February–June) as shown in Figure 6.2. The first phase utilizes a top-down approach to set macro targets, define development premises, and review the past year's revenue and expenditure trends. The second phase involves a macro-economic working group comprising economists from the Ministry of Planning, the Treasury, the Central Bank of Kenya, Kenya Revenue Authority and the government policy think tank, the Kenya Institute for Public Policy Analysis and Research (KIPPRA). MTEF requires that expenditure be allocated to prioritized national development areas (GOK, 2011a).

The macro-economic working group is responsible for the development of a suitable macro-economic framework to be used in the planning process. The group's main output is a budget strategy paper (GOK, 2011a). To achieve allocation efficiency as envisaged, MTEF segments the economy into broad sectors represented by sector working groups. For instance, the Budget Policy Statement 2015 specified 10 sectors: agriculture, rural and urban development; energy, infrastructure and ICT; general economic and commercial affairs; health; education; governance, justice, law and order; public administration and international relations; national security; social protection, culture and recreation; and environment protection, water and sanitation (GOK, 2015).

The last phase, as shown in Figure 6.2, deals with budget preparation and approval. The MTEF introduced the use of output controls as opposed to input controls to improve the allocation and usage of scarce public resources. This is meant to ensure delivery of the maximum output of specified goods and services, supporting the long-term development agenda at the lowest cost.

The Public Finance Management (PFM) Act, 2012, provides guidelines for effective management of public finances, the oversight responsibility of Parliament and County Assemblies, and the responsibilities of all the other public finance management institutions. The PFM Act caps recurrent expenditure at a maximum of 70 percent of the budget, split between emoluments and operations, and maintenance while development expenditure is set at 30 percent.

Steps in the National Government Budget Process

The Public Finance Management (PFM) Act, 2012 sections 25–27, and 35–45, provides guidelines for the national budget-making process. Before August 30 every year, the cabinet secretary of the National Treasury is required to issue a circular guiding the budget process. The circular consists of a detailed timeline schedule, format for reviewing and projecting revenues and expenditures, key priority areas, manner of public participation in the budget process, and the plan to be adopted for capturing budget data.

The National Treasury prepares a budget review and outlook paper (BROP) for approval by the Budget Committee of the National Assembly and subsequently submits the same by September 30 of every year to the National Assembly. The BROP contains an evaluation of the fiscal performance for the preceding year against the budget appropriation, discrepancies from the latest macro-economic analysis and financial forecast, and actual financial performance position from the recent Budget Policy Statement.

Section 25 of the PFM Act, 2012, requires the National Treasury to present to the Cabinet a Budget Policy Statement (BPS) not later than February 15 every year for approval. The National Treasury prepares a BPS that spells out the broad strategic priorities and policy goals guiding the national and county governments in preparing their budgets for the next financial year and over the medium term. The BPS contains an evaluation of current economic conditions and the financial situation over the medium term, and the state of affairs of Government revenues, expenditures, borrowing, and expenditure limits for the next year and over the medium term. In a nutshell the national budget process involves:

1. preparation of an integrated development plan as the basis for short and long-term planning;
2. prioritizing medium-term financial and economic focus areas;
3. providing estimates of revenues and expenditures in the form of the Budget Policy Statement;
4. approval of Budget Policy Statement by Parliament;
5. preparing and submitting of budget estimates for the National Assembly;
6. adoption of the estimates by the National Assembly;
7. enacting the appropriation bill and any other necessary laws needed to implement the budget;
8. implementing the budget;
9. accounting and evaluating all budgeted items;
10. reviewing and reporting progress after three months; and
11. promotion of public participation.

Other milestones and deadlines for every year are: April 30, when budget estimates are submitted to National Assembly and June 30, when budget estimates and the appropriation bill are approved.

Steps in the County Government Budget Process

The county government budget-making process is similar to the national process, but at a lower level. The Public Finance Management (PFM) Act, 2012 sections 117–118, 125–137 and 189 provides guidelines for the county government budget-making process. County treasuries have roles similar to those of the National Treasury. The Public Finance Management Act, 2012, tasks the management of budget process for each county to the county executive committee member in charge of finance (CECMFF). Each CECMFF is expected to issue a circular setting out guidelines to be followed in the budget process before August 30 each year.

The circular among other things specifies the timeframe for budget preparation, techniques for appraisal and projection of revenues and expenditures, key priority areas, guidelines for public participation in budget process, and the format for the documentation process in line with acceptable budget practices. Other yearly milestones and deadlines are as follows:

- September 1, county development plan is submitted;
- September 30, county BROP is submitted;
- February 28, county fiscal strategy paper (FSP) is submitted;
- April 30, budget estimates are submitted; and
- June 30, budget estimates and county appropriation bill are approved.

The County Budget and Economic Forum, comprising the Governor, County Executive Committee and representatives from a broad spectrum, marks the beginning of the budgeting process by convening a forum for a county budget consultative event that leads to the preparation of the county development plan, the county fiscal strategy paper and county budget review and outlook paper (C-BROP). The county budget-making process involves:

1. preparation of an integrated county development plan as the basis for short- and long-term planning;
2. setting priorities for medium-term financial and economic focus areas;
3. providing estimates of revenues and expenditures;
4. approval of the county fiscal strategy paper (C-FSP, containing the strategic priorities for the county government, estimates, revenue, expenditure, and deficit for the subsequent financial year);
5. preparing and submitting budget estimates to the county assembly;
6. adoption of the estimates by the county assembly;
7. enaction of the county appropriation law and any other necessary laws needed to implement the budget;
8. passing of the appropriation bill, paving the way to approval of the finance bill;
9. implementing the budget; and
10. accounting for and evaluating all budgeted items.

Figure 6.3 shows that two stages are critical in the budget preparation process, the strategic and operational phases. The strategic phase entails converting policy goals into financial terms given the prevailing social-economic situation. Revenue projections are also made in order to determine the county government financial situation This leads to submission of budget estimates to the county

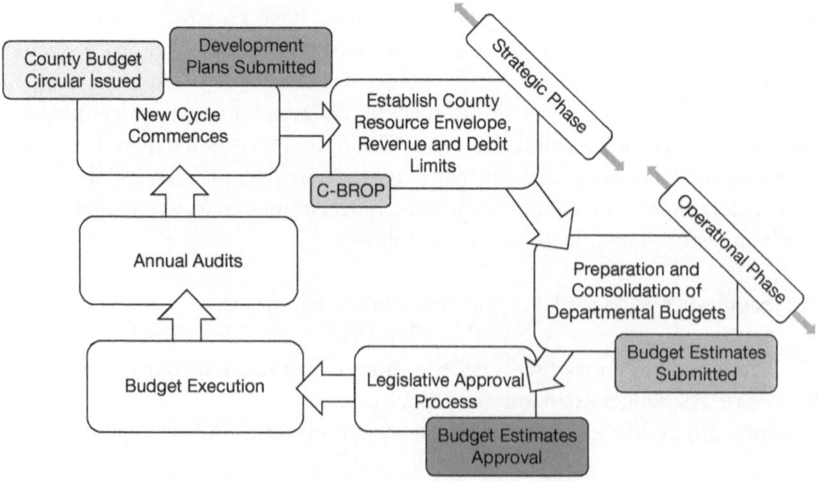

Figure 6.3 County budget cycle
Source: GOK (2014)

assembly for approval. The operational phase takes care of the actual budget preparation process.

There is limited fiscal decentralization such that counties can levy certain local taxes, which must be included in their budgets. At the county level budget preparation is more consultative and the people are given a chance to air their views and learn the priorities of the county government. However, the devolved governing structure and decentralized budgeting approach are still in formative years, and there is room for further changes and deeper engagement with the national Government on contentious issues. Recent reports show that part of the allocations received in the first quarter of the 2014/2015 fiscal year by the majority of the counties was spent on recurrent expenditure at the expense of the development agenda as stipulated in the PFM Act, 2012, and as per the requirements of the MTEF.

There are many challenges in budget preparation, approval and implementation. Some officials in the county treasuries are new and not yet fully conversant with the requirements of the law. This poses challenges and delays in the budget-making process. The county assembly members have often been cited as a stumbling block in the budget approval process where they have insisted on getting more resources to their wards than can be provided. Budget absorption especially for development purposes has been very low partly due to slow approval processes and poor planning by the county executives. These challenges are expected to lessen as county governments shape up.

The Kenya Public Budget Legal Framework

Kenya's public budgeting legal framework can be traced back from the pre-independence period to the present day. The Exchequer and Audit Act, of the pre-independence Kenyan Laws was enacted in 1955 largely borrowed from UK laws to guide the control of public funds. The act became the guiding law for the approval, control and audit of public funds and entities for many years.

As in most of the Commonwealth countries, the public budget process was therefore inherited from Westminster practices. Chapter VII of the old Constitution of Kenya (GOK, 1963) provided for the preparation of the revenue and expenditure estimates of the Government (including judiciary and Parliament) by the MOF. Those estimates of revenue and expenditure would then be tabled together with an appropriation bill to Parliament, for approval of withdrawal of funds from the consolidated fund. The constitution did not prescribe time requirements on the tabling of the estimates and the appropriation bill. However, it was standard practice for the estimates to be prepared and laid before Parliament in mid-June, before the start of the next financial year.

The constitution also allowed for the charging of certain non-discretionary expenditure to the consolidated fund. These included salaries of constitutional office holders and external debt service. All withdrawals from the consolidated fund needed the approval of the Auditor and Controller General. If, for whatever reasons, the appropriation bill did not get approval before the beginning of the next financial year, the constitution allowed for the withdrawal of funds necessary for the continuation of government services, not exceeding one-half of the tabled estimates pending approval of the appropriation bill. This overarching framework to public budgeting remained in place until the promulgation of the Constitution of Kenya, 2010, the enactment of the Public Finance Management Act, 2012 and the County Government Act, 2012.

The Constitution of Kenya, 2010

Chapter 12 of the Constitution of Kenya, 2010, retained most of the provisions contained in the old constitution albeit with greater clarity and new additions. The new constitution created new funds, offices and introduced additional requirements.

Budget Cycle

The constitution explicitly dictates the time for tabling of the budget estimates. It requires that the estimates of revenue and expenditure for the following year be tabled before the National Assembly at least two months before the end of the current financial year. These are accompanied by parliamentary and judiciary estimates.

Establishment of New Funds

In addition to the consolidated fund, the constitution created three new public funds: the equalization, contingency and revenue funds. The equalization fund was created with a requirement that 0.5 percent of all national government revenue be deposited in it. The purpose of the fund is to provide basic services to marginalized areas in order to bring them up to par with the rest of the country. The revenue fund was created for county governments to handle county government funds, while the contingencies fund was established to take care of unforeseen and urgent expenditures.

Creation of the Office of the Controller of Budget (OCB)

The office of the controller of budget (OCB) was created as a constitutional office to oversee the implementation of the budgets of the national and county governments. Under the old constitutional dispensation this role was carried out by the Controller and Auditor-General. The need for greater oversight in government expenditure led to the introduction of this vital office.

Separation of Powers and Budgeting

The constitution grants the other organs of governance, namely the judiciary and Parliament the power to prepare their own budget estimates for consideration and approval by the National Assembly. The two organs' estimates are considered for approval alongside the estimates submitted by the cabinet secretary of the National Treasury.

Creation of the Commission on Revenue Allocation

The commission on revenue allocation (CRA) was created to facilitate equitable sharing of national revenue between the national and county governments, and make suggestions and recommendations to the Senate, national and county executives and assemblies.

Financial Acts

The Public Finance Management Act, 2012

The Public Finance Management Act, 2012, was enacted to address gaps in existing laws and strengthen the public finance management practices in the Government. It is the underlying statute guiding the management of public finances by the national and county governments. The act spells out the oversight responsibility of Parliament and county assemblies, the different responsibilities of government entities, and the accountability of public officers. The act also creates the intergovernmental budget and economic council, which is a consultative forum for ensuring common understanding among the national and county governments on matters of budgeting and economic management.

The County Government Act, 2012

The County Government Act, 2012 establishes the power and functions of the county governments and their responsibilities to deliver services and other purposes.

Kenya's legal framework is made up of the constitution as the supreme law and the Public Finance Management Act, 2012. The County Government Act, 2012, entrenches budget-making requirements for county governments. The law provides both broad anchorage of the budget process and also gives detailed step-by-step requirements and responsibilities of all the parties involved. While there are no glaring gaps in the legal framework, implementation often presents challenges that can then be addressed through any necessary amendments.

The Budget Institutions

There are a number of institutions that are involved in the budget process at both the national and county levels in Kenya.

National Budget Institutions and Responsibilities

The key organs involved directly or indirectly in the preparation of budgets at the national level include the National Treasury, National Assembly, Senate, the Office of Controller of Budgets, Commission on Revenue Allocation, Kenya Revenue Authority (KRA), Central Bank of Kenya (CBK), Ministry of Devolution and Planning, Intergovernmental Budget and Economic Council (IEBEC), and Judicial and Parliamentary Service Commissions (JSC and PSC) as presented in Table 6.1.

From Table 6.1 it is discernible that 11 institutions play pivotal budgetary roles as expounded further herein.

Table 6.1 National Budget Institutions and Responsibilities

National Budget Institution	*Responsibilities*
National Treasury	Develop, execute and oversee macro-economic policies in expenditure and revenue Marshal internal and external resources with a view to cater for national and county government budgetary needs Prepare of the National Budget and coordinate of the preparation of the Judiciary and Parliamentary budgets Prepare Budget Policy Statement and Budget Review and Outlook Paper Submit estimates and draft bills for approval by Cabinet and Parliament
National Assembly	Oversee national budgets Discuss the estimates of the Judiciary, Parliament and Executive Approve budgets Appropriate government funds
Senate	Oversee County revenues Oversee revenue allocation among County Governments
The Office of Controller of Budgets	Approve withdrawal of funds from the Consolidated Fund and all other public funds
Commission of Revenue Allocation	Recommend formula for equitable distribution of revenue between the National and County Governments Develop revenue policies for marginalized counties Forward recommendations to Cabinet, Senate and Parliament
Kenya Revenue Authority	Collect taxes on behalf of the government, and advise on tax reforms and projected targets
Central Bank of Kenya	Advise National Treasury on monetary and fiscal matters
Ministry of Devolution and Planning	Facilitate in preparation of development plans
Intergovernmental Budget and Economic Council	Provide a consultative forum linking the National and County Governments
Judicial Commission	Prepare and present Judiciary estimates to Parliament
Parliamentary Commission	Prepare and present Parliamentary estimates to Parliament

The National Treasury

The National Treasury is responsible for the preparation of the national budget and coordination of the preparation of the judiciary and parliamentary budgets. The National Treasury also prepares the Budget Policy Statement, factoring in the views of the Commission of Revenue Allocation, County Governments, Parliamentary Service Commission, Judicial Service Commission, the public and other interested groups.

National Assembly

The National Assembly holds oversight authority over the budget preparation and implementation process. The National Assembly Budget Committee is the parliamentary committee tasked with budgetary issues pertaining to: discussing the Budget Policy Statement and estimates, monitoring of budgets, review of financial statements and documents, and presenting the appropriation bill to the National Assembly for approval. The parliamentary budget office is responsible for providing expert advice, preparing budget projections, considering budget proposals, publicizing budgets and facilitating analysis and approval.

Senate

Under article 96 of the Constitution of Kenya, 2010, the role of the Senate is to safeguard and address the concerns of county citizenry and oversee governance of the counties. The Senate Budget Committee is entrusted with scrutiny of the County Allocation of Revenue Bill, Division of Revenue Bill, financial statements and other documents necessary to enhance management of county financial matters.

The Office of Controller of Budget

The office of the Controller of Budget is responsible for approving withdrawals of funds from the consolidated fund and all other government funds.

Commission for Revenue Allocation

The commission for revenue allocation is responsible for developing revenue sharing and allocation criteria. It drafts the revenue sharing and revenue allocation bills in consultation with the National Treasury.

Kenya Revenue Authority

The KRA is the government's tax collection agent. It advises the treasury on level and projected growth of tax revenues, and on tax reforms, and provides government revenue estimates. A representative of the authority also sits in the macro-economic working group that develops spending ceilings for various government ministries and implementing agencies.

The Central Bank of Kenya

The CBK is responsible for formulating monetary policy, promoting price stability, and issuing currency among others (GOK, 2010).

Ministry of Devolution and Planning

The Ministry of Devolution and Planning is responsible for providing the national and county treasuries with macro-economic statistics and economic surveys (through the Kenya National Bureau of Statistics), facilitating preparation of national and county development plans and coordinating county governments' planning activities.

Intergovernmental Budget and Economic Council

The Intergovernmental Budget and Economic Council provides a consultative forum for national and county governments, on issues related to BSP, BROP and the medium-term debt management strategy, budgeting, borrowing, allocation of funds from the consolidated fund, equitable distribution of resources and other matters of mutual concern. The Deputy President is the chairperson; other members include the cabinet secretary, a representative from the National Treasury and the person in charge of intergovernmental relations, and representatives from the PSC, JSC, and Chairpersons of the Commission for Revenue Allocation and the Council of Governors.

Judicial Service Commission

The Constitution of Kenya, 2010, section 173, spells out that the Chief Registrar every year will prepare estimates of expenditure and forward them to Parliament for approval.

Parliamentary Service Commission

The Constitution of Kenya, 2010, section 127, prescribes that the PSC is responsible for preparing estimates of expenditure of parliamentary service and presenting them to Parliament for approval. The PSC is also in charge of controlling the budget.

County Budget Institutions and Responsibilities

The County Government Act, 2012, mandates the County Treasury, County Assembly Service Board (CASB) and County Planning Unit with matters relating to preparation of budgets as herein explained.

The County Treasury

Each County Treasury is responsible for the preparation and implementation of the county government's budget.

The County Assembly Service Board

The County Assembly Service Board (CASB) is responsible for preparing annual estimates of the expenditure of the county assembly service and forwarding them to the county assembly for approval, including exercising budgetary control.

County Planning Unit

The County Government Act, 2012, places great importance on development planning, and places responsibility for developing plans on the County Planning Unit. The unit is in charge of organizing and facilitating the development of integrated plans that are linked to the national planning framework. The County Government Act, 2012, envisages a five-year county integrated development plan in every county that also incorporates a 10-year county sectoral plan for every department.

There are several institutions involved in the budget process at the national and county government levels. These institutions are created and protected by law. At the budget preparation phase, the most significant institution at the national level, is the National Treasury, which controls and coordinates all the other institutions to ensure harmony in the budget preparation process. The ultimate responsibility for the timeliness, accuracy and efficacy of the budgets drawn up rests squarely with the National Treasury.

However, this responsibility must be exercised within a non-interfering and consultative and collaborative manner. At the county level, the buck stops with the County Treasury, which is in charge of ensuring the other organs move in tune with its budget timelines. At the approval phase, Parliament takes overall responsibility while the county assemblies control approvals at the county level. During implementation, the Controller of Budget has the final say on public expenditure for all ministries, agencies and departments as well as the county governments.

Revenue Sources and Expenditure Items

The budget of Kenya has evolved significantly in structure since independence, but it is still largely dependent on donor support and external loans. However, in the recent past foreign financial assistance has declined. Local taxes and domestic borrowings today account for the bulk of government revenue.

Since the year 2002, Kenya has grown its tax revenue base significantly due to major reforms undertaken by the Kenya Revenue Authority. As such, the country is very well internally financed. The country however, remains a major borrower from bilateral and multilateral partners as well as in the international financial markets. This has been necessitated by heavy investment in infrastructure development over the last decade.

Government Revenue

The major source of Kenyan Government revenue is taxation, user fees, sale of assets and dividends; other investment income forms an insignificant proportion of government revenue. The government's tax revenue sources include income tax (pay as you earn and corporate tax), excise duty, value-added tax, import duty, stamp duty, fees and charges, land rates and other levies. On the other hand the non-tax revenues include domestic and foreign borrowings, grants, dividends, surpluses from regulatory authorities, and loan repayments. Government revenue has grown tremendously over the last 10 years as shown in Table 6.2.

As is evident from Table 6.2 Government revenue generation tripled from KES309 billion in year 2005/06 to KES1 trillion by end of the 2013/14 financial year. This translates to a revenue growth rate of an average of 15 percent per annum. Total revenue to GDP averaged over 24 percent during this period. The growth in tax revenue has allowed the country to be more self-reliant in financing budgets compared to the 1980s and 1990s, when donor funding was the key determinant. Several significant reasons explain this impressive revenue performance. First, the use of fiscalized electronic devices (FEDs), especially electronic tax registers (ETRs) for collecting value-added tax (VAT) introduced in 2005 has been instrumental in growing revenue base and increasing compliance. Figure 6.4 depicts key government revenue sources over this period.

From Table 6.2 and Figure 6.4 it is clear that during the 2013/14 financial year income tax collections provided the most revenue (KES459 billion), followed by VAT (KES236 billion) then excise duty and loyalties (KES159 billion), next custom duty (KES103 billion), and lastly, other taxes and levies (KES11 billion). This may be attributed to a number of reasons. First, Government has made tax compliance an important criterion for awarding its business. Therefore, private businesses that deal with the Government must be tax compliant. Second, the introduction of mandatory annual tax returns for individuals and corporates has increased compliance. Third, the KRA has also been educating and creating awareness about the patriotic duty to pay taxes. Lastly, the formal employment sector has been growing in tandem with economic growth hence offering a strong tax base of employed workers.

Government Expenditure

The main government expenditure items remain salaries and wages for civil servants and investment in infrastructure and services delivery. As per the functional classification of expenditures, the government budget has been

Table 6.2 Government Tax Revenue Sources and Share of GDP

KES Millions	*2005/6*	*2006/7*	*2007/8*	*2008/9*	*2009/10*	*2010/11*	*2011/12*	*2012/13*	*2013/14*
Income Tax	114,629.06	130,719.00	165,155.00	193,959.00	219,496.84	272,263.87	328,908.78	378,345.09	459,300.14
VAT	79,925.91	96,497.01	115,016.50	133,882.55	141,970.69	171,880.75	176,386.07	198,409.25	236,522.99
Excise duty, royalties etc.	61,709.65	76,111.19	88,836.37	103,309.33	99,335.02	108,701.54	105,771.60	115,766.42	159,419.76
Customs duty	29,861.43	40,235.00	46,949.00	52,051.00	57,205.81	66,670.45	76,473.85	84,073.92	102,921.68
Other taxes and levies	2,542.81	3,000.94	4,590.22	5,347.06	5,624.99	7,152.14	8,347.41	9,601.06	10,916.42
Total Domestic taxes	**288,668.86**	**346,563.14**	**420,547.09**	**488,548.94**	**523,633.35**	**626,668.75**	**695,887.71**	**786,195.74**	**969,080.99**
Non-tax revenue	20,747.14	25,425.91	22,537.89	27,262.97	19,311.73	24,741.25	29,634.07	44,123.82	37,781.04
Total Revenue	**309,416.00**	**371,989.05**	**443,084.98**	**515,811.91**	**542,945.08**	**651,410.00**	**725,521.78**	**830,319.56**	**1,006,862.03**
Growth	**8%**	**20%**	**19%**	**16%**	**5%**	**20%**	**11%**	**14%**	**21%**
Percentage of Total Revenue to GDP	22%	23%	24%	25%	23%	25%	24%	24%	27%

Source: Adapted from Statistical Abstracts, Economic Surveys (2005-2014), Nairobi: Kenya National Bureau of Statistics

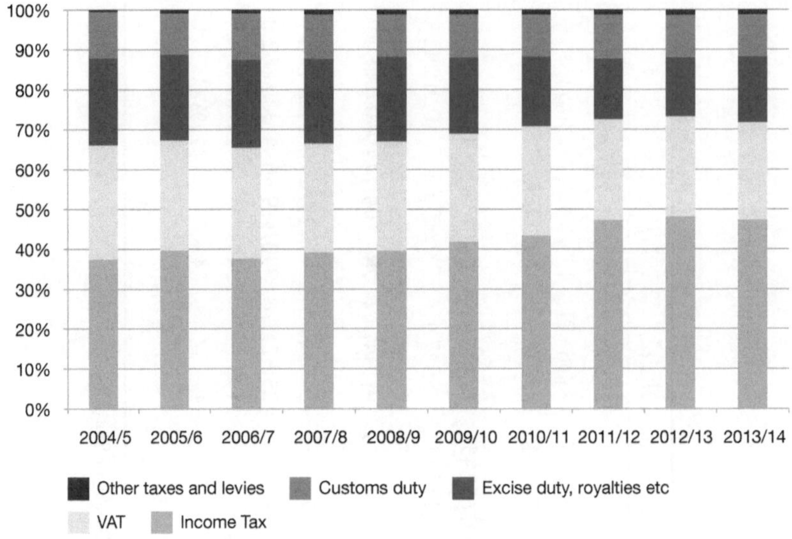

Figure 6.4 Government tax revenue by source

Source: Adapted from Statistical Abstracts, Economic Surveys (2005–2014), Niarobi: Kenya National Bureau of Statistics

changing in response to new government priorities. Since 2002, significant allocation has been made to education, following the implementation of free primary education. In 2012, partial secondary school tuition payments began to be offered, further increasing spending on education as presented in Table 6.3.

From Table 6.3 it is discernible that education accounted for 19 percent (KES302 billion) of the total government expenditure during the 2013/2014 financial year. The Government spent over KES310 billion on economic-related activities due to intensified efforts to create additional infrastructure especially in the energy sector, transport and communications, including world-class port and airport facilities and regional transit corridors.

Public order and safety took KES201 billion, general public administration pocketed KES190 billion, national defense took KES81 billion, and health at KES39 billion accounted for the lowest expenditure. With devolution, some functions of government such as health were transferred to the county governments, hence expenditure was lower at the national level in the 2013/14 financial year.

Revenue Versus Expenditure

The Kenyan Government's budget has consistently had a deficit. These deficits, which are financed out of domestic and international borrowings, are presented in Table 6.4.

Table 6.3 Government Major Expenditures by Function of Government from 2005/6 to 2013/14 Financial Year (KES millions)

Expenditure	2005/6	2006/7	2007/8	2008/9	2009/10	2010/11	2011/12	2012/13	2013/14
Gen. Public Admin	54,188.20	52,697.90	117,320.60	86,939.93	105,149.03	121,749.35	110,557.55	167,978.60	190,309.08
Economic Affairs	49,488.60	71,420.70	99,037.80	154,203.38	153,390.16	201,723.32	202,061.54	257,604.51	310,833.56
Defence	25,608.60	25,122.90	36,741.80	41,209.46	53,663.88	54,384.18	65,035.52	72,728.57	80,535.99
Education	96,027.40	109,238.90	124,908.50	151,676.86	159,339.92	189,845.78	205,510.45	220,338.08	302,173.36
Health	22,963.70	27,517.60	30,282.50	36,121.90	37,353.42	47,910.58	61,103.11	71,851.74	38,533.49
Public Order and Safety	39,804.10	41,790.90	49,825.00	65,422.53	59,945.85	74,387.74	86,956.92	102,214.62	201,206.63
Others	144,510.60	181,056.60	199,964.10	237,431.47	220,518.36	266,225.26	285,483.60	348,680.24	444,008.85
Total Expenditure	**432,591.20**	**508,845.50**	**658,080.30**	**773,005.53**	**789,360.62**	**956,226.21**	**1,016,708.69**	**1,241,396.36**	**1,567,600.96**

Source: Adapted from Statistical Abstracts, Economic Surveys (2005-2014), Nairobi: Kenya National Bureau of Statistics.

Table 6.4 shows that the budget deficit has increased over the years from KES123 billion in 2005/06 to KES561 billion in 2013/14, mainly as a result of increasing government expenditure on salaries and wages, education, economic matters and infrastructure development. The deficit however remains below 15 percent of GDP.

Government Debt

As a result of increased tax revenue, the pressure on the Government to borrow, both domestically and internationally has eased. The bulk of government borrowing has been from the domestic market as illustrated in Table 6.5.

From Table 6.5 it is evident that external loans reduced significantly from KES434 billion in 2005/06 to KES46 billion by 2013/14. Similarly, domestic borrowings dropped from a high of KES254 billion in 2005/06 to KES83 billion within the same period, due to maturity in budgeting and fiscal stability.

The Kenyan revenue base has expanded in leaps and bounds over the last five decades. This is explained partly by overall growth and development of the economy but more importantly by legal and institutional reforms in tax administration. The KRA today can be cited as a success story among peer government revenue bodies. Automation and adoption of internet technologies has improved efficiency and sealed revenue leakage avenues, thereby boosting overall collection rates.

Expenditure patterns are closely linked to the development agenda being pursued. There is significant resonance between spending priorities and the government development agenda as evidenced by the large expenditures in education since 2003 when free primary education was introduced. With devolution of certain functions we have begun to notice a shift of national expenditures away from the devolved functions such as health.

Evaluation of the Budgeting Process

In the early days, budgeting was a challenging affair due to lack of necessary personnel with adequate knowledge of the budgeting processes. Incremental and line-item budgeting approaches were commonly used in preparing budgets that were often used as tools for controlling and commanding the economy. The economy was largely government-controlled and budgets were used not only to allocate resources but also set the prices of essential commodities. At that time, government budgets were shrouded in secrecy and were often used against the citizenry by unscrupulous government officials and businessmen especially by the hoarding of essential goods and front running.

After independence, the Government of Kenya embarked on training its human resources and could, today, easily pass as the holder of the largest pool of public sector economists and accountants in the East and Central Africa region. The evolution of the budget process has been linked to this expansion

Table 6.4 Government Revenue, Expenditure, and Budget Deficit

KSh. Millions	*2005/6*	*2006/7*	*2007/8*	*2008/9*	*2009/10*	*2010/11*	*2011/12*	*2012/13*	*2013/14*
Total Revenue	309,416.00	371,989.05	443,084.98	515,811.91	542,945.08	651,410.00	725,521.78	830,319.56	1,006,862.03
Total Expenditure	432,591.20	508,845.50	658,080.30	773,005.53	789,360.62	956,226.21	1,016,708.69	1,241,396.36	1,567,600.96
Budget deficit	**(123,175.20)**	**(136,856.45)**	**(214,995.32)**	**(257,193.62)**	**(246,415.54)**	**(304,816.21)**	**(291,186.91)**	**(411,076.80)**	**(560,738.93)**
Budget deficit to GDP	–8.7%	–8.4%	–11.8%	–12.2%	–10.4%	–11.9%	–9.6%	–12.1%	–14.8%

Source: Adapted from Statistical Abstracts, Economic Surveys (2005-2014), Nairobi: Kenya National Bureau of Statistics

Table 6.5 Domestic and External Loans

KSh. Millions	*2005/6*	*2006/7*	*2007/8*	*2008/9*	*2009/10*	*2010/11*	*2011/12*	*2012/13*	*2013/14*
External Loans	434,453.00	431,236.74	397,138.75	413,460.29	11,145.88	51,068.42	42,243.13	23,970.19	46,042.01
Internal Loans	253,501.00	286,450.76	318,402.12	334,996.13	151,479.26	92,498.00	76,036.61	169,776.28	83,648.78
Total Loans	**687,954.00**	**717,687.50**	**715,540.87**	**748,456.42**	**162,625.14**	**143,566.42**	**118,279.74**	**193,746.47**	**129,690.79**

Source: Adapted from Statistical Abstracts, Economic Surveys (2005-2014), Nairobi: Kenya National Bureau of Statistics.

of the human resource pool. As such, Kenya has kept abreast of international developments in public budgeting and promptly adopted and implemented positive changes to its budget process.

Development planning has been given a high priority by the government since independence. The government structure was constantly reviewed to ensure that planning mechanisms were working. The establishment of a separate Ministry of Planning in the 1970s is a testimony to the great commitment to succeed in the planning process. The 1980s were extremely vibrant in the development of both national plans and budgeting. It has been argued that if the development plans drawn up in the 1980s, particularly the Sessional Paper No. 1 of 1986, had been properly implemented, Kenya could have acquired the status of newly industrialized country in the 1990s, joining the four "Asian tigers." Implementation and political will seems to have waned in this period and there was more rhetoric than commitment. The government of the day was more preoccupied with power retention at the expense of the economy.

The PRFB initiative was successful as far as the need to lengthen the budget period was concerned. The transition from a single-year budget to multi-year budgets helped create a future-focused outlook to planning. It also ensured that there was greater coherence between plans and the annual budgets. The main pitfall of this system was the fact that the process did not allow for consultation beyond Government and there was no oversight by Parliament since the forward estimates were not approved by Parliament (GOK, 2011a).

The budget rationalization program was intended to address resource bottlenecks caused by budget constraints. The approach failed because resources from user fees and other non-tax sources did not increase as expected, while development partners (donors and aid agencies) failed to honor their commitments (GOK, 2011a).

The public investment program was, in theory, a very good approach to budgeting and general economic management. Its adoption in 1990 created new ways of looking at government spending priorities and evaluating results and outcomes. However, the budget approach did not achieve its intended objectives because of lack of government commitment and goodwill to cut back on costs or prioritize public spending and investment programs. The budget reforms were adopted by the Government more as dictates from the Bretton Woods institutions than as acts of self-will.

The MTEF approach has been married into the Kenyan budgeting and economic management process with great success. While the MTEF adoption journey started before 2000, the heralding of new governance measures under the third president of Kenya in 2002 saw significant changes in economic management and the conduct of government affairs. Under the new Government, goodwill and commitment regained its place in the budgeting process to see the MTEF become a great success. The main reason was a raft of new governance measures under the third president that saw significant changes in economic management and the conduct of government affairs.

Conclusion

The public budgeting process is an integral part of planning in any economy. The dynamism of the process and the quality of inputs (data) determines the efficacy of the final plan. In Kenya, significant efforts have gone into understanding the economy and planning for it. In the early years after independence, there was a general lack of skilled economists to handle the task but this has since changed. Deliberate government efforts in training and retraining economists have seen a reversal of the skills gap. While competition for professional economists remains high, the Government has developed several forums to ensure skills development and retention.

Budgeting in Kenya has always been a centralized function where the Treasury serves as the key budget institution. An analysis of the evolution of the budget systems shows concerted efforts to link budgeting to planning, prioritize the development agenda, and devolve participation in the budgeting process, all attributable to a raft of legal measures developed and enacted with a view to standardize and harmonize this vital exercise.

The early days were challenging but carried significant goodwill from the government. Development planning was given a high priority by the Government. The government structure was constantly reviewed to ensure that the planning mechanisms were working. The establishment of a separate Ministry of Planning in the 1970s is testimony to the great commitment to succeed.

Transparency in public budgeting is imposed to legitimize taxation and government spending. Budget reforms in Kenya have been geared toward increasing intergovernmental consultations, encompassing civil society requirements and generally embracing public participation in the budget process. The Budget Rationalization Program (BRP) as well as the Public Investment Program were in theory very good approaches to budgeting. Their adoption created new ways of looking at economic management. However, the programs did not achieve their intended results and had to be phased out because they were mostly dictates from the Bretton Woods institutions as conditionalities for budgetary support.

The presence of political will and support from the Government ensured success both in use of the MTEF approach in budgeting and in overall management of the economy. The momentum created by the Government of the third President from 2002 continues to drive the economy more than 10 years later. The MTEF budget cycle has a clearly laid out phase for public participation both at the national and county levels which greatly enhances transparency and acceptance. This is one of the best outcomes of budget reforms in Kenya over the years.

Kenya's budgeting process has a very solid backing in law. The understanding of the new laws by public officers is still low and the effects of some of the legal requirements are likely to take time to manifest. Budget institutions enjoy the protection of the constitution and office holders enjoy significant freedom in exercise of their legal duties. The appointment of budget office holders is also an open and competitive process, thereby ensuring only the most competent get to run the affairs of those offices.

The parliamentary oversight role has been strengthened and professionalized by the establishment of the Parliamentary Budget Office, with adequately trained economists. The county government budget structure is very well articulated in the law but it will take time before the legal requirements are fully put into practice.

The public budgeting process can be viewed as being a mixed bag of successes and failures. On one hand, lack of political will in budget rationalization in the 1980s and 1990s can be cited as a low point in the budgeting process. On the other hand, the MTEF approach has worked with resounding success. Looking forward, the decentralized program-based budgeting approach under MTEF as required by the new constitution has faced initial learning-curve problems but is expected to cut teeth and work smoothly.

Recommendations for Policy and Practice

The foregoing analysis of the evolution of the budget process suggests an up-to-date review and revision program. The following recommendations have the capacity to improve the budgeting process.

The government should document and keep updating its budget practices to create a legacy of literature that can be used by future planners as a learning tool. Allowing and encouraging researchers in academia to review and criticize past practices will create an avenue for improvement since only diagnosed ills can be treated.

With budgeting at county level it may prove tricky to maintain an up-to-date review of the planning processes. It is therefore recommended that treasuries continue to spearhead planning and reforming budget approaches. County treasuries staff should be trained and retrained to ensure a smooth take-off for the decentralized budget system. County treasury staff members play a vital liaison role and if possible they should be seconded from the National Treasury on a yearly rotation basis.

Participation and political will are essential for the success of plans especially with the many approval and oversight bodies that are involved in the budget process. The Government should professionalize economic management to minimize political interference.

References

Freeman, R.J., Shoulders, C.D., Allison, G.S., Patton, T. K., & Smith, Jr. G.R. (2011). *Government and nonprofit accounting: Theory and practice*, 9th ed. Upper Saddle River, New York: Pearson Education.

Government of Kenya. Economic Survey (2005–2014). Nairobi: Kenya National Bureau of Statistics.

Government of Kenya. National development plans (1964–2001). Nairobi: Government Printer.

Government of Kenya. Statistical abstract (2005–2014). Nairobi: Kenya National Bureau of Statistics.

Government of Kenya. (1963). The 1963 Independence Constitution of Kenya. Nairobi: Government Printer.

Government of Kenya. (2003). Economic recovery strategy for wealth and employment creation. Nairobi: Ministry of Planning and National Development.

Government of Kenya. (2008a). Vision 2030. Nairobi: Government Printer.

Government of Kenya. (2008b). Medium-term plan, 2008–2012. Nairobi: Government Printer.

Government of Kenya. (2010). The Constitution of Kenya, 2010. Nairobi: Government Printer.

Government of Kenya. (2011a). MTEF manual: Kenya budget process. Nairobi: Ministry of Finance, Treasury.

Government of Kenya. (2011b). Programme-based budgeting manual. Nairobi: Office of the Deputy Prime Minister and Ministry of Finance.

Government of Kenya. (2012). County Government Act, 2012. Nairobi: National Council for Law Reporting.

Government of Kenya. (2013). County Governments Public Finance Management Transition Act, 2013. Nairobi: National Council for Law Reporting.

Government of Kenya. (2014). County PFM training module, National Treasury. Unpublished, Nairobi: National Treasury.

Government of Kenya. (2015). Budget Policy statement: Enhancing economic transformation for a shared prosperity in Kenya. Nairobi: National Treasury.

Granof, M.H., & Khumawala, S.B. (2011). *Government and not-for-profit accounting.* 5th ed. River Street, Hoboken, NJ: John Wiley and Sons.

Institute of Economic Affairs. (2007). *The citizen's handbook on the budget: A guide to the budget process in Kenya,* 2nd ed. Nairobi: Institute of Economic Affairs.

Khainga, D., Kiriga, B., Ouma, S., & Njeru, J. (2007). *Governance in public expenditure: Key issues and challenges in Kenya.* Nairobi: KIPPRA Discussion Paper No. 77. Nairobi: Kenya Institute of Public Policy Research and Analysis.

Kiringai, J., & West, G. (2002). Budget reforms and the medium-term expenditure framework in Kenya. KIPPRA Working Paper No. 7. Nairobi: Kenya Institute of Public Policy Research and Analysis.

LeLoup, L.T. (2002). Budget theory for a new century. In Khan, A. & Hildreth, W.B. (Eds.) *Budget theory in the public sector* (pp. 1–21). Westport, CT: Quorum Books.

World Bank. (1998). *Public expenditure management handbook* (1998). Washington, DC: World Bank. Retrieved on March 2, 2015.

7 Public Budgeting in African Nations: The Case of Malawi

Happy Mickson Kayuni

Introduction

Malawi, a former British colony, is a small landlocked country located in the southern region of Africa. It is bordered by Tanzania to the North, Zambia to the West and Mozambique to the South West. According to the latest national population and housing census of 2008 Malawi has a population of 13.07 million (NSO, 2008) and over 80 percent of the population live in rural areas. The country's economy is largely agro-based. With such a huge population, it is one of the most densely populated countries in Africa.

According to key development indicators, Malawi is one of the poorest countries in the world. The third integrated household survey indicated that 50.7 percent of the population live below the poverty line with one-quarter in extreme poverty (NSO 2011). According to the UNDP's Human Development Index, Malawi is ranked on position 178 out of 187 countries in the world. The Mo Ibrahim 2014 human development indicator ranks Malawi at 28 out of 52 African countries. With a poor investment climate, the *2014 Doing Business Report* ranks Malawi at 171 out of 189 countries in the world.

Politically, Malawi attained independence on July 6, 1964 and in 2014 it celebrated 50 years of independence. The country was for close to 30 years (1964–1994) ruled by Dr. Kamuzu Banda through his Malawi Congress Party (MCP). His reign was well known for his dictatorial tendencies, and it witnessed a series of serious human rights violations. Only one political party, the MCP, was allowed to operate in the country and all other parties were banned. Dr. Banda himself was declared president of the country for life. After a series of demonstrations and a call for a change in political governance, a multi-party system was introduced, and following presidential and parliamentary elections held in 1994, the United Democratic Front (UDF) led by Bakili Muluzi emerged as winner. Muluzi ruled the country until 2004 when Bingu wa Mutharika took over through UDF but later formed his own party, the Democratic People's Party (DPP). Bingu wa Mutharika died while in office in April 2011 and Mrs. Joyce Banda, who was then vice president, assumed the office of presidency until she lost in the presidential elections of May 2014 to Peter Mutharika.

This paper discusses the budgetary process in Malawi from independence to the present. The paper argues that despite numerous reforms in the budgetary process, not much has been achieved. If the current scenario continues and the critical areas that impede the process are not addressed, the budget might not meaningfully become one of the tools for national development of the country. The first part focuses on conceptual issues; the second part briefly discusses the Malawi development and budgetary process from the colonial to the one-party era (1891–1964). The final part of the paper discusses the Malawi budgetary process from 1994 to the present before concluding.

Conceptual Issues

Budgeting and Development

It is well acknowledged that there is a link between a good national budget and a country's development, hence budgeting itself is essentially a key component in a government's plans for economic growth and stability. A government's budget facilitates the process of translating national policies or goals and political commitments into tangible decisions on such matters as how to source funds and allocation of these funds in specified sectors. A weak budget system implies that the decisions are likely to be faulty, and hence worsen conditions rather than facilitate the development of the country. Since the budget has such a significant impact on the everyday livelihood of the people as well as development in general, it is no wonder that it is generally thought that it should be heavily scrutinized and debated. According to Simson (2014), studies have shown that "countries with greater budget transparency spend public funds in more progressive ways." More importantly, he also adds that "greater budget transparency allows for better public engagement in the budget process, making politicians more sensitive to broad-based public interests."

As well as looking at the budget simply as a document, it is important to focus on the stages which it goes through:

1. formulation stage, when the government in power submits the budget plans;
2. approval stage, when Parliament debates and finally approves the plan (with amendments as necessary);
3. implementation stage, which includes monitoring and control of the plan by government; and
4. oversight stage, when institutions such as the national audit and Parliament assess the actual expenditure and also ask for accountability for the expenditure made.

In 2008 the Collaborative Africa Budget Reform Initiative's (CABRI) survey of 29 African countries showed that many countries surveyed had a form of top-down approach, which in most cases led to centralized decision-making powers during the budget formulation stage. Specifically, the results also suggest "that African legislatures have, on average, less institutional capacity for financial scrutiny than their counterparts in the OECD." More importantly, the findings also highlighted the major challenges that African countries encounter, one of which is "to enhance the credibility of the budget by reducing the gap between planned and actual spending" (CABRI 2008).

Timney (1995) argues that although public budgeting theories emerged from public administration theories, the latter have stuck to the political–administrative dichotomy, which the former have abandoned. Consequently, a discussion on public budgeting cannot be divorced from the political context of the country. However, both are generally driven by the quest for efficiency in the public sector. That is why budgeting is often linked to economic and development policy analysis, which is also highly influenced by political ideologies.

Post-Independence Budgeting and Development Approaches (1964–1994)

Dominance of President Kamuzu

At independence in 1964, Malawi adopted a colonial budgeting system of two accounts: the recurrent and development accounts (Kydd & Christiansen 1981). The recurrent account was meant to meet recurrent government expenditures while the development account was meant to expand government capacity. However the reality was that the differences between these two accounts were unclear to the extent that the development account was not put to its full use. All in all, rural welfare which was meant to benefit from the development account, was not prioritized so that in the area of health, between 1964 and 1980 "health accounted for just 2.2 percent of the development account spending" (Kydd 1984, p. 311). Below is an analysis of the budgeting process as well as the challenges during the one-party era. However, it is apparent that before a comprehensive analysis is provided, the country's development policies which have a bearing on budgeting need to be explained.

It is well acknowledged that Malawi pursued development policies that were unique in the African region and Kamuzu himself was a dominant figure in the creation of these policies (Kayuni 2012; Kydd 1984; Vail 1984; Crosby 1980; Williams 1978; Thomas 1975; McMaster 1974; Pike 1968). In this regard, Chipembere (1971, p. 283) mentioned that "one could go on almost endlessly, discussing or speaking of various ways in which the policies of the present Malawi government differ fundamentally from the policies of the other black African states." Unlike Malawi's neighbors, Mozambique, Tanzania and Zambia, which pursued a brand of African Socialism, Malawi followed a form of neo-liberal capitalism. Referring to the period of the 1960s and 1970s, Chipembere (1971, p. 281) argues that Kamuzu "takes a clearly pro-western line, sometimes he is more western than the west themselves." Kamuzu's pro-capitalist approach was something that he himself cherished and "perhaps uniquely among African leaders, Kamuzu made a political virtue of his anti-protectionist views on international trade . . . as one of the benefits of his rule" (Kydd 1984, p. 305). Kydd refers to Kamazu's development approach as "African Capitalism" and Laslett (1984, p. 393) calls it a "command economy" while Kayuni (2012) calls it a "pragmatic unilateral capitalism."

Ministers were required to resign if they disagreed with the president on any significant public issue and the president held up to five Cabinet portfolios himself. To highlight his dominance in policy-making, Kamuzu once said:

> I am the boss here. Why beat about the bush? I am the boss. I am responsible for this country, the welfare of the ordinary people in the villages, men and women, boys and girls . . . Therefore, when the opinions of the officials on any subject conflict with my own opinions, my opinions should always prevail. Any official who does not like that can resign at any time. And that has been my policy all through. A leader . . . who depends on others, even his own officials or outside experts, is a prisoner.
>
> Kamuzu's public meeting speech on March 11, 1975

Public Finance Management (PFM) and Key Actors in the Budgeting Process

Since independence, Malawi's budgeting system was based on the public finance management (PFM) system, in which through the national budget, competing policy objectives, programs and activities are lined up for execution within a defined period of time, normally 12 months. Some forms of reforms were being introduced over the years such that to date, the budgeting process has gone through a lot of transformation. The major visible reforms were introduced during the adoption of a series of structural adjustment programs (SAPs) in 1980s. One of the conditions of SAPs was that the country undertakes public finance management reforms to strengthen the budgeting process (Durevall & Erlandsson 2005, p. 38).

However, even though championed by the International Monetary Fund (IMF) and World Bank as a remedy for improving Malawi's fiscal position, SAPs did not improve PFM in Malawi. Actually, actual expenditure exceeded both original and revised estimates during practically all years running up to the 1990s. Consequently the country's economic condition deteriorated. When economic performance rapidly deteriorated between 1992 and 1994 owing to recurrent drought, government over-expenditure and a reduction in donor aid among others, the Government of Malawi moved in to address the situation. It commissioned a World Bank-driven budget management review, which was carried out in 1995. The outcome of this review led to further reforms, which were taken up by the UDF-led Government in the late 1990s and beyond.

During the one-party era, policy-making and the budgeting process were highly centralized in the Office of the President and Cabinet (OPC), supported by an elaborate institutional arrangement. The OPC was the center of all budgeting, planning and implementation. The key institutions in the institutional framework for budgeting and policy-making included the following:

a) The National Development Council was responsible for planning, coordination and monitoring.
b) The National Development Planning Coordinating Committee was mandated to ensure that there was an optimal amount of consultation for all planned work in all sectors of the economy and to review all developments in the country.
c) The Department of Economic Planning and Development was responsible for planning, research and intelligence, administration of national development programs and projects and acted as a secretariat to the National Development Council and the National Development Planning Coordinating Committee.

Other supporting key institutions in the institutional budgeting and policy-making framework further included:

a) The Treasury was charged with budgetary policy, preparation of the annual budget and coordination of foreign aid and requests.
b) The Reserve Bank of Malawi was entrusted with the determination of monetary policy and played a key role in forecasting the balance of payments position.
c) The National Statistical Office provided background data for policy planning including population, industrial and agricultural statistics and so on.
d) The sectoral ministries and departments had the ultimate responsibility for initiating and implementing policies and projects for final incorporation into the Public Sector Investment Programme.
e) The District Development Committees were designed to provide the mass participatory aspect of development as forums for the discussion of development problems, priorities and plans.

Interestingly, no independent political organ including Parliament featured prominently in the budgeting and policy-making process in the one-party era. Basically participation of other stakeholders in the budgeting was very limited, if not non-existent. The single-party structures were designed to provide some semblance of participation principally as instruments of mass mobilization to support the regime's policy agenda. One key such instrument was the MCP annual convention, which was dubbed as "parliament number one" bringing delegates from every possible corner of the country to deliberate on the year's plans. The plans were outlined in the opening speech of the president who tripled as party leader, head of Government and head of state. Delegates were in principle expected to debate the plans outlined in the opening speech, and make amendments, additions and even subtractions on the basis of priorities in their respective jurisdiction. Almost always the plans were not critically debated at all; delegates simply spent the week competing with each on heaping praises on the country's leadership and endorsing the plans as specified by the president in his opening speech.

In this case, Parliament simply served a rubber-stamping role, as its agenda was determined by the MCP annual convention. Parliament was not engaged in any critical debate on issues that were tabled before it; its involvement in the budgeting and development planning process was simply to establish the legitimacy and legal standards required for such an activity.

There were some efforts, though limited, to link annual budgeting process with long-term development planning documents. Examples include:

- the 1965–1969 Development Plan;
- the 1970–1980 Statement of Development Policies;
- the 1987–1996 Statement of Development Policies.

These plans outlined comprehensively what needed to be done in each key sector of the economy over the specified time horizon. Civil society did not exist at all; a semblance of civil society prevailed within the confines of organizations appended to the MCP. The media was heavily controlled by the state and the only newspapers were owned by the head of state. More importantly, donors had limited influence on the budgeting process because Malawi was considered as a geo-strategic ally of western countries in the fight against communism.

Malawi's Budgeting System from 1994 to the Present

Introduction of Medium-Term Expenditure Framework

As mentioned above, a study was carried out in late 1995 to review the PFM and according to Simwaka (2006, p. 3), this review revealed several weaknesses and problems in the budgeting process, some of which were also highlighted in the 1990 public expenditure review (PER). The first central problem was failure to link policy-making and planning to the recurrent budget. Thus, although the development budget was generally well prepared by planners and based on overall government policy and planning, the recurrent budget was not planned and was prepared on an incremental basis (i.e. simply adding a certain percentage to the previous year's estimates). The process did not involve reviewing whether the particular activities were in line with government priorities. The second central problem was that budgeting was focused on the short term rather than the medium to long term. In other words, not only were budgets prepared for one year, the recurrent and development budgets were subject to separate analysis. This led to a strong upward bias in development expenditure (reinforced by donor pressure) and a shortfall in recurrent expenditure.

To address these and other challenges, the Government initiated several measures that would facilitate a long-lasting improvement in the budgeting process as recommended by the budget management review. The most important measure was the introduction of a Medium-term Expenditure Framework (MTEF) as the basis for a more strategic approach to public expenditure planning. The Malawi Government adopted a phased approach in implementing MTEF. The first phase included five key ministries, those of Agriculture, Education, Sports and Culture, Health and Population, and Works and Supplies. In the 1997/98 financial year, the framework was rolled out to all ministries, departments and agencies (MDAs). Since then, the budgeting process in Malawi has been based on the principles of MTEF.

Adopted in several African countries including Malawi, the MTEF is a specific way of conducting the budgeting process that involves a three-year rolling program process based on costed strategic priorities and an output-focused approach with the objective of developing an integrated realistic budgetary framework. It is a tool that ensures that budgets are program- or activity-based and ceilings on expenditure are set in sectors based on priority areas. MTEF allows the integration of planning and budget programs over a medium term of three to five years and ensures adequate allocation of resources to priority areas as determined by Government from time to time. MTEF therefore, facilitated a complete departure from incremental budgeting.

However, by 1999, it became clear that MTEF had not meaningfully transformed the national budget into an effective allocative and management tool. This was because sector policies remained unaffordable and resources were spread too thinly across many activities, substantial off-budget expenditures were still taking place and there were significant divergences between priority expenditures as expressed in approved budgets and actual expenditures. As a result, MTEF failed to achieve aggregate fiscal discipline and adequate direction of resources to strategic priorities. The fiscal position of the country did not improve.

Consequently, in the 1999/2000 fiscal year, the Government decided to assess MTEF through a comprehensive review of MTEF (Simwaka, 2006, p. 4). At the outset of the MTEF review, it was determined that it would not be sufficient to focus only on the planning and MTEF budget formulation processes but the full PFM cycle. Following the review, it was concluded that the national budget was not operating as an authoritative and credible fiscal management tool. The recommendations from this review have continuously informed the design of the subsequent MTEF reform programs and since this review, a number of steps have been taken to improve the budgeting process. Many of the recommendations arising from the review have guided Malawi's budgeting process since the 2000/01 budget. The budgetary reforms have also manifested in the process itself, which is meant to be on a par with internationally recognized practices in democratic states hence linked to good governance ethos.

Decentralized Budgeting and Other Reforms

The relationship between central Government and local councils is such that the central Government supports local councils with policy guidance, financial and technical assistance. However, in Malawi, local councils are required by law to prepare their own budgets. Section 51 (1) of the Local Government Act (1998), requires local councils to prepare detailed estimates of revenue and expenditure for each financial year. Local councils therefore, prepare national budget estimates in a similar way as central ministries and departments. The Act further subjects the local councils to monitoring by the National Local Government Finance Committee (NLGFC). The NLGFC was established by the Republican Constitution and is mandated to supervise and audit accounts of local councils subject to the recommendations of the Auditor-General. Under the Act, the councils are obliged to submit their final accounts to the NLGFC. The NLGFC also submits the copy of the final accounts to the Auditor-General. The Auditor-General is mandated to carry out surprise audit investigations or any other audit considered necessary.

In terms of financing, the Government of Malawi ensured that a sound local government financing mechanism was instituted. Therefore, local councils have two main revenue sources: locally generated revenues (traditional), and central government transfers.

Currently, it is the responsibility of ministries and departments, which are still devolving their activities, to work closely with local councils to ensure that adequate resources are provided to meet their intended purposes at community level. Ministries and departments are required to ensure that quality and standards are maintained in the provision of goods and services in the local councils. At budget hearings for key sectors such as health, the NLGFC is usually represented.

Another reform in the budgetary system was the introduction of an Integrated Financial Management Information System (IFMIS). Currently IFMIS has been implemented and rolled out to most MDAs including local councils. IFMIS has enhanced expenditure control as expenditure cannot be made outside the budget. All payments are executed electronically through banks. Budgeting in Malawi is now more focused on program results and outputs than mere activities. The Government is in the process of migrating to program-based budgeting (PBB) as part of a broader PFM reforms package with the expectation that PBB will be rolled out across all MDAs in the 2016/17 financial year. This will ensure budgets are tied to programs, strategic plans, organizational performance agreements and the national development strategy.

The Malawi Legal Budgetary Framework

Though involving various actors, PFM and the budgeting process is undertaken within a well-entrenched legal framework as guided by the Constitution of the Republic of Malawi, the Public Finance Management Act (2003), the Public Audit Act (2003), the Public Procurement Act (2003) and Treasury Instructions. Specifically, these instruments play the following roles.

According to the Constitution, the Government of Malawi has a duty to raise or levy revenue by or for the purpose of the Government or any local government authority. The revenue raised, levied and imposed is paid into and from one fund known as the consolidated fund. The main objective of Public Finance Management Act (2003) is to foster and enhance effective and responsible management of public resources. The Public Audit Act (2003) aims at promoting accountability of the Government to the public through the National Assembly by making available to it for scrutiny information on public expenditure, revenues, assets, liabilities and the management of public money. The mandate of the Public Procurement Act (2003) is to regulate public procurement of goods, works and services. The Directorate for Public Procurement is the main authority responsible for the monitoring and oversight of public procurement activities, and for the development of the related regulatory and legal framework and professional capacity of public procurement. The Secretary to the Treasury issues Treasury Instructions from time to time advising ministries and spending agencies on how public moneys and public resources are to be managed. Instructions are issued under section 92 of the Public Finance Management Act.

Apart from the various actors that take part in the budgeting process, and the coherent legal framework that guides PFM in Malawi, the processes are also enshrined within institutionalized control mechanisms. When the national budget is approved by Parliament, it is assumed that financial resources will be applied to their proper uses. This assumption is based on an ideal scenario of financial and management probity. In reality however, implementing agencies tend to manage complex operations, making it difficult to share information validating the use of the financial resources. Budget controls are therefore put in place to ensure that planned and approved expenditures materialize, and hold responsible officers accountable.

In Malawi, budgetary controls may be exercised at four levels: First, the Presidential exercises controls mainly via the Office of the President and Cabinet through policy direction. Second, the Executive (Government) controls mainly by the Treasury (Ministry of Finance) and the Auditor-General. Third, Parliament controls through various committees such as the Public Accounts Committee, and Committee on Finance and Budget. Finally, citizens control through civic lobbies, advocacy and whistle-blowing in the event of financial mismanagement by government offices.

Revenue and Public Expenditure Framework

The fiscal performance in Malawi from the 2005/2006 fiscal year to date can be divided into at least four phases:

1. 2006 to 2010: steady growth and stable macro-fiscal environment;
2. 2011 to 2012: macro-economic imbalances, falling donor in-flows and slow growth;
3. May 2012 to 2013: the launch of new policies to restore macro-economic balances, donor in-flows, and growth;

4. From 2013/2014 to date: the economy has been beset by a tightened fiscal envelope due to falling donor in-flows and withdrawal of direct budget support. These events have greatly impacted the budgeting process in terms of budget planning and execution. Consequently, revenue generation and public expenditure have both been shaped by these events even though the trends in the national budget demonstrate that there has been a steady increase in public expenditures during periods of high economic growth and performance and economic contraction. The dynamics of revenue generation and public expenditure in Malawi are as described below.

Revenue Generation

The principal means by which the Government finds financial resources to implement its activities is by revenue collection through the MRA. Through MRA, income tax, customs duty, surtax and value-added tax, fuel levies, corporate tax, departmental receipts and dividends are collected and deposited into Government Account Number One held by the RBM. As portrayed in the table below, domestic revenue is largely dependent on tax revenue, and is boosted by non-tax revenue. Non-tax revenue includes: departmental receipts, levies, dividends, and RBM profits while tax revenue includes: taxes on income and profits, taxes on goods and services and taxes on international trade. Practically, taxes on goods and services have continued to be the dominant source of revenue generation in all years.

Table 7.1 shows that the 2013/14 fiscal year witnessed exceptional tax revenue performance as compared to the previous year. This was on account of good VAT performance, which significantly improved due to the introduction and enforcement of electronic fiscal devices by MRA. In Malawi, grants and budget support have been erratic since 2010 (GoM, 2012).

Overall, from 2010/11 to 2013/2014 domestic revenues performed well both in absolute and relative terms, with 21.8 percent of GDP registered in 2012/13. The general trend projected to the 2013/14 fiscal year is the same. It must be pointed out that the significant improvement in performance of tax revenue over the years is due to a number of factors ranging from strengthened tax administration to increased economic activity due to resumption in availability of fuel and foreign exchange reserves.

The Public Expenditure Framework (2012–2015)

Similarly, the PER of 2013 highlights that the major budget expenditures items continue to be in social, economic and community services. This is consistent with the Government's commitment to ensure that sufficient resources are made available to the social sector in line with the Malawi Growth and Development Strategy paper (MGDS) II particularly in agriculture, health and education in order to meet the MDGs. Closely competing with social and community services are expenditures on general public services, which increased to 8.6 percent of

Table 7.1 Central Government Domestic Revenue 2012/13–2014/15 Financial Year (in MWK millions)

	2012/13	*2013/14*	*2014/15*
A. GROSS TAX REVENUE	276,008.4	393,530.8	482,448.3
1. TAXES ON INCOME & PROFITS	131,872.2	183,707.3	229,852.6
Companies	36,764.8	47,698.5	59,679.9
Individuals	69,761.1	99,256.8	124,189.1
Non Resident Tax	1,736.1	3,319.8	4,153.7
P.A.Y.E.	65,116.8	91,442.0	114,411.4
Withholding Tax	22,724.7	33,715.1	42,184.0
Fringe Benefit Tax	2,908.2	4,495.0	5,624.1
Other*	25,346.3	36,752.0	45,983.6
2. TAXES ON GOODS & SERVICES	110,731.5	168,306.9	200,583.9
VAT	82,192.6	126,049.2	147,711.4
Excise Duties	28,538.9	42,257.7	52,872.4
3. INTERNATIONAL TRADE TAXES	33,404.7	41,516.6	52,011.8
Customs Duties	33,404.7	41,516.6	52,011.8
Import Duties	32,865.0	41,061.2	51,442.1
Miscellaneous Duties	539.7	455.4	569.8
4. *Less:* TOTAL TAX REFUNDS	7,067.4	5,171.0	12,311.2
5. NET TAX REVENUE	268,941.0	388,359.8	470,137.1
B. NON TAX REVENUE	27,683.2	53,236.0	55,183.6
Stabilization Fund			
Departmental Receipts	10,927.2	10,660.8	14,290.5
Other Revenue (dividends etc.)	2,472.2	8,221.5	17,955.0
Receipts from PIL	7,276.1	24,643.6	10,415.1
Rural electrification levy	5,816.3	8,302.8	11,073.0
Storage levy	1,191.4	1,407.4	1,450.0
GROSS DOMESTIC REVENUE	303,691.6	446,766.8	537,631.9
NET DOMESTIC REVENUE	296,642.2	441,595.8	525,320.7
Percent of GDP			
GROSS TAX REVENUE	16.5	18.0	18.3
Taxes on Income and Profit	7.9	8.4	8.7
Taxes on Goods and Services	6.6	7.7	7.6
International Trade Taxes	2.0	1.9	2.0
NET TAX REVENUE	16.1	17.8	17.8
NON-TAX REVENUE	1.7	2.4	2.1
GRAND TOTAL	18.1	20.5	2.4

Source: Ministry of Finance
*2014/15 period is based on budgeted estimates

GDP in the 2013/14 fiscal year from 6.7 percent in the 2012/13 fiscal year, accounting for the second largest share of the recurrent expenditure. Allocations to social-community services were 9.6 percent of GDP in the 2013/14 fiscal year. Despite the above, agriculture, health and education are the major stand-alone public expenditures items by sector. See Table 7.2 below.

From Table 7.2, it is apparent that the education sector has increasingly accounted for the largest share of public expenditure (19 percent in 2013/2014). Government resources have grown by an average of 25 percent per annum while pooled development partner resources have increased enormously by over 200 percent. Similarly, since the launching of the farm input subsidy program (FISP) in the 2005/2006 fiscal year, public expenditure in agriculture has considerably

Table 7.2 Functional Classification of Central Government Recurrent Expenditure 2012/13–2014/15 Financial Years (in MWK)

	2012/13	*2013/14*	*2014/15*
General Public Services	112,784.8	187,727.5	164,398.0
General Administration	72,403.8	144,790.3	126,858.2
Defence Affairs	11,603.0	20,381.4	16,527.2
Public Order and Safety Affairs	28,778.0	22,555.8	21,012.6
Social and Community Services	159,729.3	208,474.7	224,004.5
Education Affairs and Services	77,246.0	102,101.2	109,706.9
Health Affairs and Services	52,269.1	75,175.5	80,775.5
Social Security and Welfare Affairs Services (social protection)	22,449.2	23,833.1	25,608.5
Housing and Community Amenity Services	6,734.9	5,976.3	6,421.4
Recreational, Cultural & Other Social Services	1,030.1	1,388.7	1,492.1
Economic Services	124,686.8	152,807.5	157,764.9
Mining and Manufacturing and Environmental Protections	3,391.2	4,849.8	5,211.1
Agriculture and Natural Resources	72,067.4	85,951.6	92,354.3
Tourism Affairs and Services	901.2	7,277.6	1,372.8
Transport and Communication Services	13,687.5	12,671.2	13,615.1
General Economic, Commercial and Labor Affairs	1,501.4	2,589.8	2,782.7
R & D Economic Affairs and Public Debt	33,138.0	39,467.4	42,428.8
Total Recurrent Expenditure	397,200.8	549,009.7	546,167.4
GENERAL PUBLIC SERVICES	6.7	8.6	6.2
SOCIAL AND COMMUNITY SERVICES	9.5	9.6	8.5
ECONOMIC SERVICES	7.4	7.0	6.0

Source: Ministry of Finance
*2014/15 period is based on budgeted estimates

increased to reach about 19 percent of total budget expenditure. Managed by the Ministry of Agriculture, Irrigation and Water Development, FISP has left the ministry with very little fiscal space as the program has absorbed 69 percent of its financial and human resources since inception and over 40 percent of total public spending. The health sector has also witnessed increased sector spending (with a notably significant boost of external finances) while facing decreasing funding levels from the national budget.

Suffice to say that the wage bill in Malawi is the single largest expenditure item in the national budget appearing under general public services in Table 7.2. The wage bill has risen from about 5.4 percent of GDP and 22 percent of the total expenditures in 2005/06 to about 7.2 percent of GDP and 26 percent of total expenditures in 2011/12 and was projected to reach 8.6 percent of GDP in the 2013/14 fiscal year. The budgeted wage bill was 8.1 percent in the 2012/13 fiscal year. This is on account of increased civil service salaries and wages.

According to the 2013 PER, weak expenditure control continues to be an important cause of over-spending and poor fiscal outcomes. Others are loss of data and errors due to human intervention, budget templates that do not take into account the MDAs' outputs, budget virements done outside the normal system functionality, no clear link from the budget to the MDAs' plans or to MTEF, and inaccurate budget report figures. Finally, Malawi continues to accumulate large arrears due to poor expenditure management and fiscal reporting. MDAs frequently acquire goods and services on credit with no repercussions.

In view of the issues discussed in this chapter and within the context of tightened budget over the medium term, the Government aims to achieve fiscal sustainability by strengthening revenue mobilization and restraining growth in public expenditures while prioritizing spending in social, economic and community services in order to achieve MDGs as embedded in the MGDS II. With strong projected tax and non-tax revenue and declining grants, the fiscal accounts indicate that overall expenditure would have to be reduced by 2016. Going forward, the next phase of PFM reforms should include restructuring of the IFMIS so that transactions occur with little manual intervention.

Have Reforms Improved Budgeting System in Malawi?—A Critique

The transition to multi-party democracy provided a huge opportunity for the renewal of budgeting and policy-making processes in the country. There was the potential that the budgeting processes would not only be opened to a wide range of stakeholders beyond the president and bureaucracy but would also be procedurally different with qualitatively different outcomes. In this case, several stakeholders have indeed emerged including the following:

1. political parties;
2. civil society (the church, citizen groups, NGOs and professional associations);

3. the media (print and electronic);
4. international organizations (international financial institutions and donor agencies);
5. the three branches of government (legislature, executive, and judiciary); and
6. the public at large.

The key question is how have these groups faired in the budgeting and policy-making processes since 1994?

According to the Open Budget Survey, which produces the Open Budget Index (based on elements of budget transparency, budget participation and budget oversight), Malawi's performance has significantly improved from 42 in 2006 to 52 in 2012[1]. Specifically, in 2006 Malawi scored an index of 42 and in 2008 it went down to 28 only to pick up significantly in 2010 when Malawi scored an index of 47 and further improved to 52 in 2012. One of the reasons for significant improvement in the 2010 and 2012 scores is that the Government started to publish in-year reports and a year-end report as well as producing and publishing a citizens' budget. A citizens' budget is a non-technical outline of the government budget and aims at ensuring that the general public, especially those not conversant with public finance, are able to understand it and ably engage in these matters of public finance. In the 2008 survey by Collaborative Africa Budget Reform Initiative (CABRI) of 29 African countries, Malawi was ranked fourth in relation to fiscal transparency. Despite these noted improvements, there are numerous challenges.

First, the major challenge that Malawi is facing in relation to the budget processes is the mismanagement of the transition from a single-party to multi-party system of governance. The notable consequence of the mismanaged transition was the dramatic decline in the Government's capacity to formulate, articulate and implement budget policy alternatives. The situation was compounded by widespread neo-patrimonial tendencies and practices that characterized the running and management of the civil service. Most government ministers surrounded themselves with their own people, side-lining senior technocrats in a way that demotivated them and ultimately reduced administrative efficiency. In other words, the civil service came to be dominated by party loyalists who were not competent at all to make use of the technically oriented policy and budgetary analysis. The fairly honest, disciplined, well paid, professional and hardworking civil service of the one-party regime was replaced by a lax, demoralized and underpaid civil service distracted by private business activities and more easily corrupted.

Second, the decline in the government's budgetary planning capacity resulted in almost a complete loss of state business, with the following consequences:

1. Donors take advantage of the weakened capacity or non-existent technical capacity of the Government to step into the vacuum and coordinate policy

formation to the extent that sometimes actions by donors settled budgetary decisions.

2. Policy-making and implementation was often subjected to polarized ideological leanings and orientations of donors instead of being guided by the unique circumstances and needs of the country. These ideological leanings have a bearing on the budgetary process.
3. A multiplicity of grand policy documents underpinned by an absence of real implemented and implementable policies beyond the short term created a scenario in which budgetary priorities are often confused.

Third, there is a limited culture of valuing evidence in budgetary and policy development and as such the budget is often not evidence-based. This is worsened by the following factors:

a) Lack of resources has a demoralizing effect on government budgetary institutions, which as a result respond to and follow a "what gets paid for gets done principle." There is also a pervasive lack of resources in the departments entrusted with preparing budgets and organizing research information and stakeholders in the process of doing their work. The producers of research outside the Government are underfunded and find few entry points to engage with the Government in the deliberation and formulation of budgetary options.
b) A deep-rooted tendency for "podium policies" makes life difficult for technocrats since they have to work retrospectively to give shape and form to these policies in the budget. Furthermore, the challenge is to create a system in which politicians and top bureaucrats will be less tempted to influence budgetary decisions according to their political or personal preferences.

Fourth, although budget evaluation has some level of independence and credibility, monitoring and evaluation (M&E) reports are not adequately utilized. Experience has shown that evaluations of the budget are mainly used by the MoF to assist in resource allocation and disbursement. However, effective budget monitoring and evaluation is being hampered by a number of challenges, which include:

a) Inadequate capacity to monitor and evaluate the whole national budget—the M&E Section in MoF does not have the required capacity to monitor and evaluate the entire budget. This is because the section does not have enough officers to prepare the budget and and monitor it at the same time.
b) Lack of skills and expertise in budget evaluation—no wonder there is little evaluation being done on the budget as officers mostly focus on monitoring. The PERs have contributed on the evaluation of the budget but since most of them are donor-driven and usually done by consultants, there is no skills transfer.

c) Resistance of MDAs to being monitored and evaluated—since they usually wrongly perceive these activities as auditing. Most MDAs are therefore reluctant to participate in M&E activities. Therefore, there is reluctance to submit budget progress reports, which makes it difficult for MoF to follow up on outputs being delivered by MDAs.
d) Lack of an M&E database system that can coordinate information for all the M&E units in government. Reports from MDAs are usually hard copies, which can be misplaced easily.
e) Lack of feedbac—M&E data must be fed back into MDAs to guide the implementation of ongoing activities and planning of future ones. However, little feedback goes to the implementing agencies.

Fifth, although the decentralization process in Malawi was among other things meant to enhance the accountability and effectiveness of the budgetary process at local level, not much has been achieved. For instance, from April 2005 up to May 2014, there were no local council elections, hence the elected positions of councillors were vacant. This vacuum has created a number of problems rendering the decentralized budgetary process merely a fiasco. Based on several research findings, it has been argued that the local councils themselves are institutions which have traditionally witnessed infighting between the secretariat and elected councillors and also between councillors and traditional authorities. Such kinds of scenario have rendered the whole institutional set up a hostile environment that is not conducive to proper budgeting.

Finally, there are several other overriding institutional and practical challenges to the budgeting process in Malawi that can be summarized as follows:

1. A clearly defined framework to enable precise predictions of revenue is lacking; this affects the implementation of planned activities.
2. In recent years up to the present, lack of budget support from development partners is compromising the effective implementation of the national budget, which has traditionally been substantially financed by development partners. Traditionally 40 percent of the national budget has always been financed by development partners.
3. IFMIS is not fully rolled out to some MDAs due to connectivity challenges, hence failures to detect excessive payments, increased workload of civil servants, fraud and theft in the agencies concerned continue.
4. Detailed budget documents are not properly understood by most stakeholders including the citizenry especially because the documents are generally too technical.
5. Since the output-based budget document is the only reference material, lack of clearly defined output indicators makes budget monitoring and evaluation difficult and of little value.
6. Unstable fuel and fertilizer prices on the international market have tended to affect the budgeting process as changes in the prices of these materials have long-lasting triple effects on the economy.

Conclusion

From independence to the present, budgeting in Malawi has always been associated with national development endeavors; hence several reforms have taken place in this arena. Despite major transformations and reforms in public finance management and the budgeting process, Malawi still faces a myriad of challenges that pose huge obstacles to the successful implementation of national development programs as specified in the national budget. These challenges continue to restrict the smooth execution of the budget itself, thereby negatively affecting public-service delivery. Although budget monitoring and evaluation in Malawi is considered vital for the purposes of accountability and transparency in the use of public finances and for guiding implementing agencies on budget execution, it has not adequately assisted in enhancing the same. Budget evaluation still faces a number of challenges that need to be addressed in order to yield better results.

Note

1 The official statement of the Open Budget Survey says that "Open Budget Survey examines 100 countries in the world in the areas of budget transparency, budget participation and budget oversight. It is the only independent, comparative, and regular measure of budget transparency, participation, and oversight in the world. It is the culmination of analyses conducted by a global network of hundreds of researchers over a two-year period."

References

Chipembere, H. 1971. Seminar Address at University of California at Los Angeles, February 1, 1971. Reprinted in Baker, C. 2008. *Chipembere: The Missing Years*. Zomba, Malawi: Kachere Series. pp. 281–300.

Collaborative African Budget Reform Initiative (CABRI). 2008. *Budget Practices and Procedures in Africa 2008*. Pretoria: Collaborative Africa Budget Reform Initiative and African Bank.

Crosby, C. 1980. *Historical Dictionary of Malawi*. London: The Scarecrow Press.

Durevall, D., & Erlandsson, M. 2005. *Public Finance Management Reform in Malawi*. Stockholm: SIDA Country Economic Report.

Government of Malawi. 2012. 2012/2013 Draft Financial Statement. Lilongwe: Ministry of Finance.

Kayuni, H. 2012. Malawi's Economic and Development Policy Choices from 1964 to 1980: An Epitome of Pragmatic Unilateral Capitalism. *Nordic Journal of African Studies*, 20(2): 112–131.

Kydd, J. 1984. *Malawi in the 1970s: Development Policies and Economic Change*. Proceedings of a Seminar held in the Centre of African Studies (Seminar Proceedings No. 25), University of Edinburgh, May 24 and 25. pp. 293–375.

Kydd, J., & Christiansen, R. 1981. Structural Change and Trends in Equity in the Malawian Economy 1964–1980. Income Distribution Project Working Paper No. 2.

Laslett, R. 1984. *An Account of Malawi's Economy and Economic Policy in the 1970s*. Proceedings of a Seminar held in the Centre of African Studies (Seminar Proceedings No. 25), University of Edinburgh, May 24 and 25. pp. 381–406.

McMaster, C. 1974. *Malawi: Foreign Policy and Development*. London; New York: Friedman.

NSO. 2008. National Population and Housing Census. Zomba: National Statistical Office.

NSO. 2011. National Integrated Household Survey. Zomba: National Statistical Office

Pike, J. 1968. *Malawi: A Political and Economic History*. London: Pall Mall.

Simson, R. 2014. *Transparency for Development: Examining the Relationship Between Budget Transparency, MDG Expenditure, and Results*. International Budget Paper. http://internationalbudget.org/wp-content/uploads/Transparency-for-Development.pdf.

Simwaka, C. 2006. Malawi: Lessons from First Reforms Lead to New Approach. *OECD Journal on Budgeting*, 6(2): 1-22.

Thomas, S. 1975. Economic Developments in Malawi since Independence. *Journal of Southern African Studies*, 2(1): 30–51.

Timney, M. 1995. The Asynchronism of Public Administration and Budget Theories. *Administrative Theory & Praxis*, 17(2): 41–51.

Vail, L. 1984. Peasants, Migrants, and Plantations: A Study of the Growth of Malawi's Economy. *Journal of Social Science*, 11:1–36.

Williams, T. 1978. *Malawi: The Politics of Despair*. Ithaca: Cornell University Press.

8 Public Budgeting in African Nations: The Case of South Africa

Gerrit van der Waldt and Shikha Vyas-Doorgapersad

Orientation

Budgeting approaches and processes in African nations are context sensitive. Each country is shaped and molded by its history, political and government system, culture, demographics, geographical realities, and current events and trends. These realities can of course be analyzed from various vantage points. Economists, for example, would be interested in broad macro-economic policies, and economic growth trajectories, as well as international treaties and bilateral and multi-national agreements; political scientists would be attracted to the system of government and the political dynamics shaping individual countries; and social scientists would be fascinated by the heterogeneous demographical realities and diverse cultures of the region. Only once these, and other, perspectives are combined, does a fuller picture emerge. It is thus important not to embark on an investigation of public budgeting in African nations with a narrow, silo mentality. Only comparative and multi-disciplinary perspectives reveal complex realities shaping budgeting processes.

The purpose of this chapter is to enhance understanding of public budgeting on the African continent by investigating the country on its southernmost tip, South Africa. The chapter will contribute in this sense by an exploration of the "what," "why," and "by whom" dimensions of public budgeting in South Africa. For this aim, the chapter will first contextualize financial management and budgeting in South Africa's system of government. Thereafter, the politics of budgeting and the South African budgeting architecture and associated key actors will be explored. The chapter will furthermore accentuate budget reforms, the budget cycle, and the country's legislative framework. Lastly, particular revenue sources as well as the frameworks and methods of budgeting will be investigated.

Contextualing Financial Management and Budgeting in South Africa's System of Government

Resource allocation and distribution in any country ultimately boils down to its broader dominant governance philosophy and ideology. In shaping the broad contours of a country's strategic direction and development trajectory, philosophy and ideology generally culminate in a country's strategic socio-economic disposition, its monetary and fiscal policy, and its financial arrangements. A country's historical perspectives, its geographical realities and its demographical challenges all shape decisions regarding the allocation of resources—including finances. The purpose of this section is to investigate the way these realities sculpted public finance in general and budgeting processes in particular in a South African governance frame.

South Africa has a highly sophisticated financial sector. The international Open Budget Survey for 2010 ranked South Africa's budget process number one in the world. The survey covers 94 countries and is conducted on a biannual basis. South Africa further complies with internationally accepted comparative measures of budget transparency and budget criteria developed by the IMF (International Monetary Fund), OECD (Organisation for Economic Cooperation and Development) and INTOSAI (International Organisation of Supreme Audit Institutions). As far is the Open Budget Index (OBI) is concerned, the average global score for countries is 42 out of 100. South Africa obtained a score of 92 on this index.

In spite of this seemingly encouraging picture, South Africa is branded by exceptionally high levels of poverty, unemployment, and crime. Its economy is characterized by highly developed first-world infrastructure and systems in major city centers, but at the same time also with a large so-called third- and even fourth-world component. This duality in the economic system makes financial planning, policy design, and strategic orientation in government a highly complex endeavor. Only 3.3 million people out of an estimated total population of 54 million pay 99 percent of all income tax, while approximately 16.7 million people receive social grants from the South African Social Security Agency every month. These facts strain the revenue base of the state severely. Although there is ample evidence that South Africa's budget process has improved significantly over the last two decades, there are, however, also perturbing signs of high levels of corruption and a general inability of the executive to effectively, efficiently and economically implement the budget. Once expenditure priorities are established, it is up to each government department to deliver a targeted outcome using the funds allocated. That is generally not happening, especially in key areas such as safety, education, and healthcare.

On the local sphere of government, where South Africa's 278 local, district, and metropolitan municipalities are at the forefront of basic service delivery, the picture is even more distressing. A recent statement (March 4, 2015) by the Minister of Cooperative Governance and Traditional Affairs, Pravin Gordhan, revealed that one in three municipalities in South Africa are dysfunctional. This finding was based on a survey conducted utilizing four measurement criteria: economic position, tax viability, financial capability, and dependence on intergovernment transfers. The factors that generally led to dysfunctionalism include political instability, institutional mismanagement, maladministration, and serious challenges associated with service delivery.

Colonial Legacies: The Westminister System of Government

Just like so many other countries on the African continent, South Africa did not escape the imperialistic ideals of other nations. South Africa's first contact with the Western world came when Jan van Riebeeck, a Dutch explorer, landed in the Cape on April 6, 1652. Van Riebeeck was commissioned by the Dutch East India Trading Company to establish a posting station for passing ships en route to the East. The Dutch settlers in the Cape were tasked with supplying merchant ships with fresh fruit, vegetables and meat. The settlers soon established trade relationships with the indigenous population, mainly of Khoikhoi extraction. However, this relationship then turned into antagonism leading to stock raiding and armed conflict. The Dutch colonial authorities allotted farms to Europeans and soon more Dutch settlers arrived, followed by immigrants from all over Europe. This eventually led to full colonization and occupation of the Cape Colony by the Dutch. The Cape Colony remained under Dutch rule until 1795, when it fell to the British Crown. After the occupation of the territory by the British, approximately 10 thousand Dutch settlers (the so-called "boers" or "voortrekkers") trekked north-east, to escape British rule. They founded two independent republics, the Transvaal Republic and the Republic of the Orange Free State.

Diamonds and gold were discovered (1867) in the northern areas of the country and soon immigration to these areas intensified. The indigenous inhabitants of the area were mainly used as laborers to work in the diamond and gold mines. The British rulers in the south were determined to unite their colony (the Cape) with the two Boer republics and thereby seize control of the gold mines in the north. The Boers resisted British encroachment and on February 11, 1899 the Anglo-Boer War broke out. The British army managed to seize control over major areas in the republics and on May 31, 1902 a peace treaty was signed.

Since the first contact between Europeans and the native inhabitants of the country tension was always present. The political environment was characterized by policies of separate development and racial segregation. The right to vote was not extended to the black majority. This led to the establishment of the African National Congress (ANC) in 1923, and the formation of its military wing, *Umkhonto we Sizwe* (Spear of the Nation) in 1961. The ANC deemed itself a force of national liberation, and its famous leader, Nelson Mandela, was imprisoned in 1962 for acts of treason. Upon his release in 1990 and following general national elections, South Africa became a full democratic constitutional democracy in 1994 with Mr. Mandela serving as President.

An analysis of the legacies of South Africa's colonial past probably depends on the truism that where one sits often determines what one sees and how one reacts. British government officials would probably argue that their rule brought considerable benefits to the country, notably education, technology, economic and infrastructure development, rule of law, and a sophisticated system of government. As far as the latter is concerned, the Westminster democratic parliamentary system brought to South Africa was modeled after the politics of the United Kingdom. It is most commonly applied in Commonwealth countries. The Westminster system of government, as applicable to South Africa, generally has the following features:

- a head of state, elected by the members of parliament;
- separation of powers between the executive, legislative and judiciary branches of government;
- the executive branch, led by the head of state, i.e. president, prime minister or premier, is headed by a cabinet of ministers as political heads of departments;
- permanently appointed civil servants who serve in an independent civil or public service that implements policy decisions;
- regular democratic elections;
- an independent judiciary upholding statutory and common law in the country.

South Africa has a rather complex system of government characterized by interrelated and interdependent, yet autonomous spheres of government layered on national, provincial, and local levels. Furthermore, it has characteristics of both unitary and federal systems with decentralized operations and centralized decisions. The process for the sharing of revenue raised nationally among the national, provincial, and local spheres of government is regulated by the Intergovernmental Fiscal Relations Act 97 of 1997.

The Politics of Budgeting

A country's budget is generally regarded as a financial plan to assure fiscal integrity and as a control mechanism over government functions and operations (see Chen et al., 2009, p. 145). As a systematic financial plan it outlines the utilization of resources, including prioritized spending and strategic direction. Budgets thus have planning and controlling purposes at their roots (see Khan and Hildreth, 2003, p. 508). Decisions that shape a budget and operations that follow to spend the budget, i.e., general expenditure and supply chain processes, are ultimately molded by political dynamics. It is this political arena in which tensions between clashing ideologies, priorities, and strategic direction are highly visible. For example, a budget as planning instrument brings questions such as the expected outcomes of the plan, the general goodness of the plan, for whose benefit is it intended, and who should be involved, to the fore. As controlling instrument a budget is characterized by political questions such as: which mechanisms are utilized to exercise control over whom? and who decides whether expenditure was authorized and within the ambit of law? In this regard, Gildenhuys (1993, p. 3) confirms that any analysis of public budgeting should have as point of departure the philosophical premises of government as well as the dominant political ideologies that underpin financial decisions.

A budget can be regarded as an expression of political wishes that allows a government to plan in such a way that political goals are achieved. Budget decisions are complex in nature and involve different actors in and outside government (see Musell, 2008, p. 23; Bandy, 2015, p. 42). Consultations can strengthen legitimacy of government expenditure, legislative scrutiny, and public accountability. This makes all budget-making inherently a political sensitive process. The overall strategic direction and ideals of a state, for example, to be more interventionist and developmental in nature, ultimately have to be funded and hence have a direct bearing on the budget of the state. Furthermore, the political and strategic vantage points of budgeting, i.e., more free-market, capitalistic approaches versus state interventionism and socialistic approaches, ultimately influence the redistribution of wealth and growth imperatives. It should also be noted that the macro-economic framework within which budgeting occurs, the setting of monetary policies, as well as the establishment of fiscal targets, are all highly political in nature. In short, a budget can be regarded as the translation of political priorities into monetary terms. It is not merely a technocratic exercise.

To further reveal the inherent political nature of public budgeting, it is helpful to analyze the budgeting process in its respective phases. The budgeting process generally comprises of a strategic planning phase, a decision-making phase, a design phase, an execution (expenditure) phase, and an accounting phase. It should be noted that the use of terms such as phases and stages do not exclude the reality that the process is iterative, calling for extensive back-and-forth interaction between the phases and stakeholders. An analysis of these phases quickly exposes the political underpinnings of each.

Strategic Planning Phase

In the national sphere the budgeting process is guided by legislation such as the Public Finance Management Act 1 of 1999 and various National Treasury regulations, including general regulations (Gazette No. 27388, March 2005) and regulations dealing with specific aspects such as the supply chain management framework (Gazette 25767, December 2003) and the alignment of strategic planning with budgeting (Gazette No. 29644, February 2007). Budgeting generally commences with a political process, namely the strategic session of Cabinet called the *legotla*. In the provincial sphere the budget process starts with a Finance *Makgotla*.[1] The Office of the Premier, through the Planning Commission, generally coordinates provincial budget processes based on the outcomes approach adopted by Government. It is thus evident that the strategic planning phase of budgeting is highly reliant on political direction and priorities.

Decision-Making Phase

Once the strategic (political) input is obtained, the next phase in the budgeting process is to refer it to the respective medium-term expenditure committee

(MTEC) meetings annually during September. The primary objective of the MTEC discussions is to evaluate the budget submissions, spending proposals and to determine the extent to which departments have justified and reprioritized their expenditure for the current financial year and the medium-term expenditure framework (MTEF) baselines. In particular, these meetings are utilized to assess departmental outcome plans for the next financial year, to ensure that provincial outcome plans are aligned with national outcomes plans, to identify suitable projects, to analyze personnel and infrastructure requirements, and to perform a revenue analysis. As such, these discussions are influenced by political decisions regarding spending priorities and departmental outcomes. Various budget forums, in turn, focus on assessing departmental plans and budgets in the context of the outcomes approach. The approach aims to ensure that resources are allocated to specific projects and programs that may impact on the outcomes set. The analysis is based on the draft budget documents submitted by departments to the respective provincial treasuries.

Preparation Phase

During the budget preparation phase political trade-offs and prioritization of government programs are made to ensure that the budget fits government overall policies and strategies. In this phase of the budgeting process all the departmental budgets are consolidated in preparation for the tabling of the provincial budget. The budget documentation is finalized during this phase, which includes the following:

- an appropriation bill that reflects allocations to departments per program and economic classification;
- estimates of provincial revenue and expenditure;
- cabinet and explanatory memoranda;
- a socio-economic review, which provides a detailed analysis of socio-economic indicators that impact on the overall quality of life for citizens;
- the budget speech prepared by the office of the Member of the Executive Council (MEC) for Finance;
- a budget booklet, which is an easy-to-use guide to the budget;
- budget inserts, which may include key information published in the various newspapers to inform the citizens about the budget; and
- the Government Gazette, which reflects the transfers framework and allocations to municipalities, schools and hospitals.

All the documents mentioned above are subjected to intense political scrutiny in the sense that they are submitted to the relevant standing committees of the provincial legislature for their consideration and adoption. It should be noted that the respective provincial budgets are again consolidated and added to the respective national departments and entities to eventually become the final budget of the Government. The Minister of Finance finally tables the budget in Parliament, in short succession to the State of the Nation Address by the President.

Accountability Phase

A budget can be regarded as a spending plan that indicates how available public funds will be used by Government to address societal needs. The accountability stage is about assessing how effectively, efficiently and economically money was spent. This stage again accentuates the political nature of budgeting since it is undertaken by means of official annual reporting on the progress made during budget implementation (Bandy, 2015). Politicians provide an important monitoring and oversight function over departmental expenditure. The budget cycle is concluded by annual reports that are produced for submission to the Auditor-General (AG) and other stakeholders.

In terms of the statutory framework, the principles of political oversight are embedded in the South African Constitution. Section 1 of the Constitution requires a system of democratic government to ensure accountability, responsiveness and openness. Section 41 furthermore calls for all spheres of government and all organs of state within each sphere to provide effective, transparent, accountable and coherent government. Legislation such as the Public Finance Management Act 1 of 1999, the Municipal Finance Management Act 56 of 2003, and the Public Audit Act 25 of 2004 further provide for monitoring and political oversight over the expenditure of government institutions. The budget reporting framework is prescribed by the National Treasury, which is obliged to gazette a statement of actual revenue and expenditure with regard to the National Revenue Fund 30 days after the end of each month. According to the Municipal Finance Management Act (MFMA), the cabinet member responsible for local government must, as part of the report referred to in the Municipal Systems Act, report annually to Parliament on actions taken by MECs for local government to address the issues raised by the AG in audit reports on financial statements of municipalities and municipal entities. Furthermore, the AG, as the Supreme Audit Institution (SAI) of South Africa, exists to strengthen the country's democracy by enabling oversight, accountability and governance in the public sector through auditing. The AG is mandated with the responsibility of auditing all three spheres of government, all municipalities and any other institution or accounting entity required by national or provincial legislation to be audited.

Parliament, in turn, has the power to scrutinize, amend, adopt, or reject legislation. In terms of political oversight, it also has the power to monitor and hold the Executive to account for compliance with legal instruments and for their general performance. In terms of its budgetary powers Parliament does not have the power to scrutinize, amend, adopt, or reject the Executive's budget proposals. It has, however, the power to monitor budget implementation and to hold the Executive branch to account for using funds as authorized and for value for money achieved. There are two dimensions to Parliament's oversight obligations: financial or fiduciary (through scrutiny of financial forecasts, monitoring of the use of money, and scrutiny of financial outturns) and non-financial results (the scrutiny of forecasts of expected achievements, achievements during the spending year, and actual achievements).

Although the South African Government prepares budgets on an annual cycle basis, events outside this cycle, such as macro-economic realities, should also be taken into account. Wildavsky (1986, p. 317) cautions against an isolated annual budget process by stating that:

- only the next year's expenditure is reviewed;
- since huge disbursements in future years are generally hidden, it may lead to over-spending; and
- because government programs tend to be viewed in isolation rather than in comparison to their future costs, it may lead to parochialism.

To overcome this potential state of affairs, multi-annual considerations should be incorporated including future recurrent costs of capital expenditure, the funding needs of entitlement programs, and contingencies that may result in future spending requirements. It is exactly due to these considerations that the South African Government adopted a medium-term (i.e.three years) budgeting outlook to make provision for adjustments in expenditure priorities and realities. The MTEF thus overcomes the challenges associated with more conventional or classic budget planning.

South Africa's Budgeting Architecture and its Key Actors

Within the framework of South Africa's system of government, specific financial arrangements and budgeting processes take shape. A basic assessment of the governance architecture of the South African Government is thus necessary to appreciate top-down and bottom-up cascading decisions regarding finances in national, provincial, and local spheres. This architecture further reveals the political and technical interface in relation to budget and policy decision-making.

The Constitution establishes three spheres of government and assigns them specific functional responsibilities. The Constitution furthermore prescribes a framework to align the three spheres by coordinating their fiscal responsibilities. Revenue is shared between the three spheres of government to finance the administration of these concurrent functions. In particular, health and basic education are financed through a combination of the provincial equitable share and conditional grants to provincial governments.

As far as the fiscal alignment between the three spheres is concerned, three aspects deserve special attention. The first aspect is the continuous interface between the provincial and national budget processes. Provinces have different priorities and spending patterns, which make the interface a challenging endeavor. Failure to take full account of diverse needs and spending pressures in other spheres can result in priorities identified in the national budget being diverted to fund provincial or municipal priorities. The national budget process must therefore include extensive engagement with all spheres to ensure that priorities are shared and agreed upon. A second aspect that demands constant attention is that intergovernmental fiscal transfers should be structured in such a way that they successfully set into operation national policy objectives in a cost-effective manner. A third aspect is to ensure that provincial and local governments have sustainable funding so that they can continue to deliver their service mandates. In particular the sphere of local government struggles to maintain a steady stream of revenue mainly due to poor revenue collection practices, non-payment of services, and general service boycotts and protests.

The South African Government's budget currently exceeds one thousand billion rand (ZAR). The budget process aims to ensure that resources are allocated to meet South Africa's political priorities and to improve the quality and effectiveness of spending within sustainable fiscal limits. Through the budget process, a large number of public institutions plan, collaborate, negotiate, and decide together on a comprehensive plan for spending public resources over three fiscal years (National Treasury, 2014b, p. 21). In the section below, some of the key actors in this process are identified.

Key Actors and Structures in the Budgeting Process

The budget process is led by a number of political structures, which report to Cabinet for final approval of all budget decisions. Cabinet exercises oversight over the budget and its related processes to ensure that key government priorities are achieved (National Treasury, 2014b, p. 23). Cabinet reviews the proposed allocation of national resources and provides final approval for them to be tabled in the budget. The political structures involved in the budget process include:

- **Ministers' Committee on the Budget (MINCOMBUD):** The Minister's Committee on the Budget is constituted as a cabinet committee. Its mandate includes consideration of budget allocations to be included in the national budget, the MTEF, and the division-of-revenue framework. It also considers issues related to the determination of expenditure allocations, including the economic assumptions underpinning the budget, fiscal policy objectives, and tax proposals. The MINCOMBUD is convened and chaired by the Minister of Finance. The President on recommendation from the Minister of Finance appoints its members.
- **Budget Council:** The Intergovernmental Fiscal Relations Act 97 of 1997 established the Budget Council, which consists of the Minister of Finance and the MECs for finance of each province. The Budget Council is the body where national and provincial governments consult on any fiscal, budgetary or financial matter affecting the provincial sphere of government.

Any proposed legislation or policy that has a financial implication for the provinces is also discussed in the Budget Council, as is any other matter concerning financial management and the monitoring of the finances of provinces.

- **Joint MINMEC[2]:** The Joint MINMEC comprises the Minister of Finance, Members of the Executive Council for Finance from nine provinces, heads of department of provincial treasuries, representatives from departments within a particular sector, and senior officials from National Treasury. The Joint MINMEC generally considers recommendations relating to the resourcing of relevant policy outcomes and make proposals to the MINCOMBUD.
- **Local Government Budget Forum:** The Local Government Budget Forum comprises the Minister of Finance, the MEC for finance of each province and five representatives of the South African Local Government Association (SALGA) at national level, as well as one representative of SALGA from each province. The Budget Forum is a body in which the national government, the provincial governments and organized local governments consult on any fiscal, budgetary or financial matter affecting the sphere of local government.

Over and above the above-mentioned political structures, there are also a number of technical structures involved in the budget process. Below, some of the core actors in this regard are highlighted.

- **Medium-Term Expenditure Committee (MTEC):** MTEC is a committee of senior officials that makes recommendations to MINCOMBUD regarding budget allocations in the MTEF, taking into account government priorities, funding available, alternative funding sources, and the division of revenue among the three spheres of government. It is composed of the directors-general of the following departments:
  - National Treasury (Chair)
  - Planning Commission
  - Performance Monitoring and Evaluation
  - Cooperative Governance
  - Public Service and Administration
- **Technical Committee on Finance (TCF):** TCF is a committee of the heads of all provincial treasuries and is chaired by the Deputy Director General (DDG) of the Intergovernmental Relations division of the National Treasury. The TCF considers intergovernmental finances and the division of revenue and may make recommendations to the Budget Council, Budget Forum and MTEC. If agreed in these forums, matters are referred to MINCOMBUD. The TCF is consulted on all significant changes proposed to intergovernmental transfers, to ensure that the interests of provinces have been taken into account. SALGA should also be consulted on any changes impacting local government.

- **MTEC sub-committees:** the National Treasury appoints budget group leaders, who are responsible for engaging with institutions and preparing reports to the MTEC for each budget group. They convene in so-called "budget bilaterals" to prepare reports to the MTEC. The MTEC responds to the recommendations presented to MINCOMBUD.

Various other actors (i.e. structures and mechanisms) are involved in the budget process. Table 8.1 below shows some of these actors as well as the main budget instruments utilized to facilitate an integrated budgeting process for the three spheres of government.

This concludes the brief exposition of the architecture of the budgeting process in the three spheres of government as well as the key actors and structures involved. In the next section focus shifts to particular public financial and budgeting reforms in South Africa.

Table 8.1 Key Actors and Budget Instruments Per Sphere of Government

Sphere of Government	*Budget Instruments*
National:	
Ministry of Finance	State of the Nation Address
National Treasury	National Development Plan: Vision 2030
Ministry of Finance and Minister's Committees on the Budget	Government's Program of Action Minister of Finance Budget Speech
Auditor-General	Medium-Term Strategic Framework
Parliament Oversight Committees e.g. Standing Committee on Public Accounts (SCOPA)	Medium-Term Expenditure Framework
Medium-Term Expenditure Committee	
South African Revenue Service (SARS)	
Financial and Fiscal Commission	
South African Reserve Bank and commercial banks	
Local Government Budget Forum	
Provincial:	
Provincial Treasury	State of the Province Address
Provincial Legislature	Provincial Growth and Development Strategies
MEC Finance	
Intergovernmental Forums	Provincial Budget
MINMEC	
Local:	
Portfolio Committee for Finance chaired by the MMC Finance	Integrated Development Plan Municipal Budget
Municipal Public Accounts Committee	Service Delivery Budget Implementation plans ('top-layer' and departmental)
Chief Financial Officer	
Internal Audit	
Audit and Risk Committee	
Representative of the Auditor-General	

Public Financial and Budgeting Reforms

The African continent is facing a number of administrative crises. The recent decline of public administration on the continent has forced some African countries to reassess their governance systems. Their public-service reforms are evidence of the emergence of new public management (NPM) for improved public financial management structures and operations (Vyas-Doorgapersad, 2011, p. 1). These reforms coincided with the global crises (especially in the oil sector during 1970s), that led the way to "enormous deficit of the public budget" (Kickert, 1997, p. 17), and hence created financial pressure upon governments around the world. The financial crisis is considered to be a major factor: "adoption of new reforms in the public sector was essential to do public tasks with less money. Adoption of new reforms was also a way to review government's role in public service delivery" (Keita, 2014, p. 1). These reforms are the indication that the governments of African countries (and globally at a broader scale)

> strive to realise predetermined goals by attaining more concrete objectives and fixed short-term targets, and . . . money is needed to cover the costs of these objectives and targets. The prevailing political ideology of the ruling party . . . always has a significant influence on the government's financial policy. The original philosophy . . . was contained in the tenets of the *laissez-faire* system where government intervention in private, economic and social activities was taboo . . . through a capitalist economic system, a greater awareness emerged of the needs of the less privileged individuals . . . this awareness led to the concept of a social welfare state with socialism as the underlying ideology . . . the social welfare state idea is based on the so-called 'mixed economy' . . . also emphasises the collective and communal base of the state . . . failures of the social welfare state forced . . . to return to what may be termed an economic welfare state.
>
> Gildenhuys, 1993, p. 21

Despite these ideologies, Gildenhuys believes that:

> A rational approach towards identifying the objectives of modern government is to learn from the mistakes of the past and to identify and bring together the positive aspects of all approved systems. By following such an approach, it is obvious that the broad goals of modern government should be the creation of a good quality of life for each of their citizens.
>
> Gildenhuys, 1993, p. 21

This approach requires that the financial management of any country aims to do the following:

> [sustain and] maintain macroeconomic stability and fiscal discipline (neither over- nor under-spending), allocative efficiency (appropriate prioritisation, resulting in the optimal welfare . . . within given budget constraints)

> and operational efficiency (obtaining the maximum amount of goods and services of a given quality from a given quantum of public resources).
>
> Ajam & Fourie, 2014, p. 45; see also Schiavo-Campo & Tommasi, 1999; Schick, 1998

It moreover requires "increased financial accountability, and political oversight; improved transparency and citizens' access to information; more focus on policy priorities; ensuring of budget stability and human development; and more efficient control mechanisms" (Deutsches Institut für Entwicklungspolitik, 2011, p. 1; Fölscher and Cole, 2006, p. 3; Qwabe, 2014, p. 189), and in addition it requires equity and equality for sustainable economic development.

There were additional factors that led to the financial and budgetary reforms in South Africa:

> an agreed set of priorities in the form of a clear, integrated statement of overall public sector policy goals and outcomes has been often lacking. The budget and financial management processes have frequently failed to generate adequate information to assist political decision-making.
>
> Republic of South Africa, 1998, p. 162; see also Fourie, 2005, p. 678

> [Additionally,] horizontal fiscal coordination across ministries and departments tended to be poor. Often there was no link between the national vision and the annual departmental priority setting and budgeting processes. Frequently there was little or no link between budgeting and micro-economic framework . . .[.] The lack of effective budgetary guidance by treasuries to spending agencies was often accompanied by poor budgetary preparation by spending agencies. Budget implementation was frequently characterized by rigidity in the release of funds; excessive reliance on central controls; and the absence of reliable cost, output and efficiency data . . . Some of the reform initiatives identified are: the introduction of effective aggregate expenditure control frameworks to promote greater fiscal discipline and macroeconomic stability; the introduction of medium-term expenditure frameworks to promote improved planning and greater stability and continuity in the budgetary process, and to overcome some of the well-known problems associated with annual incremental budgeting; and . . . decentralisation of greater managerial autonomy at the operational level, to promote flexibility and responsiveness to local needs.
>
> Visser & Erasmus, 2009, p. 16–19

Public financial management, in the new dispensation, therefore, transacts "with the management of people's money." This money has been entrusted to Government. "It involves decision-making regarding the needed financial resources to implement government programs and projects; where to obtain these resources; how to collect and utilize the resources; and how to control all financial processes within given time frames" (Nsingo in Moeti et al. 2007, p. 40; Majam, 2014, p. 27).

Legislative Frameworks Regulating Public Budgeting in South Africa

As explained in the previous section, since democratization in 1994 South Africa embarked on a comprehensive financial and budget reform process. This reform process culminated in the design of a comprehensive statutory and regulatory framework to guide all financial and budgeting processes. The purpose of this section is to briefly elaborate on the most significant legislative and regulatory documents shaping praxis of public finance and budgeting.

The Constitution of the Republic of South Africa, 1996, and the Public Finance Management Act, 1999, are key legislative documents that anchor budgeting and financial management at large. The National Treasury, as the custodian of budgeting and fiscal control, upholds and supports this process through issuing budgetary guidelines and control mechanisms to the policymakers and managers in the public service.

No government institution, including public entities and parastatal organizations, may collect or spend money before obtaining authorization from the legislative structures of the state. This principle forms the cornerstone of an accountable and responsible government (Thornhill, 2012, p. 192). Table 8.2 below, briefly lists some of the most significant legislation and its primary purposes.

Formats and Methods of Budgeting

Budget formats "establish the rules by which the budgeting game is played (the decision rules) . . . [and] . . . create the standards by which success is measured (rules of evidence)" (Morgan, 2002, p. 71; see also Oxford University Press [global.oup.com], undated, p. 1). Budget formats are significant aspects of public budgeting that guide the manner in which the information regarding budgeting "is structured, the kind of information that is required to justify budget requests, and what kind of questions are asked during the budget review process" (Morgan, 2002, p. 71; see also Oxford University Press [global.oup.com], undated, p. 1). The most common budget methods are:

- **Line-item budgeting:** This is the commonly used and simplest form of budgeting. It aligns the inputs to the system with minimal information regarding purpose within the financial system.
- **Program budgeting**: This method of budgeting requires decision-making related to allocation of resources to fund a program.
- **Program planning budgeting system:** This method serves as an aligning link between the line-item and program-budgeting methods. It is a more advanced and long-term decision-making method that aligns the funding of programs with their facilitation.

Table 8.2 South African Financial Legislation

Legislation	*Purpose*
Constitution of the Republic of South Africa, 1996	As the highest authority in the country, the Constitution of the Republic of South Africa, 1996 sets the broad philosophical and operational parameters for public financial management and government budgeting processes. Chapter 13 of the Constitution, General Financial Matters, prescribes the establishment of a National Revenue Fund, aimed to receive all money from the national government, and the determination of equitable division of revenue that is raised nationally. It further provides for the perseverance of financial allocation to provincial and local governments; purposefulness of national, provincial and local governments budgets; the establishment of a national treasury; the implementation of a procurement policy; the determination of government guarantees; as well as the determination of remuneration packages for public servants. Other matters provided for include the establishment of a Financial and Fiscal Commission; regulation of the South African Reserve Bank; the establishment of a Provincial Revenue Fund for each province, as well as the determination of provincial taxes and local government loans.
Public Finance Management Act 1 of 1999	The Act (PFMA) aims to promote financial transparency, cost-effective manner of service delivery, and efficient utilisation of financial resources. The Act sets good financial management practices and uniform financial norms at national, provincial and local spheres of government. It further provides for expenditure control measures and oversight responsibility over the revenue funds. The Act makes a significant contribution to hold public managers accountable and to eliminate the waste and corruption in the use of public assets (National Treasury, 2014a, p. 1–2).
Municipal Finance Management Act 56 of 2003	On the local sphere of government this Act regulates financial governance, accountability and reporting in metropolitan, district and local municipalities. It is aligned with the PFMA to create seamless financial and budgeting processes across the spheres of government.
Inter-governmental Fiscal Relations Act 97 of 1997	The main purpose of this Act is to promote co-operation between the national, provincial and local spheres of government on fiscal, budgetary and financial matters. It also prescribes a process for the determination of an equitable sharing and allocation of revenue raised nationally.
Financial and Fiscal Commission Act 99 of 1997	This Act was promulgated with the specific purpose to give effect to the constitutional requirements relating to the role and responsibilities of the Financial and Fiscal Commission.
Division of Revenue Act 1 of 2001	The Act regulates the equitable division of revenue raised nationally among the national, provincial and local spheres of government. It furthermore stipulates reporting requirements for such allocations as well as the withholding and the delaying of such payments. The Act also makes provision for the liability for costs incurred in litigation in violation of the principles of co-operative governance and intergovernmental relations.

Table 8.2 continued

Legislation	*Purpose*
Preferential Procurement Policy Framework Act 5 of 2000	This Act, as amended by the Preferential Procurement Regulations (2001), provides for the establishment of a framework for the implementation of the procurement policy contemplated in section 217(2) of the Constitution.
Public Audit Act 25 of 2004	The main aim of this Act is to establish the Office of the Auditor-General. The Act covers matters such as "the finalisation of audits, audits that the AG opted to perform/not to perform and standards applicable to audits for the current financial year" (Fakie, 2005, p. 25). According to Thornhill (2012, p. 194) it is imperative to have a "general policy that sets out in broad terms how public institutions are to be financed." Therefore, there must be rules and prescribed control measures to ensure that they can give account in public regarding the collecting and spending of public moneys.
Division of Revenue Act 2 of 2013 (as amended by Act 10 of 2014)	This Act has the specific purpose to provide for the equitable division of revenue raised nationally among the national, provincial, and local spheres of government, the determination of each province's equitable share and allocations to provinces. It also makes provision for other allocations to local government and municipalities from national government and the responsibilities of all three spheres pursuant to such division and allocations.

Note: A more comprehensive list of legislation is available at www.gov.za.

- **Incremental budgeting:** The most common and often used method of budgeting in South Africa is incremental budgeting. In the medium-term expenditure framework (MTEF), the Government compiles the financial statements, which run over a three-year cycle. The other two years include the projected estimates on listed items. The aim is to adjust the budget based on inflation. This method of budgeting is appropriate to cover operational costs.
- **Zero-based budgeting:** Zero-based budgeting is a modern and modified approach that reverses the common approach of budgeting that combines line-item budgeting and incremental budgeting. In zero-based budgeting finance managers review and reassess each item of the budget starting from a zero base then vote for the items.
- **Performance-based budgeting:** Performance-based budgeting is intended to measure the success or failure levels of organizational performance. It is defined as an "approach [that] seeks to present a clear relationship between the input of resources and the output of services" (Griesemer, 1983, p. 17). Performance data is used annually in the preparation of the budget as the basis for increasing or decreasing the number of personnel and the related operating expenses of a given department required performing the service it renders (Shabalala, 2005, p. 36).

The reality is that "the multiplicity of governmental purposes makes it difficult, if not impossible, for any single budget classification system to satisfy all the varied purposes of budgeting" (Kim, 2007, p. 17). Thus, it is advisable in a developing country such as South Africa to combine program budgeting with performance-based budgeting, with clearly articulated indicators and targets to measure and assess the outcomes of the Government's service delivery.

> [However,] clearly linking the budget and performance management system and presenting this linkage through the budget document would seek to improve accessibility and user-friendliness of the budget. The program classification structure serves to highlight the direction of government policy and shows the areas in which each ministry is also linked to the PMS. It will also be desirable for the budget documents to add narrative as well as quantitative information including information on key trends for gauging performance.
>
> Kim, 2007, p. 128

These instruments are moreover crucial to improve transparency and accountability in the financial management system in South Africa.

Main Revenue Sources of Government

How does a government attend to its statutory and moral obligations? How does it implement its developmental objectives and core outcomes? The answer to these questions is that it requires significant revenue. It goes without saying that there is a direct correlation between the tax base of a country, the ability to generate revenue, and the competence of its government to render services. No government can compile a budget without a clear indication of the amount of revenue that will be generated. For purposes of this chapter it is thus important to investigate typical sources of revenue of the South African Government to design appropriate mechanisms for its collection and eventual budget allocation.

In South Africa sources of revenue differ between the respective spheres of government. For the national sphere, section 213 of the Constitution requires that all money received by the national government be paid into the national revenue fund. Various sources of revenue are paid into this fund. Below, some of the most significant sources per category are outlined.

Category 1: Taxes on Income and Profits

- *Personal income tax (PAYE)*: Income tax is the government's main source of income and is levied in accordance with the Income Tax Act. All individuals earning an annual taxable income above ZAR60 000 have to register with South African Revenue Service (SARS) as taxpayers. The number of registered individual taxpayers currently is estimated at 5.2 million. Non-residents are taxed on their income from a South African source. Tax is based on taxable income, which, in essence, consists of gross income less exemptions and allowable deductions. On average around 95.5 percent of taxes on persons and individuals are from PAYE (pay as you earn).

- *Corporate income tax (CIT):* The number of companies registered for income tax currently tops 1.5 million. Companies are taxed at an average rate of 30 percent. A special tax formula applies in the case of gold mining companies.
- *Capital gains tax (CGT):* Introduced in October 2001, CGT forms part of the income tax system and is levied on capital gains made on the disposal of assets.
- *Secondary tax on companies (STC):* STC is levied at a rate of 10 percent on profits of companies distributed by way of dividends.
- *Other:* Other sources of revenue include interest charges on overdue tax.

Category 2: *Taxes on Payroll and Workforce*

- *Skills development levy:* The skills development levy is a compulsory levy to fund the training of employees. SARS administers the collection of this levy in consultation with the Department of Labor. The current rate is 1 percent of a company's total payroll and it is payable by employers that are registered with SARS for employee tax purposes and that have an annual payroll of more than ZAR500 000.

Category 3: *Taxes on Property*

- *Donations tax:* Donations tax is levied at a rate of 20 percent on the value of the donation. The first ZAR100 000 donated in each year by a natural person[3] is exempt from donations tax.
- *Estate duty:* Estate duty is levied on the estates of citizens when they die. An estate consists of all property of the deceased including items deemed to be property, such as life insurance policies and payments from pension funds wherever situated. It only applies to estates as South African assets.[4] The duty, at a rate of 20 percent, is calculated on the dutiable amount of the estate.
- *Uncertificated securities tax (UST):* UST is payable in respect of changes in beneficial ownership of listed securities. It is currently levied at a rate of 0.25 percent.
- *Transfer duties:* Transfer duty is payable by individuals when they acquire property at a rate of 5 percent of the value above ZAR500 000 and at 8 percent of the value exceeding ZAR1 million. When property is acquired by a person other than an individual, such as a company or trust, transfer duty is payable at a rate of 8 percent of the value.

Category 4: *Domestic Taxes on Goods and Services*

- *Value-added tax (VAT):* VAT is levied at a standard rate of 14 percent on most goods and services subject to certain exemptions, exceptions, and zero-ratings, provided for in the Value-Added Tax Act (1991). VAT is also levied on the importation of goods and services into South Africa.

- *Excise duties:* Excise duties are levied on certain locally manufactured goods and on their imported equivalents. This duty is levied as a specific duty on tobacco and liquor, and as an *ad valorem* duty on cosmetics, televisions, audio equipment and motor cars.
- *Fuel levy:* The fuel levy is a specific excise tax imposed in accordance with the Customs and Excise Act (1964). Relief is available through a diesel refund system for farming activities, forestry, mining, offshore vessels, harbor vessels, locomotives used for rail freight, and large electricity generation plants.
- *International air passenger departure tax:* Fee-paying passengers departing on international flights pay a tax per passenger.
- *Environmental levy:* The current environmental levy is essentially a tax on certain types of plastic shopping bags. The levy aims to encourage the sustainable use of these bags.

Category 5: Taxes on International Trade and Transactions

- *Customs duties:* Customs or import duties are levies imposed on goods imported into South Africa. Import duties are imposed as a means to protect certain local producers. They also include anti-dumping and countervailing duties.
- *Miscellaneous customs revenue:* This primarily comprises customs duties that have yet to be allocated to the appropriate duty types. South Africa, for example also collects customs and excise revenue on behalf of the Southern African Customs Union.

Category 6: State Miscellaneous Revenue

This is revenue received by SARS in respect of taxation that cannot be allocated to specific revenue types, and includes:

- *Unemployment insurance fund (UIF) contributions:* The UIF provides short-term relief to workers when they become unemployed or are unable to work because of maternity or adoption leave, or illness. It also provides relief to the dependants of a deceased contributor. The bulk of contributions to the UIF is collected by SARS and transferred to the fund, which is administered by the unemployment insurance commissioner.
- *Road accident fund (RAF):* SARS is responsible for the collection of the RAF levy on petrol and diesel.

In the provincial sphere of government, the Constitution, Chapter 13, section 226 (1)(2) requires that all money received by a provincial government via the provincial treasury must be paid into the provincial revenue fund. The provincial revenue (budget) is derived from the following sources:

- allocation from the national government and the National Treasury known as the equitable share, calculated according to a formula based on the population of the province;
- conditional grants from the National Treasury, given with certain conditions attached. For example, a conditional grant to construct houses can only be used to do just that, without deviation;
- own revenue collected by the province and supplementary revenue collected by the provincial government. This includes gambling and betting taxes, hospital patient fees, and vehicle license fees.

Finally, in the local sphere, municipalities must ensure that there will be adequate money to pay for their planned expenditure as per their integrated development plans. There are various sources of income that can be used by municipalities to finance this expenditure. These sources can be categorized in terms of capital budget financing and operational budget financing. As far as the capital budget financing is concerned, some of the most significant sources include the following:

- *External loans:* External loans from a bank or other financial institution are an expensive form of financing for the capital budget because of the high interest rates in South Africa. Loans should only be used to finance major capital items such as roads, buildings, sewerage works and water systems.
- *Internal loans:* Many municipalities have internal savings funds such as capital development funds or a consolidated loan fund. These funds can make internal loans to the municipality for the purchase or development of capital items, usually at a lower interest rate than for an external loan. The municipality pays the interest back to its own savings fund, which can later be used for another capital project.
- *Contributions from revenue:* When purchasing a small capital item, the cost can be paid for from the operating income in the year of purchase. This financing source is known as "contributions from revenue." In most municipalities, this source of financing is used to pay for smaller capital items, such as one or two items of furniture and equipment.
- *Government grants*: Municipalities may apply to national government for grants for infrastructure development. The two main funds available are the Consolidate Municipal Infrastructure Programme (CMIP) and water services projects.
- *Donations and public contributions*: Local and foreign donors may sometimes donate a capital item or money to be used specifically for the purchase of a capital item, in a disadvantaged area.
- *Public-private partnerships*: Capital costs can be paid for by means of partnerships between the private sector and the municipality. In most cases

the private-sector partner will have a profit motive in the services and capital being financed, so the terms and conditions must be carefully defined to protect the community's interests.

As far as the second category of revenue sources is concerned, namely operational budget financing, some of the most significant revenue sources include the following:

- *Service charges or tariffs:* Users have to pay for specific services such as water, electricity or approval of building plans. This only applies to services where the exact usage of the service can be measured.
- *Property rates:* All people and businesses who own fixed property such as land, houses, factories, and office blocks, in the municipal area have to pay property rates. A property rate is a yearly tax based on the value of each property.
- *Fines:* Fines typically include traffic fines and penalties for overdue payment of service charges.
- *Equitable share*: The equitable share is an amount of money that a municipality gets from national government each year. The constitution says that all revenue collected nationally must be divided equitably (i.e. fairly) between national, provincial, and local spheres of government. The local government equitable share is meant to ensure that municipalities can provide basic services and develop their areas. The amount a municipality gets depends mainly on the number of low-income people in the area—rural municipalities usually get more.

One of a municipal council's greatest responsibilities is approving and regularly monitoring a municipal budget that provides money for implementing its visions. Without adequate revenue sources to implement the policies, a municipal council cannot serve its communities adequately. Effective financial management ensures that there are funds available to implement council policies. Good financial management and budgeting practices are thus key drivers for local service delivery. In a constitutional democracy like South Africa, it is vital that citizens understand the principles of good municipal finance and effective budgeting so that they can engage council and political representatives on the bigger debates about spending and development priorities.

Process of Public Financial Management in South Africa

In South Africa, there is an apparent paradigmatic shift in financial management from a line-item and incremental approach to a more outcome-based approach. The implementation of the Public Finance Management Act (PFMA) has allowed that:

> all budget planning . . . be based on the strategic and operational-or-business-plans of an institution: the strategic plan indicates the strategy

> and structure that will be followed in producing the output facilitating the desired outcomes. The strategic plan in the PFMA regime covers a period of three years and forms the basis for the operational plan; the operational plan covers a period of one year and provides the detail on how the work will be done. The operational plan should furnish sufficient detail as to the resources to be used and the expenditure to be incurred. The operational plan should also provide for the allocation of specific responsibilities with timelines, to ensure efficient and effective service delivery.
>
> Pauw et al., 2007, p. 56–57

It must be noted that the South African Government:

> formulates budgets to ensure that public expenditure is focused on social and economic priorities such as transformation or growth. The competing needs for resources [must] be balanced against the budget constraints determined by the economic environment and by macroeconomic policies. Such policies may include enhancement of economic growth, job creation and infrastructure creation.
>
> Pauw et al., 2009, p. 57

According to Graham (2006, p. 32), in a decentralized unitary state, "PFM reform can provide the necessary financial information (for example, on unit costs of service delivery) and performance information on service delivery outputs and outcomes (relative to national norms and standards) to enhance accountability." It must nonetheless be cautioned that budget and financial reforms, when they happen rapidly, may make

> deepening of such reforms difficult; weak coordination among oversight, constitutional bodies and central government that dilute the force of the work done by some agencies must be avoided at all cost; adopting a system where sub-national government has extensive expenditure responsibilities, but no revenue-raising powers.
>
> Wildeman & Jogo, 2012, p. 5

This resulted in unsuccessful fiscal decentralization with incapacitated local government and poor service delivery.

Budget Cycle

In the budget cycle various decisions are taken regarding the budget at different levels. In terms of budget allocation, the national government decides how much of the revenue (raised nationally) must be allocated to the three spheres of government. These three spheres then decide the manner of allocation of budget to all departments. Departments, therefore, take decisions regarding allocation of budget to varied programs within their departments. The budget cycle comprises four phases:

PHASE I – *The Drafting Phase*

This is a planning phase whereby the Cabinet is responsible for drafting a budget plan with the support of the National Treasury. The steps during this phase involve:

- *Policy prioritization*: During the month of February each year, the State of the Nation Address (SONA) incorporates the medium-term priorities that emerged from the MTEF. These priorities are considered by the MINCOMBUD to establish the allocation of resources to economic sectors. In order to accommodate the needs of local government, the established priorities are furthermore assessed by the MINCOMBUD in association with the Budget Council and the SALGA. The provincial executive committees take care of the resource allocations to provincial departments.
- *MTEF budget submission*: The National Treasury establishes a uniform template and guidelines for the national and provincial departments to prepare their MTEFs. However provincial treasuries prepare their own guidelines for provincial departments' MTEFs, which are reviewed by the National Treasury. The SALGA participates in the consultative process organized between the National Treasury and local government to discuss issues regarding local government grants. This consultation is imperative for the national departments to submit their MTEFs, including conditional grants to provincial and local governments.
- *Medium-term allocation process*: The MTEFs submitted by the national and provincial departments, and departmental priorities are reviewed in hearings by the MTECs. Crucial issues for MTEC hearings include "the proposed revisions to a department's medium-term plans and how they link to government's policy priorities and the key challenges identified for each sector; the credibility of the costing and affordability of the new proposal; the department's ability to implement new proposals over the MTEF period, based on past performance and expenditure trends" (National Treasury, 2015, p. 23). The recommendations based on the review are then submitted by the MTEC to the MINCOMBUD and the Cabinet. The provincial MTEC hearings take place at the end of September. The national MTEF submits the recommendations to the MINCOMBUD in early October. The National Treasury then prepares a medium-term budget policy statement (MTBPS), which after approval by the Cabinet is placed in front of Parliament in late October. In order to decide the final allocation of resources to the provincial departments, the provincial treasuries conduct MTEC hearings again in December. The National Treasury then compiles estimates of national expenditure and guides the Budget Review Process. The provincial treasuries follow the guidelines provided by the National Treasury to document their budgets.

The drafting phase therefore embraces the significant documents, such as Departmental Annual Strategic Plans; Medium-Term Strategic Framework; Medium-Term Budget Policy Statement. In addition, the drafting phase includes the State of the Nation Address in which the President of South Africa reports on the status of the nation, exploring the priorities and goals set by the Government for the coming year.

PHASE II – The Legislative Phase

This is an authorization phase whereby the budget prepared by the Executive is debated in the Parliament for accountability and transparency. Secondary participants in policy-making (citizens, media, organized interest groups) are involved in discussion and debate sessions during public hearings. These debates pave the way toward making changes in the budget through amendment of money bills if required. This phase emphasizes citizen participation in the budget process, in accordance with the Money Bills Amendment Procedure and Related Matters Act 9 of 2009. This requires the finance committees of the National Assembly and National Council of Provinces to organize fiscal framework and revenue proposal hearings; the Appropriation Committee of the National Assembly to organize a Division of Revenue Bill, Appropriation Bill, and other money bill hearings; and the Finance Committee of the National Assembly to organize Revenue Bill hearings. The legislative phase therefore embraces key documents such as the Division of Revenue Bill and Appropriation Bill that form part of the national budget.

PHASE III—The Implementation Phase

During this phase the budget is enacted by Parliament. The legislature authorizes the Executive, which, through government departments and state-owned enterprises, is responsible for implementing the budget and providing service delivery. Expenditures, performance and deliverables are stated in reports reviewed by the accounting officers, ensuring that expenditures match outputs.

PHASE IV—The Evaluation Phase

This is an auditing phase whereby the Auditor-General is responsible for assessing the final budget documents. The Auditor-General reviews the year-end reports and provides comments on the status of financial statements and management.

Fiscal and political oversight are required to ensure the effective and efficient implementation of the budget by all three spheres of government. This can be achieved through the establishment of political and technically inclined forums with diverse opinions exploring financial issues, creating an accountable financial system and transparent budget process, resulting in a sound financial management system in South Africa.

Concluding Remarks

Despite all the above-stated mechanisms and procedures for creating a sound financial management system in the country, fiscal analysis reveals the existence of challenges that require prompt attention. The World Bank Group states that due to the slow recovery and restricted progress made in the post-apartheid period,

> South Africa remains a dual economy with one of the highest inequality rates in the world, perpetuating inequality and exclusion . . . [and] . . . the unresolved set of complex socio-economic challenges has locked South Africa into a low-level equilibrium of low growth, persistent poverty and widespread exclusion and unemployment.
>
> World Bank Group, 2015, p. 1

This indictment is substantiated by the view of Lungisa Fuzile, Director-General, National Treasury, who in his review of the 2014 budget emphasized that although the democracy is almost two decades old, the country is still facing challenges in reconstruction and development.

> South Africa has high levels of poverty, inequality and unemployment. Joblessness among young people is of great concern. In many parts of the country, public services are uneven or of poor quality. Our economy is not growing fast enough to meet the challenges we face.
>
> Republic of South Africa, 2014a, p. v

However, there is a more fundamental issue that needs to be addressed in the future management of South Africa's fiscal affairs, i.e., what the state should look like in a global environment of secular stagnation, which is increasingly becoming a possibility that cannot be ignored (Laubscher, 2014, p. 3). This concern was raised by Nhlanhla Musa Nene, Minister of Finance, during his budget inaugural speech when he stated that "the challenge of governance is to choose wisely between competing alternatives" (Hassen, 2015, p. 1). This statement is a reflection of the depreciated South African fiscal environment, whereby "the rupture in responses to Budget 2015 shows a deep division of opinion about the purpose of the South African economy. It is reflected in shorthand descriptions of economic policymaking, demonstrating typical 'polarisation paralysis' and a 'leadership deficit'" (Hassen, 2015, p. 2). In order to improve the fiscal environment, "maintaining a stable long-term relation between expenditures and revenues is one of the key requirements for a stable macro-economic environment and a sustainable economy . . . If economic agents do not expect current and future policies to operate within the inter-temporal budget constraint, then the fiscal process would be unsustainable" (Jibao et al., 2012, p. 1).

The Medium Term Budget Policy Statement of 2014 (Republic of South Afria, 2014b, p. iii), states that "national, provincial and local government will need to continue identifying savings and improving the way they spend money. Key social programs will be protected. Government will continue to roll out its capital investment program. We will encourage private-sector participation in infrastructure delivery" to deal with social-economic and structural challenges. The Government has therefore established a 2030 National Development Plan with an aim of combating poverty, reducing unemployment and enhancing development. Nene in his inaugural national budget speech, the fifth in the country's democratic Parliament, delivered on February 25, 2015 (Media Club South Africa, 2015, p. 7) concluded that: "implementation of the budget . . . is the collective outcome of the activities of all South Africans. It is my privilege to table these proposals for the consideration of all South Africans, and to reaffirm our commitment to work together with all South Africans in pursuing a better future." However, the poor citizens are not interested in the policies, programs and statistics tabled by the minister. The challenge for the minister in the existing scenario of economic uncertainty is "to provide human-size budget information" (Van Zyl, 2015, p. 1). The analysis of 21 years of fiscal management and cross-country comparative data reveals that the financial bodies and systems have ensured that public money needs to be invested largely "in adequate service delivery. If government can find ways to deepen budget transparency to provincial and local government and can engage citizens in budget implementation, then the rest of us will find it much easier to support this quest" (Van Zyl, 2015, p. 2) for participatory, inclusive, and integrated public budgeting in South Africa.

Public budgeting in South Africa has witnessed a paradigm shift from a traditional centralized approach to a decentralized inclusive manner of managing budget. This shift has brought outcome-based demands to bear on the Government, requiring a transparent and accountable financial management system. In addition a need arises for the Government to introduce performance-based budgeting in delivery of services in a cost-effective manner. The fiscal analysis provides assessment of the budget utilized, but the lack of monitoring fails to determine the manner in which objectives set are achieved; the level of performance of service delivery cannot be measured in financial terms. This is an area of continuous fiscal assessment for sustaining social-economic development in South Africa.

Notes

1 Courts of law.
2 Ministers and Members of the Executive Council.
3 A natural person is a human being, as opposed to be a legal person, granted with fundamental rights of country.
4 Only land and residences in South Africa are included.

References

Ajam, T., & Fourie, D.J. 2014. The role of the provincial treasury in driving budget reform in South Africa's decentralised fiscal system. *Administratio Publica*. 22(3): 43–61.

Bandy, G. 2015. *Financial Management and Accounting in the Public Sector*. 2nd ed. New York: Routledge.

Chen, G.G., Forsythe, D.W., Weikart, L.A., & Williams, D.W. 2009. *Budget Tools: Financial Methods in the Public Sector*. Washington, DC: Sage.

Deutsches Institut für Entwicklungspolitik. 2011. *Reforming public financial management systems in developing countries as a contribution to the improvement of governance*. www.die.gdi.de/CMSHomepage/openwebcms3.nsf/.

Fakie, S. 2005. *The Public Audit Act, 2004* (Act No. 25 of 2004). http://reference.sabinet.co.za/webx/access/electronic_journals/imfo/imfo_v6_n1_a9.pdf.

Fölscher, A., & Cole, N. 2006. South Africa: Transition to democracy offers opportunity for whole system reform. *OECD Journal of Budgeting*. 6 (2): 1–37.

Fourie, D.J. 2005. The utilisation of the budget as a strategic and managerial tool. *Journal of Public Administration*. 40(4.1): 677–686.

Gildenhuys, J.S.H. 1993. *Pubic Financial Management*. Pretoria: Van Schaik.

Graham, J. 2006. *Accountability in a Federal State: Challenges and Prospects for Canada*. Ottawa: Institute on Governance.

Griesemer, J. 1983. *Accountants and Administrators Guide: Budgeting for Results in Government*. New York: Ronald Press.

Hassen, E-K. 2015. *Minister Nene's Budget 2015 exposes South Africa's poor economic policymaking agenda*. www.polity.org.za/article/minister-nenes-budget-2015-exposes-south-africas-poor-economic-policymaking-agenda.

Jibao, S.S., Schoeman, N.J., & Naraidoo, R. 2012. *Fiscal regime changes and the sustainability of fiscal imbalance in South Africa: a smooth transition error-correction approach*. www.scielo.org.za/scielo.php?pid=S2222–34362012000200001&script=sci_arttext.

Keita, H. 2014. *Furthering new public management principles through financial reforms in post-1999 South Africa*. Master's dissertation (unpublished manuscript). University of Stellenbosch: Faculty of Management Science.

Khan, A., & Hildreth, W.B. 2003. *Case Studies in Public Budgeting and Financial Management*. 2nd ed. New York: Marcel Dekker.

Kickert, W.J.M. 1997. Public Management in the United States and Europe. In Kickert, W.J.M. (Ed.) *Public Management and Administrative Reform in Western Europe*. London: Edward Elgar, pp. 1–25.

Kim, J.M. 2007. *From Line-item to Program Budgeting Global Lessons and the Korean Case*. Korea: Korea Institute of Public Finance.

Laubscher, J. 2014. *Mini budget: Fiscal realism required*. www.fin24.com/Budget/Mini-budget-Fiscal-realism-required-20141021.

Majam, T. 2014. A nexus between public financial management and public leadership. *Administratio Publica*. 22(4): 26–39.

Media Club South Africa. 2015. *South Africa's Budget 2015: the full text*. www.mediaclubsouthafrica.com/economy/4165-south-africa-s-budget-2015-the-full-text.

Moeti, K., Khalo,T., Mafunisa, J., Nsingo, S., & Makondo, T. (Eds.). 2007. *Public finance fundamentals*. Cape Town: Juta.

Morgan, D. 2002. *Handbook on Public Budgeting*. Portland, OR: Portland State University, Hatfield School of Government.

Musell, R.M. 2008. *Understanding Government Budgets: A Practical Guide*. New York: Taylor & Francis.

The National Treasury. 2014a. *Public Finance Management Act*. Pretoria: National Treasury.

The National Treasury. 2014b. *Medium Term Expenditure Framework (MTEF)*. Pretoria: Government Printers.

The National Treasury. 2014c. *MTEF Technical Guidelines for the preparation of expenditure estimates for the 2015 Medium Term Expenditure Framework*. June. Pretoria: Government Printers.

The National Treasury. 2015. *The Budget Manual*. Pretoria: Government Printers.

Oxford University Press. n.d. Budget Formats. http://global.oup.com/us/companion.websites/fdscontent/uscompanion/us/static/companion.websites/9780195387452/Budget%20Formats%204–10.pdf.

Pauw, J.C., Woods, G., Van der Linde, G.J.A., Fourie, D., & Visser, C.B. 2009. *Managing Public Money: Systems from the South*. Johannesburg: Heinemann.

Qwabe, B.R. 2014. Integrated financial management information system in the South African government: a multidimensional framework. *Administratio Publica*. 22(3): 186–201.

Republic of South Africa. 1998. *Presidential Review Commission Report*. Pretoria: Government Printer.

Republic of South Africa. 2014a. *Budget Review 2014*. Pretoria: National Treasury.

Republic of South Africa. 2014b. *Medium Term Budget Policy Statement 2014*. Pretoria: National Treasury.

Schiavo-Campo, S., & Tommasi, D. 1999. *Managing Government Expenditure*. Manila: Asian Development Bank.

Schick, A. 1998. *A Contemporary Approach to Public Expenditure Management*. Washington, DC: Economic Development Institute, World Bank.

Seidman, A. 1986. *Money, Banking and Public Finance in Africa*, London: Zed Books.

Shabalala, M.P. 2005. *Budget allocation and expenditure patterns of government with specific reference to government communication and information system (GCIS) for the period 1998–2001*. Master's dissertation (unpublished manuscript). Pretoria: University of South Africa.

Thornhill, C. 2012. *JJN Cloete's South African Public Administration and Management*. Pretoria: Van Schaik.

Van Zyl, A. 2015. *Help us help you, Minister Nene*. http://groundup. org.za/article/help-us-help-you-minister-nene_2721.

Visser, C.B., & Erasmus, P. W. 2009. *The Management of Public Finance: A Practical Guide*. Johannesburg: Oxford University Press.

Vyas-Doorgapersad, S. 2011. Paradigm shift from New Public Administration to New Public Management: theory and practice in Africa. *TD: The Journal for Transdisciplinary Research in Southern Africa*. 7(2): 235–250.

Wildavsky, A. 1986. *Budgeting: A Comparative Theory of Budgetary Processes*. New Brunswick, NJ: Transaction Books.

Wildeman, R., & Jogo, W. 2012. *Implementing the Public Finance Management Act in South Africa: How Far Are We?* Pretoria: Idasa.

World Bank Group. 2015. *South Africa Overview*. www.worldbank.org/en/country/southafrica/overview.

9 Public Budgeting in African Nations: The Case of Uganda

Benon C. Basheka

Introduction

Public budgeting attracts two strands of usage. The first is as a field of practice, which has moved side by side with the journey of human civilization. The second is as a field of study (theory), which is relatively young as compared to the field of practice. As a field of practice, public budgeting is part of public financial management (PFM) which remains a core function of any government whether the country concerned is a developed or a developing one. Public administrators are directly or indirectly involved in public budgeting at some or all of formulation, implementation, accounting and reporting stages as well as oversight. As a field of academic study, public budgeting remains at the heart of the broad discipline of public administration but more specifically within public finance and public procurement (supply) specializations. PFM broadly encompasses the mobilization of revenue and the allocation of these funds to various activities intended to deliver public services. In any country, Uganda inclusive, the instrument used to attain the objectives of government is a public budget. The term public budgeting covers the processes and intricacies involved in formulation and development, implementation, accounting and reporting about the budget as well as the oversight functions of a public entity's budget. The existence of the above two strands used to describe public budgeting implies that the term public budgeting has an academic connotation beyond just the practice. The theoretical understanding of how the public budgeting process is undertaken and the forces that come into play to produce a budget for a country, the disciplines that shape our understanding of public budgeting, the various approaches as well as whatever is done to prepare people in schools and universities to effectively undertake the process of public budgeting fall within the domain of public budgeting.

Public budgets affect all citizens of a country directly or indirectly whether or not the citizens are involved in the processes of making the budgets. Public budgets affect citizens differently as some are affected negatively through increased taxation of their income and others positively through mobilized resources as long as such resources are used to deliver commonly used inclusive public services. The process of public budgeting therefore often attracts different interests. Businesses for example analyze budget policy in order to make appropriate investment decisions that impact on the growth, profitability and sustainability of their investments.

Government looks at the budget not only as an economic policy tool, but also as a communication and governance tool. The spending and taxation policies of public jurisdictions, regardless of size, have economic impacts on entire government operations. Once the budget has been adopted by the legislature and signed into law, agency administrators and staff members become the recipients of budget information. Importantly, each of group affected perceives the budget differently. Citizens of a country depend on the government to provide crucial public services, goods and infrastructure. Whether new roads are built, whether children have good schools, whether healthcare facilities exist, and whether all other public services are adequately provided to a large extent depends on the effectiveness with which government raises its revenues and allocates money to meet various competing and sometimes conflicting needs through its budget. The budget remains the most important economic policy tool of a government and provides a comprehensive statement of the priorities of a nation.

An effective legislature of a country plays a fundamental role in distributing government resources to meet national priorities and the aspirations of all citizens in a country. As the closest institution to the people, the national legislature ensures that the budget optimally matches a nation's needs within the available resources. There are certainly competing forces between the interests of the executive and what the legislature should aspire to see in a country's budget. Effective legislature participation in the budget process establishes needed checks and balances crucial for transparent and accountable government thereby facilitating efficient and effective delivery of public services. Kiragu (1999, p. 68) clearly and rightly demonstrates how effective financial management is a critical feature of any public administration system. He argues that the key objectives of an effective public financial management system include:

- proper planning and budgeting for public expenditure;
- effective and efficient administration of government revenue;
- proper use of budget resources;
- effective control of public expenditure;
- accounting and reporting on public finance; and
- full accountability for all public spending.

All the elements of effective public financial management systems touch the scope of public budgeting process. Public financial management involves general governmental fiscal issues, although it also covers the full spectrum of social, economic and political dimensions. The assumption here is that the fiscal operations of government are a reflection and culmination of the dynamic interaction between all these dimensions within a particular time frame (Visser and Erasmus, 2011, p. 1).The budget provides the means for a government to pursue its policy objectives and the public budgeting process should offer a legitimate place for academic scholarship. Unfortunately as Hoque and Hopper (1994) have demonstrated, the developing country context has been neglected in accounting studies. A need to pay more attention to this context in academic discourse is a matter of necessity. Most literature on public budgeting in Africa has been written by western scholars with a few exceptions—studies on specific countries, but these are usually commissioned by international financial institutions as part of their policy agenda. These still use international experts, an approach that always leaves contextual information gaps that hinder the understanding of unique issues within developing countries. Nurturing country scholarships by local scholars has also become a matter of necessity.

This chapter on public budgeting in Uganda joins effort by African scholars to theorize on the subject of public budgeting using local country knowledge and context, as well as universal knowledge on the subject. Indeed, the chapter covers the elements of effective public financial management systems. Public budgeting involves the taxation and the expenditure processes of public finances in a democracy and has to be conducted within democratic principles. While the structures and processes may differ from country to country due to the nature of government (parliamentary or presidential), the principles of public budgeting remain largely the same. While most budgets in most African nations raise the hopes of citizens at their reading, their implementation often leaves disappointing traces of failure. The chapter begins with a discussion of the conceptual and theoretical issues regarding public budgeting, including its philosophical foundations and the meaning of the budget itself. The chapter then turns to the budget process in Uganda, with a detailed account of key stages and stakeholders involved. The chapter finally gives an analysis of the budget implementation challenges before concluding remarks are made.

Theorizing and Conceptualizing Public Budgeting

Conceptually, public budgeting is discussed in this chapter within the context of a democracy including the politics–administration interface within democratic governments. Its meaning needs to be clarified here to contextualize the debate to a democracy. The meaning of the word "budgeting" stems from the Middle English word for the king's purse, "budget," which contained the public funds (Schiavo-Campo and Tommasi, 1999, p. 33). From other sources, the word budget was also derived from the French word "bougette," which meant a small bag, portfolio or purse (Cowden, 1969, p. 283). In Britain it was used to mean the leather bag in which the Chancellor of the Exchequer carried the statement of the government's need for resources to the Houses of Parliament for the parliamentary session (Gildenhuys, 1997, p. 393). The leather bag contained statements on public finances, including the revenue and expenditure items and the purposes for which the expenditure items were to be utilized.

Today, a budget refers to the document containing the revenue and expenditure proposals of a public authority. Public budgeting is a field of study within public administration but more specifically in the public finance and supply sub-fields. The formative years of the development of public administration as an academic subject provides appropriate guidance to our debate. The politics–administration dichotomy debate (1887–1926), championed by Woodrow Wilson, laid the foundation for the discipline of public administration, and hence public budgeting. Woodrow Wilson's dichotomy made a clear distinction between the roles of politicians (policy-making) and administrators (implementing policies). Political questions were regarded quite differently from administrative questions. While politicians were to make policies (including budgets) administrators were to implement the policies. Several writers contributed to this contentious debate, concluding with Leonard D. White with his book *Introduction to the Study of Public Administration* (1926). The book was based on four assumptions; the last of these, which is core to our debate, is the assumption that public administration was not yet a science but had shown signs of being a science. This shaped the next paradigm in the evolution of the discipline of public administration.

In an attempt to respond and quite robustly address the challenge White had posed, scholars embarked on the journey to make public administration a scientific discipline. The second paradigm—the principles of administration (1927–1937)—saw scholars' efforts directed at developing principles of administration that would make public administration a science. In 1927, Willoughby, in response to the daunting challenge posed by White that administration was not yet a science, wrote a book, *Principles of Public Administration*, which had a progressive tone. He argued that administration was indeed a science whose study needed to focus on five specializations: general administration, organizational theory, personnel, supply, and finance (Basheka, 2012, p. 27). This delineation of the specializations gave public finance a natural home.

The public finance and supply specializations provide the locus for the debate in the public budgeting discipline. To date, public finance remains a key specialization in public management programs and even in financial management academic studies the hard aspects of public finance are covered under public sector accounting and financial management. Within public administration curricula, public finance is taught from an administrative point of view to describe the philosophical foundations of managing public moneys as informed by different ideologies. In business management courses, focus is on the hard aspects of accounting and book keeping. Public budgeting provides one of the avenues for managing public finances in a democratic society.

Visser and Erasmus (2011, p. 14) note that various approaches and theories with regard to governmental fiscal affairs developed especially during the twentieth century. Historically, budgets were developed as instruments for the compilation of executable programs; to serve as meaningful documents through which programs could be approved by the legislative authority; and to serve as instruments of control of the execution of approved programs by the administrative authority and for their revision, should their results require it

(Gildenhuys, 1997, p. 417). An effective budget maintains fiscal discipline and assists in allocating resources in accordance with policy priorities and hence it facilitates efficient delivery of public services. In order for budgets to contribute to the attainment of objectives they should contain a macro-economic framework, revenue forecast, a discussion of budget priorities, planned expenditure and past outturns, a medium-term outlook and details on budget financing, debt and the government's financial position. In this regard, as Thornhill (1984, p. 13) suggests, the most important features of a budget if it is to attain these objectives include those listed below:

1. The budget after its approval by the legislative authority is enforceable. The individual taxpayer is compelled to pay taxes and other amounts owing and has to comply with any other requirement contained in the budget or flowing from it.
2. The results of most of the objectives to be realized by the budget are not quantifiable. Therefore the taxpayer cannot always deduce the advantages to be received from a specific budget from the approved amounts of money.
3. The budget brings together a number of considerations. It may therefore be found that the budget has seemingly disparate public objectives, or the budget may have some objectives that may not be advantageous to the larger part of the community.
4. As the objectives of action taken by public institutions differ widely from those of private organizations, the process for determining the contents of a public budget are therefore unique. Revenue is not compared with expenditure in order to establish the productivity of the product or service. Instead a comparison has to be made between the costs, on the one hand, and the political, economic and social benefits that the community may derive, on the other hand.
5. Authorities do not always adapt their expenditure to fit their available revenue. As public goals are aimed at the promotion of the welfare and economic well-being of the community, authorities usually set out to determine what services will be necessary to realize these goals.

Budgets are regarded as public programs expressed in monetary terms (Mikesell, 1986, p. 32). Public budgets translate politics into reality through providing needed public services. The legislature in a democracy is assumed to have original authority (Gildenhuys, 1997, p. 87). It is composed of people's representatives and their decisions are assumed to have the blessing of the citizens. This position cements the role of the legislature in budgeting. Gildenhuys (1997, p. 88) clearly demonstrates how the ultimate authority to allocate funds undoubtedly rests with the legislature of a country and this principle is normally adhered to in all democracies. Uganda is not an exception.

William Ewart Gladstone (1891) once remarked that the finance of the country is ultimately associated with the liberties of the country and if the House of Commons by any possibility loses the power of the control of the grants of public money, the very liberty would be worth very little in comparison. This is possibly one of the strongest statements ever made about the importance of public finance in a democracy and particularly the role of administrators and politicians in running a functional democracy. Gladstone's work is one of the classic works regarding the theoretical foundations of the centrality of the legislature in public financial management within democratic societies. This leverage known as the power of the purse mandates the legislature (however it is named) to control a country's public finance infrastructure.

The struggle to ensure consent to taxation has historically presented itself as one of the major battlefields in the evolution of parliament in England. To guard against despotic royal rule, parliament sought to limit the monarch's powers to impose taxes so as to curtail their ability to maintain a standing army beyond times of war and immediate external threat (Harris 1975). The principle of parliamentary consent to taxation gained constitutional recognition when it was enshrined in the Magna Carta—a list of concessions to the barons that King John signed at Runnymede in 1215. But this agreement did not resolve the conflict over the power to impose taxes, which continued to simmer throughout the following centuries.

The Public Budgeting Process in Uganda

As in in any other democratic country, the Uganda Government's forecast of revenue and planned expenditure is laid out in its budget, usually produced on an annual basis and enacted into law by the Legislature, which authorizes the Government to spend funds in accordance with a set of appropriations, in accordance with the Constitution. A collection of laws and regulations regulate how the approved budget should be executed. The budget process facilitates the provision of public services. Within the public sector this process fulfills the same task as an economic market because it establishes what public services are to be supplied to the public, which individuals or groups will receive the public services, how these public services will be delivered and with what costs (Gildenhuys, 1997, p. 391).

In the early 1990s, Uganda's priority was to establish macro-economic stability, following a lapse in fiscal discipline occasioned by the misrule that the country witnessed during the turbulent years in the 1970s under the dictatorial regime of Idi Amin. The National Resistance Movement (NRM), which came to power in 1986, embarked on an uphill task of correcting the ills of the Amin era. By 1995, a new Constitution had been put in place and democratic institutions for public budgeting were ushered in. Several reforms were subsequently undertaken to manage both politics and the economy. Specifically as a result of these reforms, the merger of the ministries of finance and planning and the introduction of instruments including the medium-term budget famework (MTBF) as a means to control aggregate public expenditure resulted in a reassertion of macro-economic discipline.

In 1995 the medium-term expenditure framework (MTEF) started to be used as a tool for addressing the inter- and intra-sector composition of budgeted expenditures and expenditure outturns. Throughout its development, the MTEF was strongly linked to the budget process and all actors were compelled to follow the established procedures while preparing their public budgets. Agencies were encouraged to start planning and budgeting on a sector-by-sector basis and from the mid-1990s sector wide approaches (SWAPs) were promoted as a means of improving strategic planning and implementation in the roads, education, and health sectors. The Government later introduced output oriented budgeting (OOB), linked to the new public management (NPM) initiatives. NPM favors the use of market principles and ideologies. It is centered on a set of managerial principles and the economic principles of privatization, liberalization, stabilization, and creation of private-sector-driven economies. These various developments had direct implications on the legal and institutional architecture for public budgeting. New developments have taken place in public financial management in general and public budgeting in particular. These developments shape the public budgeting process in Uganda.

Uganda's budget process is currently regulated and managed under the new Public Financial Management Act assented to by the President of the Republic of Uganda on February 23, 2015. The Act establishes the processes for the preparation, approval and management of a transparent national budget. It also elaborately describes the various actors and their roles and responsibilities during the budget-making process. Quite importantly, the Act provides for a mechanism for managing oil revenues, owing to the country's ascendance among the oil-producing countries. It creates an oil fund, deposits to and withdrawals from which are highly regulated and elaborately detailed.

The budgeting process describes how public actors (administrators and politicians) in the country plan and interface to produce a national budget which determines how finite public resources are to be shared among competing demands. Budgeting is defined by Uganda's Public Financial Management Act as the process by which Government sets levels to efficiently collect revenue and allocate the spending of resources among all sectors to meet national objectives. The National Development Plan of Uganda (2010) grouped the country into four major clusters:

1. primary growth sectors, which include agriculture, forestry sector, tourism, mining, oil and gas sector, manufacturing, information and communication technology, and housing development;
2. complementary sectors, which include science and technology, transport, energy, water for production, land management and administration, physical planning, urban development, trade development, financial services, and cooperatives;
3. social sectors including population, labor and development, education and sports, skills development, health and nutrition, water and sanitation, and social sectors; and

4. enabling sectors including legislature, law and order, national defense and security, public sector management, and others.

The budgeting process has to see the money distributed to these sectors. Logically the budget process in Uganda, just like other countries, progresses through four core activities or stages that include:

1. budget formulation,
2. budget execution or implementation,
3. accounting and reporting,
4. external oversight.

Each stage deals with particular issues and has key stakeholders. Preparation of the budget is at the heart of the political process: it concerns the decisions on how to allocate the state's limited resources to competing demands. Indeed, Gildenhuys (1997, p. 393) demonstrates how the budget process is always a political process characterized by inherent tension between politics and scientific analysis. (The interaction often causes tension between the various actors.) Preparation of the budget takes many months and involves all public institutions. The Ministry of Finance, Planning and Economic Development manages and coordinates the budget process at the macro level while individual accounting officers manage the process within their own entities. The Cabinet, President, and budget committee set or approve the policy priorities in which line ministries plan and advocate for their resource needs. The Legislature reviews and approves the final plan.

The budget process, the actors and their major roles are listed in Table 9.1 (p. 222).

Budget Formulation

Similar to other countries of the British Commonwealth, the first step in budgeting in Uganda is the budget formulation process, which combines top-down direction and bottom-up planning involving different actors. The overall budget envelope, and sector and ministry spending ceilings are usually set by the Ministry of Finance and the Cabinet in accordance with the policy objectives of the Government. These are then communicated to the line ministries, which are responsible for preparing their respective sector budgets through a consultative process. This process often involves debate and bargaining and the outcome is a sector and ministry consolidated budget. This is then submitted to the Ministry of Finance, Planning and Economic Development, which consolidates all sector and ministry budgets into one government consolidated budget. The proposed consolidated budget is then presented to the Legislature, where it is debated and negotiated with the executive and eventually passed into law. Once passed into law, the budget has to be implemented.

Table 9.1 Budget Cycle, Issues and Actors at each of the Stages

Stage	*Issues*	*Actors*
Budget Formulation	Budget preparation Expenditure frameworks Capital expenditure	Cabinet Ministry of Finance Spending agencies Parliament
Budget Execution	Cash and commitment management including: – Adjustments – Payroll – Procurements – Transfers – Internal control – Automation	Ministry of Finance Spending agencies PPDA
Accounting and reporting	Accounting Reporting Budget monitoring	Spending agencies Ministry of Finance
Oversight	Audit Legislative scrutiny Legal reform	Ministry of Finance Office of Auditor General (OAG) Parliament Spending agencies

Budget Execution

This is referred to in some circles as the fine art of spending. Once the budget has been approved and the new fiscal year begins, spending agencies and the Ministry of Finance embark on its implementation. Some government agencies, especially the Uganda Revenue Authority, contribute to budget execution through collecting revenue. Other agencies contribute to revenue generation through various fees, levies and taxes they charge on services they offer. The spending ministries, departments and agencies (MDAs) use the resources allocated to them on salaries for public servants, running costs for their offices, such as rent and electricity, and goods and services delivered to their beneficiaries. The Ministry of Finance manages the flow of funds, and monitors and makes in-year adjustments to ensure compliance with the budget and PFM rules. The Ministry of Finance ensures the budget is executed in accordance with appropriations and rules.

The budget execution process is usually divided into four steps:

1. **Commitment controls**
   In order to effectively manage the government's cash flow and prevent arrears from accumulating, it is important to monitor the pipeline of future payments. Commitments are obligations to make future payments but the exact definition varies between countries, and the practices of recording

and tracking commitments are equally varied. How commitments are defined and monitored is therefore a central topic in budget execution literature.

2. **Cash management**
In order to ensure central control over cash, governments are advised to operate a single treasury account set of linked accounts where all government revenue is deposited before it is allocated for expenditure purposes. There are different methods of managing transactions linked to this account (or accounts): countries may centralize all payment transactions through the single account, centralize cash balances only but channel funds to spending agency accounts for payment purposes or operate an imprest system, whereby spending agencies are given advances which they clear on a regular basis.
3. **Budget alterations**
Substantial changes to the budget may require a budget supplemental. Preparing a supplemental is essentially a mini-budgeting process whereby an amendment to the budget is prepared and submitted for legislative approval. The Ministry of Finance is responsible for monitoring and managing in-year changes to the budget. Unforeseen circumstances or poor budgeting may make it necessary to adjust the budget. Rules govern transfers between budget categories (virements).
4. **Public procurement**
Procurement rules aim to ensure the government receives the best value for money when buying goods and services, without incurring excessive transaction costs. Procurement resembles a reverse auction, whereby suppliers compete to offer the lowest price for goods or a service. To balance value for money against excessive transaction costs, procurement procedures vary for different expenditure categories and the value of the purchase. While low-cost readily available goods can usually be procured according to relatively simple procedures, larger and more complex contracts require competitive bidding.

Accounting and Reporting

Accounting is the practice of recording, classifying and summarizing financial transactions. It is a means of assuring compliance with budget rules and demonstrating that public funds are being used for their intended purposes. Throughout the fiscal year, each spending agency records its expenditures in accounts. These accounts are consolidated centrally by the Ministry of Finance. At the end of the fiscal year, the Ministry of Finance issues a report that demonstrates how the budget was implemented.

Financial reporting is a key post-execution activity. Financial reports aim to improve budget compliance. They provide a means for internal or external actors to assess government performance. Financial reporting entails extracting and presenting data from the accounting system in ways that facilitate analysis.

The Government produces a range of reports for internal and external consumption. Typical reports include daily flash reports on cash flows, monthly reports on budget execution, revenue reports, mid-year reports, and annual financial statements or fiscal reports. To gain an understanding of how public funds have been utilized, and how they contribute to government policies, it is important to monitor the results of expenditure. This has led to the establishment of a government budget monitoring and evaluation (M&E) unit, which has developed its own systems.

External Oversight

The Office of the Auditor General, an independent government body, reviews the Government's revenue collection and spending and issues its own statement on the execution of the budget and the strength of the PFM systems. This report is presented to the Legislature for further scrutiny and follow up. The Public Accounts Committee (PAC) invites accounting officers to respond to audit queries raised by the Auditor General. Once this process is done, the PAC makes recommendations and presents them to the full legislature and recommendations are adopted.

Important components of the budget process in Uganda are the budget framework papers (BFPs), which are prepared at the national, sectoral and local government levels. They are three-year rolling frameworks used to streamline and guide the budget process, setting out planned outputs and their associated expenditures in the medium term.

The steps and timelines shown in Table 9.2 apply to every financial year. Typically, the budget cycle has four phases. The first consists of policy planning and resource analysis and includes revenue estimation. The second phase, policy formulation, includes the negotiation and planning of the budget. The third phase, following budget adoption, is policy execution i.e. budget execution—the implementation and revision of budgeted policy. The fourth phase encompasses the entire budget process, but is still considered its fourth phase. This phase is auditing and evaluating the entire process and system. The phases and steps of the budget process at national and sub-national levels are shown in Figure 9.1.

The budget cycle is a year-round process involving formulation (establishing budgetary policies, parameters and allocation priories) by the executive, legislative approval by Parliament, implementation involving MDAs and even civil society organizations, and evaluation and audit, in which the Auditor-General has a significant role. The cycle covers a number of steps involving the Ministry of Finance as the co-coordinating ministry, other implementing ministries, Cabinet and Parliament as the legislative body. Participation in the annual budget process is a two-stage process. As well as the process at the national level, there is also one at the local government level, which is aimed at broadening participation and consultation in the budget process. Local governments are required to prepare budget framework papers and update a

Table 9.2 The Current Public Budgeting Process in Uganda

S/N	*Activity*	*Deadline in the new PFM law*	*Practical timelines for FY 2015/16*
1	Submission of Annual Budget Performance Reports for the FY 2013/14 by Sectors to MoFPED	By End of July	By End of July 2014
2	Local Government Negotiations with Sectors	By 3rd October	By 3rd October 2014
3	Draft Budget Strategy Paper for next Financial Year	By 3rd October	13th October 2014
4	Provision of Macro Framework and Resource Envelope for the next financial year with detailed underlying Assumptions	By 6th October	23rd October 2014
5	Permanent Secretaries' Meeting on the Budget Strategy for FY 2015/16	By 10th October	23rd October 2014
6	Issue the First Budget Call Circular	By 20th October	29th October 2014
7	Consultations with Local Governments	27th October–11th November	27th October–11th November 2014
8	Consultative Workshop on Service Delivery	24th November	1st December 2014
9	Cabinet Retreat on the Budget Strategy/ OPM Retreat on Annual Government Performance Report of the previous year	25th–27th November	2nd–4th December 2014
10	National Consultative Budget Conference	By 28th November	5th December 2014
11	Sector Working Groups Consultations	October / November	By end of December 2014
12	Submission of Sectoral Budget Framework Papers and Detailed Budget Estimates by Accounting Officers to the Minister of Finance, Planning and Economic Development [Section 8 (2)]	By 15th November	By 31st December 2014
13	Inter-Ministerial Consultations (Technical and Policy Levels)	November/ December	27th–30th January 2015
14	Meeting with Development Partners	By 12th December	5th February 2015
15	Consultations with the Presidential Advisory Committee on the Budget	December	Mid-January to February 2015
16	Meeting with The President on the National Budget Framework Paper	By 15th December	Monday 9th February 2015
17	Submission of the National Budget Framework Paper to Cabinet	By 22nd December	Monday 16th February 2015

Table 9.2 continued

S/N	*Activity*	*Deadline in the new PFM law*	*Practical timelines for FY 2015/16*
18	Submission of the National Budget Framework Paper with the Preliminary Detailed Estimates to Parliament [Section 8 (4)]	By 15th January	By 20th February 2015
19	Submission of Semi-annual Performance Reports by MDAs to MoFPED	By End of January	By 13th March 2015
20	Issue the Second Budget Call Circular	1st February	By 20th February 2015
21	Submission of half-year financial statements by Accounting Officers to the Accountant General	By 15th February	By 13th March 2015
22	Approval of the National Budget Framework Paper by Parliament [Section 8 (5)]	By 20th February	By 20th March 2015
23	Incorporate the Parliamentary Comments into the Budget Framework Paper	N/A	Within 5 days after receiving comments from Parliament
24	Revised Macro Framework and Resource Envelope with detailed underlying Assumptions	25th February	20th March 2015
25	Cabinet Retreat on Half-Annual Gov't Performance Report	26th–27th February	26th–27th March 2015
26	Report on Fiscal Performance by the Hon. MoFPED to Parliament [Section 16 (1)]—semi-annually	By 28th February	By 28th February 2015
27	Issue the Third Budget Call Circular	By End of February	31st March 2015
28	Submission of the Final Detailed Budget Estimates by MDAs to MoFPED	By End of February	By 7th April 2015
29	Submission of Half-Year Financial Statements by the Accountant General to Secretary to the Treasury [Section 47 (3)]	By 15th March	By 15th March 2015
30	Submission of Detailed Draft Budget Estimates and Ministerial Policy Statements to Parliament (Section 11)	1st April	By 10th April 2015
31	Publication of the National Budget Framework Paper on the MoFPED Website [Section 8 (6)]	Within 30 Days after Parliamentary Approval	Within 30 Days after Parliamentary Approval
32	Consideration and Approval of Budget by Parliament [Section 12 (1)]	By 31st May	By 31st May 2015
33	Finance Bill and Budget Appropriation	31st May	31st May 2015
34	Meeting with HE The President on the Budget Speech	By 1st June	By 1st June 2015
35	Appointment of Accounting Officers	10th June	10th June 2015
36	Presentation of the Budget Speech in Parliament [Section 11 (2)]	By 15th June	4th June 2015

Table 9.2 continued

S/N	*Activity*	*Deadline in the new PFM law*	*Practical timelines for FY 2015/16*
37	Presentation of Vote on Account in Parliament	N/A	N/A
38	Processing of Q1 Warrants by the Auditor General	By 30th June	By 30th June 2015
39	Budget Execution Circular	By 30th June	By 30th June 2015
40	Budget comes into operation [Section 11 (3)]	On 1st July	On 1st July 2015
41	Publication of the Approved Budget Estimates by the Hon. MoFPED [Section 11(9)]	By 1st July	By 1st July 2015
42	Submission of Work Plans and Requisition for Committed Funds by MALGs	15th July of the next financial year	15th July of the next financial year
43	Repayment of uncommitted funds from the previous financial year into the Consolidated Fund [Section 15 (2)]	By 5th July of the next financial year	By 5th July of the next financial year
44	Re-voting of unspent funds from the previous financial year by Parliament [Section 15 (4)]	By 31st August of the following financial year	By 31st August of the following financial year
45	Submission of Annual Budget Performance by MDAs to MoFPED	End of July of the next financial year	End of July of the next financial year
46	Report on Fiscal Performance by the Hon. MoFPED to Parliament [Section 16 (1)]—Annually	By 31st August of the following financial year	By 31st August of the following financial year
47	Submission of Accounts by Ministries to the Accountant General	31st August of the following year	31st August of the following year
48	Submission of Consolidated Accounts by the Accountant General to the Hon. MoFPED and Auditor General [Section 49 (1)]	30th September of the following financial year	30th September of the following financial year
49	Completion of Auditing of Accounts by the Auditor General	By 28th February of the following year	By 28th February of the following year
50	Submission of Charter of Fiscal Responsibility to Parliament [Section 6 (5)]	Within 30 days of Commencement of the first session of Parliament	Within 30 days of Commencement of the first session of Parliament
51	Publication of the Charter of Fiscal Responsibilityusing appropriate Media [Section 6 (6)]	Within 30 days after Parliamentary approval	Within 30 days after Parliamentary approval
52	Submission of the deviation report on Charter of Fiscal Responsibility to Parliament [Section 7 (3)]	Within 30 Days after Parliamentary approval	Within 30 Days after Parliamentary approval

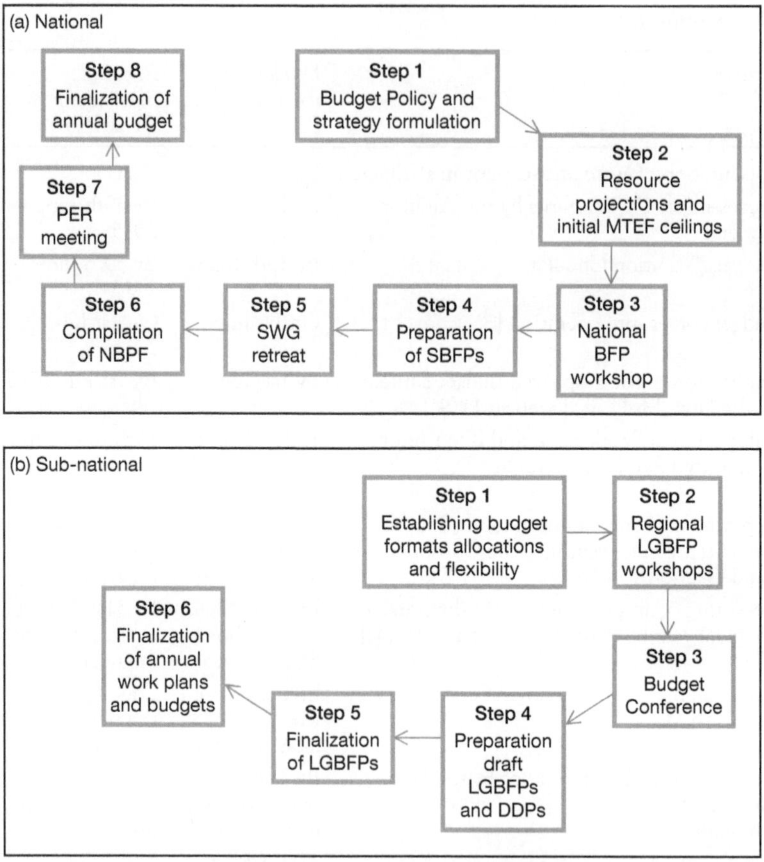

Figure 9.1 Budgeting phases of national and sub-national units

Note: Local Government Budget Framework Paper (LGBFP), National Budget Framework Paper (NBFP), Sector Budget Framework Paper (SBFP), Sector Working Group (SWG)

district development plan, which feeds into the sector budgets at the national level. The Ministry of Finance reviews the preliminary sector estimates and compiles the national BFP and the updated MTEF allocation, which are forwarded to Cabinet between January and March for approval. The final estimates of recurrent and development grants are sent to the sector ministries and local governments, who finalize the detailed estimate proposals consistent with the revised MTEF. Local governments prepare work plans for recurrent and development grants.

Major Actors and Forces in Public Budgeting Process in Uganda

Uganda was colonized by Britain and its public administrative systems including public budgeting have been shaped by the Anglophone tradition. Lienert

(2003, p. 3) drives this point home clearly by stating that most African countries have inherited either French-based or British-based public expenditure systems. The major actors in public budgeting have been shaped by the numerous public financial management reforms in the country. Uganda has been a public sector reform leader in Africa. It was one of the earliest countries to initiate reforms on the continent in the 1980s and was an early adopter of many interventions that are now ubiquitous on the continent. These include independent revenue agencies, MTEFs, public expenditure tracking surveys, and results-oriented management mechanisms (Andrews & Bategeka, 2013, p. 4).

The two most important players in the budget process are the legislature and the executive. Their respective roles and power are influenced by political context as well as the legal and procedural aspects of the budget process itself and internal legislative structures and processes. The constitutional division of power between executive and legislative branches and the doctrine of checks and balances are major factors. The legislative role in budgeting has evolved over centuries. The independent exercise of the "power of the purse" was a primary anchor of the legislature's emerging role in the governance process. Determining the allocation of resources among competing claims was critical to establishing the legitimacy and authority of the legislature as an institution competing with the monarchy (in the UK).

The budget in Uganda is prepared by the Ministry of Finance, Planning and Economic Development (MoFPED) on the authority of the President. The process starts between October and December with cabinet approval of the resource projection and the initial indication of the medium-term expenditure ceiling. MoFPED then organizes a national budget framework paper (BFP) workshop where the outlook and government priories and the initial resource ceiling are made known. This leads to the updating of the macro-economic framework and the issue of the budget guidelines, also known as the "budget call circular"; the guidelines reflect ceilings approved by Cabinet and they are distributed in September to all MDAs and local governments. The circular outlines the indicative ceilings for each vote and requires preparation of BFPs for each sector, and preliminary budget estimates consistent with sector resource ceilings.

Public Budget Implementation Pitfalls and Performance Analysis

Kuteesa et al. (2006) describe budget reforms in Uganda through a historical account of the country's economic recovery journey. They argue that Uganda's economic history has gone through four distinct episodes since independence. Between 1960 and 1970, Uganda had one of the most vibrant economies in sub-Saharan Africa. Real GDP grew at an average rate of 4.8 percent and GDP per capita grew at 3 percent per annum. The national savings rate averaged 13.4 percent of GDP, which was sufficient to finance a moderate level of capital accumulation amounting to 13 percent of GDP. The growth of manufacturing played a key role in maintaining economic growth, and by 1971 industrial output accounted for 14 percent of GDP. By 1987 real GDP was declining by 2.7 percent annually, and inflation was in at three-digit levels. The currency was heavily overvalued, and both the current and capital accounts were controlled, as were interest rates and commodity export prices. All sectors of the economy were operating below capacity. Gross domestic investment halved from its peak of 16 percent of market price GDP in 1971, to an average of 7.8 percent in the period until 1986. Gross domestic savings fell from a post-independence peak of 17 percent of GDP in 1970, to negative 0.4 percent of GDP in 1980, averaging just 6 percent for the period 1972–86 despite a significant boom in coffee prices in the late 1970s (World Bank, 2007). Numerous reforms were initiated in the 1980s and since then have had successes and failures almost in equal measure.

Andrews and Bategeka (2013, p. 6) recently stated that there is no doubt that PFM reforms had yielded major gains including the adoption of new laws, management systems, and administrative processes. The MTEF, public expenditure tracking surveys, outcome- and output- oriented budgeting, and a new IT system (IFMIS) are among the key reforms that have demonstrated the country's strong performance on globally recognized measures of PFM system quality. Kuteesa et al. (2006) have also reported how in the endeavor to enhance fiscal discipline and enhance the necessary smooth operation of the budget, in 1992/93 the government began formulating its annual budget within a three-year rolling budgetary plan otherwise known as the MTEF. Initially, the MTEF was a fiscal policy tool, but in 1998 it was formally anchored as a tool integrating budgeting and planning. The objectives of the MTEF are to:

- match expenditures with available resources;
- guide sectoral allocation of expenditure;
- facilitate strategic sector planning; and
- improve efficiency and effectiveness in resource use.

Uganda's governmance is not as good as it looks. In practice, the reforms in many areas have actually been limited to impressive appearance and do not yield the kind of action and effectiveness needed for a developing country with major problems getting basic services delivered, and addressing significant poverty challenges, and socio-economic deficiencies (Andrews & Bategeka, 2013, p. 10). An assessment report from the Government issued in 2014 gives insight into actual budget performance. Using selected sector statistics, a state of the budget implementation is delineated. Table 9.3 summarizes the performance of each sector in terms of progress made against key annual output targets, and in view of the budgets released by the halfway stage in the financial year. It further shows which sector output targets were likely to be achieved by the end of the financial year at the current rate of implementation, those that may be achieved with additional effort made, and those that are unlikely to be achieved at the current

Table 9.3 Government-wide Progress at the Mid-year Point in FY 2014/15

Sector	*% Likely to be Achieved*	*% May be Achieved*	*% Unlikely to be Achieved*	*% No Data*	*% of GoU Approved Budget Released*
Accountability	48	24	28	0	58.9
Agriculture	54	7	39	0	61.4
Education	47	3	38	13	44
Energy and Mineral Development	49	15	29	7	23.2
Health	54	21	25	0	62.5
ICT	64.29	7.14	7.14	21.43	51
Justice, Law and Order	63	10	24	3	54
Lands, Housing and Urban Development	63	16	21	0	62.9
Legislature	50	10	40	0	51
Public Administration	77	10	10	3	54
Public Sector Management	55	8	14	23	50
Security	95	5	0	0	41
Social Development	66	6	26	3	47
Tourism, Trade and Industry	68	12	17	3	48.1
Water and Environment	50	14	28	8	39
Works and Transport	55	26	17	2	46.4

rate of implementation. The table also shows the percentage of the approved budget (Government component only, excluding donor contributions) released to sectors by mid-year point (first two-quarters of the financial year).

The table illustrates that budget releases to sectors and their constituent MDAs are uneven at the mid-year point. Sectors such as agriculture, health, ICT, accountability, justice, law and order, legislature, lands, housing and urban development, public administration and public sector management all received over half of their annual budgets (government component only, excluding donor contributions) in the first two-quarters, while others have received considerably less than expected. Among these, education, energy and mineral development, security, and social development have all received no more than 45 percent of their annual budgets by the half-year stage. Good progress was being made by the security, public administration, justice, law and order, agriculture, social development, ICT, tourism and industry, and lands, housing and urban development sectors. In three of the sixteen sectors, the progress against outputs was unrelated to their financial resources, with all having low releases. This could mean that either their targets have been set too low, or contributions outside of the government budget (donor component of the budget or extra-budgetary resources) are being utilized to achieve the results.

The Budget Monitoring and Accountability Unit established in 2008 physically monitors priority programs and projects. This is a government-funded project unit, with contract staff members. The unit focuses on nine areas: health; education and sports; water and environment; agriculture; industry; ICT; microfinance; energy; and roads and transport. It is evident from numerous reports produced by this office and other government departments that the performance of the public budget does not meet citizens' aspirations. While large amounts of money are spent, service delivery is not generally speaking commensurate with the heavy expenditure. Indeed, Andrews and Bategeka (2013, p. 13) drew this conclusion when they asserted that whereas reforms have produced a PFM system in which laws and processes comply with over 70 percent of the "good international practices" measured in the multi-donor Public Expenditure and Fiancial Accountability (PEFA) assessment, actual implementation complies only 50 percent with these practices.

Conclusions and Policy Implications

In any country, budgets provide an important instrument for distributing public resources. The process of public budgeting considers competing demands and forces in an attempt to share the scarce resources. There are a number of actors and institutions involved in the formulation, execution, monitoring, accounting, reporting, and oversight of a country's budget. The legislature and the executive are the two most important institutions in budget-making. In Uganda, the Public Finance Management Act (2015) provides detailed guidance on how the country's budget is to be prepared and executed. Specific timelines are clearly stipulated and it remains a critical challenge to fully abide by the timelines. Once a budget has been approved, implementation, accounting, and reporting as well as oversight are critical activities. Central to the success is budget monitoring. Budget monitoring aims to verify the information in the quarterly performance reports and assess the link between financial performance and physical performance.

Quarterly budget monitoring reports present findings and high-level recommendations to the different actors. The Budget Directorate at the Ministry of Finance uses the information to engage with spending agencies on performance issues. Each sector is required to submit a written response explaining areas of under-performance. The reports are aimed at individuals working in Parliament (including the Parliamentary Budget Office), government officials and development partners. The unit also has a direct reporting line to senior management in the ministry and this implies that priority concerns can be flagged. The work of this unit complements that of other government agencies, such as the Auditor General, the Accountant General, Office of the Prime Minister and the Inspector General of Government. To have effective public budgeting, independence in role performance is critical. The different constitutional bodies for managing public budgets must be allowed to perform their duties without any interference. Professionalism needs to be jealously guarded by all actors especially the administrators. The role of politicians and administrators in public budgeting must be maintained as per established procedures.

References

Andrews, M., & Bategeka, L. (2013). *Overcoming the limits of institutional reform in Uganda*. WIDER Working Paper No. 201.

Basheka, B.C. (2012). The paradigms of public administration re-examined: A reflection. *Journal of Public Administration*, 47(1): 8–25.

Cowden, J.W. (1969). *Holmes's Local Government Finance in South Africa*, 2nd ed. Durban: Butterworth.

Gildenhuys, J.S.H. (1997). *Public Financial Management*. Pretoria: J.L. van Schaik.

Harris, G. L. (1975). *King, Parliament, and Public Finance in Medieval England to 1369*, Oxford: Clarendon Press.

Hoque, Z., & Hopper, T. (1994). Rationality, accounting and politics: a case study of management control in a Bangladeshi jute mill. *Management Accounting Research*, 5: 5–30.

Kiragu, K. (1999). Public Financial Management. In Adamolekun, L. (Ed.) *Public Management in Africa: Main Issues and Selected Country Studies*. Ibadan: Spectrum Books.

Kuteesa, F., Magona, I., Wanyera, I., & Wokadala, J. (2006). Uganda: A Decade of Budget Reform and Poverty Reduction. *OECD Journal on Budgeting*, 6(2): 1–25.

Lienert, I. (2003). A comparison between two public expenditure management systems in Africa. *IMF working paper (WP/03/02)*, International Monetary Fund.

Mikesell, J.L. (1986).*Fiscal Administration: Analysis and Application for the Public Sector*. Homewood, IL: The Dorsey Press.

National Development Plan. (2010). National Planning Authority, Kampala, Uganda.

Public Financial Management Act. (2015). Ministry of Finance, Planning and Economic Development, Kampala, Uganda.

Schiavo-Campo, S. (2008). *Of mountains and molehills: The Medium-Term Expenditure Framework*. Conference on Sustainability and Efficiency in Managing Public Expenditures, p. 7.

Schiavo-Campo, S., & Tommasi, D. (1999). *Managing Government Expenditure*. Manila: ADB.

Thornhill, C. (1984). *Die begroting in die openbare finansiele administrasie*. Pretoria, J.L. van Schaik.

Visser, C.B., & Erasmus, P. W. (2002). *The Management of Public Finance: A Practical Guide*. Oxford: Oxford University Press.

Visser, C.B., & Erasmus, P.W. (2011). *The Management of Public Finance: A Practical Guide*. Goodwood, South Africa: Oxford University Press, Southern Africa.

White, L.D. (1926). *Introduction to the Study of Public Administration*. New York: Macmillan, 1926.

Willoughby, W.F. (1927). *Principles of Administration: with special reference to the national and state governments of the United States*. Washington, DC: Brookings Institution.

World Bank. (2007). UGANDA Moving Beyond Recovery: Investment and Behavior Change, for Growth, *Country Economic Memorandum Volume II: Report No.* 39221-UG, Washington, DC.

10 Public Budgeting in Zimbabwe: Trends, Processes, and Practices

Gideon Zhou, Ricky Munyaradzi Mukonza, and Hardlife Zvoushe

Introduction

The chapter takes a decade-focused review of trends, processes and practices of public budgeting in post-independence Zimbabwe. Analysis of public budgeting over the four decades since independence strongly suggests that the colonial legacy has remained a pervasive subterranean force directly informing and influencing how Zimbabwe addresses the core political questions of who gets what, how and when in the body politic. Public budgetary processes in each decade point to a post-colonial state making political calculations and choices in a bid to reconcile the unfolding socio-economic pressures within its unsustainable inherited historical realities. In fact, one can read the state of politics and the economy by merely looking at the contents of the budget decisions over the decades. The political and economic challenges experienced by the nation since the dawn of independence are clearly mirrored in its national budgets. Guided by this framework of reasoning, this chapter specifically interrogates the following sub-issues in its bid to sniff out the structural and situational forces influencing budgetary trends, process and practices in Zimbabwe:

- the constitutional, legislative and institutional basis of public budgeting;
- the impact of pre- and post-independence dynamics on budgeting;
- critical institutional actors in national budgeting;
- core national value considerations and principles that have influenced prioritization of budget targets, allocation and fiscal measures;
- dominant revenue mobilization and expenditure control strategies enunciated in national budgets;
- challenges disabling the effectiveness of public budgets as instruments of promoting economic and fiscal management;
- measures that should be adopted to strengthen the effectiveness of public budgeting; and
- lessons that can be gleaned from budgeting experiences in Zimbabwe.

Information relating to these sub-thematic issues was gathered through a combination of desk and field research. Desk research entails review of relevant published material, government policy documents (national budget statements, mid-term fiscal policy statements, parliamentary statements), and internet searches. Field research involves interviews with relevant actors in the fiscal sector such as fiscal authorities (at both the policy-making and policy execution level), academic experts and local think tanks. The study seeks to ensure a balanced review of public budgetary process by gathering data from both state and non-state sources. This is critical because fiscal authorities interact with relevant private actors during budget formulation. While non-state actors do not own the public budgeting processes, they nevertheless influence these processes.

The Geo-Political Contexts of Zimbabwe

It is instructive to note that a country's geographical conditions have a direct bearing on public budgeting processes. It influences the way the national cake is distributed across the competing development centers of the country. In fact, each geographical area constitutes an expenditure zone in need of budgetary support. For example, a country with some of its geographical regions highly prone to perennial bouts of droughts is bound to have drought-mitigating fiscal measures featuring in its national budgets.

Zimbabwe is a southern African landlocked country occupying a land space of 390,730 square kilometres between Zambia to the north and north-east, South Africa to the south, Mozambique to the east and Botswana to the south-west. Its population, which in 1979 stood around 7,260,000 (Government of Zimbabwe, 1981, p. 7) is currently around 13 million. Its land space falls into five ecological zones with zone one comprising high rainfall areas suitable for intensive farming and zone five being drought-prone areas largely unsuitable for agricultural use. For administration purposes, Zimbabwe is divided into 10 provinces comprising two metropolitan provinces (Harare and Bulawayo) and eight non-metropolitan provinces (Midlands, Masvingo, Matabeleland North, Matabeleland South, Mashonaland West, Mashonaland Central, Mashonaland East, and Manicaland).

Its historical existence dates back to a century of settler colonialism (1890–1980) in which it existed as Southern Rhodesia (1890s–1965) and Rhodesia (1965–1979). Its independence was attained in 1980 following a gruelling seven-year armed struggle against the white settler regime. Since independence, a black government led by ZANU PF has been in power with Robert Gabriel Mugabe as its first serving Prime Minister (1980–87) and President (1987 to date). This is despite notable competition from the Zimbabwe Unity Movement (ZUM) in the mid-1990s and Movement for Democratic Change (MDC) in 1999. ZANU PF represents a political merger in 1987 between ZANU and ZAPU, the two main political groups that waged the liberation struggle as ZANLA and ZIPRA, respectively. It should be noted that following the formation of the Movement for Democratic Change (MDC), national politics in Zimbabwe became home to unending political strife and unbridled polarization along party lines. This strife nosedived after the fiercely contested results of the 2008 harmonized elections to the extent that the Southern African Development Community (SADC) had to intervene by negotiating a global political agreement (GPA) between ZANU PF and the two MDC political subgroups (MDC-T led by Morgan Tsvangirai and MDC led by Arthur Mutambara).

These political developments had a deleterious effect on public budgeting processes as they left little room for broad-based consultation and long-range fiscal policy planning. The boundary between state authority and political party authority became blurred, with informal structures (party structures) seemingly holding sway over formal structures (Zhou & Zvoushe, 2012). Politically influenced budgetary allocations were also very visible during this period. Interestingly, it was during this period that some of the hotly contested policies such as access to information and protection of privacy (AIPPA) and the Public Order and Security Act (POSA) were crafted. One reads from these policies attempts by the state to protect itself from what it perceived as intrusive forces from within and outside. Although socio-economic situation significantly stabilized during and after setting up of the inclusive government in 2009, Zimbabwe is yet to recover from some of the bruising sustained during the decade of political instability. The veil of secrecy that characterized fiscal policy processes during this period had far-reaching ripple effects on budget processes.

Legal Frameworks

Legal frameworks serve as the authority and regulatory contexts of budgetary processes. They prescribe what procedures should be followed as well as proscribing unwanted behavioral practices. In this way, they lend predictability to national budgetary processes. Public budgeting in Zimbabwe is executed within specific constitutional and legislative provisions. It is principally executed within the supreme law of the country, Chapter 17, section 305(1–2) of the Constitution of Zimbabwe Amendment (No. 20) Act 2013, and an Act of Parliament, the Public Finance Management Act (Chapter 22:19), supported by an array of ancillary legislation such as the Appropriations Act and the Finance Act. These legal provisions vest powers relating to the management of the finances of government in the Minister responsible for finance. As the principal manager of public funds, the minister is obliged by the Constitution of Zimbabwe to prepare the national budget and lay before Parliament, "on a day on which Parliament sits, before or not later than thirty days after the start of each financial year Estimates of the Revenue and Expenditure of Zimbabwe for that financial year" (section 305 (2). Section 305 (1) of the national Constitution stipulates that "every year the Minister responsible for finance must present to the National Assembly a statement of the estimated revenues and expenditures of the Government in the next financial year" while section 2 lays down that:

> The estimates of revenue and expenditure must be presented to the National Assembly in terms of subsection (1) on a day on which the assembly sits

before or not later than thirty days after the start of each financial year, but if Parliament is dissolved and it is impossible to lay estimates before the Assembly by the time, then they must be laid before the Assembly within thirty days after the Assembly first meets following the dissolution.

Part II (section 7) of the Public Finance Management Act outlines the duties and powers of the Minister of Finance while Part III makes specific reference to the national budget and submission to Parliament of annual estimates of revenues and expenditures. Part IV refers to preparation and reporting of annual financial statements by ministries, preparation and reporting of quarterly financial statements, preparation and reporting of monthly financial statements, and consolidation of financial statements, among others.

The Budget Process

Although budget presentations mostly take place in mid-November, budget consultations start as far back as April, when all ministries and government departments are invited to submit bids. Spending ministries are expected to conduct wide consultations with relevant stakeholders so that their bids are a true reflection of the financial requirements of the ministry or department. By July, all bids are expected to have been submitted to the Ministry of Finance. Extensive inter-ministerial consultations ensue during this period, spending ministries and departments defending their bids where queries are raised. This verification process is critical as ministries often inflate their bids. A series of pre-budget public hearings (consultations) are conducted in provinces by the Minister of Finance around October before these bids are consolidated into a budget white paper for presentation in Parliament in November. There is also active involvement of parliamentary portfolio committees at this stage. After presentation in Parliament, post-budget reviews follow in which budget estimates of expenditure are thoroughly scrutinized before Parliament approves the Finance Bill and Appropriations Bill. These Bills are then passed to the President and if assented to, become the Finance Act and Appropriations Act, respectively. These acts sanction spending and collection of revenue by the state. The Zimbabwe Revenue Authority (ZIMRA) is the sole revenue collection agent.

As is typical in Westminster budget models, the Minister of Finance plays a key role in budget planning with Parliament exercising approval powers. It is instructive to note that while Parliament has powers to reject the budget, these powers are more visible in principle than in practice as they are yet to be exercised in post-independence Zimbabwe. Notwithstanding this, since the 1990s there has been a shift from a secretive budgetary process to a relatively more open and participatory process with active involvement of parliamentary committees in the pre- and post-budget preparation stages. There has also been an emerging culture of budget hearings—frameworks that have provided space for public participation in budget processes. The public budget cycle is illustrated in Figure 10.1.

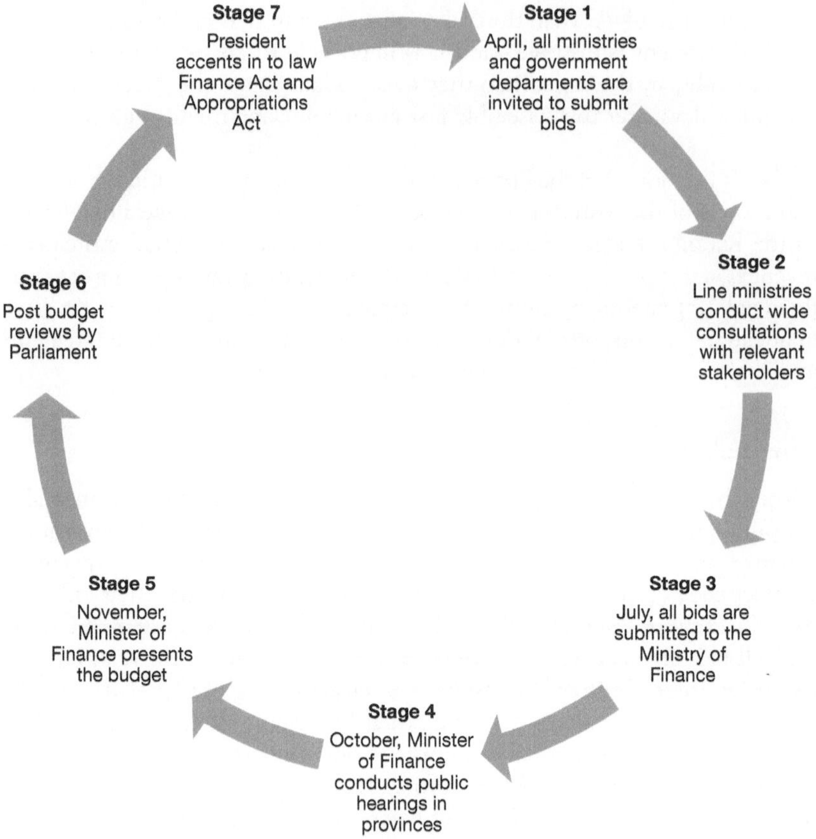

Figure 10.1 Public budget cycle in Zimbabwe

The Colonial Development Strategy and Fiscal Policy

Reviews of post-colonial literature on Zimbabwe generally reveal that the dawn of independence in 1980 did not immediately translate into overall control of key state apparatus by the new black government (Agere, 1998; Bratton, 1981; Dashwood, 2000; Herbst, 1990; Mandaza, 1986; Zhou 2000). In the words of Herbst (1990, p. 30), "in 1980 the ZANU PF black government took over a bruised but not defeated settler state" while Bratton also notes that:

> the ZANU PF leadership constituted a thin veneer atop a largely untransformed state apparatus. The Cabinet found itself in a fragile position because institutions wholly or partially controlled by groups of dubious loyalty were interposed between the leadership and its popular base.
>
> Bratton, 1981, p. 452

The import of these observations is that the colonial state poised a potent potential center of resistance in the post-independence transformative development drive.

On the economic front, although colonial Zimbabwe had experienced accelerated industrialization, with the manufacturing sector being the fastest growing sector, this growth did not translate into a significant growth in employment (Government of Zimbabwe, 1981). Gross domestic product experienced growth between 1975 and 1978 but thereafter experienced negative growth due to the escalation of the war and tightening of sanctions. International economic isolation reduced foreign direct and portfolio investment by severely restricting access to external capital and money markets that could have supplied funds to finance public investment programs. The physical infrastructure had been ravaged by war while the economic infrastructure had suffered half a decade of international isolation. The costs of the war in terms of infrastructure, general economic growth and development as well as human lives were substantial. The impact of the armed struggle was particularly devastating in the rural areas with much of the rural social and physical infrastructure either partially or totally destroyed by military action of one kind or another. Water supplies, dip tanks, contour ridges, schools, clinics, roads, and bridges were military targets for damage or destruction. Rehabilitation of this infrastructure emerged as a dominant consideration in post-independence fiscal planning.

Income and wealth distribution was skewed along racial lines with much of the economic development significantly biased in favor of the modern sector and, within that sector; the distribution of economic benefits was highly skewed in favor of a small elite (Government of Zimbabwe, 1981, p. 15). In fact, it was a classic dual economy that on one hand had a fairly advanced and sophisticated modern commercial industrial and agricultural sector and, on the other an under-developed rural subsistence sector. The nation was highly unequal with very high levels of poverty in both rural and urban communities. Public and private investment was concentrated in the modern sector while the rural sector generally received little investment. This, in the long term, generated gross inequalities in income distribution and in income-earning opportunities between inhabitants and workers in the modern and rural sectors. Per capita income in the modern sector was at least twenty times that in the rural sector although there were significant differentials within the modern sector; 1979 average earnings for black workers in the modern sector were USD1,180 per person per year and USD11,950 for other workers (Government of Zimbabwe, 1981, p. 16). This skew was evident in the allocation of public employment and national resources. In the public service, as stated by Murapa (1986, p. 62), only 3,368 of the 10,570 established officers inherited by the new Government in 1980 were black, with no blacks holding positions above the senior administrative level. The land sector experienced extensive land alienation with the settlers occupying the larger and more fertile tracts while the peasantry were forced into the more marginal lands, which, under the growing population, could not sustain the farming systems (Moyo, 1992, p. 166). The Land Apportionment Act (1930) and other policies had largely put a seal on the development of production among the peasantry, which had no access to the inputs necessary for technologically advanced and productive farming. Seidman (1986) even laments that while the Grain Marketing Board had twenty-seven depots before independence, only one (in Murewa), specifically served communal sectors. This skewed development was most manifest in the education sector, where policy execution served as an instrument for sustaining white power and consolidating white control in the key positions of successive colonial governments from the BSAP Company to the Rhodesia Front (Zvobgo, 1986, p. 319).

On the whole, colonial budget policy had served as a key facet of a broader strategy aimed at promoting settler supremacy in key sectors such as agriculture, public service, investment, education, health, and social welfare (Mlambo, 1997; Seidman, 1986; Zhou & Masunungure, 2006, 10–11; Mandaza, 1986, p. 15; Zhou, 2001, p. 231). Racial colonial fiscal policies left behind a huge current budget deficit and a USD 700 million debt (Zimbabwe Europe Network, Eurodad & Jubilee Debt Campaign, 2011, p. 6) with a large proportion of total government expenditures arising from defense expenditures. For instance, in 1971 defense and internal security claimed 18 percent of aggregate budget (Zimbabwe Coalition on Debt and Development, 2001, p. 21).

Post-Independence Budget Imperatives, Budgeting Trends and Practices

First-Decade Public Budgeting (1980–1989)

The transition from colonial rule to independence not only ushered in a new political configuration of power but also marked a paradigmatic change in the national development agenda in which public budgeting served as a vehicle for engineering sustainable socio-economic development. This entailed promoting balanced regional development, integrated programs for rural development, equitable distribution of resources, nation building, reconciliation (peaceful co-existence), rehabilitation, post-war reconstruction, land resettlement, rural and agricultural development, and general economic and social development. Fiscal policy formulation focused on aggressively diluting and gradually obliterating colonially wrought negative practices in the distribution and allocation of national economic resources. Actually, fiscal policies as distributive, allocative and economic management tools complemented the vision espoused in the wider macro-policy frameworks and national development plans. They served as instruments for achieving the wider developmental goals and objectives of the Government.

Post-independence fiscal policy formulation carefully considered the skewed inherited colonial system that pervaded every fabric of economic and social life in the country. A cursory review of this colonial system is necessary for better appreciation of the fiscal policies that were subsequently formulated.

The year 1980 marked the end of colonial rule in Zimbabwe after seven years of protracted armed struggle, ushering in black majority rule. There were structural bottlenecks in almost every sector of the economy, which served effectively as impediments to the socio-economic and political development of the black majority. Marginalization of the black population was carefully calculated to maintain a status quo of disequilibrium in social and economic life along racial lines. This manifested in acutely limited access to basic social services and infrastructure. Service provision basically followed patterns of white settlement such as urban areas, commercial farms and mining centers (Makumbe, 1996). Furthermore, colonial legislation such as the Land Apportionment Act of 1930, the Land Husbandry Act of 1951, and the Land Tenure Act of 1969 were used to allocate land on racial lines, disregarding the racial composition of the population which comprised 96 percent African and 4 percent European, Asians and Coloureds. And yet all prime land was allocated to a minority population. All these developments provide the backdrop against which post-independence government spending was premised, especially with the objectives of reducing colonially established bottlenecks and inequality.

Colonial imbalances and asymmetries greatly influenced national fiscal policy choices across sectors in the decade 1980–1989. The majority government mainly used the national budget as an instrument to undo negative colonial creations and improve living standards, access to basic services, and social infrastructure. Consequently, the budgetary practice automatically became predominantly reactive, top-down, pro-poor, expansionary and welfare-centric in focus (Zhou and Zvoushe, 2013, p. 49). This was reflected in a consistent trend in high budgetary allocations to social sectors such as education and health. These sectors formed part of the developmental priority list of the new government, whose broader vision was captured in the national development plans and macro-economic policy frameworks such as Growth with Equity (1981), Transitional National Development Plan (1982–1985) and the First Five-Year National Development Plan (1986–1990). In all these blueprints and macro-economic policy frameworks, the Government was consumed by the pressure to establish a socialist and egalitarian society. The desire to establish social equity and development stirred government generosity, resulting in subsidization of basic services in social sectors and transfer of government grants to public enterprises and other state-owned entities. Subsidies and grants were a common feature of budget statements in the first decade of independence. Subsidization was largely in keeping with the socialist ideals embraced by the government at independence. It went a long way in widening access to basic social services and reducing levels of marginalization. The social welfarist bias of the government was demonstrated by its continued commitment in the areas of health and education, which continually received high government support even in the face of economic recession and a balance of payment crisis.

Due to the consistent government commitment to radically improving social sectors, there was a wide expansion in access to education from primary through to tertiary levels. Public capital expenditure on education averaged about

USD18 million a year between 1980 and 1985, compared to USD8.9 million in 1979/80 (Chung, 1988, p. 121). Even during the period of economic recession from 1982 to 1984, funds allocated to the Ministry of Education continued to increase. The government provided free education for all through the education-for-all policy. School enrollment increased by 47 percent in the years 1980–1981. Enrollment in primary schools increased from 819,000 in 1979 to 2,229,000 in 1985 (Dashwood, 2000, 41) Enrollment in secondary schools increased from 73,000 in 1979 to about 500,000 in 1985 (ibid). University education enrollment also increased by 120 percent between 1980 and 1984. Numbers of technical colleges also went up. Between 1980 and 1984 about 1,000 primary schools were built, mostly in rural areas (Sigobodhla, 1988, p. 170). Rapid construction of new schools had obvious implications on the demand for qualified teaching staff. There was a critical shortage of skilled personnel especially in the early years of independence, and this unavailability of qualified staff presented a fresh handicap for the government's education program. However, to cater for shortfalls in the numbers of required teaching staff, the government recruited expatriate teachers. The number of expatriate teachers increased from 300 in 1981 to 1,300 in 1984 (ibid. p. 171).

Significant spending was also witnessed in the health sector for much of the first decade. The government allocated considerable resources toward the extension of training facilities for health workers. As a result, the health sector grew in real terms by an average of over 6 percent annually from 1980 to 1984, and employment in the sector increased substantially from 14,800 in 1979 to 19,800 in 1984 (ibid. p. 172). Expenditure patterns in the health sector were almost similar to those in the education sector:

> In 1979/80, USD53.5 million was allocated to health, and by 1985/6, the amount had reached $195 million. The Ministry of Health's budget share increased from 4.6 percent in 1979/80 to 5.6 percent in 1981/2. Although the Ministry of Health received less during the economic downturn of 1982 to 1984, by 1985/6 its budget share had increased to 5.3 percent.
>
> Dashwood, 2000, p. 43

In the early years of independence there was a deliberate bias towards allocating financial resources to rural areas, which had previously been marginalized in terms of access to basic services. For example, Parirenyatwa Hospital used to receive 31 percent of the total health budget before independence, but that figure was reduced to about 13 percent in post-independence years. From 1980 to 1985, there was a 58 percent increase in the provision of rural health centers (Herbst, 1990, p. 174). The number of health centers rose from an average of 9.5 per 100,000 people in 1980 to 15 per 100,000 people in 1985 (ibid. p. 44). Government spending in the health sector was mainly directed towards the salaries of health personnel, supplies, and grants for upgrading all mission hospitals and clinics and local government health services. The number of grant-aided hospitals increased by 100 percent from 53 in 1979 to 105 in 1984 (Sigobodhla, 1988, p. 172). As well, district council clinics increased from 242 to 381 in the same period. In the health sector, the government also invested in the reconstruction and upgrading of war-damaged clinics and staff houses in eight provinces. Implementation of the Preventive Health Care scheme resulted in the construction of 163 new health centers and the upgrading of primary health care clinics. To further realize the objective of widening access to basic services, the government, in 1980, introduced free health care for those earning less than USD150 per month.

There was also significant investment in the land resettlement program and in the construction of dams and roads. The government also gave loans to mining companies that were experiencing difficulties because of rising production costs. The government loaned USD6.7 million and USD8 million to the mining sector in the years 1982/1983 and 1983/1984 respectively. Elsewhere, subsidies and advances to major parastatals amounted to USD1,719.6 million from 1986 to 1990. The tables below show the sectors that received the highest budgetary allocations from 1979 to 1992. Table 10.1 below shows budget allocations to various sectors while Table 10. 2 following expresses those budget allocations as percentages of the national budget.

Table 10.1 Budget Account Expenditure: Major Categories, Z$mn (Current)

Budget Year	*Education*	*Defence*	*Health*	*Total*
1979/80	119.1	266.2	53.5	1,155.2
1981/2	315.0	290.3	106.1	1,897.3
1983/4	473.9	415.1	138.9	2,866.1
1985/6	651.6	504.6	195.0	3,688.4
1987/8	862.8	671.9	287.3	5,206.1
1989/90	1,200.0	840.3	352.8	6,937.7
1990/1	1,672.7	1,036.9	566.8	9,085.3
1992/3	2,487.7	1,342.6	802.5	21,426.3

Table 10.2 Budget Allocations as Percentages of the National Budget

Budget Year	*Education (%)*	*Defence (%)*	*Health (%)*
1979/80	10.3	23.0	4.6
1981/2	16.6	15.3	5.6
1983/4	16.5	14.5	4.8
1985/6	17.7	13.7	5.3
1987/8	16.6	12.9	5.5
1989/90	17.3	12.1	5.1
1990/1	18.4	11.4	6.2
1992/3	16.3	8.8	5.2

Source: *EIU*, *Zimbabwe: Country Profile* (various years), cited in Dashwood, H.S. (2000: p. 42)

During the first decade after independence, budgetary practice was centrist and marked by pervasive state interventionism. This could be the result of an implied assumption that in achieving the goals of raising living standards, widening access to basic services, and stimulating economic growth and post-war reconstruction, it was the role of the state to single-handedly drive the whole development agenda in the country. This practice had a negative impact on stakeholder participation in national budget formulation. On the one hand, there were very low levels of parliamentary participation and citizen involvement in ex-ante budget preparations, and on the other, a pervasive hand of the state dictating budget priorities and allocations. This observation is echoed in Moyo's (1992, p. 66) analysis:

> The Zimbabwean budget process . . . tended to be one-dimensional, driven by a top-down approach with politicians, especially the President, basically telling everyone what they think is good for the country. In the ensuing budgetary milieu, bureaucrats in sectoral ministries, particularly in the Ministry of Finance, Economic Planning and Development, have tended to adopt an "office boy" mentality wherein they view their budgeting role as merely an accounting process of facilitating and implementing policy whims and caprices of Cabinet without considering fundamental value questions.

Generally, involvement and inclusion of critical stakeholders and the general citizenry in the design of policies and plans was uncharacteristic of the first decade. The planning, formulation and designing of national policies was predominantly a technocratic exercise by bureaucrats in line ministries. Lack of parliamentary participation in the budget formulation processes meant that the budgetary process automatically became shrouded in secrecy and very exclusive in focus, making the whole process strictly executive business and monopolistic in nature. The Legislature was relegated to a mere rubber-stamping unit where its role was merely to approve national budgets. Real budgetary business and fiscal policy formulation revolved around two main institutions: the Ministry of Finance and the National Economic Planning Commission (NEPC). The NEPC was a department operating in the Office of the President, and at national level. It was mandated with carrying out economic planning to spearhead national development with short-term, medium-term and long-term foci to national planning. In making national budget formulation a business of only a coterie of political and bureaucratic elites, the crucial elements of transparency and democracy were sacrificed. The government also never attempted to synchronize national development plans and the national budget as the main instrument of its implementation (ZHDR, 2000, p. 35).

The centralized economic and fiscal planning of the first decade was part of the undoing of the government's espoused vision of stimulating economic growth and development across sectors of the economy. The combined effect of state interventionism and centrist economic planning was the establishment of pricing regimes that were unresponsive and insensitive to market dynamics; stalling of investment and trade flows; an increased culture of borrowing; and stunted, stagnating economic growth. Central government debt increased to 71 percent of GDP, of which 36 percent constituted external debt (Zhou and Zvoushe, 2013, p. 50). The budget deficit also amounted to 10 percent of GDP. The average annual growth rate was 4.1 percent between 1980 and 1985, and 4.6 percent between 1985 and 1990 (CPIA, 2005, p. 127).

Zimbabwe experienced a major economic boom in the first two years of independence. According to CPIA (ibid. p. 126), this was enabled by access to international assistance and lending, favorable terms of trade and increased aggregate demand arising from agricultural and wage incomes. Though the economic boom of the early years was short-lived, it gave the government some optimism and security, which inspired the adoption of liberal policies of foreign exchange allocation, remittance of dividends and an expansionary incomes policy (ibid. p. 127). The direct effect of these policies, however, was macroeconomic instability in the ensuing years. As highlighted in the Zimbabwe Human Development Report (2000, p. 33), the liberal economic policies resulted in the deepening of the current deficit from USD157 million in 1980 to USD440 million in 1981. The budget deficit rose sharply after the early 1980s, largely because of the huge increases in social spending and the payments of subsidies to parastatals (Dashwood, 2000, p. 49). Throughout the 1980s, the budget deficit ranged between 10.6 to 13.3 percent of GDP (ibid). The sustainability of the government's high level of spending on social programs became questionable. In the years after the two-year economic boom, the government started periodically rolling out national development plans. The first five-year national development plan (1986–1990) placed more emphasis on productive sectors. Of the planned investment for the period 1986–1990, 47 percent was meant for productive sectors (Sigobodhla, 1988, p. 173). The five-year plan had the objective of transforming, controlling and expanding the economy as well as improving employment levels and land utilization.

Emerging Salient Budget Features of the Decade

Vividly emerging from the review of the first decade of public budgeting is that issues of nation building, infrastructure rehabilitation and equitable provision of social services to previously neglected areas and groups took center stage in fiscal policy planning. Fiscal policy had a clear social spending slant with sectors such as education, health and welfare receiving very visible prioritization in budget allocations. Transfer expenditures (subsidies, grants, welfare outlays) constituted key features in aggregate expenditure such that by the end of the decade, subsidies accounted for 10 percent of GDP. Although aggregate public expenditure rose from ZWD1,057 million in 1980 to ZWD10,959 million by 1990, capital expenditures were generally lower than current expenditures.

Although the first two years after independence experienced an economic boom, overall economic growth was subdued in subsequent years. GDP grew by

2.7 percent per year, lagging behind the population growth rate of 2.8 percent. Employment creation lagged behind demand for employment such that by 1989, unemployment had reached 26 percent. The budget deficit continued to increase such that by 1989 total public sector debt had shot up to 90 percent of GDP while debt payments gobbled up 34 percent of GDP.

Budget formulation processes had a noticeably centrist bent, with subdued stakeholder and parliamentary participation during the early days of the formulation processes. Despite the top-down nature of fiscal policy planning, welfare considerations were clearly decisive in budget allocations and choice of fiscal instruments. The net picture is that there existed a very strong convergence of interest between the new black government and its citizens during the first decade of independence. Memories of colonial policies and liberation struggle hardships were still fresh in the minds of the political leadership. Some key members of the political leadership had not completely shaken off socialist thinking and rhetoric—hence the populist thrust of fiscal policies. It should also be noted that the period under review (1980–1989) was the period when the influence of the global interventionist development orthodoxy underpinned socio-economic planning in most developing countries.

Second-Decade National Budgeting (1990–2000)

As highlighted above, first-decade national budgeting was driven by state interventionism and pressing nation-building needs. Fiscal policies were markedly expansionary and characterized by pervasive social welfarism, which manifested in huge social sector spending, grants and subsidization of public goods and services in parastatals and state-owned enterprises. Second-decade national budgeting makes a significant departure from the budgetary practice of the first decade. There is a clear paradigm shift from state interventionism to economic liberalization, which advocated a lean government and fiscal austerity. Under the dictates of the liberalization paradigm, state frontiers had to be rolled back and social spending, subsidies and grants drastically reduced or removed to make way for cost recovery, privatization, deregulation, and demonopolization of service provision by the state.

This paradigm shift came against the background of a poorly performing economy—a situation which was attributed to the cumulative effects of state interventionism and weak fiscal management strategies (Zhou & Zvoushe, 2013, p. 50). There was widespread realization of the need for reforms to revamp the economy. Such reforms were expected to boost depressed investment, streamline labor regulations, create employment and stimulate export growth (ZHDR, 2000, p. 35). At the international level, the IMF and the World Bank had been exerting pressure on the government to adopt economic reforms, especially trade liberalization. This was noted for instance, in 1987, when the World Bank refused to sign an agreement for the extension of an export revolving-fund until measures were taken to liberalize trade (ibid. p. 37). Eventually, in July 1990 the government released a document entitled *Economic Policy*

Statement together with the 1990 national budget. The document spelt out the government's intention to launch major market-based reforms. A year later, the document *Zimbabwe: A Framework for Economic Reform (1991–1995)* was released. It detailed the specifics of the reform strategies to be adopted in that five-year period.

Generally in the second decade the government adopted three reform programs namely: the Economic Structural Adjustment Programme (ESAP), Zimbabwe Programme for Economic Transformation (ZIMPREST) and the Three Year Medium-Term Development Plan (TYMTDP). The reform programs had far-reaching implications on the direction and orientation of national budgeting.

Economic Structural Adjustment Programme

This reform program aimed at doing away with state interventionist policies in the economy, replacing them with market-based reform strategies. ESAP sought to: achieve annual GDP growth of 5 percent during 1991–95; reduce the budget deficit from over 10 percent of GDP to 5 percent by 1995; reduce inflation from over 17 percent to 10 percent by 1995; raise savings to 25 percent of GDP; raise investment to 25 percent of GDP; and achieve export growth of 9 percent per annum during 1991–95 (GoZ, 1991). Unfortunately, ESAP did not achieve its objectives (Mlambo, 1997). Instead, during the reform period the average annual growth rate was less than 1 percent; the budget deficit remained high, increasing to 123 percent of GDP in 1994–95; inflation rose to 42 percent in 1992; parastatal losses continued unabated (ZHDR, 2000, p. 37). During ESAP there was a lack of fiscal discipline that resulted in excessive borrowing, which, in turn, fueled inflation and exacerbated poverty (ibid.). Overall, ESAP drastically affected some of the achievements recorded in health and education sectors in the previous decade. De-emphasizing subsidies, grants and high social spending meant a radical departure from the very strategies that had initially led to realization of successes in social sectors.

Furthermore, ESAP was not without its effects on national budgetary practice. Following its adoption, fiscal policies had a visible contractionary bent and were devoid of the welfarist flavor. The years 1991–1997 actually marked the decline of social welfarism (Dashwood, 2000, p. 166). ESAP emphasized the adoption of growth-oriented economic policies and cuts in social expenditure. The reform program foregrounded expected economic benefits without due consideration of the social costs it generated. In addition, IMF and World Bank conditional ties attached to reform programs literally constricted the possible fiscal space for deliberations by the national fiscal authorities. By default such authorities ceded their autonomy and decision-making power over fiscal matters to the international financial institutions. Realizing the various weaknesses and failure of ESAP, the government went ahead and developed yet another reform programme—the Zimbabwe Programme for Economic and Social Transformation (ZIMPREST).

Zimbabwe Programme for Economic and Social Transformation (ZIMPREST)

ZIMPREST was launched in April 1998. The intention was to take note of the shortcomings and unintended consequences of ESAP and try to rectify them. For instance, by 1998 61 percent of the population was living in poverty. This automatically made poverty reduction a policy target under ZIMPREST. The new program sought the following:

> Urgent restoration of macro-economic stability (low inflation and interest rates, and a stable exchange rate); facilitating of public and private savings and investment needed to attain growth; and pursuing economic empowerment and poverty alleviation by generating opportunities for employment and encouraging entrepreneurial initiative.
>
> GoZ, 1998b

Table 10.3 shows the ZIMPREST targets for the years 1996–2000.

ZIMPREST did not fare any better than its predecessor ESAP. The budget deficit remained very high, and real GDP growth decelerated from 8.5 percent in 1996 to a negative 2 percent in 1999; export growth in USD terms collapsed from about 12 percent in 1996 to –20 percent in 1999; forex reserves deteriorated from 4.2 months' cover in 1995 to 1.6 months' in 1999 (ZHDR, 2000, p. 38). Various weaknesses accounted for the failure of ZIMPREST. The program had a five-year lifespan (1996–2000), yet it was only launched in 1998—two years behind schedule. ZIMPREST was also launched at a time when resources had already been allocated through the three-year rolling budget system (ibid.). Moreover, the national budget did not allocate resources according to priorities set out in the program. One outstanding weakness was the fact that ZIMPREST was not only over-ambitious in its policy targets, but it also failed to consider the budgetary implications of the policy objectives it spelled out.

Three-Year Medium-Term Development Plan (TYMTDP)

This plan covered the period 1998–2000. It was introduced as a tool to facilitate implementation of Vision 2020. One notable weakness in the formulation of

Table 10.3 ZIMPREST Targets

Years	*1996*	*1997*	*1998*	*1999*	*2000*
GDP growth (%)	7.3	4.5	6.3	6.1	6.3
Inflation (%)	19.3	21.2	22	18.5	8
Budget deficit (% p.a)	9.4	6.4	7.9	6	5
Expenditure (% p.a)	34.2	33.2	33.7	35.5	35
Revenue (% p.a)	24.8	26.8	25.7	29.5	30
Employment (millions)	1.46	1.39	1.33	1.39	1.46
Capital inflow (US$m)	135	620	490	435	335

Source: ZIMPREST, Government of Zimbabwe, 1998

reform programs since ESAP was their failure to capture and reflect the aspirations of the people. The TYMTDP sought not only to include the people's aspirations but to involve, engage and consult them in policy planning, design and formulation. According to Zhou and Zvoushe (2013, p. 52), TYMTDP:

> mainly sought to translate the broad strategic issues in Vision 2020 into actionable activities by addressing macro-economic instability, low and unsustainable economic growth, weak linkages between plans and budgeting, inequitable land redistribution and ownership, inadequate human resource base and relevant skills, and insufficient infrastructure development.

Parliamentary Involvement

In the period around 1998, parliamentary reforms were introduced with the main aim of strengthening the role of the parliament in pre- and post-budget processes. This was after the Parliamentary Reform Committee had carried out a research toward "strengthening parliamentary democracy in Zimbabwe" (GoZ, 1998a). The Committee found out that there was public disquiet about the exclusion of MPs and the public in the budget-making processes. It was felt that MPs must be "involved in the drafting of the budget and should be given enough time to consult their constituencies before debating it" (ibid. p. 56). The committee recommended that consultations between Parliament and the Executive on the budget should take place on an ongoing basis before, during and after the budget period (ibid.). All these recommendations made by the Parliamentary Reform Committee were taken up and earnestly implemented, resulting in the entrenchment of a culture of wide consultations between the Parliament, Executive, private sector, the public and other relevant stakeholders. Legislative participation in budgetary processes became more pronounced than before.

Emerging Salient Budget Features of the Decade

Second-decade public budgeting was within the rubric of the IMF- and World Bank-initiated Zimbabwe Framework of Economic Reform (1991–95), a blueprint that drew its theoretical and intellectual thinking from the global doctrine of liberalism. Within this framework, national budgets served as key instruments through which the cardinal concerns of liberalism (trade liberalization, domestic deregulation, aggregate expenditure cuts and fiscal austerity) were enforced. To this end, fiscal policy measures generally recommended a reduction in aggregate public expenditure through cuts in the public employment costs, grants, and subsidies. Unlike first-decade fiscal policy-making in which the state was the central actor, there was direct donor involvement in second-decade budget formulation and implementation. Domestic ownership and stakeholder involvement in the formulation stages of these economic and fiscal blueprints were visibly reduced.

Equally worth noting is that although fiscal policy planning was informed by the doctrine of austerity with its emphasis on lean state expenditures, overall aggregate expenditure, as observed by Zhou (2012, p. 42) "remained sticky downwards as expenditure outturns frequently surpassed expenditure targets." Aggregate expenditure, which in 1989 stood at around ZWD10,959 million, had by 1999 expanded to ZWD342.5 billion. Fiscal measures aimed at instilling a ministerial culture of living within vote limits scored little success as evidenced by frequent recourse to supplementary budgets. Reducing the budget deficit by 5 percent from its 1990 level of 10 percent of GDP proved a daunting task, as it had only dropped to 9 percent of GDP by 1999.

Despite the economic recovery thrust of second-decade fiscal policies, capital expenditure allocations played second fiddle to recurrent expenditures. A comparison of the two expenditures shows that whereas capital expenditure in 1996 was 6 percent of total budget, recurrent expenditure was 13.6 percent. In the 1997 financial year, capital expenditures constituted 12 percent against 4.2 percent recurrent expenditure. In the 1998 budget, capital expenditure was at a 2.4 percent low against a recurrent expenditure figure of 9 percent, while in 1999 the capital–recurrent expenditure allocation was 2.4 percent against 11.8 percent.

The decade also experienced a noticeable drop in the health vote and per capita spending. The health vote slumped from 6.2 percent in the 1991 to 4.2 percent in 1996 while per capita spending dropped from ZWD58 in 1991 to ZWD36 in 1996. These developments were particularly disturbing when viewed against the background of the adopted government policy of "health for all by 2000" and the AIDs pandemic.

Overall the tax revenue base remained subdued due to a combination of factors such as reduction in corporate and individual tax rates in 1994, and company closures and attendant employee retrenchments coupled with weak revenue collection systems.

Budgeting in the Third Decade (Post-2000 Era)

The post-2000 era presents a typical case of public budgeting under conditions of stress, turbulence and uncertainty. These conditions were a result of the political, economic and social meltdown that ensued during the decade. For analytical purposes, this period can be divided into three main phases: the pre-inclusive government (IG) phase, the IG phase, and the post-IG phase (2013–2015). The pre-IG phase dates from 2000 to the later parts of 2008, the IG phase covers 2009–2013, and the post-IG phase covers 2013 to date. This distinction is primarily on the basis that while the pre-IG phase is characterized by an exclusively ZANU PF dominated executive arm of government, the IG phase, owing to a power-sharing agreement in 2008 between ZANU PF and the two wings of the MDC resulted in the formation of the inclusive government in February 2009.

Pre-inclusive Government Phase (2000–2008)

Zhou and Zvoushe (2013, p. 26) correctly observe that in Zimbabwe, after 2000 national budgeting was influenced by emerging disenchantment with liberalism, the socio-economic meltdown, and strained relations between the Government, the Western world, and the donor community. To these factors it is also important to add domestic political pressures that were a result of the emergence of the MDC. For example in the 2002 national budget, at a time when the country was faced with a depreciating currency and escalating inflation, the Minister of Finance announced a 108 percent increase in public spending and the equivalent of USD 400 million in tax cuts (Integrated Regional Information Networks, 2001). 2002 was a presidential election year at a time when Robert Mugabe, the candidate of the ruling party, ZANU PF, was being seriously challenged by the MDC candidate Morgan Tsvangirai and it is plausible to argue that the above budgetary pronouncement, which is difficult to justify from an economic point of view, was motivated by the desire to attract voters. Furthermore it can be argued that some of the factors that influenced national budgeting can be traced back to the later part of the second decade. Sachikonye (2002, p. 14) and United Nations (2002, p. 123) pick up on two of those: first, authorization by the President of huge unbudgeted pay-offs of above ZWD5 billion for war veterans who sought a payback for their role in the liberation struggle, and second, military intervention in the Democratic Republic of the Congo in mid-1998 to shore up the Kabila government. These two major decisions had serious economic ramifications that arguably can be said to have affected the nation's financial status going into the third decade. Sachikonye (2002, p. 14) paints a bleak picture for Zimbabwe on the economic front at the turn of the century:

> In 2001, it (the economy) shrank by minus 5 percent, and in 2002 it is projected to shrink by a further 7 percent (as projected by the Budget Statement, 2001). In addition, there was hyper-inflation, which climbed above 110 precent in the first quarter of 2002, while domestic debt levels shot to $3.5 billion and foreign debt to $4.5 billion during the last quarter of 2001.

In 2005, even after a supplementary budget, an overall budget deficit of ZWD6.0 trillion or 8.6 percent of GDP was recorded (GoZ, 2005).

Public budgeting was conducted within the framework of a cocktail of hastily crafted national development programs, notable ones being the Millennium Development Goals (MDGs), the Millenium Economic Recovery Program (MERP) of 2000, the National Economic Revival Plan (NERP) covering 2003 to 2004, and the National Economic Development Priority Programme (NEDPP) of 2006. MERP sought to promote economic recovery through a series of domestic-initiated solutions and resources within the time frame of 2002 and 2003. NEDPP sought to promote economic development and stability within a tight target time frame of six months. MDGs, which had a very distinct poverty reduction thrust, prioritized human development as a critical ingredient for economic recovery. However, the hasty way in which these national development programs were formulated coupled with a very jittery socio-economic environment had a deleterious effect on their implementation as most were abandoned halfway through.

The inflation rate, which in 2002 was around 100 percent, had by 2006 risen to 619.5 percent, and by the close of 2008 had reached an unparalleled level of 231 million percent. These hyper-inflationary conditions distorted fiscal policy planning processes, as budget figures galloped from millions to billions, from billions to trillions and from trillions to quintillions within a short space of time: 2002 budget: ZWD342.5 billion; 2003 budget: ZWD770.2 billion; 2004 budget: ZWD6.250 trillion; 2006 budget: ZWD824 billion; 2007 budget: ZWD4.5 trillion; 2008: unquantifiable quintillions. In presenting the 2008 budget, the Minister of Finance singled out the twin challenges of economic contraction and high inflation as impacting negatively on potential economic growth (GoZ, 2008, p. 5). Making reference to the tumultuous period, the same minister further remarked that "Budget implementation is equally undermined as frequent adjustments to prices of goods and services erode the purchasing power of Ministries' allocations, compromising delivery of essential services" (ibid. p. 7).

Another striking feature of third decade public budgeting was the active engagement of the Reserve Bank of Zimbabwe (RBZ) in both monetary and fiscal activities through off-budget quasi-fiscal spending interventions. The post 2004 year saw the bank's governor usurping responsibilities traditionally the reserve of the Minister of Finance. Within this quasi-fiscal framework, the governor was involved in the mobilization and allocation of foreign currency for the purchase of basic goods and critical agricultural inputs and equipment under the parastatals and local authorities re-orientation programme, productive sector support facility and the basic commodity supply side intervention (BACOSSI) program. These developments blurred the authority boundaries between the Governor of the Reserve Bank and the Minister of Finance. While debate is still raging on whether or not Zimbabwe emerged better off with these quasi-fiscal financing interventions, it is indisputable that reconciliation of the revenue and expenditure components of the budget became extremely problematic during this period. Quasi-fiscal activities also had a deleterious effect on the budgetary and supervisory roles of the Treasury. Notwithstanding this, fiscal and monetary policy statements of this decade shared a common zero-tolerance posture on corruption. They explicitly exhorted sound institutional and corporate governance, fiscal discipline, and zero tolerance to corruption and off-budget quasi-fiscal activities (Zhou, 2007, p. 10). This posture was echoed in the macro-economic policy framework (2005–2006) and national budget statements of 2004, 2005, 2006, 2007, and 2008. This, among other things, led to the establishment in 2004 of an anti-corruption and anti-monopolies post in the Office of the Presidency and Cabinet as well as the passing of the Anti-corruption Commission Act (16/2004). Notwithstanding this fiscal policy stance, buttressed with the adoption of a cash budgeting framework, "line ministries, local authorities and parastatals violated treasury regulations and exhortations with impunity" (Zimbabwe Parliamentary Report, Volume 31, No. 8 of October 2004 cited in Zhou, 2012, p. 156). Unbudgetd expenditures and supplementary budgets remained perennial features of public budgeting. For instance, in 2000, the Ministry of Finance ended up with a supplementary budget of ZWD35.5 billion which was 37 percent above the approved budget. The issue of supplementary budgets became even more problematic following recourse to off-budget quasi-fiscal activities.

The period also experienced company closures, surging unemployment levels, an increasingly informal economy, and de-industrialization. According to the African Economic Forum (2003), around 500 companies wound up between 2000 and 2001, offloading around 25,000 employees. These developments generated negative ripple effects on individual and corporate tax revenue collection. Closure of companies and de-industrialization also led to declines in exports, deteriorating balance-of-payments-deficit scenarios and shortages of basic commodities. In a bid to curb the persistent increases in the prices of goods and services, and to protect public welfare, the Government introduced price controls by passing Statutory Instrument 302 then Control of Goods (Price Freeze) Order. This statutory instrument outlined goods and services whose prices had to be frozen. Although the intention of price control measures was good, their enforcement not only worsened shortages of basic commodities but also led to the emergence of a thriving parallel market. The Government reacted to this by implementing the (BACOSSI) program, in which basic commodities were distributed to the people through what were called "people's shops" where goods were sold below the market price.

The country's souring relations with the Western world during this decade also did not assist in improving the economic conditions. The government kept insisting that the economic misfortunes of Zimbabwe were a direct consequence of "illegal sanctions" imposed on the country by Britain and its allies, who were against the fast-track land reform program. The Western countries argued that these were merely "restrictive measures" targeted at Zimbabwe's leadership as a result of its lack of respect for human rights. From their point of view, these measures were intended to force the Government to "return to democracy." The net effect of this disagreement was both the tacit and explicit isolation of Zimbabwe from the international community. While the disagreement is not the primary focus of this chapter, it certainly exposes some of the sources of economic pressures that impacted on the implementation of the public budgets. This particularly had a negative impact on potential sources of revenue for the Government, as foreign direct investment and continued payments from multilateral institutions such as the World Bank and International Monetary Fund became restricted.

Notwithstanding these resource limitation challenges, there were visible efforts to render support to the agricultural sector, in particular the "new farmers" who had just acquired land under the fast-track land reform program. In 2007 the Government, through concessionary loan facilities under the Reserve Bank quasi-fiscal financing activities, made available to farmers 2,500 tractors, over 70 combine harvesters, and scores of other farm implements and machinery. Over 70,000 ox-drawn farm implements were also made available to communal farmers (GoZ, 2008, p. 7). In spite of this support agricultural production continued to be erratic, with production in 2007 of key crops such as maize falling to 953,000 tonnes compared to the 2006 crop of 1,485,000 tonnes. In the same year winter wheat production decreased to144,000 tonnes, as compared to 163,000 tonnes in 2006.

Salient Features of the 2000–2008 Phase

The 2000–2008 phase is arguably one of the saddest chapters in Zimbabwe's post-independence history. The policy environment was in ferment in the political, economic, and social arenas. A combination of inflation rates at stratospheric levels, an absence of offshore budgetary support, and a highly polarized environment characterized by contested elections of 2002, 2005, and 2008 inflicted far-reaching negative ripple effects on fiscal planning, implementation and management. The hyper-inflationary environment, which by 2008 had scaled unparalleled levels of 231 million percent, inflicted serious inflationary spiral effects that saw gross government expenditures graduating from billions in 2002 and 2003 to trillions in 2006 and 2007 and then quintillions in 2008. The Zimbabwean dollar was losing value on a daily basis. Although fiscal authorities initially responded by shifting budget projections from the long range (one year) to the short term (initially six months and later three months), this was to no avail. By late 2008, the Zimbabwean dollar had been rendered valueless. The Government had no option but to replace it with a foreign multi-currency basket of the US dollar, Botswana pula and South African rand. It is instructive to note that when a country ditches its own currency for the currencies of other countries, its economic sovereignty is inevitably compromised.

Tax revenue performance remained subdued throughout the period despite concerted efforts at widening the revenue base through the establishment of the Zimbabwe Revenue Authority (ZIMRA) as the sole revenue collection agency in 2002 and the introduction of value-added tax (VAT) in 2004. This was attributed to a number of factors including porous tax revenue systems, which in turn created room for tax evasion and leakages, closure of companies, retrenchments, and increased informalization of the economy.

Although the introduction of price controls and the BACOSSI programme (through which goods and services were availed through designated "people's shops" at very affordable levels) was meant to protect the public from predatory pricing, it made things worse in the form of increased shortages of basic commodities and the emergence of parallel markets. By 2008, most state institutions such as government ministries, state universities, schools, hospitals and clinics were operating at unsustainable levels as their vote allocations could hardly last a week. Public budgeting during the period can thus at best be described as budgeting under extreme socio-economic stress and uncertainty.

Budgeting Under the Inclusive Government Phase (2009–2013)

The period from 2009 to 2013 presents an interesting experience in Zimbabwe's post-independence public budgeting history. For the first time since independence, Zimbabwe was governed under an executive power-sharing framework comprising the traditional ruling party (ZANU PF) and the two opposition political parties (the MDC-T led by Morgen Tsvangirai and the MDC led by Arthur Mutambara). National governance and economic and fiscal policy planning was thus undertaken within the context of a Global Political Agreement (GPA) signed by these three political parties in 2008. A minister drawn from the opposition party (MDC-T) was responsible for the finance portfolio. The Reserve Bank of Zimbabwe, the monetary authority of the finance ministry, had been stripped of most of its known traditional functions. There was also a climate of hope in the air. On the political front, there was hope for a new political dispensation characterized by a shared vision on national issues among the political leadership. On the economic front, there was hope that re-engagement with the donor community and the discovery of diamonds in Manicaland province would result in increased external and domestic revenue in-flows into treasury coffers and in the long term broaden the fiscal space.

Against this backdrop, post-2009 national budgeting had a distinct turnaround and inclusive growth character. The national budget was primarily viewed as a steering tool for restoring macro-socio-economic stability and growth. The national budget premised two major policy initiatives, the short-term emergency recovery programme (STERP) and the Medium-Term Plan (2011–2015), whose central thrust was the restoration of economic stability through reduction in inflation rate, promotion of food security, agricultural productivity, infrastructural development, and delivery of health and education services. The budgetary thrust sought to change fiscal priorities from consumption to wealth creation through increased support to the agriculture, mining, and manufacturing sectors, whose operational capacity was below 30 percent in January 2009 (Zhou & Zvoushe, 2013, p. 42). These goals and objectives informed the declared themes of IG national development plans and national budgets. The medium-term plan of 2011–2015 ran under the theme "towards sustainable inclusive growth, human centered development, transformation and poverty reduction" (GoZ, 2011b). This was echoed in the 2011 national budget statement, whose theme was "shared economy, shared development, shared transformation: creating the fair economy" (GoZ, 2011a). This thematic thread was also manifest in the 2012 national budget, which ran under the theme "sustaining efficient and inclusive growth with jobs" (GoZ, 2012a).

Recurring throughout these economic and fiscal policy statements was the need to create a stable, modern, dynamic, democratic, and developing state. This yearning is not surprising when compared with what the nation had experienced during the tumultuous 2000–2008 phase.

The prevailing circumstances, as rightly argued by Zhou and Zvoushe (2013, p. 42), demanded that public budget processes be informed by the principles of realism and fiscal prudence. Public budgets during the IG phase appeared to pursue the more realistic principle of living within the country's means. Government sought to align expenditures with actual revenues under what was popularized by the then Minister of Finance, Tendai Biti, as the "We eat what we kill or we eat what we gather" cash budget framework. The framework, promoted innovation and creativity among public institutions, as spending ministries were not expected to "eat" beyond what they could "gather" through collection of taxes, and fees, and so on.

The IG phase experienced noticeable stabilization of the economy in the first two years. The adoption of a multi-currency regime induced stability in the pricing of goods and services and availability of basic goods and services. Fiscal policy planning reverted to year-long projections as the rate of inflation significantly dropped from its 2008 level of 231 percent to 7.7 percent by the end of 2009. Capacity utilization also improved to above 30 percent from below 10 percent in 2008 (GoZ, 2010). The first years saw GDP improving from 5 percent in 2009 to 8 percent in 2010. Revenue in-flows also improved from 4 percent of GDP in 2008 to 19 percent (USD973 million) of GDP in 2009, though falling short of the targeted USD 1.9 billion. This was attributed to the performance of VAT, which had the highest contribution of 39 percent. In fact, subsequent years up to 2013 saw ZIMRA generally surpassing its revenue targets.

Equally noticeable throughout the IG phase was an evolving culture of pre- and post-budget consultations. These were conducted in all the 10 provinces, targeting a wide spectrum of stakeholders such as individual citizens, professional groups, labor unions, industrial organizations, farmers unions, and members of parliament. This approach lent a participatory edge to the budgetary process. The language used was also simple enough to be understood by a cross section of society.

Notwithstanding these noted improvements in tax revenue in-flows, the fiscal space remained subdued throughout the IG phase. In fact this was one of the most recurrent issues in all IG national budgets. Out of the budgeted USD800 million as offshore financing, only USD360 million was received (GoZ, 2010). Gross government debt, which at the onset of the IG in 2009 was estimated to be around USD5.84 billon, had by 2010 increased to USD6.9 billion. Although by 2011 it had slightly dropped to USD6.4 billion, by the dissolution of the IG in July 2013, it was estimated to be around USD7.6 billion (GoZ, 2012a, p. 4). Of the total USD6.9 billion debt as of December 2010, USD 2.504 billion was owed to multilateral institutions as follows: World Bank USD1.126 billion (45 percent); the International Monetary Fund USD550 million (22 percent);

the African Development Bank USD529 million (21 percent); the European Investment Bank USD 221 million (9 percent); and others (3 percent). By the dissolution of the IG in July 2013, Zimbabwe's external debt accounted for 118 percent of GDP. The issues of interest payments and arrrears clearance remained thorny in fiscal management during the lifespan of the IG as the Government had limited fiscal space to make payments. In the 2011 national budget a token amount of USD 30.8 million was allocated toward interest servicing out of the gross interest bill of USD 687.8 million (GoZ, 2011a, p. 103).

An equally recurrent issue in all IG national budgets was the unsustainable salaries and wages bill. In his 2012 budget statement, the Minister of Finance described employments costs as "an elephant in the living room" (GoZ 2012a, 124) The civil service wage bill, which in 2009 accounted for 25.4 percent of the USD 1.9 billion budget had by 2010 risen to 60 percent and by 2011 to 69 percent. In the 2012 financial year, employment costs stood around 73 percent with a sector spread of education 44.7 percent, security 33.8 percent, health 9.0 percent, agriculture 4.6 percent and others 4.6 percent. It is instructive to note that while the civil service establishment was estimated to be around 235,000 during the period of the IG (GoZ, 2012a), the size of the civil service salaries and wages bill remained a thorny issue as many civil servants earned below the poverty datum level of around USD500. The issue of the civil service employment bill is further complicated by unconfirmed reports of around 75,000 ghost workers in the civil service.

Another recurring budget feature of the IG phase was the issue of unsustainable foreign travel costs, crowding out essential social services and economic sectors. Foreign travel costs cover foreign trips to regional and international events, mainly by the President, government ministers and senior officials. As made clear in statements by the then IG Minister of Finance, Tendai Biti, these unsustainable costs were a result of both too many trips and (usually) the size of the delegations accompanying the President—the daily per diem subsistence payments generally ranged from USD500–900, depending on the region visited.

Obscurity in the handling of revenue derived from the country's mineral resources also became a bone of contention during this period. This was seen as an impediment to central planning and budgeting. A case in point is the discovery of diamonds in 2006 in the Chiadzwa village of Marange in the Manicaland province. Since the start of operations the diamond revenue head had generally underperformed, the Minister of Finance ascribing this to "transparency challenges over diamond revenue streams from mining at Chiadzwa and the rest of the mining sector" (GoZ, 2012a, p. 68). In fact the MDC accused ZANU PF of running a parallel treasury with revenue obtained from the Marange diamonds. Throughout the IG phase there were no official figures on the actual size of the diamond fields, number of carats of diamond produced per year, amount realized from sales and the percentage remitted to the Treasury (ibid. p. 29). A 2012 Global Witness Report alleged the existence of parallel structures that were clandestinely financed from diamond revenues (www.sokwanele.com.July 8, 2012). Tendai Biti, the then Minister of Finānce, reportedly stated that although diamonds worth USD456 million were sold, the Treasury received a paltry USD41 million. A 2011 parliamentary report cited in Zhou (2012, p. 30) revealed that around USD200 million in diamond revenues was being siphoned out of Zimbabwe each month by the three companies operating at Chiadzwa. The *Financial Gazette* of December 16–23, 2010, claimed that Zimbabwe was losing around USD1.2 billion per year in potential revenue from the mining sector due to smuggling and tax evasion. The emerging picture as gleaned from budget statements during the lifespan of the IG strongly suggests that diamond mining activities were shrouded in secrecy, the bulk of diamond revenues were not being remitted to the Treasury and the responsible ministry was not in control of the national revenue systems (GoZ 2009, 2010, 2011a, 2012a).

Besides these challenges, public budgeting in the IG phase also suffered from the tug of war between the MDC and ZANU PF, dubbed the new problem. The Finance portfolio, which was held a member of MDC, became a battle ground especially in relation to the allocation of financial resources; for example defense portfolio, which was held by a ZANU PF deployee and had previously enjoyed generous allocations, complained of inadequate budget allocations during the entire IG period. Writing about economic developments during this period, Zhou (2013, p. 156) notes that the production sector continued to experience financing and power supply challenges while the mobilization of external financing emerged as a major challenge to the inclusive government, the donor community generally opting to channel aid through non-governmental organizations rather than through government structures.

Blame-shifting among parties in the IG, especially in relation to the allocation of financial resources, became commonplace. A vivid example was when the President blamed the Minister of Finance for not allocating adequate resources to the agriculture ministry. The President is quoted as saying:

> They say we don't have money, but they are the ones in charge of the Finance ministry. If it were a Zanu PF government, without these other partners, do you think you can tell that to the people? A government can dare not say we have no money to give people to grow food for the country. We can't say that. We must have the capacity even to borrow. No government does without borrowing from others.
>
> *NewsDay*, November 12, 2012

This statement was made despite the known fact that the President has to give his assent to the budget before it can be implemented. This blame-shifting exposes the political nature of public budgeting, as argued by various scholars (Moeti, 2014; Denhardt & Denhardt, 2009).

During the IG phase, social sectors received more public resources than before, but their share of the total government budget was well below their pre-2000 levels. The World Bank (2011, p. 18) states that in 2010, budgeted resources to social sectors reached 11.6 percent of GDP, almost twice as much as in 2009. This predictably helped the Government to resume essential social service delivery. It also observed that social sectors in 2011 represented only 35 percent of the budget (basic education 17.1 percent, higher education 5.7 percent, health 9.3 percent, and social protection 2.9 percent), well below the level of 45 percent during the first half of the 2000s (World Bank, 2011, p. 19). A serious challenge that negatively impacted social sectors during this phase was that they suffered drastic cuts when revenue failed to materialize as expected, for example in 2009 the health sector received 65percent of the budgeted allocation (World Bank, 2011, p. 19).

Post-IG Phase (Post July 2013)

After the July 31, 2013 elections ZANU PF became the exclusive party directing the executive arm of government. Public budgeting was undertaken within the context of the Zimbabwe agenda for sustainable socio-economic transformation (Zim Asset), which is expected to run from October 2013 to December 2018. These developments signaled a significant change in the policy direction of government. Zim Asset was expected to set Zimbabwe on a new trajectory of accelerated growth and wealth creation (GoZ, 2013b, p. 6). Judicious exploitation of human and natural resources was expected to see the country dealing with some of the socio-economic problems that had bedeviled it particularly in the third decade of independence. In addition, Zim Asset identified four strategic clusters that would ensure sustainable economic growth: food security and nutrition; social services and poverty eradication; infrastructure and utilities; and value addition and beneficiation (or mining of metals) (GoZ, 2013b). The importance of the national budget as a fiscal instrument to buttress Zim Asset cannot be over-emphasized. As Denhardt and Denhardt (2009, p. 238) point out, national budgets are fiscal instruments and are primary expressions of government priorities just as much as they are a record of decisions made concerning various public choices. While the intentions of Zim Asset are good, the issue of where to find capital to fund the proposed programs remains the elephant in the room. The domestic economic prospects remain bleak with high levels of unemployment, below-capacity production levels, and company closures. All this coupled with an unpredictable policy environment, especially with relation to the indigenization drive of the country, which has been a major impediment in efforts to attract investment, do not bode well for the country's economy. The *Zimbabwe Independent* of December 24, 2014 carried a story in which Youth, Indigenization and Economic Empowerment Minister Christopher Mushowe contradicted the Vice President Mr. Emmerson Munangagwa on the Government's policy position on indigenization. Mushowe stated that the Government could compel foreign-owned companies to relinquish as much as 99 percent of ownership to Zimbabwean locals; on the other hand Munangagwa had earlier pronounced that the Government would relax the controversial indigenization policy in 2015 to attract much-needed foreign investment. Such mixed signals from high-ranking government officials do not inspire any confidence for potential new entrants into the economy. Expected assistance from the traditional so-called friendly allies such as Russia and China has not yielded much despite numerous promises reported in the media. The net effect of all this, is that the Government has had little or no fiscal space to maneuver.

The way budget expenditures have been distributed in the post-2013 phase has a direct bearing on the extent to which the budgets are poised to stimulate socio-economic recovery. Table 10.4 lists allocations to selected items from 2013 to 2015.

A quick look shows that there was a steady decrease in allocations to health: of total budget allocations per year it received 9.87 percent in 2013, 8.2 percent in 2014 and 6.3 percent in 2015. There is however a contrasting picture when it comes to defense, which in 2013 received USD26.2 million. The allocation shot up to USD 368 million in 2014 and 380 million in 2015. It can also be observed that similar rises in allocations occurred with the Home Affairs Ministry and the Office of the President and Cabinet. What is common about these three government departments is that they house the country's security apparatus, and as earlier mentioned, the post-IG phase is characterized by a prioritization

Table 10.4 Budget Allocations of Selected Items from 2013 to 2015 (US$)

2013		*2014*		*2015*	
Item	*Allocation USD*	*Item*	*Allocation USD*	*Item*	*Allocation USD*
Total budget allocation	*3.8bn*	*Total budget allocation*	*3.6bn*	*Total budget allocation*	*4.1 bn*
Education	1bn	Education	1.198bn	Education	919m
Health	381m	Health	337m	Health	301m
Agriculture		Agriculture	155.2m	Agriculture	225m
Industry and Commerce	7.7m	Industry and Commerce	7.4m	Industry and Commerce	23m
Office of the President and Cabinet	36.3m	Office of the President and Cabinet	206m	Office of the President and Cabinet	190m
Defense	26.2m	Defense	368m	Defense	380m
Home Affairs	2.1m	Home Affairs	364m	Home Affairs	485m
Energy and power development	20.8m	Energy and power development	23.4m	Energy and power development	10m

Source: Extracted from the GoZ 2013c, 2014, 2015 budgets

of the security of the state. On a positive note, the budget allocations to education seem to remain relatively high, giving the picture that despite limited resources education remains a priority for the Zimbabwean Government. Meagre allocations to energy and power development do not reflect the dire state of affairs in this sector. With the strategic importance of energy and power in driving economic development, it goes without saying that future allocations to this sector need to be higher.

As was the case in the IG phase, employment costs have remained a recurring issue in post-2013 national budgets. The public employment establishment increased from 315,000 in 2009 to 554,000 in 2015 (*The Herald*, March 25, 2015; *Zimbabwe Independent*, March 27 to April 2, 2015), a rise that has left Government struggling to raise money to service its public wage bill. In the 2015 budget, employment costs accounted for 80 percent of the aggregate expenditure. In 2014 the Treasury failed to pay civil servants their November bonus and ended up staggering the payments in the early months of 2015. The *Daily News* of March 11, 2015 reported that the Foreign Affairs permanent secretary, Joey Bimha, in his oral presentation to the parliamentary portfolio committee revealed that the Government was struggling to pay salaries and other operational costs for its 40 embassies and free consulates across the world. According to this report, budgetary support of USD4.1 million is needed by these embassies. The ministry owes these embassies USD6, 669,900 in salary arrears as of December 2014. Government is also in school fees arrears of USD376,900 for diplomats' children. The Foreign Affairs permanent secretary was also said to have informed this parliamentary committee that as of March 6, 2015, the Treasury had provided the January monthly salary of USD2.7 million without taking into account the requested operations budget of USD543,750. On March 13, 2015, 900 prisoners at Chikurubi Maximum Prison rioted over the issue of food. On March 17, 2015, staff at state universities in Zimbabwe went on strike, demanding outstanding salary payments for February and bonuses, a development that saw the University of Zimbabwe temporarily closing until March 24, 2015. The net picture emerging from these events is of a Treasury that is extremely stressed in terms of fiscal capacity. In March 2015, the Treasury embarked on an audit of the establishment of government employees in a bid to reduce what it views as an unsustainable wage and salary bill. However, this development sets the ZANU PF-led Government on a collision course with its own election promise of 2013 to create 2.2 million jobs before the next elections in 2018.

In an article, "Government struggles to fund SADC summit," the *Zimbabwe Independent* of March 27 to April 2, 2015, wrote:

> the broke ZANU PF government already struggling to meet its financial obligations, has extended a begging bowl to local companies—battling for survival in a hostile economic environment—to help it out by funding an extraordinary SADC Summit set for Harare next month (April).

On page 2 the paper detailed the expenses and donations of the summit as follows.

EXPENSES

- USD8,157 for the conference meeting of the standing committee of senior officials;
- USD12,375 for the April conference package for the council of ministers; and
- USD28,000 conference package for the extraordinary meeting on April 29.

DONATIONS

- 700 golf tee shirts
- 500 round-neck tee shirts
- 40,000 units of mineral water
- 26,000 liters of petrol
- 16,000 liters of diesel
- 2,000 units of Mazoe
- 500 units of beverages and fruit juices
- suits for 150 drivers, 50 liaison officers and 50 ushers.

Foreign travel expenditure, as in the IG phase, was another thorny issue, gobbling up a significant chunk of the national budget at a time when the Treasury was experiencing serious fiscal capacity limitations. Its topicality is attributed to the size of this expenditure as a fraction of the budget, the frequency of trips, the size of delegations and the amount spent on each trip, which since 2013 have at least been monthly. A latest case in point is a report that was carried in the *Zimbabwe Independent* of March 13 to 19, 2015 in which President Robert Mugabe is alleged to have traveled with a huge delegation of around 100 during an eight-day trip to Japan via Singapore, which started on March 10, 2015. As stated in the paper, a delegation of 100 people was set to consume a total of USD1 million, as delegates received an allowance of USD900 per day. These concerns certainly seem to hold water when viewed against actual foreign travel expenditure figures in post 2013 national budgets. Budget figures point to huge spending on foreign travel. For instance, in the 2014 budget year, USD38 million out of the total budget of USD4.1 billion was spent on travel and accommodation. In the 2015 budget funding for presidential foreign trips was prioritized over economic ministries. The Office of the President was allocated USD190 million while vote allocations to economic ministries were as follows: industry and commerce USD23 million; mines and mineral development USD18.3 million; energy and power development USD10 million; tourism USD3 million (GoZ, 2015). These costs are concerning when viewed against the background of a severely stressed Treasury, an unemployment rate of around 80 percent and a Zim Asset program that needs an injection of USD27 billion for implementation. *NewsDay Zimbabwe* of March 25, 2015 ran a story with the headline "Mugabe blows USD10 million on foreign travels since January 2015" in which it claimed that the President was allocated USD600,000 as incidental cover allowances per trip while each aide received USD500 per day. It further claimed that the President, within a short space of time, undertook the following trips, some of which were less than two days apart: to Zambia to attend the inauguration of President Edgar Lungu, Ethiopia to attend the Africa Union Summit, Asia for medical check-ups, South Africa to attend a UN World Conference on Disaster Risk Reduction, Namibia for the inauguration of the new president, and Algeria. Debates are raging on, with some critics expressing concern given that the Treasury has been struggling since January 2015 to pay government employees and also support the crumbling health sector. Questions have also been raised whether some of these trips are so critical that they cannot be attended by ministers, at a lower cost to the budget (*NewsDay*, March 26, 2015).

These spiraling expenditures are taking place at a time when the country's trade deficit is on an unsustainable and deteriorating course. Zimbabwe's trade deficit, which in 2014 was around USD2.9 billion had by 2015 reached USD3.3 billion (accounting for 23.9 percent of GDP) (GoZ, 2015). Since the move to an international currency, the country's import bill has been growing faster than its receipts from exports. For the month of January 2015, aggregate imports were around USD538 million, a 10 percent increase from January 2014 levels (ibid.). This increase was attributed to imports of food, cotton-wool, fuel, medicines, motor vehicles, motor vehicle parts, fertilizer, and capital goods. Zimbabwe is going through an unsustainable course of de-industrialization coupled with low capacity utilization, which dropped from its 2011 level of 57.2 percent to 36.3 percent in 2014. These unfolding scenarios point to a country that is fast turning into a traders' market.

A cursory review of the circumstances under which the 2015 national budget was presented to Parliament, its contents and post-budget events vividly present a case story of public budgeting under fragility. The USD4.1 billion 2015 national budget, besides being the first budget since 1980 to be presented without allocations to government ministries, was also presented against a background of the absence of offshore financing and a budget deficit of USD386 million. Total debt was around USD8.39 billion as of the end of 2014, with a profile of USD1.1 billion domestic debt and USD7.2 billion external debt. Eighty-one percent of external debt was accounted for by accumulated arrears. Vote allocations reflect skewed spending priorities and huge under-funding variances. A critical and probably honest description of the budget is given by one of the opposition leaders, Elton Mangoma, who wrote in the *New Zimbabwe.com*:

> a flat and uninspiring fiscal plan that has no ingredient to inspire any form of investor confidence that the country is desperately in need of. While the economy is shrinking, revenue collection continues to decline and is way behind what was collected in 2013.
>
> Mangoma, 2015

In 2014, net revenue collected stood at USD3.6 billion against the expected USD3.82 billion, pointing to a negative variance of six percent. This depressed situation is set to continue in 2015. As of March 26, 2015, Zimbabwe's domestic debt had risen from its January level of USD3.9 billion to USD4.2 billion, a 6.16 percent growth in domestic debt (*Daily News*, March 26, 2015; *The Herald*, March 26, 2015). In the absence of support from offshore credit lines, due to defaulting in servicing arrears to several multilateral and bilateral creditors, and declining revenue in-flows, due to company closures and retrenchments, the Treasury has largely relied on domestic borrowings to finance the budget deficit, mainly through issuance of treasury bills. These budget figures, besides highlighting the extreme difficulties under which public budgeting is undertaken in the ZANU PF-led Government, also suggest that the Treasury has a daunting task in its efforts to restore national creditworthiness.

A quick comparison of vote allocations to the social, economic and security ministries in 2015 points to prioritization of the security ministries over social and economic ministries. The Ministry of Defense emerged with the highest vote allocation of USD368 million while the Ministry of Health, which has traditionally enjoyed one of the top three positions, received USD301 million, the fifth position in terms of vote allocation. Security ministries emerged with an aggregate vote allocation of USD1 billion when compared to economic ministries such as industry and mining, which received USD23.2 million and USD18 million respectively. This vote allocation to the Ministry of Health at 6.8 percent of the national budget is a far cry from the 15 percent threshold stipulated in the 2012 Abuja Declaration, to which Zimbabwe is a signatory.

A capital-versus-recurrent-expenditure analysis of the budget also points to budgeting that is largely consumption driven. Of the USD4.1 billion total budget, 92.5 percent is recurrent expenditure and within this expenditure, 81 percent covers employment costs. The USD798 million allocated to cover expenses relating to operations, debt service, and capital development, a paltry 2 percent (USD341 million) of the total expenditure, is allocated towards capital expenditure. This runs counter to the national economic recovery drive. This trend is also manifest in vote allocations to the key economic ministries of industry and agriculture, which are far less than allocations to the security ministries.

This skewed spending was also reflected in the 2014 national budget, in which the Office of the President and Cabinet received USD206 million, which was 5.6 percent of the total budget of USD3.6 billion and also six times the 2013 budget allocation during the IG period, and even exceeded the sum of the vote allocations of the five key economic ministries of commerce, industry, mines, energy, and agriculture. The net impression is of a budget where political considerations are prioritized over economic issues.

Conclusion

In conclusion, this chapter has described how public budgeting in Zimbabwe has been dynamic, responding to the ever-changing broader socio- political and economic environment in the country and beyond. In the three and a half decades that Zimbabwe has been independent, public budgetary processes have been heavily influenced by and also in turn have influenced socio-political developments in the country. In fact it can be argued that a public budget can be seen as a mirror of a country's present conditions and future aspirations. From the foregoing discussion various factors impacting public budgeting can be identified and these include: the dominance of the Executive, partisan politics, a large pool of relatively unskilled parliamentarians, and the excessive application of the party whipping instrument, among others.

In the first decade after independence public budgeting in Zimbabwe was generally typical of experiences in post-colonial Africa , with national budgeting largely a matter of state largesse. There was visible goodwill within the multilateral and bilateral donor community. In these contexts, fiscal policy planning had an expansionary and welfare edge—subsidies, grants, welfare transfers, and social spending were highly prioritized issues in national budgets.

During the second decade of national budgeting, the state was in economic and fiscal crisis. Budgets were formulated under IMF and World Bank-initiated ESAP conditions, which, as pre-designed interventions, had a "one size fits all" approach. As a result, national budgeting was generally lacking in transparency, domestic ownership and transformational thrust, and national budgets and national development plans had a very low achievement score in terms of meeting budgetary targets.

The third decade showed public budgeting reflecting two distinct periods, the 2000–2008 phase of socio-economic meltdown, and the 2009–2012 period of relative socio-economic stability. The tumultuous period between 2000 and 2008 had very serious effects on public budgeting, at some points rendering it a ritual bereft of any significance. The inflationary conditions obtaining during this period made public budgeting extremely difficult to undertake. The value of local currency and prices of commodities were changing by the day, which in turn affected budgetary estimates for revenue collection and expenditure.

Like the third decade, the fourth decade can be divided into two periods: the IG phase (2010–2013) and the post-IG phase (2014 to date). The IG period, though relatively stable, remained encumbered by the socio-economic challenges of the previous period (2000–2008). National budgets had a very visible thrust to turn the economy around and to align expenditures with actual revenues under the "We eat what we kill or we eat what we gather" cash budget framework; limited fiscal capacity and lack of inter-party support put paid to these goals.

The current period appears to be something of a return to the pre-IG period, as public budgeting is taking place in adverse economic conditions that are characterized by massive company closures, astronomical unemployment figures, low levels of foreign direct investment and so on. Even though public budgeting is guided by the ambitious economic blueprint Zim Asset, constricted revenue sources and high expenditure demands make it an unenviable task in Zimbabwe. There has also been a visible prioritization of the security sectors over economic sectors.

In light of the above, we recommend that the Government take a more realistic as opposed to populist approach to public budgeting. The cash budgeting approach appears to be a suitable one given that Zimbabwe has limited revenue sources. In the long term, efforts must be made to ensure that economic and political stability is achieved, as these have a bearing on public budgetary processes.

References

Books and Articles

Agere, S. (Ed.) 1998. *Zimbabwe Post-Independence Public Administration: Management Policy Issues and Constraints*, Dakar: CODESRIA.

Bratton, M. 1981. Development in Zimbabwe: Strategy and tactics. *Journal of Modern African Studies*, XIX: 447–76.

Centre for Peace Initiatives in Africa (CPIA). 2005. *Zimbabwe: The Next 25 Years*. Harare: Benaby Printing and Publishing.

Chung, F. 1988. Education: Revolution or Reform? In Colin Stoneman (Ed.) *Zimbabwe's Propects*. London: Macmillan, pp. 118–132.

Dashwood, H.S. 2000. *Zimbabwe: The Political Economy of Transformation*. Toronto: University of Toronto Press.

Denhardt, R.B., & Denhardt, J.V. 2009. *Public Administration in Action: An Action Orientation*. Boston: Wadsworth.

Herbst, J. 1990. *State Politics in Zimbabwe*. Princeton: Princeton University Press.

Integrated Regional Information Networks. 2001. *Makoni presents election budget*. www.irinnews.org/report/28010/zimbabwe-makoni-presents-election-budget.

Makumbe, J.M. 1996. *Participatory Development*. Harare: University of Zimbabwe.

Mandaza, I. (Ed.) 1986. *Zimbabwe: The Political Economy of Transition 1980–1986*. Harare: Jongwe House.

Mangoma, E. 2015. *2015 national budget is nothing but hot air*. www.newzimbabwe.com/columns-19696–2015+budget+nothing+but+hot+air/columns.aspx.

Mlambo, A.S. 1997. *The Economic Structural Adjustment Programme: The Case of Zimbabwe, 1990–1995*. Harare: University of Zimbabwe.

Moeti, K.B. 2014. *Public Finance Fundamentals*. Cape Town: Juta.

Moyo, J.M. (Ed.) 1992. *The Politics of the National Purse: Public Budgeting as Public Policy in Zimbabwe*. Harare: SAPES Trust.

Murapa, I. 1986. Race and Public Service in Zimbabwe 1980-83. In Michael, G. Schatzberg (Ed.) *The Political Economy of Zimbabwe*. Praeger, New York, pp. 41–62.

Sachikonye, L.M. 2002. Whither Zimbabwe? Crisis & Democratisation. *Review of African Political Economy*, 91:13-20. http://ir.uz.ac.zw/xmlui/bitstream/handle/10646/513/Sachikonye-whither-zimbabwe.pdf?sequence=1.

Seidman, A. 1986. *Money, Banking and Public Finance in Africa*. London: Zed Books.

Sigobodhla, A.M. 1988. Our economy, trends and policy at six years. In Arthur Jim Patsanza (Ed.) *Our Zimbabwe: An Element of Political Economy*. Harare: Govazvimwe Mukuruwenzira Publishing House, pp. 15–17.

United Nations (UN). 2002. *Economic Report on Africa, 2002: Tracking Performance and Progress*. Geneva: United Nations Publishing.

World Bank. 2011. *Challenges in Financing Education, Health, and Social Protection Expenditures in Zimbabwe*. World Bank Poverty Reduction and Economic Management Unit Africa Region.

Zhou, G. 2000. Public Enterprise Sector Reforms in Zimbabwe: A Macro Analytical Approach. ZAMBEZIA *Journal of Humanities of the University of Zimbabwe*, 27(2): 195–219, Harare: University of Zimbabwe Publications.

Zhou, G. 2001. From Interventionism to Market-based Management Approaches: The Zimbabwean Experience. ZAMBEZIA: *The Journal of Humanities of the University of Zimbabwe*, 28(11): 229–262, Harare: University of Zimbabwe Publications.

Zhou, G. 2007. The Corporate Governance Question in Zimbabwe: Experiences from the Corporate Sector. ZAMBEZIA *The Journal of Humanities of the University of Zimbabwe*, 34(i/ii): 1–20, Harare, University of Zimbabwe Publications.

Zhou, G. 2012. *An Assessment of the Policy, Legal and Institutional Framework Governing the Mining of Gold, Diamonds and Platinum in Zimbabwe. Annual State of Corruption Report 2012: A Look at the Mining Sector in Zimbabwe—Gold, Diamonds and Platinum.* Harare: Transparency International Zimbabwe.

Zhou, G. 2013. The Challenges of Public Administration under Inclusive Models of Governments: The Case of Zimbabwe. *International Journal of Humanities and Social Science*, 3(12): 154–164.

Zhou, G., & Masunungure, E. 2006. *An Analysis of the Objectives and Effects of Privatisation on the Public Sector and the Role of the State in Zimbabwe*. Harare: Zimbabwe Coalition on Debt and Development & Southern African People's Solidarity Network.

Zhou, G., & Zvoushe, H. 2012. Public Policy Making in Zimbabwe: A Three Decade Perspective. *International Journal of Humanities and Social Science*, 2(8): 212–222.

Zhou, G., & Zvoushe, H. 2013. Interrogating the trajectory of Zimbabwe national budgeting. *Global Business and Economics Research Journal*, 2(3):26–49.

Zimbabwe Europe Network, Eurodad and Jubilee Debt Campaign. 2011. *Uncovering Zimbabwe's Debt: The Case for a Democratic Solution to the Unjust Burden*. London: The Town Press.

Zimbabwe Human Development Report (ZHDR). 2000. Harare: UNDP, Poverty Reduction Forum and IDS.

Zvobgo, R. 1986. The Education and the Challenge of Independence. In Ibbo Man'daza (Ed.) *Zimbabwe: The Political Economy of Transition 1980–1986*. Harare: Jongwe House, pp. 319–354.

Reports and Government Documents

African Economic Forum. 2003. A special Report on Zimbabwe. http:www.aficconoutlook, search/zimbabwe

Government of Zimbabwe. 1981. Zimbabwe Conference on Reconstruction and Development. Government Printers: Salisbury.

Government of Zimbabwe. 1990. Economic Policy Statement: Macro-Economic Adjustment and Trade Liberalisation. Harare: Government Printers.

Government of Zimbabwe. 1991. Second Five-Year National Development Plan, 1991–1995, Government Printers: Harare.

Government of Zimbabwe. 1991. Zimbabwe: A Framework for Economic Reform, 1991–1995. Harare: Government Printers.

Government of Zimbabwe. 1998a. Strengthening Parliamentary Democracy in Zimbabwe: A Foundation Report by the Parliamentary Reform Committee, Volume 1: Findings and Recommendations. Harare: Parliament of Zimbabwe.

Government of Zimbabwe. 1998b. ZIMPREST: Zimbabwe Programme for Economic and Social Transformation, 1996–2000. Harare: Government Printers.

Government of Zimbabwe. 2005. National Budget Statement, Harare, Printflow.

Government of Zimbabwe. 2008. National Budget Statement, Harare, Printflow.

Government of Zimbabwe. 2009. Budget Estimates. Harare: Printflow.

Government of Zimbabwe. 2010. National Budget Statement, Harare, Printflow.

Government of Zimbabwe. 2011a. The 2011 National Budget Statement. Harare: Printflow.

Government of Zimbabwe. 2011b. Zimbabwe: Medium Term Plan 2011–2015. Harare: Printflow.

Government of Zimbabwe. 2012a. The 2012 National Budget Statement. Harare: Printflow.

Government of Zimbabwe. 2012b. Accelerated Arrears Clearance, Debt and Development Strategy. Harare: Printflow.

Government of Zimbabwe. 2013a. Constitution of Zimbabwe Amendment No. 20. Act 2013. Harare: Printflow.

Government of Zimbabwe. 2013b. Zimbabwe Agenda for Socio-Economic Transformation: Towards an empowered society and a growing economy. Harare: Government Printers.

Government of Zimbabwe. 2013c. National Budget Statement. Harare: Printflow.

Government of Zimbabwe. 2014. National Budget Statement. Harare: Printflow.

Government of Zimbabwe. 2015. National Budget Statement. Harare, Printflow.

Zimbabwe Coalition on Debt and Development. 2001. Harare: ZIMCODD.

Reports in Newspapers and Websites

Business Reporters. 2014. Stop cash leakage. *The Herald.* Harare.

Gumbo, L. 2015. Varsity lecturers down tools. *The Herald.* Harare.

Mangudhla, T. 2014. Mushowe contradicts Mnangagwa. *Zimbabwe Independent.*

Mushava, E. 2012. Mugabe attack on Biti senseless. *NewsDay*

11 Public Budgeting in African Nations: The Case of Rwanda

Dominique E. Uwizeyimana

Introduction and Background

The purpose of this chapter is to describe the status of public budgeting and public finance management (PFM) reforms in Rwanda. Rwanda's population was estimated at about 10 million people and its national budget at EUR1.2 billion in 2011 (Klingebiel & Mahn 2011, p. 1). In the 2013–2014 "Citizen's Guide to the National Budget" Claver Gatete, the Minister of Finance and Economic Planning defined the term "national budget" as "an instrument through which Government policies are translated into action" (Gatete 2014, p. 3; see also MINECOFIN 2014a, p. 3). The Government of Rwanda (GoR)'s fiscal year or financial year (FY) runs over a period of 12 months, from July 1 to June 30 every year. Literature tells us that a "government budget is a document presenting what government's revenues and spending are going to be for the coming financial year" (Wikipedia, 2015). Each year, most governments' "revenue and expenditure proposals are passed by the legislature, approved by the chief executive or president and are often presented to the nation by the Finance Minister as the national budget" (Internet source 2015, p. 1). Also in the case of Rwanda, once the budget has been passed (adopted or approved) by Parliament at "central government and local councils at the District level of government, it becomes a law which is published in the official Government Gazette and/or in all budget agencies" (Gatete 2014, p. 27). Thus public budgeting is essentially about working out the government income (or revenue) from different sources and deciding on the priorities that the Government wants to spend money on (prioritizing and allocation). The purpose of government budgeting is to ensure that government's expenditure does not create huge deficits. A budget deficit occurs when government spending exceeds revenue and a budget surplus occurs when revenue exceeds expenditure (Gwartney et al. 2009).

In line with this budgeting process,

> Rwanda's national budget was stated to be also the result of a budgeting process in which the GoR proposes how to raise money (revenue or income)

> and how this money will be allocated through different government spending agencies in order to address basic needs

of Rwanda's citizens within a specified timeline (Gatete 2014, p. 6; MINECOFIN 2014a, p. 26).

Most Government expenditures are often divided into recurrent expenditures (also known as operating expenditure budget) and development expenditures (also generally known as a capital or project expenditure budget) (Gatete 2014, p. 16). Whereas the operating budget (recurrent budget) relates to government's expenditure.

> [This is] incurred on or in connection with the provision of benefits (in the form of goods/products and/or services) which are immediately consumed (such as paying salaries and wages, rent, materials and supplies, transport expenses, repairs and maintenance of equipment etc.); development or capital expenditures are expenses used for acquisition of assets such as the construction of roads, rehabilitation or construction of water and electricity installations, schools, hospitals, etc.
>
> Gatete 2014, p. 15–16; MINECOFIN 2014a, pp. 15–16; Auriacombe & Van der Waldt 2015, p. 69

According to the budget strengthening initiative (BSI) (2012, p. 3–4) "the GoR introduced the process for defining budget ceilings" (revised in 2007) in order to strengthen the role of the Cabinet and ensure "a comprehensive overview of recurrent and capital budget ceilings for all the budget agencies" (see also Versailles 2012c, p. 3). In the 2014/5 financial year, the GoR recurrent budget stood roughly at 51 percent while the capital and development budget stood roughly at 49 percent of the total government's national budget (Gatete 2014, p. 16).

The following paragraphs go into details to discuss the goals of the GoR PFM reforms and strategies, the important processes and pillars of Rwanda's PFM reforms, and the key institutions involved and their roles. They describe the financial legal framework and different policies that guide PFM reforms in Rwanda. A special emphasis is put on the link between Rwanda's Vision 2020, the Economic Growth and Poverty Reduction Strategies (EDPRS), Sector Strategic Plans (SSP), District Development Plans (DDP), Annual Action Plan (AAP), Performance Contracts (*Imihigos*) and the Medium Term Expenditure Framework (MTEF).

The discussion proceeds with clarification of the linkages between planning and aid coordination, and between planning, budgeting, and the MTEF, and how all of this fits into Rwanda's budget calendar. The chapter ends with a discussion of Rwanda's internal revenue collection and management systems and issues of budgetary financial reporting, and internal and external scrutiny as well as some major challenges encountered in the PFM reform processes.

Goal of the Government's PFM Reform Strategy

Virtually all PFM reform programs strive to implement initiatives that are designed to improve cash management. According to MINECOFIN (n.d., p. 1):

> The ultimate goal of the GoR's PFM Reform Strategy is to ensure efficient, effective and accountable use of public resources as a basis for economic development and poverty eradication through improved service delivery.

To achieve this objective, the PFM system must be effective. Morgner (2013, p. 7) observes that some of the typical interventions that are used to improve the cash and expenditure management are:

> 1) Moving to a Single Treasury Account (STA) to replace individual (ministries', other spending units') bank accounts; 2) the introduction of an (IT-based) Integrated Financial Management Information System (IFMIS); and 3) integration of revenue and expenditure management in a single system.

STA and IFMIS are part and parcel of PFM reforms because they "make accounting, control and oversight easier, and do even allow for automated processes" (Morgner 2013, p. 7). Following is a brief discussion of the STA and IFMIS in Rwanda.

The Single Treasury Account (STA)

There are three organizational aspects of budgeting, namely bringing the whole budget under the responsibility of the National Budget Directorate (Versailles 2012c, p. 2), the creation of one STA, and assigning responsibility for the implementation of Rwanda's PFM. For example, in terms of STA, until 2006, according to Versailles (2012c, p. 2), "the Development budget was prepared separately by the Central Bureau for Public Investments and External Funding (CEPEX)" (see also BSI 2012, p. 2). According to BSI (2012, p. 4) "CEPEX was a semi-autonomous body responsible for supporting the implementation of development projects and improving projects' financial management, procurement, monitoring and evaluation" (also in Versailles 2012a, p. 4). Before its abolishment in early 2010, as BSI (2012, p. 2) continued to argue, "CEPEX was also in charge of the Public Investment Programme (PIP) and the preparation of the annual report on project implementation and disbursements (which was known as the CEPEX Development Projects Implementation report)" (also in Versailles 2012c, p. 2). Besides being in charge of the PIP and the development budget reporting, CEPEX is said to have been also "responsible for monitoring and reporting on, pipeline (non-signed) projects as well as NGO-funded projects" (BSI 2012, p. 2; Versailles 2012c, p. 2). However, in 2006, according to Versailles (2012c, p. 2), "the responsibility for preparation of the development budget was shifted from CEPEX to the National Budget Directorate (NBD), within the Ministry of Finance" (Versailles 2012c, p. 2). From 2006 to 2010, "CEPEX role was limited to supporting the NBD in preparing the development budget and for preparing what was then known as the 'Development Budget execution report'" (BSI 2012, p. 2; Versailles 2012c, p. 2). After CEPEX was abolished in 2010 the "responsibility for monitoring of externally financed projects was moved to the responsibility of the Director-General for National Budget (DGNB)" (BSI 2012, p. 2). There is a view that such shifting of responsibilities under the aegis of DGNB led to a strengthening of the oversight of the whole budget process (Versailles 2012c, p. 2).

In addition the reform also entailed assigning responsibilities for the PFM reforms. Currently, according to ECORYS (2012, p. 25), the "Implementation of the PFM Reform Strategy in Rwanda is overseen by the PFM Reform Steering Committee, which is supported by a PFM Reform Secretariat reporting to the Permanent Secretary of the Ministry of Finance and Economic Planning (MINECOFIN)." In addition "The Development Partners have to date supported the PFM reforms in Rwanda mainly via the Public Sector Capacity-Building Project (PSCBP), the Multi-Donor Trust Fund (MDTF) for PFM reforms, and via the PFM Reform Basket Fund" (ECORYS 2012, p. 25). Thus the implementation of the PFM Reform Strategy is overseen by "a Steering Committee, Technical Committee and PFM Reform Portfolio" (MINECOFIN 2014a).

Finally, the PFM reforms in Rwanda entail the introduction of a single treasury account (STA). The main purpose of the STA is to achieve budget integration. Versailles (2012c, p. 1) defines "budget integration" as "the process of bringing the recurrent budget and the development budget under one uniform structure." Before 2000, Rwanda's expenditure budgeting was based on dual budgeting (Versailles 2012a, p. 4). Dual budgeting, according to Versailles (2012c, p. 1), is "when the expenditure side of the national budget is divided into two categories, namely the recurrent budget and the development budget" (BSI 2012, p. 1). The former refers to the "ongoing expenditures while the latter refers to once off (or project) expenditure" (Versailles 2012c, p. 1–2). Because over 50 percent of Rwanda's national budget is financed by external donors, both the ongoing and project exepnditures are jointly financed by Government and external donors, that is, the recurrent budget and project funding are both internally financed but also both receive external budget support (Versailles 2012c, p. 2).

In terms of internal revenue collection, the Rwandan Revenue Authority (RRA) was established in 1998 and is responsible for all kinds of revenue (tax, custom duties, and other forms of revenue). The World Bank Central Finance Agency (WBCFA) reported that, by 2011, the RRA had the power both to formulate tax policies and to collect taxes (Murara 2011, p. 2).

A Steering Committee, Technical Committee and PFM Reform Portfolio, which oversee the implementation of the PFM Reform Strategy, are often credited with having helped Rwanda to improve its PFM on 28 public expenditure and financial accountability (PEFA) indicators. With budget integration, the Government is said to have been able to "strengthen the transparency, comprehensiveness, effectiveness and accountability of the national budget" (Versailles 2012c, p. 1). Some of the strong and concrete steps that have been taken by the Government in order to strengthen its budget integration since 2000 are well summarized by IMF Country Report (2011:197), which argues that, in line with the global trend:

> The PFM Reform strategy focuses on building human resource capacity, putting in place modern and effective systems and procedures for effective financial management and reporting and strengthening the institutional framework in accordance with international best practices for a more efficient and transparent PFM system. It also aims at increasing effective coordination of various reforms, sequencing the reforms to the priorities of the country consistent with both the Economic Development and Poverty Reduction Strategy (EDPRS) and the Vision 2020, and to ensure effective implementation.
>
> IMF 2011

In order to achieve these objectives the PFM reform in Rwanda has focused on the following four important processes.

The Integrated Financial Management Information System (IFMIS)

Through the IFMIS, according to BSI, the Government is able to:

> monitor the execution of project-financed expenditure through the same process as the domestically financed budget. [The IFMIS is] critical to the improvement of PFM and the consolidation of internally and externally raised revenues in Rwanda because it has a specific module which has been developed to allow managers of externally financed projects to enter the information on project expenditure in the IFMIS.
>
> BSI 2012, p. 3

Furthermore, proper implementation of this system has the benefits of allowing "improved and comprehensive monitoring of project expenditure, and will enable the relevant budget agencies to provide timely reports on externally financed budget execution" (BSI 2012, p. 3). All of this helps them to remain within the limits of the Budget Law (Versailles 2012c, p. 1). Evidence tends to suggest these PFM teams are being successful in turning around Rwanda's IFMIS systems and that the PFM reforms are achieving good results.

As a result of this comprehensive reform program, the second PEFA analysis conducted in December 2010 showed major improvement in all four phases of the budget cycle, namely preparation, execution, monitoring and auditing

(Klingebiel and Mahn 2011, p. 2). Rwanda's rating for 18 of the 28 PEFA indicators ranged from "good to very good" in 2010 (Klingebiel and Mahn 2011, p. 2). The PEFA analysis framework allows international comparisons, and the 2010 analysis showed that Rwanda was doing better than its neighboring countries especially in terms of external control mechanisms such as the Office of the Auditor-General (OAG) (Klingebiel & Mahn 2011, p. 2).

Four Important Pillars of Rwanda's PFM Reforms

A review of available literature suggest PFM Reforms in Rwanda have focused on four important processes: a) "Allocation of public resources, b) Revenue collection and management, c) cash and expenditure management, d) accounting and financial reporting, e) external audit and public oversight" (Morgner 2013, p. 5). These processes or four pillars under which Rwanda's PFM Reform Strategy is being implemented are complemented by "twelve distinct complementary components" (MINECOFIN 2011, p. 7; see also ECORYS, 2012, p. 11). The four pillars and 12 distinct complementary components of Rwanda's PFM reforms are listed in Table 11.1.

Key Institutions Involved in Rwanda's PFM Reforms

According to Klingebiel and Mahn (2011, p. 1) the PFM reform agenda was developed by the Government. Thus, PFM reforms were not imposed upon the

Table 11.1 Four Pillars and Twelve Distinct Complementary Components of Rwanda's PFM Reforms

Pillars	*Components*
Economic and Budget Management	Economic Management Budget Formulation and Preparation Domestic Revenue Generation Intergovernmental Fiscal Relations Public Investment Policy
Financial Management and Reporting	Accounting & Reporting Treasury Management Implementation of an Integrated Financial Management Information System (IFMIS) Implementation of an Integrated Payroll and Pension System (IPPS)
Public Procurement	Public Procurement
Budget Execution Oversight	Internal Audit External Audit

Source: Borrowed from MINECOFIN 2011. Available at: www.minecofin.gov.rw/fileadmin/templates/documents/Public_Financial_Management.pdf.

country by western donors. However, because funding for Rwanda's national budget is heavily dependent on western donors it could also be safely argued that Rwanda's donors have influenced the country's budgeting reforms and all aspects of PFM. About 50 percent of Rwanda's national budget is provided by donors (or development partners). The donors' influence is exemplified by the fact that the Rwanda's PEFA reforms are generally in line with the Paris Declaration on Aid Effectiveness (2005) and the Accra Agenda for Action (2008) (Klingebiel & Mahn 2011, p. 1). In addition, Rwanda's EDPRS is a direct result of the IMF and World Bank funding program. Thus donors are important actors in shaping Rwanda's PEFA reform and stakeholders in its implementation. The "prominent donors who provide direct support for the implementation of Rwanda's PFM reforms include Germany, Britain's DfID, World Bank, the European Union (EU), USA, Japan and Sweden among many others" (Klingebiel and Mahn 2011, p. 3).

However, while these PFM reforms have been largely driven and funded by donors, the Government has wholeheartedly embraced and supported these PFM reforms, and has been generally commended for so doing. Morgner (2013, p. 2) identifies the following factors as being evidence of Rwanda's concrete actions to support to the PFM reforms:

- Strong political will, commitment and support by the national government
- Coordination of reform activities (and for this to happen, also coordination of the donor agencies' implementation plans)
- Adaptation of best practices to the specific context in the country
- Domestic ownership of the reform process, including parliament and the public (civil society, business, media)

Morgner 2013, p. 2

There is a view that the above was possible because of the "shared common interest" between western donors and the Government. Because of such shared common interests, there is a joint funding mechanism known as a "basket fund" (Klingebiel & Mahn 2011, p. 3). The common interest and the basket funding led to the establishment of a "strong PFM steering committee" whose responsibility is to oversee the PFM reforms strategy and basket fund (Klingebiel & Mahn 2011, p. 3). The dialog regarding funding and implementation of the PFM strategies also includes the Rwandan national Government (Ministries of Finance, Economic Development and Planning and so on), the OAG, the district authorities and civil societies (Klingebiel & Mahn 2011, p. 3). The involvement of district authorities and civil society is largely driven by the western donors' desire for decentralization of power and development to local authorities.

Because of the strong decentralization emphasis from the donors, according to Klingebiel and Mahn (2011, p. 1), "budgets and budget responsibilities are increasingly being shifted to the country's thirty districts." These districts receive about 30 percent of the national budget (Klingebiel & Mahn 2011, p. 2); thus explaining why it is "both imperative to strengthen the PFM systems at these subnational levels and inclusion of them into the PFM design and implementation strategies" (Klingebiel & Mahn 2011, p. 2).

Public Participation in Budgeting and Implementation Processes

Morgner (2013, p. 4), citing www.participatorybudgeting.org/aboutparticipatory-budgeting/where-has-it-worked, states that some donors rely on civil society organizations and citizens in their attempts to increase transparency in budget planning at the sub-national level. Public participation ensures that the money is allocated in a fair and effective manner. The most common form of public participation in budget planning processes "is the so-called participatory or community budget" (Morgner 2013, p. 4). Community budgeting allows the public to directly participate in the budget planning exercise in order to jointly decide over government spending priorities (Morgner 2013, p. 4). Community budgeting is widely practiced on a local government level in over 1,500 cities in all continents. Examples include Latin America, North America, Asia, Africa, and Europe (Morgner 2013, p. 5).

There is a view that participatory budgeting is likely to reduce corruption in PFM as it eliminates opportunities to cut deals about budget allocations among insider-officials, and it can also be expected to increase the motivation for the public to monitor budget implementation more closely (Morgner 2013, p. 4). According to Rwanda's Ministry of Finance and Economic Planning (MINECOFIN 2014a, p. 26), "the national budget preparation process in Rwanda is an annual participatory process that involves the central and local government agencies, development partners, parliament, private sector as well as the civil society organizations at different levels" (also Gatete 2014, p. 26). Citizens' participation is viewed as a major contribution to the Rwanda's budgeting process in the sense that it "orients government programs appropriately" (Gatete 2014, p. 26). Therefore, not only are citizens (in this case Rwanda's citizens) "encouraged to participate in the national and local/district level budgets, government must create conditions for the local community to participate in the affairs of the municipality, including specifically the preparation of its budget" (Auriacombe & Van der Waldt 2015, p. 36).

In terms of citizens' participation strategies, according to MINECOFIN, the Government encourages its citizens to participate in one or more of the following channels:

- Attend or follow-up budget hearings both at National and at your respective District;
- Attend accountability days, participate in Joint Action Development Forum meetings, *Imihigo* validation and evaluation events, as well as open days whenever they are held;

- Attend other events that can give you an opportunity to meet with your leaders during community work (Umuganda);
- Visit your nearest administrative head offices for instance at Sector or District level and meet the leaders to discuss your concerns;
- Attend annual tax payers days whenever they are held;
- Get a hard or a soft copy of this guide or National budget at Ministry of Finance and Economic Planning website or the website of respective government spending agency.

Gatete 2014, p. 26–27; MINECOFIN 2014a, p. 26–27

Rwanda's Financial Legal Framework

Murara (2011, p. 1) argues that Rwanda has made major strides in establishing a comprehensive and modern legal framework for budget and PFM. A report on the "public financial management (PFM) reforms in developing and post conflict countries" such as Rwanda conducted by Matthias Morgner of International Transparency in 2012 also asserts that Rwanda has made major progress in terms of its Budget Organic Law (Morgner 2013, p. 5). Among the laws enacted are the 2003 Constitution (as amended to date), and the 2006 Organic Budget Law and "accompanying financial regulations which have been passed in 2006" (Versailles 2012c, p. 1). These laws provide clarity on the "powers, roles and responsibilities of the institutions responsible for the budget, namely Parliament, Cabinet, the Ministry of Finance and Economic Planning (MINECOFIN), and the Office of the Auditor General (OAG)" to name but a few (Versailles 2012c, p. 1). In doing so, these laws "clarify the separation of power between the executive and the legislative branches of government" (Murara 2011, p. 1).

In addition, Rwanda's legal framework determines the budget preparation procedures and requires such preparation to be consistent with international standards (Murara 2011, p. 1). The following is a summary of some of the main components of the legal framework for the budget and PFM in Rwanda.

Constitution of the Republic of Rwanda

The Constitution of the Republic of Rwanda was adopted by Parliament on the June 4, 2003. The Constitution has been amended four times since 2003. "The first amendment was published on December 2, 2003, the second on December 8, 2005, the third on August 13, 2008 and the fourth on June 17, 2010" (Republic of Rwanda 2010, p. 1).

A number of articles in Rwanda's Constitution deal with critical PFM issues. For example, Rwanda's Constitution outlines the roles and responsibilities in respect of submission of the draft Finance Law by the Cabinet, adoption of the Finance Law by Parliament and the submission of the budget execution reports by Auditor General.

Some of the key features of this article include "the Chamber of Deputies shall adopt the State finance Law every financial year"; in order for the Chamber of Deputies to do its job, "the Cabinet shall submit to both Chambers of the Parliament the finance bill for the next financial year"; the submission of this bill must be done in every State financial year and the bill's submission must be done before "the commencement of the session devoted to the examination of the Budget" (Republic of Rwanda 2010, p. 33).

Article 79 of Rwanda's Constitution also assigns responsibilities to different actors in the budget process in the following manner:

- The responsibility to examine relevance of the State finance bill lies with the Chamber of Deputies.
- Parliament shall receive the Budget implementation report for the first semester of the current financial year presented to it by the Cabinet before examining the budget of the next financial year.
- Every financial year and before the commencement of the session devoted to the examination of the Budget, the Auditor General of State Finances shall submit to the Parliament the audited State consolidated financial statements of the previous financial year.
- Before the final adoption of the Budget, the Senate must provide the Chamber of Deputies with its opinion on the State finance bill.

Republic of Rwanda 2010, p. 33

In terms of Article 79 Rwanda's Constitution it is the "State Finance Law which determines the revenue and expenditure of the State in accordance with conditions provided for by an Organic Law." In addition to the determination of the State's "revenue and expenditure" (i.e. budget) the Organic Law also "determines the date of the presentation of the annual budget before both Chambers of Parliament" (Republic of Rwanda 2010).

According to Article 80 of the 2010 Rwandan Constitution:

> In the event that the Finance bill is not voted and promulgated before the commencement of a financial year, then the Prime Minister shall authorise by an Order a monthly expenditure on a provisional basis of an amount equal to one-twelfth (1/12) of the budget of the preceding year.
>
> Republic of Rwanda 2010, p. 34

Such a ministerial order is intended to keep the government machinery running while waiting for the final approval of the budget of that year. According to Article 80 of the 2010 Constitution "the budget must be accompanied by the report on the implementation of the previous budget, certified by the Auditor General, when presented to Parliament and Chamber of Deputies." Rwanda's Constitution also sets "certain limitations on what parliament can do in terms of Budget" (Republic of Rwanda 2010). For example, Article 91 of the

Constitution limits "the legislature's ability to modify the Finance Act" by stipulating that:

> bills and statutory amendments, which have the potential to reduce Government revenue or increase state expenditure, must indicate proposals for raising the required revenue or making savings equivalent to the anticipated expenditure.
>
> Republic of Rwanda 2010, p. 39–40, also cited in Versailles 2012c, p. 1

The Constitution does not make provision for what to do when the Legislature proposes an increase in state revenue or a reduction in state expenditure. This is unfortunate because an increase in state revenue could mean an increase in taxes, while a reduction in state spending could have a negative impact on service delivery. However, such limitations seem not to have an effect on Parliament's powers over the Government on other budget-related matters.

Besides approving the draft budget, MPs have also the responsibility to hold the executive to account at the end of the fiscal period (Morgner 2013, p. 5). For example, Article 128 of Rwanda's Constitution "makes provisions for Parliament to obtain information and exercise oversight of activities of the government" (Republic of Rwanda 2010, p. 58). There is therefore a "need to strengthen the technical capacity of Members of Parliaments (MPs) in order to perform their constitutional mandate" (Morgner 2013, p. 5).

Finally, "Article 183 defines the role of the Office of the Auditor General of State Finances, its independence and financial and administrative autonomy." (Versailles 2012c, p. 1). However, in terms of Rwanda's Constitution, according to MINECOFIN (2014a, p. 28) "the overall monitoring and evaluation of the government finances is carried out by the Auditor General who submits the annual report to the parliament" (also Gatete 2014, p. 28). The Auditor General's monitoring is carried out under the terms of Article 184 of Rwanda's Constitution, which states:

> Subject to the provisions of Article 79 of the Constitution, the Office of the Auditor General of State Finances shall submit each year to both Chambers of Parliament in joint session prior to the commencement of the session devoted to the examination of the budget of the following year, a complete report on the balance sheet of the State budget of the previous year. This report must indicate the manner in which the budget was utilized, unnecessary expenses which were incurred or expenses which were contrary to the law and whether there was misappropriation or general squandering of public funds.
>
> A copy of the report shall be submitted to the President of the Republic, the Cabinet, the President of Supreme Court and the Prosecutor General.

> The Parliament, after receiving the report of the Auditor-general referred to in this Article shall examine it and take appropriate decisions within six (6) months.
>
> Institutions and public officials to which a copy of the annual report of the Auditor-general is addressed are obliged to implement its recommendations by taking appropriate measures as regards irregularities and other shortcomings which were disclosed. The Parliament may request this Office to carry out a financial audit of State institutions or with regard to the use.
>
> Republic of Rwanda 2010, pp. 87–88

Rwanda's Constitution is supplemented by the statutory framework discussed in the following paragraphs.

Organic Budget Law and Regulatory Framework

The overarching objective of Rwanda's Organic Law (ROGL) is "to establish principles and the basis of planning, budgeting and monitoring of state resources and the sound management of State Budget" in line with international best practice. One of the main instruments supporting Rwanda's Constitution is the Rwandan Organic Budget Law (ROBL) on State Finances and Property, which was promulgated on September 12, 2006. This law "was updated in 2008 in order to accommodate changes resulting from the transition to the East African Community fiscal year" (Versailles 2012c, p. 2). The ROBL establishes principles that govern state property and other financial resources that apply to both the national government and decentralized government entities such as districts and the basis for allocating state resources to state functions and reporting adjustments.

The ROBL also establishes documentations that must be submitted to Parliament in support for the proposed budget (Versailles 2012c, p. 2). Extracts from Article 39 of Rwanda's Organic Law 37/2006 of September 12, 2006 on State Finances and Property prescribe that the State budget document submitted to the Chamber of Deputies shall contain:

1. A statement on the projected macro-economic assumptions, the medium-term budget framework and policy priorities and new revenue and expenditure policies proposed to be enacted in the context of the annual budget;
2. Analytical summaries of revenues and expenditures including financing of the budget balance if a deficit is projected; if a budget surplus is projected and a statement on how the surplus is to be used shall be provided. The summaries should include:
   a) the actual data for the year before the current year;
   b) budget estimates for the current year;
   c) data projections for the two years following the budget year.

3. Detailed documents of:
    a) the expected revenues and expenditures including expectations in the following budget year;
    b) the actual data on the use of the budget of the previous year;
    c) the use of the budget of the current year and its revision.
4. Projections relating to public debt.

With regard to constitutional public institutions that use revenues not generated in procedures provided for by this organic law, self-raised and self independently retained revenues shall be subject to reports submitted in the same manner as that prescribed under point 2° of this article.

Article 39, Republic of Rwanda 2006

In addition, Article 40 of Rwanda's Organic Law 37/2006 prescribes that the budget document submitted to local councils by local administrative entities should contain:

1. Analytical summaries of the achievements of the previous financial year and the priority activities for the new financial year as well as projections for the following two years;
2. Detailed estimates of revenue and expenditures as well as projections for the following year, actual data indicating how the budget of the previous year was used and the use of the budget of the current year and its revision.

Article 40, Republic of Rwanda 2006

Furthermore, Article 41 of Rwanda's Organic Law 37/2006 prescribes a list of "annexes to provide additional detailed information" that must "be attached to the central Government budget document." These annexes include the following:

1. Summaries of expected revenues and expenditures which are not reflected in the budget as well as funds provided in the public enterprises;
2. Consolidated summaries of revenues and expenditures of local administrative entities;
3. The document indicating the general picture of:
    a) Country loans, all interests to be paid on those loans, period of payments, how to repay foreign loans, how the loan was used and how it served the nation to achieve its goals;
    b) All donations the Government received during the year proceeding the budget year, where they came from and how they were used;
    c) Securities seized by the central Government in general, Government enterprises, financial institutions and local administrative entities.

Article 41, Republic of Rwanda 2006

It also emphasizes that "The budget document of local administrative entities shall include summaries of their revenues and expenditures" (Article 41, Republic of Rwanda 2006).

Finally, the law requires that the annual budget documents that must be submitted to Parliament by Cabinet in support of their budget request, must include a draft Finance Law. According to Versailles (2012c, p. 4) "the Draft Finance Law is a very short document of about twenty-eight pages which details the main spending and revenue categories." Rwanda's Constitution requires that the draft Finance Law be "submitted to Parliament in June of each year" (Versailles 2012c, p. 4).

One of the other documents that must accompany the draft Finance Law is the "Explanatory Note to the Draft Finance Law" (Versailles 2012c, p. 2). The Explanatory Note to the Draft Finance Law is an "an updated overview of the Budget Framework Paper" that "gives a detailed overview of the main spending and revenue categories as well as the explanation of the main policy changes that are proposed in the budget" in the next financial year (i.e. the year for which the budget is being requested) (Versailles 2012c, p. 4). A number of supporting documents are submitted with the draft Finance Law. For example, the documents that were:

> submitted to Parliament in order to give much more detail on spending and expenditure categories proposed in the draft Finance Law submitted to Parliament in June 2011 (for the budget 2011/12) [include]:
>
> - Annex I: State Revenues 2011–2014
> - Annex II-1: 2011/12 Detailed Expenditure by Budget Agency
> - Annex II-2: 2011/12 Budget by Programme, sub-programme and economic category
> - Annex II-3: 2011/12 Development Budget by Agency, Project and Funding Type
> - Annex II-4: 2011/12 Budget by Agency and Economic Classification
> - Annex II-5: 2011/14 Budget by Agency, Programme and Sub-programme
> - Annex II-6: 2011/14 Budget by Budget Agency
> - Annex II-7: 2011/14 Budget by Budget Agency and by Economic Category
> - Annex II-8: 2011/14 State Expenditure by Division and Groups
> - Annex II-9: 2011/14 State Expenditure by EDPRS Prioritiessee also Versailles 2012c:4
>
> Article 41, Republic of Rwanda 2006

Finally, according to Murara (2011:1), these documents must include:

> the macro-economic assumptions on which the budget projections are based, MTEF documents, revenue projections, proposed spending as well

as information on the progress made in the implementation of the current Financial Year's budget. . . . Institutions not covered by the government's budget are required to submit their financial reports and proposals covering their activities in terms of the Organic Law.

The Rwanda Organic Law and the Budgeting Process

A closer look at the above documents shows clearly that budgeting in Rwanda is based on what is known in the literature as program based budgeting (PBB). Developed and developing countries are increasingly moving from an input-based budgeting system toward formulating their budgets on the basis of output-based programs in order to achieve policy priorities. Input-based budgeting is also known as line-item budgeting. PBB is a budgeting system "that is more focused on outcomes and places emphasis on results" (CABRI 2013, p. 1), rather than the inputs used to produce results. The assumption underlying the increasing use of PBB is that, unlike line-item budgeting, public budgets could be used "more effectively and more efficiently if spending is no longer allocated to purchase an input to a certain public service delivery; but instead to achieving satisfactory outputs on the service delivery" (Morgner 2013, p. 5). A classic example used by Morgner is: "the budget is allocated to a school for the agreed output of XY pupils graduating" (i.e. throughput) at the end of a specific academic period; rather than allocating "teacher's salaries according to a pupil-per-teacher quota" (Morgner 2013, p. 5).

However, some commentators such as Morgner argue that "the process is far from comprehensive and meaningful in terms of budget accountability purposes" (Morgner 2013, p. 5). For example, according to BSI (2012, p. 2–3) "since the start of programme budgeting system in Rwanda in the early 2000 . . . the same programme structure has been used for both recurrent and capital expenditure budgets" (see also Versailles 2012c, p. 2–3). The problem with "this reporting structure is that it did not differentiate whether what was reported as being project funding either financed the recurrent or investment/project expenditure" (BSI 2012, p. 2; Versailles 2012c, p. 3). The weakness in this system "gave rise to the introduction of the new Chart of Accounts in 2007" (BSI 2012, p. 2).

With the new Chart of Accounts it became possible to separate recurrent from capital expenditures and to recognize that some projects are financed by both recurrent and investment expenditure. Following the introduction of this new method of expenditure budget classification, "all projects, whether internally or externally financed, have split their expenditures between capital and recurrent" (MINECOFIN 2010, cited in Versailles 2012c, p. 3 and BSI 2012, p. 3).

However, while the Chart of Accounts is a very useful tool in terms of budget presentation, and was a necessary reform in order to separate recurrent and capital expenditure budgets, the PBB is still a useful tool in Rwanda's budget formulation phase. The budget formulation process entails the transfer of individual ministries' and government units' political priorities into budget allocations (Morgner 2013, p. 4). This process is governed by a particular detailed policy framework, which is briefly discussed below.

The National Budget and Government Policies

The development and management of any country's budget is directly influenced by the socio-economic context in which the country finds itself. "The Rwanda's budget is influenced by Government policies (also known as government priorities)" and the dominant socio-economic context (Gatete 2014, p. 1). For example, Rwanda's national budget and government policies have to take into account the fact that "Rwanda is among the poorest countries in the world" (Gupta 2013, p.3). Although Rwanda is now slowly getting back on track in terms of the millennium development goals (MDGs), with good progress on lowering infant and under-five mortality; and even the cleanest urban roads by African standards "the average Rwandan still lives on less than $0.70 per day (US dollars), with a typical epidemiological profile for Sub-Saharan Africa" (Rusa et al. 2009, p. 191). In total, around 60 percent of the population were living under the poverty line in 2000 (Sangano, Naanzabaganwa & Mpyisi 2003, p. 1). By 2012, this had dropped to about 44.9 percent (Republic of Rwanda 2012, p. 3).

However, despite this economic improvement, malnutrition remains serious (45 percent of children under five are chronically malnourished), fertility rates are high (the total fertility rate is 6.1 percent), and maternal mortality is about 750 deaths per 100,000 live births (Rusa et al. 2009, p. 191). "The HIV adult prevalence rate is also about 3 percent overall and 3.6 percent for women" (Rusa et al. 2009, p. 191). In summary, according to the 2007 UNDP report entitled "Turning Vision 2020 into Reality: From Recovery to Sustainable Human Development":

> Rwanda's head-count poverty rate has decreased from 60.2% to 56.9% from 2001 to 2006, but there are 600,000 more Rwandans living in poverty than there were five years ago. Despite a decrease in acute malnutrition among children under five, from 7% to 4%, chronic malnutrition has increased from 43% to 45% of children in the past five years. 78% of Rwandan households present some vulnerability in access to or consumption of food. [In general] 28% of Rwandan households are food insecure. In Bugesera, South of Kigali, 40% of households are food insecure. [Therefore,] Rwanda needs to quadruple its investments in agriculture to USD 15 per capita per year if it is to break the cycle of hunger and poverty needed to meet MDG 1.
>
> UNDP Report 2007, p. 8

However, despite these socio-economic realities, the leadership of Rwanda and its people have shown a desire to create a brighter future for themselves in the next few decades as described in Vision2020 (Rusa et al., 2009, p. 191). At the same time, the Government recognizes that "there is never enough money to do all the things that the government would like to do for its citizens" (Gatete 2014, p. 7; MINECOFIN 2014a, p. 7). Therefore, it uses the budget as a tool "to weigh up various needs and decide how to allocate the available scarce resources according to priorities" MINECOFIN (2014a, p. 7). Thus "the priorities identified and reflected in the budget reflect the goals to which Government is most committed" (Gatete 2014, p. 7, MINECOFIN 2014a, p. 7). All government policies are influenced by Rwanda's dream and objective to become a middle-income country by the year 2020 (Gatete 2014, p. 1).

According to Gatete (2014, p. 3) Rwanda's budget follows the practices advocated by the Open Budget Initiative global program. In this, the Government is guided by three important documents: Vision 2020, the Economic Development and Poverty Reduction Strategy (EDPRS) first adopted in 2007 with a five-year horizon, and the MTEF (Klingebiel and Mahn 2011, p. 1; Murara 2011, p. 1). These are the main three policy documents that set out the overarching objectives and priorities that guide the budgeting and planning processes in Rwanda (Murara 2011, p. 1).

Rwanda's Vision 2020

The President of the Republic of Rwanda, Paul Kagame, describes Vision 2020 as a "reflection of Rwandans' aspiration and determination to construct a united, democratic and inclusive Rwandan identity" (Republic of Rwanda 2012, p. i). "Vision 2020 sets the longer term perspective and objectives for Rwanda" (Republic of Rwanda 2012, p. i). The aim of this vision, according to Kagame, is "to transform the country into middle-income nation in which Rwandans are healthier, educated and generally more prosperous, united and competitive both regionally and globally" (Kagame, cited in Republic of Rwanda 2012, p. i).

In order to achieve these objectives, Vision 2020 identifies six interwoven pillars, namely, "good governance and an efficient State, skilled human capital, vibrant private sector, world-class physical infrastructure and modern agriculture and livestock, all geared towards prospering in national, regional and global markets" (Republic of Rwanda 2012, p. i, also available at http://rwandamilitaryhospital.rw/archives/1320?&session-id=52c183bf734e872487f6e1d20d301047).

In addition, "together with these six pillars are the three cross-cutting areas, namely: gender; environment and climate change; and science and technology" (Republic of Rwanda 2012, p. 14). As a long-term planning tool for the country "Vision 2020 presents the overarching framework for all Government activities which guides budgeting and planning at all levels of government (national and district) and sectors of the Rwandan socio-economic life" (Versailles 2012b, p. 1).

Table 11.2 Pillars of Vision 2020 and Associated Cross-cutting Areas

Pillars of Vision 2020	*Cross-cutting areas of Vision 2020*
1. Good governance and a capable state	1. Gender equality
2. Human resource development and a knowledge-based economy	2. Protection of environment and sustainable natural resource management
3. A private sector-led economy	3. Science and technology, including ICT
4. Infrastructure development	
5. Productive and market-oriented agriculture	
6. Regional and international economic integration	

Source: Republic of Rwanda 2012, p. 8.

The six pillars and the three cross-cutting areas through which Vision 2020's aspirations are expected to be realized are depicted in Table 11.2.

As indicated in Table 11.2, any effort to achieve any of the six pillars of Vision 2020 must take into account the three cross-cutting areas.

Economic Development and Poverty Reduction Strategies (EDPRS)

The Government recognizes that no country in the world can pursue a developmental agenda without a vibrant and strong economy to provide the financial means necessary to address poverty. The World Bank and other western development partners for Rwanda (i.e. donors) also put much emphasis on economic development in their funding. Therefore, in line with the views of the World Bank and other western donors to Rwanda as well as the willingness of Rwanda's authorities, government budget spending generally focuses on growing Rwanda's economy. Rwanda's desire to grow its economy and alleviate its citizens' socio-economic conditions are the main thrusts for the country's EDPRS. The EDPRS is considered to be an important document in public budgeting and the national development of Rwanda because "it is a result of in-depth participatory poverty assessments and broad consultation of Rwanda people and development partners who provide funds for its implementation" (Versailles 2012b, p. 1). Versailles (2012b, p. 1) states that "the EDPRS for Rwanda was first adopted by Government in 2007 and since then it has been updated annually through the EDPRS annual reports." To date Rwanda has had two EDPRS's. The first, EDPRS I, was implemented between 2008 and 2012 and the second, EDPRS II began to be implemented in 2013/14 and is expected to last until 2017/18. It is said that both EDPRS (I) and EDPRS (II) are "critical for Rwanda's development because they prioritize sectors with high growth in order to achieve an economic growth" (MINECOFIN 2014a, p. 4).

The funding for government priorities proposed in EDPRS (I & II) comes from external donors and nationally raised funds. According to Klingebiel and Mahn (2011, p. 1) "about 50% of Rwanda's National Budget is external donor funded and about half of that comes in the form of direct budget support . . . about 46% of the budget comes from tax revenues and the balance (i.e. 4%) is collected from non-tax revenue such as fees, fines." Almost all the external funding has been used to fund EDPRS II thematic areas in the 2013/2014 financial year (Gatete 2014, p. 13).

According to the Citizen's Guide to the 2013–2014 national budget provided by MINECOFIN, "there are four EDPRS II thematic areas" (Gatete 2014, p. 13; MINECOFIN 2014a, p. 13).

The first is "Economic Transformation" (Ministry of Finance and Economic Planning 2015, p. 1). According to Rwanda's Ministry of Finance and Economic Planning "the key objective of this thematic area (i.e. 'economic transformation') is to ensure a sustainable rapid economic growth and to facilitate the process of economic transformation" (Gatete 2014, p. 13). Achieving these "twin objectives is expected to increase the internal and external connectivity of the Rwandan economy" (MINECOFIN 2014a, p. 16). Since economic transformation is considered to be the most important theme of Vision 2020, it receives the highest share of the national budget. For example, the economic transformation thematic area received 28 percent of the national budget in the 2013/2014 financial year. This is far higher than any of the other three thematic areas of EDPRS as the following paragraphs demonstrate.

The second EDPRS II thematic area is "to achieve sustainable poverty reduction by improving land use, agriculture productivity; enabling graduation from extreme poverty as well as connecting rural communities to economic opportunity through improved infrastructure" (Gatete 2014, p. 13, MINECOFIN 2014a, p. 13; MINECOFIN 2015b, p. 1). The rural development thematic area received 10 percent of the national budget in the 2013/2014 financial year.

The third thematic area is "Productivity and Youth Employment" (Gatete 2014, p. 14). The purpose of this thematic area is "to transform Rwanda from an agriculture-based economy to an industry and services-based economy" (Gatete 2014, p. 14; MINECOFIN 2014a, p. 14). The Productivity and Youth Employment thematic area received 10 percent of the national budget in the 2013–2014 financial year (MINECOFIN 2014a, p. 14).

The fourth thematic area is "Accountable Governance," the objective of which is "to enhance good governance by promoting citizen participation and mobilization for better service delivery and strengthening public accountability" (Gatete 2014, p. 14; MINECOFIN 2014a, p. 14–15). This thematic area received 2% of the total national budget in the 2013/4 financial year (Gatete 2014, pp. 13–14).

Linking EDPRS, Sector Strategic Plans (SSP), District Development Plans (DDP), Annual Action Plans (AAPs), Performance Contracts, and the MTEF

The second step in the budget allocation process, after the thematic areas, is allocations to the sector strategies (also known as foundational sectors). About 50 percent of Rwanda's national budget is allocated to "foundational sectors such as health and basic education, macro-economic stability, PFM, justice, peace and stability, food security, nutrition and decentralization" (Gatete 2014, p. 15; MINECOFIN 2014a, p. 15). Both the EDPRS and the sector strategic plans "define the MTEF objectives (up to 5 years) and Government's priorities at national and sectoral levels and describe/define performance indicators that will be used to measure the results of each and every sectorial program" (Versailles 2012b, p. 1–2).

Other important plans that must be clearly and directly linked with the EDPRSs are the SSPs, the DDPs, the AAPs and the performance contracts (also known as the *Imihigo* in Kinyarwanda, the Rwandan language). In other words, all the national, regional and local plans must seamlessly talk to each other and be directly linked to the Government's annual budget (Versailles 2012b, p. 2). For example, the DDP is a five-year plan at district level that provides the link between local priorities and national priorities as outlined in other higher level plans such as the EDPRS (at national level), the SSP (at sectoral level) and the AAPs (at the level of budget agencies such as line ministries, provinces, semi-autonomous institutions fully or partly funded through the national budget).

The AAPs are about the activities to be carried out each year by the budget agencies (Versailles 2012b, p. 2). Generally, as Versailles (2012b, p. 2) states, the activities in the AAPs are finalized and adopted at the end of each fiscal year and must be in line with the MTEF and National Budget as adopted by Parliament. The performance contracts (*Imihigos*) outline the key targets and objectives of the district or ministry for the coming year, and for the purpose of monitoring must include targets and measurable indicators related to the delivery of key services (Rusa et al. 2009, p. 191–2). Signing of the *Imihigos* by the President and the mayors at district level can be said to be a service delivery and performance evaluation tool similar to the Management By Objectives (MBO) initiative of 2006 (Rusa et al. 2009, p. 191–2). Table 11.3 shows Rwanda's 2014–16 Planning and Budgeting Calendar.

Coordinating Vision 2020, EDPRS, SSPs and MTEF Funding

All the plans and objectives discussed above are financed by nationally raised or externally donated funds. Thus our brief summary of Government revenue sources suggests that the budgeting process in Rwanda involves two major processes that must be closely coordinated in order to come up with the national budget. These processes are: the collection of revenue internally and the coordination of donor funding from outside the country.

Table 11.3 Rwanda's 2014–16 Planning and Budgeting Calendar

Timeframe	*Week*	*MINECOFIN*	*Ministry*	*Districts*
SEPTEMBER	2nd	Issue the 2013/14 Backward looking JSRs TORs Conduct trainings for planners and budget Officers (Two weeks)	Participate in the trainings of planners and budget officers	Participate in the trainings of planners and budget officers
		Technical support in preparation of backward looking JSRs provided to sectors	JSR preparatory meetings organized	Elaborate an approach to update and harmonize DDPs with national strategies
		Issuance of 1st Planning & BCC	Dissemination of P&BCC to Agencies Developing internal planning roadmaps, review, identification of gaps and Emerging Priorities	Dissemination of P&BCC to Districts Developing internal planning roadmaps, review, identification of gaps and Emerging Priorities Continuous updating of DDPs
		Ministerial and Governors high level meeting conducted to kick start the planning process(Central & local Government, TBC)	Ministerial and Governors high level meeting conducted to kick start the planning process (Central & local Government, TBC)	
	3rd and 4th	Provide technical support in drafting of plans Provide technical support & quality assurance of JSR Reports	Drafting 2015/16 Plans and investments Conduct 2013/14 Backward Joint sector reviews Draft JSR Reports produced and JSR Meetings conducted Incorporate feedback and produce the Final JRS report for submission to MINECOFIN	
OCTOBER	1st	Joint training of district councillors on key components of PFM(Planning, Budgeting and Financial regulations)		District Councillors Training

Table 11.3 continued

Timeframe	*Week*	*Minecofin*	*Ministry*	*Districts*
	2nd and 4th	Provide technical support & quality assurance of plans and investments	Submission of JSR signed reports Ministries' and Agency consultations on plans and investments Consultations with the Private Sector on plans and investments conducted	Preparation of PPDs, PIP forms and Projects Selection
			Central and Local government Consultative meetings coordinated by MINALOC/ LODA in 3 Clusters (Economic, Social and Governance)	Central and Local government Consultative meetings coordinated by MINALOC/ LODA in 3 Clusters (Economic, Social and Governance) Continuous updating of DDPs
NOVEMBER	1st	Quality assurance of plans and investments	First Draft Ministries' plans submitted to MINECOFIN for Quality assurance	First Draft Districts' plans , PPDs and PIP forms submitted to the joint planning team of MINALOC & MINECOFIN for quality assurance through LODA
			Revise Ministries and Agencies plans and investments based on the feedback provided by MINECOFIN	Revise Districts' plans and investments based on feedback provided from joint planning team led by LODA Analyse possible gaps in DDPs and update them accordingly
	2nd	Joint Planning session between central and local Government Including Infrastructure needs Forum	Joint Planning session between central and local Government Including Infrastructure needs Forum	Joint Planning session between central and local Government Including Infrastructure needs Forum
	3rd and 4th	Coordinate the submission of the Second Draft Plans	Adjust Plans and Investments with reference to outcomes from joint planning session btn CG & LG including Infrastructure needs Second Draft Ministries' plans submitted to MINECOFIN	Adjust Plans and Investments with reference to outcomes from joint planning session btn CG & LG including Infrastructure needs

Table 11.3 continued

Timeframe	*Week*	*Minecofin*	*Ministry*	*Districts*
		Phase 1 Planning Consultations	Phase 1 Planning Consultations	
DECEMBER	1st and 2nd	Phase2 Planning Consultations	Phase2 Planning Consultations	Submit the updated plans to the joint team through LODA
		Preparation for National Dialogue	Preparation for National Dialogue	Finalize draft version of updated DDPs and submit to JADF(including private sector representatives and other stakeholders)
				Preparation for National Dialogue
		National Dialogue (TBC)	National Dialogue (TBC)	National Dialogue (TBC)
	3rd and 4th	Support ministries and Agencies, and districts in Budget Revision	Budget Revision	Budget Revision
		Prepare Phase 3 Planning consultations briefs a head of planning consultations	Prepare for Phase 3 planning consultations	
JANUARY	1st and 2nd	Analyze sector Reports on performance against big priority outputs in the 2014/15 budgets	Submit sector Reports on performance against big priority outputs in the 2014/15 budgets	Submit Imihigo progress reports
		Phase 3 Planning consultations	Phase 3 Planning consultations	
		Support Ministries to adjust Plans	Incorporate planning consultations recommendations in the plans	
	3rd	Preparation for Public Investment Committee(PIC)	Preparation for Public Investment Committee(PIC)	Joint consultative forum on LG Projects
		Public Investment Committee(PIC) to agree on projects to be funded in 2015/16	Public Investment Committee(PIC) to agree on projects to be funded in 2015/16 at MINECOFIN	Finetune PPDs, PIP forms for submission to MINECOFIN
		Preparation of summary plans for submission to Cabinet	Adjust Plans and Investments with reference to PIC Recommendations	Adjust Plans and Investments with reference to feedback from consultative forum
		Submission of summary plans and Budget outlook paper to Cabinet		

Table 11.3 continued

Timeframe	*Week*	*Minecofin*	*Ministry*	*Districts*
		Issuance of the 2nd BCC	Dissemination of 2nd BCC to Agencies	Dissemination of 2nd BCC to Districts
	4th	Training of MDA's Staff on budget Data Entry Requirements Analyzing draft submissions of Budget and MTEF and quality assurance	Preparation of Budget proposals including earmarked transfers to districts Submission of Budget proposals, earmarked transfers and MTEF Data entry in IFMIS	Preparation of Budget proposals Finalising the MTEF, LPP and approval Submission of Budget proposals and MTEF Data entry in IFMIS
FEBRUARY	1st and 2nd	Support Ministries, Agencies and Districts in Data Entry in Smart IFMIS	Data Entry Into Smart IFMIS	Data Entry Into Smart IFMIS
	3rd and 4th	Budget Consultation Meetings with Agencies on Budget Priorities and Resource Allocations	Budget consultations	
		Adjustments from budget consultations	Adjustment from budget consultations and submission of IMIHIGO outputs	Adjustment from budget consultations and submission of IMIHIGO outputs
		Leadership retreat (TBC) preparations	Leadership retreat (TBC) preparations	Adjust budget as per budget consultation recommendations Leadership retreat (TBC) preparation
		Leadership retreat (TBC)	Leadership retreat (TBC)	Leadership retreat (TBC)
MARCH	1st and 2nd	Preparation of the Budget Framework Paper (BFP) Finalization of Budget Framework Paper and submission to cabinet Technical support in preparation of forward looking JSRs provided to sectors	Conduct 2015/16 forward looking Joint sector reviews	Prepare 1st Imihigo Draft (TBC) in consultation with stakeholders
		Quality assurance of submitted 2015/16 forward looking draft JSR Reports	Incorporate feedback and produce the JSR Final report for submission to MINECOFIN	

Table 11.3 continued

Timeframe	*Week*	*Minecofin*	*Ministry*	*Districts*
	3rd	Preparations for commemoration of 21st Anniversary of Genocide against the Tutsi	Preparations for commemoration of 21st Anniversary of Genocide against the Tutsi	Preparations for commemoration of 21st Anniversary of Genocide against the Tutsi
	4th	Preparation of Public Investment Programme(PIP) 2015/16–2017/18	Submission of Signed Forward Looking JSR reports	
APRIL	1st and 2nd	21st Genocide commemoration Submission of Draft BFP to Parliament Approval of the Budget Framework Paper	21st Genocide commemoration	21st Genocide commemoration
	3rd and 4th	Joint Quality assurance on Draft Imihigo for ministries & Districts (In collaboration with PMO, PRESREP &MINALOC)	Incorporate feedback and produce the Final draft of Imihigo	Incorporate feedback and produce the Final draft of Imihigo
MAY		Submission of draft Finance Law to parliament Hold DPCG meetings Communication of Firm Commitments by Development Partners	Participation in DPCG	
JUNE	1st and 2nd	Budget hearings in Parliament Submission of Final Draft imihigo	Budget hearings in Parliament Produce final imihigo draft	Budget hearings in Parliament Produce final imihigo draft
	3rd and 4th	Finalization of Public Investment Programme(PIP) 2015/16–2017/18 Preparation of the Budget speech and finalization of the finance law Presentation of Finance Law to the Parliament	Approval of Finance Law by Parliament	District Council Scrutiny and Approval of Annual Budget and IMIHIGO

Source: MINECOFIN 2014b, available online at: www.minecofin.gov.rw/index.php?id=152&L=data%3A%2F%2Ftext%252.

In order to coordinate funding for the "long-term aspirations of the Vision 2020" the Vision's aspirations are translated into medium-term Economic Development and Poverty Reduction Strategies (EDPRS) at the national level (Republic of Rwanda 2012, p. 16). In turn, "the EDPRS is operationalized through sector strategies and DDPs. Both the SSPs and DDP as well as the EDPRSs are implemented through the MTEF" (Republic of Rwanda 2012, p. 16). The Republic of Rwanda (2012, p. 16) argues that in order to ensure smooth implementation of Vision 2020 and increase the chances of achieving the envisaged aspirations described in it, it must be reflected in the whole planning process and, "particularly, in the medium-term operational instruments" such as the MTEF.

Hence, the MTEF is often described in Rwanda as "three-year fully integrated budgets that mainstream the Public Investment Programs (PIP) of all the agencies and translate into concrete action plans." It is these agencies' action plans that are "costed through annual budgets" (Republic of Rwanda 2012, p. 16).

It can therefore be argued that the first stage in the process of allocating public resources in Rwanda is strategic planning. This relies heavily on the MTEF. The MTEF is the "most popular instrument to improve budget planning over a multi-year perspective and to align the budget framework with policy planning" in Rwanda (Morgner 2013, p. 4). The MTEF is a popular tool at the strategic planning stage because it allows the budget to be drafted in a manner that reflects political priorities of the ruling party as well as donors' objectives (Morgner 2013, p. 4).

Thus there is a close and direct link between MTEF, Vision 2020 and EDPRS. The poverty reduction targets to be achieved through the MTEF are closely monitored and usually "feed back into the elaboration of national strategies, sector strategies and district plans" every year (Republic of Rwanda 2012, p. 16). The relationships between EDPRS, the various plans and the MTEF are succinctly summarized in the "2015/16 Planning guidelines extract" provided by MINECOFIN:

> It is important to note that the relationship between both the EDPRS and SSPs and between SSPs and DDPs is an interactive and iterative process. The EDPRS sets the framework for other plans but is also a product of those plans. Similarly, while SSPs set the policy framework for DDPs, subsequent revisions will take note of local priorities as specified in DDPs. That is, for Ministries, MTEFs should translate the overarching Sector strategies to individual institutional 3-year plans and provisional resource allocations while districts' MTEFs should reflect DDP priorities.
>
> MINECOFIN 2015a, p. 1

The links between Rwanda's Vision 2020, EDPRS, SSPs, DDPs, and the MTEF is nicely summarized in Figure 11.1Vision 2020.

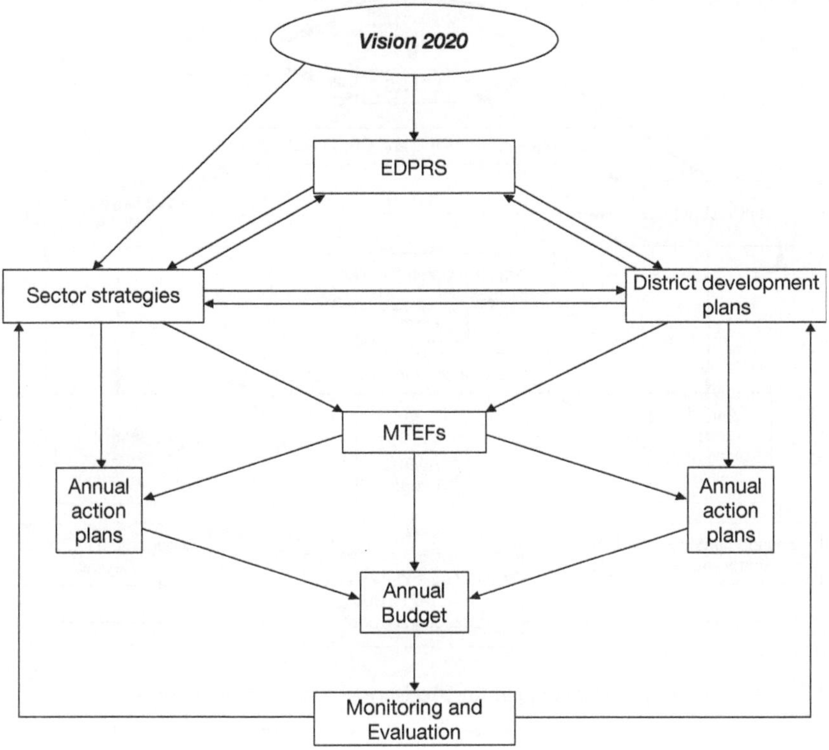

Figure 11.1 Converting Vision 2020 into reality
Source: Republic of Rwanda 2012, p. 25

Linkages between Planning, Budgeting and Aid Coordination

Figure 11.2 illustrates for the complex "linkages between planning, budgeting and aid coordination" (Versailles, 2012b, p. 2) in Rwanda.

Figure 11.2 shows that all planning is directed by the overarching objectives of Vision 2020 and that the aspirations of Vision 2020 are articulated in EDPRS. EDPRS is however implemented through various sector strategies that are executed at district level and by various agencies. Each implementing agency must have a clear action plan for how it will operationalize the set EDPRS objectives, which are linked to performance objectives (*Imihigo*). It is the SSPs, DDPs, AAPs and the *Imihigos* that are funded through the MTEFs.

While the MTEF projects funding for more than one year, actual funding for service delivery is provided on one-year basis (annual budget) in order to allow continuous monitoring and evaluation of progress and to take corrective measures where problems arise. All the steps are closely monitored and regular execution reports are one of the various instruments used for monitoring and evaluation of the budget implementation process by different stakeholders.

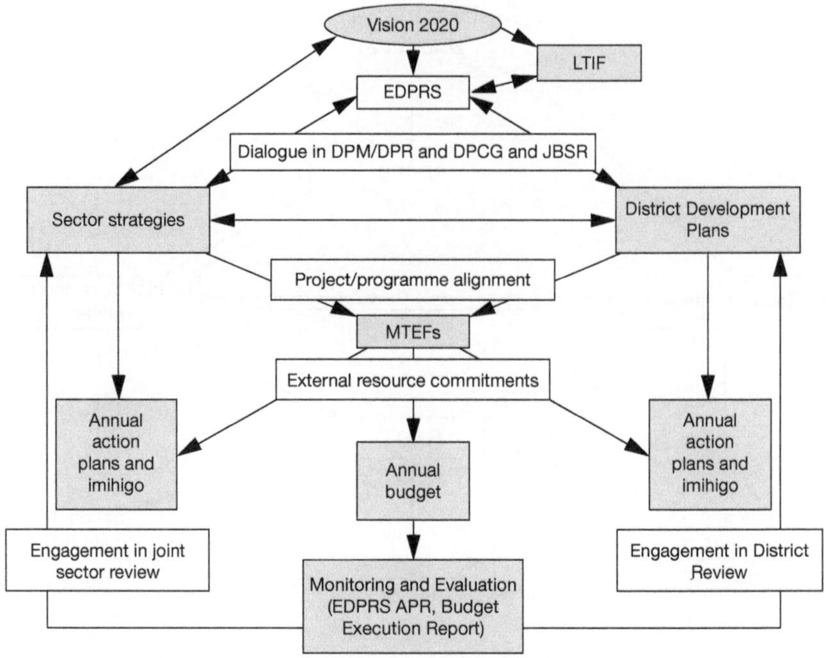

Figure 11.2 Linkages between planning, budgeting, and aid coordination
Source: Versailles 2012b, p. 2, Country learning notes: www.budgetstrenghening.org

Linking Planning, Budgeting and the MTEF

In order to maintain high standards in the PFM, the Government has developed a comprehensive financial legal framework. The MTEF is one of the major instruments used to strengthen the budget preparation process. The MTEF is also considered to be the key instrument in linking planning and budgeting in many countries (Versailles 2012b, p. 3). "The MTEF was first rolled out in 2002 with the objective of making the National Budget an effective and efficient tool for implementing 'the plans and reach the EDPRS' objectives" (Versailles 2012c, p. 4). It is therefore used as a tool for enhancing the integration of both the recurrent and development budgets in one plan.

Some of the successes that can be linked to the introduction of the MTEF in Rwanda's budgeting and planning processes include:

- enhanced quality of macro-economic planning and budget ceilings;
- improved budget preparation process and negotiations between MINECOFIN and budget agencies which is demonstrated by enhanced budget submissions; and
- enhanced quality of medium-term forecasting of internal and external revenue (Versailles 2012b, p. 4).

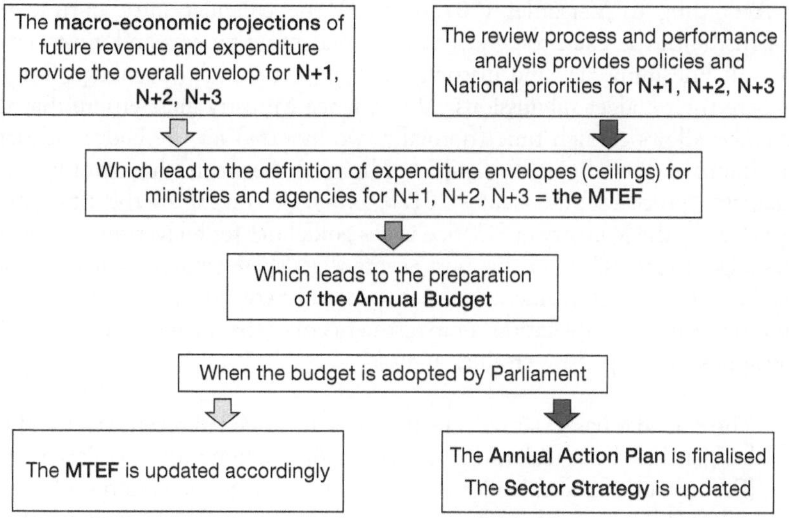

Figure 11.3 MTEF as link between planning and budgeting

Source: Borrowed from Versailles 2012b, p. 4

Another important document in terms of linking planning and budgeting is the budget framework paper (BFP). The BFP sets out the Government's medium-term strategic thinking and is usually developed a month before the submission of the budget to Parliament. Finally, another important tool which has been developed alongside the METF in terms of the budget preparation process is the strategic issues paper (also known as SIPS). Normally SIPS are prepared by the budget agencies and provide background and justification for ministries' budget submissions. SIPS summarizes the main current policy issues,.the overall focus being what exactly the priority areas should be. This focus is considered to be important in terms of helping planning and budgeting to be more of strategic use than a historical process. Figure 11.3 illustrates the key role of the MTEF in facilitating the links between policies and priorities (i.e. planning) and the annual budget (Versailles 2012b, p. 4).

Rwanda's Budget Calendar

The new ROBL deals with the issues of budget preparation by setting out clear deadlines for the national budget preparation cycle, clarifying the responsibility of each actor and minimum content of the budget documentation submitted to Parliament. The Rwandan Organic Budget Law (ROBL) requires the Ministry of Finance to provide a detailed calendar for the budget preparation and planning process (Article 28). All documents must be submitted according to a clearly defined budget calendar that outlines when, where, and by whom these processes must be started and completed.

According to Versailles (2012b, p. 4) the calendar must outline the responsibilities of each role-player in the budgeting process and must ensure that all line ministries and districts (budget agencies) have enough time to prepare their budget submissions. The Finance Ministry must ensure that the calendar allows enough time (normally two months) for the budget agencies to "improve the alignment and coordination between the planning and budgeting processes" (Versailles 2012b, p. 4). According to the BSI (2012, p. 3) "when the Ministry of Finance issues guidelines for budget submissions to all budget agencies," he or she must ensure that "these guidelines give stronger emphasis to the complementarity between recurrent and capital expenditure and the recurrent implications of investments over the medium term" (see also Versailles 2012c, p. 3). Versailles argues:

> The calendar has so far been relatively well applied in recent years and the budget has been submitted in time for examination by Parliament. [Furthermore,] the calendar is designed to allow participation of different stakeholders at political level, in particular through the adoption of the budget ceilings by Cabinet and the inter-ministerial consultative meetings on final draft budget allocations.
>
> Versailles 2012b; Government of Rwanda 2010

In order to "foster a more inclusive budget process, the calendar must also provide relevant information to civil society" (Versailles 2012b, p. 4). Figure 11.4 is an example of Rwanda's budget calendar.

Figure 11.4 shows that "budget preparation runs for a period of 12 months in line with Rwanda's financial year (1 July–30 June)" (MINECOFIN 2014a, p. 6). As Figure 11.4 shows, budgeting starts with the "revision of the macro-framework in July of every year and ends with the presentation of the draft budget to parliament in June of the following year" (see also MINECOFIN 2014a, p. 6). A great many planning and budgeting processes have to take place simultaneously between MINECOFIN, line ministries at national level and districts in order to finalize the budget that is finally approved by Parliament and executed by the various line ministries and district agencies.

Budget Financial Reporting: External Audit and Parliamentary Scrutiny

The improvement of accounting standards is the most commonly "applied tool of PFM reform programs next to the improvement of budget implementation through STA and IFMIS" (Morgner 2013, p. 8). Improving accounting standards has tended to focus on making government accounting compliant with International Public Sector Accounting Standards (IPSAS) and the move from cash-based accounting toward accrual accounting. Morgner says, "unlike the traditional cash-based accounting, the accrual accounting applies the principles of private-sector accounting to the public sector" (2013, p. 8). In addition, while

TIME-FRAME	MINECOFIN	LINE MINISTRIES	DISTRICTS	NON-STATE ACTORS/DEV PARTNERS	CABINET/ PARLIAMENT
July	Update of macro-framework	Preparation of financial statements	Preparation of financial statements		
	Preparation of budget execution report				
August	Preparation of budget outlook paper	Preparation of annual reports	Preparation of annual reports		Cabinet retreat and approval of BFP
September	Issuance of First Budget Call Circular to communicate Sector MTEFs and request for preparation of Sector BFPs	Review of Ministerial expenditures	Review of District expenditures	Preparation of District expenditure reviews	
October	National budget consultative workshop to officially launch the budget process	Joint Sector Review & preparation of Sector BFPs	District Expenditure Review & preparation of District BFPs	Participation to the National Budget consultative workshop	
	Local government consultative workshop				
November	Training of budget staff on new utilities of SmartGov				
	Joint Budget Review (JBRs) & update of macro-framework	Participation in the JBR	Consultation with Ministers on District BFPs	Participation in the JBR	
December	Issuance of the second Budget Call Circular with revised MTEF & agency ceilings	Training of Budget Officers on the use of SmartGov			
	Preparation & submission of the Revised Budget to Cabinet	SWG Retreat to consolidate Sector BFPs		Participation to the SWG Retreat	Approval of Budget by Cabinet
January	Submission of Reviewed Budget to Parliament	Online Budget Submission by Budget Agencies	Estimation of District resources and preparation of District Budgets	Communication of Indicative Commitments	Approval of Revised Budget by parliament
February	Inter-Ministerial Consultative Meeting on Budget Priorities & Resource Allocation	Revised budget data input in the SmartGov			
	Beginning of the EAC Pre-Budget Consultative process		Budget date input in the SmartGov		
March	Preparation & submission of the National BFP and draft Budget to Cabinet				Cabinet approval of the BFP and Draft budget
April	BFP presented to Parliament not later than April 5				
	Draft Budget submission to Parliament				Discussion of BFP and the Draft Budget by Parliament
	Communicate the draft budget estimates to CBMs		District Council scrutiny and approval of Annual Budget		
May	Joint Budget Review (JBR)	Participation on the JBR		Participation in the JBR	
	EAC Ministerial Consultation on tax policy issues				
June	Preparation of the Budget Speech and finalisation of the draft budget				
	Presentation of the draft Budget to Parliament			Communication of firm commitments	Approval of the budget

Figure 11.4 Example of Rwanda's budget calendar (FY 2012)

cash-based accounting considers the date of payment of the corresponding expenditure, accrual accounting only "takes note of the actual consumption of a good or service" (Morgner 2013, p. 8).

Improving accounting standards have often gone hand in hand with strengthening the internal and external oversight bodies. According to Morgner (2013, p. 8), PFM reforms "usually aim at strengthening the functions and capacities of countries' supreme audit institutions as well as of parliament oversight committees." In addition, civil society may also play an instrumental role in overseeing the activities of these bodies.

In terms of improving external scrutiny, the post-1994 Government made an effort to replace its "old Francophone tradition of centralized administration with an Anglophone system based on checks and balances based on parliamentary authority" (Klingebiel & Mahn 2011, p. 2). The first general accountant of Rwanda (GAR) was appointed in 2005 and the Office of the Auditor General (OAG) was established in 2000 (Murara 2011, p. 1). These two British-styled institutions replaced the pre-1994 French-styled *cour des comptes*, which is said to have failed to produce an audit during its 43 years of existence "due to limited capacity and an entrenched lack of culture of accountability that characterized the pre-1994 era" (Murara 2011, p. 1).

Another important step in terms of the Parliamentary scrutiny was the establishment of the Public Account Committee (PAC). According to Pendo (2012, p. 1),

> PAC was established in April 2011 as a requirement of East African Community bloc. Uganda, Kenya and Tanzania already have them. [PAC is responsible for] consideration, study, and submission of reports on general accounts of institutions that use national budget and patrimony [and] performance of such other duties related to the use of national budget and patrimony within public institutions.
>
> Ministry of Agriculture and Animal Resources 2015, p. 1

In performing its duties, "the committee is supposed to ensure that every cent spent by the executive goes for the right cause" (Pendo 2012, p. 1).

Rwanda's Key PFM Reform Challenges

The first PEFA analysis in 2006/7 highlighted some challenges that led to the introduction of the 2008–2012/3 PFM Reform Strategy (PFMRS). Rwanda's PFM reforms usually get good-to-very-good ratings in PEFA international comparative indices (Klingebiel & Mahn 2011, p. 2). But some challenges remain. These challenges include lack of capacity at district levels, where 30 percent of the national budget is spent (Klingebiel & Mahn 2011, p. 2). Because local governments (districts) have important service delivery responsibility in Rwanda, improving PFM and good governance at these sub-national levels is critically important in order for the PFM initiatives and strategies to succeed (cited in World Bank 2014, p. 1).

Another challenge is that about 50 percent of Rwanda's national budget is donor funded (and about half of this is direct national budget support) but donors tend to be slow at turning their pledges into action and in providing timely information on development cooperation projects in order to help government improve its budget planning (Klingebiel & Mahn 2011, p. 2, ECORYS 2012, p. 11). While the Government's budget strategy is aligned to its national strategies such as 2020 Vision, "aid fluctuations constrain implementation of government expenditure programmes" (cited in World Bank 2014, p. 1).

Since PFM reform is relatively new in Rwanda, it is still work in progress. Many lessons are still being learned and the process will require continuous monitoring and improvement with time. Despite numerous challenges, there is political willingness, and donors' support has been very helpful. There is hope that the PFM reforms in Rwanda will bring about improvements with time and Rwanda might achieve the performance level of modern countries.

Conclusion

The purpose of this chapter was to describe the status of public budgeting and PFM reforms in Rwanda. The discussion above shows that Rwanda's budgeting process and PFM reforms are heavily dependent on national objectives such as those set out in Vision 2020 and strategic documents such as the EDPRS. Budgeting and planning at different levels of Government and implementing agencies are enabling functions for Vision 2010 and the EDPRS. The Government has made tremendous progress in the sense that it has established a modern legal framework to govern its PFM reforms and budgeting processes. There is also strong evidence of proper linkages between budgeting and planning and of various instruments for internal and external control to increase accountability.

However, PFM reforms are still work in progress and many challenges still exist, but Rwanda's authorities and their development partners are doing all that is possible to deal with them.

References

Auriacombe, C., & Van der Waldt, V. 2015. *Section B Municipal Finance Management: Budgeting*. Unpublished internal handbook. Johannesburg: University of Johannesburg.

Budget Strengthening Initiative (BSI). 2012. *Rwanda: Integration of the National Budget*. http://static1.1.sqspcdn.com/static/f/1349767/18085925/1336475379787/Rwanda+integration+of+national+budget.pdf?token=s0%2BfNZHBb4DrGk9SdqUFnjByUpM%3D.

Collaborative Africa Budget Reform Initiative (CABRI). 2013. *Programme Based Budgeting*. www.cabri-sbo.org/what-we-do/systems/programme-based-budgeting.

ECORYS. 2012. *Rwanda: Independent Evaluation of the Implementation of the PFM Reform Strategy 2008–2012*. Final Report. Kigali, November 2012. www.swedenabroad.com/ImageVaultFiles/id_7083/cf_347/PFMRS_Evaluation_Final_submitted_-_A.pdf .

Gatete, C. 2014. *The National Budget: A Citizen's Guide 2013-2014*. www.minecofin.gov.rw/fileadmin/templates/documents/Fiscal_Decentralisation_Unit/Budget_Citizen_Guide/2013-2014/2013-14__Budget_Citizen_Guide-_English.pdf.

Government of Rwanda (GoR). 2010. "PFM Performance Report—PEFA" Final report, November 30, 2010. www.minecofin.gov.rw/webfm_send/1394.

Gupta, N. 2013. *One of the World's Tiniest, Poorest Countries is Redefining HIV Care*. www.theatlantic.com/international/archive/2013/12/one-of-the-worlds-tiniest-poorest-countries-is-redefining-hiv-care/281937/.

Gwartney, J.D., Stroop, R.L., Sobel, R.S., & Macpherson, D.A. 2009. *Macroeconomics: Private and Public Choice*, 12th ed. US: Cengage Learning.

IMF. 2011. *Rwanda: Poverty Reduction Strategy Paper: Progress Report*. IMF Country Report No. 11/154. https://books.google.co.za/books?id=hNh8-jXbuZsC&pg=PT268&lpg=PT268&dq=.

Klingebiel, S., & Mahn, T. 2011. *In the Fast Lane: Rwanda's Public Finance Management is Improving Fast*. http://dandc.eu/en/article/rwandas-public-finance-management-improving-fast.

MINECOFIN. n.d. *Public Financial Management: Objectives of the Public Financial Management (PFM) Reform Portfolio*. www.minecofin.gov.rw/fileadmin/templates/documents/Public_Financial_Management.pdf.

MINECOFIN. 2010. *The Budget of Rwanda—a Citizen's Guide 2010–2011 Kigali, June*. http://www.minecofin.gov.rw/fileadmin/templates/documents/LG_DIstricts/Budget_Citizens_Guide/2010-2011/2010-11%20Budget%20Citizen%20Guide%20in%20English.pdf.

MINECOFIN. 2014a. *The Budget of Rwanda: a Citizen's Guide 2013-2014*. www.minecofin.gov.rw/fileadmin/templates/documents/Fiscal_Decentralisation_Unit/Budget_Citizen_Guide/2013-2014/2013-14__Budget_Citizen_Guide-_English.pdf.

MINECOFIN. 2014b. *2014–2016 Planning and Budgeting Calendar*. www.minecofin.gov.rw/index.php?id=152&L=data%3A%2F%2Ftext%252.

MINECOFIN. 2015a. *Public Financial Management*. www.minecofin.gov.rw/fileadmin/templates/documents/Public_Financial_Management.pdf.

MINECOFIN. 2015b. *EDPRS2 (Both main and abridged)*. www.minecofin.gov.rw/file admin/templates/documents/NDPR/EDPRS_2_Abridged_Version.pdf.

Ministry of Agriculture and Animal Resources. 2015. *The Parliament's Committee on Public Accounts (PAC) visits RAB Rubona centre*. www.minagri.gov.rw/index.php?id=469&L=0&tx_ttnews%5Btt_news%5D=997&cHash=ae49246f4b9074ff909eec95dad9ce52.

Morgner, M. 2013. *Public Financial Management Reforms in Developing and Post Conflict Countries*. www.transparency.org.

Murara, L. K. 2011. *Rwanda: A Decade of Difficult but Sustained Public Financial Management Reforms*. www.blog-pfm.imf.org/pfmblog/2011/08/rwanda-a-decade-of-difficult-but-sustained-public-financial-management-reforms.html.

Pendo, A. 2012. *Rwanda Public Accounts Committee Releases First Report, Cites Massive Irregularities*. www.newsofrwanda.com/irembo/2694/rwanda-public-accounts-committee-releases-report-cites-massive-irregularities/.

Republic of Rwanda. 2006. *Organic Law on state finances and Property: Official Gazette of the Republic of Rwanda*. No. 37/2006 of 12/09/2006. Year 45 no. special of 12 September 2006. https://repositories.lib.utexas.edu/bitstream/handle/2152/5080/4172.pdf?sequence=1.

Republic of Rwanda. 2010. *Rwanda: Constitution (2010)*. http://e-tegeko.com/wp-content/uploads/2012/04/CONSTITUTION-of-RWANDA-3-Languages-with-amendments.pdf?&session-id=52c183bf734e872487f6e1d20d301047.

Republic of Rwanda. 2012. *Rwanda Vision 2020: Revised 2012*. www.minecofin.gov.rw/fileadmin/templates/documents/NDPR/Vision_2020_.pdf.

Rusa, L., Schneidman, M., Fritsche, G., & Musango, L. 2009. Rwanda: Performance-based financing in the public sector. In R. Eichler, R. Levine and the Performance-Based Incentives Working Group (Eds.) *Performance Incentives for Global Health: Potential and Pitfalls*. Washington: Center for Global Development.

Sangano, K., Nsanzabaganwa, S., & Mpyisi, E. 2003. *Rwanda Country Position Paper. Section A: Summary Overview of Status of National Poverty Policy and Strategy*. Regional Workshop on Ageing and Poverty. Dar es Salaam, Tanzania. http://www.un.org/ageing/documents/workshops/Tanzania/rwanda.

UNDP. 2007. *Turning Vision 2020 into Reality: From Recovery to Sustainable Human Development*. National Human Development Report: Rwanda 2007. http://hdr.undp.org/sites/default/files/rwanda_2007_en.pdf.

Versailles, B. 2012a. *Budget Strengthening Initiatives: Country Learning Notes: Rwanda: Integration of the National Budget*. http://static1.1.sqspcdn.com/static/f/1349767/18004663/1336052328690/Rwanda+integration+of+the+national+budget.txt?token=3Ra8nf2Gv7BbPas1EclxHiJ74%2B8%3D.

Versailles, B. 2012b. *Budget Strengthening Initiatives: Country Learning Notes: Rwanda: Legal and Institutional Frameworks for Public Finance Management*. Overseas Development Institute (ODI). http://static1.1.sqspcdn.com/static/f/1349767/18085926/1336475380730/Rwanda.

Versailles, B. 2012c. *Budget Strengthening Initiatives: Country Learning Notes: Rwanda: Budgeting & planning process*. http://static1.1.sqspcdn.com/static/f/1349767/18085923/1336475378620/rwanda-budgeting-and-planning.pdf.html.

Wikipedia. 2015. Government budget. http://en.wikipedia.org/wiki/Government_budget.

World Bank. 2014. *Rwanda: World Bank Helps Boost Public Financial Management and Enhance Nutrition and Food Security for Rural Farmers*. www.worldbank.org/en/news/press-release/2014/10/31/rwanda-world-bank-helps-boost-public-financial-management-and-enhance-nutrition-and-food-security-for-rural-farmers.

12 Public Budgeting and Service Delivery in Tanzania

Denis J. Kamugisha and John S. Kihamba

Introduction

In a democracy, the budget provides the means for the government to pursue its policy objectives—increasing access to quality services to a majority of citizens. Effective access to quality services largely depends among others on well-functioning public budgeting institutions as well as agencies of service delivery. Public budgeting is a prerequisite to improving the quality of life and the well-being of the population. A budget establishes what public services will be supplied to the public, which individuals and groups will receive the public services, how the public services will be delivered and how and with what the cost public services will be financed (Gildenhuys 2010). Clearly the budget is a most important statement of government policies, and implemented to increase access to quality services. Also it gives citizens a sense of ownership and control over the use of public financial resources, among others.

However, experience has shown that delivering public services that are consistent with citizens' preferences is not an easy task in developing countries particularly in Tanzania. It requires effective and efficient management of fiscal resources at both national and local levels. Management of fiscal resources in many developing countries particularly Tanzania is faced with a number of challenges, as shown by the Controller and Accountant-General (CAG) report for 2006 to 2014, including among others: over-estimation of revenues, unfriendly revenue collection techniques, unwillingness to pay taxes on the part of the taxpayers, unreliable or untimely disbursement of approved foreign financial resources to support national budgets, poor sources of revenue assigned to local government authorities, and mismanagement of allocated scarce resources by public officials.

In light of the foregoing, government plans to improve quality service delivery through annual budgets have not been realized despite the fact that people in both rural and urban areas largely depend on services rendered by public institutions such as health care, education, water, among others. The quality of these services is still low despite a government initiative to reform its budgetary system from line-item budgeting to program-based budgeting (PBB). The Aadoption of PBB was expected to increase credibility of the budget by ensuring accurate costing of priority areas (URT 2013). The introduction of results-based management was also expected to improve service delivery (ibid.). However, budgeting based on PBB is not adequately addressing the challenges of the mismanagement of fiscal resources. Efforts to mobilize public financial resources (tax and non-tax revenues), accounting, and reporting are still below expectation, according to CAG reports in 2013, 2014, 2015.

This situation has a negative impact on the quality of services delivered by public institutions; many citizens are discouraged by the quality of some social services such as health care, education, and so on. The most affected are those with low incomes, people with disabilities, and other marginalized groups who are not capable of acquiring such services from the private sector. It has to be noted that the public budget in Tanzania is always considered to be a panacea for a number of ills, including a lack of access to quality services. Public services are either provided freely to some groups or are provided at lower cost, because the government budget provides subsidies to enable the majority of the Tanzanian population to easily access services such as health care and education. These services are considered as of national importance, and are largely financed through public budgeting. About 82 percent of the actual recurrent transfers in the years 2010/11, 2011/12 and 2012/13 were directed to financing national priority sectors (education and health) with only 17 percent being directed to other sectors (URT 2012a, 2013). Despite the significant share being allocated to finance these sectors the quality of services has not improved enough (URT 2014).

In principle, addressing citizens' preferences requires democratic decisions on how the state solicits revenue and expends it. However, the practice in Tanzania has been that significant fiscal decisions are made by the executive branch while the parliamentarians play a more or less approving role. This implies that parliamentarians are unlikely to be sensitive and responsive to public demands rather than to those of the appointing authority. This state of affairs forces them to react positively to the legal and executive orders of the appointing institutional authority.

While there is a consensus in the literature that the budget process plays an important role in providing citizens with public services, in Tanzania, there is little or no impact on the service provided. It is therefore imperative to explain why the budgeting process in Tanzania does not clearly address service delivery issues. In every financial year Tanzania undertakes budgetary process with a view to allocating scarce resources to improve access to quality services. The situation on the ground has not significantly changed in many areas and in some it has declined. Agencies of service delivery have not been able to provide quality services such as education, health, water, agriculture, among others (URT 2011, 2012a). In this regard, ensuring equitable access to quality public services in Tanzania constitutes a key challenge throughout the budgetary process at national and local levels. Evidence suggests that many of the citizens are disproportionately affected by the barriers to quality services, compounded by inadequate funding of priority sectors and mismanagement of disbursed funds.

Therefore this chapter sets out to explain why public budgeting in Tanzania does not effectively address issues related to access to quality services. It covers introductory remarks; conceptual issues; guiding principles for resource allocation and its dynamics; budgeting dynamics; and service delivery. It compares approved against actual budgets with regard to service delivery. It takes into account challenges affecting fiscal management such as revenue collection and allocation and how they relate to the current state of service delivery. Lastly, it considers policy implications and the way forward.

Conceptual Issues

This section sheds light on key concepts and underpinning principles. Delivering quality services that meet citizens' preferences requires well-functioning budgeting institutions. Efficient and effective public budgeting is the life blood of the public sector, for it improves access to quality services. The credibility and legitimacy of the public sector depends on its capability to effective manage fiscal resources and deliver quality services. Gildenhuys (2010) clearly states that a budget stipulates goods and services to be supplied by government authorities, although the services can be supplied by the private sector. Peters (1988) argues that all resources in society are available to government. Therefore, the government's role is to effectively manage—soliciting and allocating scarce resources to address citizens' preferences. However, effective fiscal management is not easy.

Budgeting as a Concept and its Dynamics

According to Marais (1980), a budget in its physical appearance is the collection of various official documents. For Vocino and Rabin (1981), it is a document indicating how a public institution spends resources in order to realize specific public goals. Gildenhuys (2010) states that a budget, in the ordinary sense of the word, is a financial statement that contains the estimates of revenue and expenditure over a certain period of time. It is the document containing revenue and expenditure proposals of a public authority. It involves two key elements, *revenue* and *expenditure*. According to Henry (2007), revenue is the money that the government collects to expend in support of public policies. Expenditure (outlays) is the money that governments spend to fund public policies. Since central government plays a major role in ensuring public services are provided, it incurs enormous public costs. This is possible only when there is sufficient public revenue. Without it there cannot be expenditure. Public revenue is obtained from taxes, borrowings, debts (internal and external), international investments, profit from public enterprises, equities and funds from international monetary agencies, internal financial institutions, and deficit-financing (Narayan 2002). Despite these sources of funding, developing countries, including Tanzania, always operate in budget deficit. Mikesell (1986:25) agrees. He states that public institutions "... operate with haphazard budget processes." This implies that the aforesaid revenue sources are not enough to finance the expenditure the government wishes to make. The reasons for that funding gap are discussed using the Tanzanian case in the following pages.

There are two types of fund in which revenues are held to be used to finance public activities: the general fund and the special fund (Henry 2007). The general fund holds revenue that can be expended for any purpose the government chooses. This is normally tabled in parliament for approval. The approval stage involves a lot of friction. Henry (2007) asserts that when a budget battle erupts in parliament or a local legislature, it is the general fund that is typically at stake. According to Thomson (2005), budget battles provide an x-ray of values and priorities, which vary from person to person. He (ibid.) argues that this diversity leads to ferocious (brutal) political battle. Because approving a budget is a political process, fierce battle is unavoidable. Without it a budget cannot be feasible. Gildenhuys (2010:393) holds that the "budget as a political process is characterized by an inherent tension between politics and scientific analysis."

The Special funds are used to hold revenues that may be expended only for specific pre-established purposes. Some special funds support public policies. Social security is an example. Special funds require protection from political tides and their accompanying opportunities, which tend to divert special funds to other lesser but popular purposes (Henry 2007). Although governments use social security funds to support public policies, it takes long time to fund social security administration. As a result organizations and individual retirees are affected.

Tanzania's budgetary system uses a public fund and special funds. Some people get confused between a budget and a budget system. According to Thornhill (1984), while a budget refers only to the documents within which financial (revenue and expenditure) proposals are contained, the budget system shows the interface between the stages that are followed in compiling the budget documents. This process is known as budgeting.

Budgeting is the means by which public officials raise and allocate resources in order to achieve social objectives (Thomson 2005:51). Specifically, each government institution, on whatever level of authority, pursues predetermined goals, objectives and targets that are reflected in its annual operational and capital budgets (Gildenhuys 2010:3). Peters (1988), states that the budgetary process provides a means of allocating the available resources among the competing interests to which they could be applied. This involves both public and private organizations.

Thornhill (1984) says that a public budget is different from a private budget. First, the public budget is enforceable after its approval by the legislative authority. Citizens are compelled to pay taxes and comply with any other requirements contained in the budget. Second, most public budgets are not quantifiable, especially as some aspects of public budgeting are difficult to estimate accurately. As a result, taxpayers are often unable to assess the rationale behind public expenditures . Third, the public budget brings together a variety of considerations. So, those citizens who need more help can receive it. Fourth, its content is unique. Its purpose is not to ascertain the profitability of a product by comparing costs and revenue. Rather, it compares costs and the political, economic and social benefits that might accrue for the community. It is important to note that the approved budget tasks cannot be assessed in fiscal terms alone, but also in the extent to which they realize the goals of the government (or other authority). Fifth, the government does not always align their expenditure with the available revenue. This is because the government always seeks to determine what services will be necessary and how much money will be needed to promote the welfare and economic well-being of the community.

On the basis of the foregoing, it is safe to argue that the public budget is a compromise between the services in demand by the community and the ability of the community to pay for them. This notion leads on to a number of key budget questions, one of which was raised by Key: "On what basis should it be decided to allocate x dollars to activity A instead of activity B" (Key 1940: 1137). Peters (1988: 103) raised two further questions, both of which are implied by Key's fundamental question. His first question is concerned with system-level allocation between the public and private sectors:

> How many activities or problems justify government intervention into the economy for the purpose of taxing and spending? Could the best interest of society as a whole be served by keeping the money in private hands for the investment decisions and allowing some possible beneficial programs in governments to go unfunded? Or do the equity, equality, and economic growth produced by a public project justify the use of political capital by officials to pass and collect an additional tax or to increase an existing tax?

As Haruna stated in Chapter 1, his second budget question is about how the available resources should be allocated. Thomson (2005) is of the opinion that the bedrock questions of politics can be settled through budgeting. For Dye (1981) and Key (1940), the fundamental political question revolves around who gets how much, for what purpose and who pays for it? There is no clear evidence that budgeting always sheds light on the bedrock questions of politics, although it deals with the process of soliciting and expending resources in order to improve the delivery of goods and services. It remains a fact that allocation of financial resources aims at increasing access to quality services to meet citizens' expectations.

Budgeting as a Function of Resource Allocation

Budgeting as a function of resource allocation carries with it three administrative functions (Cowden 1969, p. 283). First, it is the basis on which the tax policy for the budget period is devised. Second, it is the basis on which financial control is exercised in order to ensure that the financial policy made by the legislature authority is adhered to. Third, it is a financial program through which revenue and expenditure are harmonized to realize certain public objectives. It provides an opportunity to determine what choices have been made and on what basis certain actions will be taken.

According to Gildenhuys (2010), there are five functions of a budget First, it is a control instrument. It involves both a priori control (predetermined budget objectives before execution) and *ex post facto* control (evaluation of budget results after execution). Second, it is a policy document in which the elected political representatives, as the legislature, express the measure to which they wish to execute the mandate received from their constituencies. It contains proposed public services by parliament or councils. Third, it serves as the most important source of information for everyone concerned, particularly the administrative authority for execution of its functions. Fourth, it is an instrument for coordination and integration of overall government activities for it contains all information, objectives and activities of the government. Fifth, it is an operating program from which every department bases its operational activities to ensure that government goals especially the tangible ones are effectively and efficiently realized.

One of the important functions of public budget is the redistribution of wealth between the "haves" and "have nots" (ibid.: 413). This notion can be understood by applying the socialist doctrine (principle): "pay according to one's ability and receive according to one's need." This is reflected in tax collection system known as "pay as you earn" (PAYE). Hakielimu and the Policy Forum (2008:53) consider the case of Tanzania. Those well-salaried undertake very challenging and numerous tasks. Comparatively, they pay more tax. The graduated tax rate structure under which individual income tax is charged, is applied each year for every person who earns income from employment, business or investment. The tax rate structure for two recent tax years is shown in Table 12.1.

Table 12.1 Individual Income Tax Rates for the Years 2007/08 to 2008/09 (T/Shillings)

2007/08		*2008/09*	
Income Interval	*Tax Rate*	*Income Interval*	*Tax Rate*
0–80,000	0%	0–100,000	0%
80,000–180,000	15%	100,001–360,000	15% (amount above 100,000)
180,000–360,000	20%	360,001–540,000	20% (amount above 360,000) plus T.sh. 39,000
360,001–540,000	25%	540,001–720,000	25% (amount above 540,000) plus T.sh. 75,000
540,000 and above	30%	720,000 and above	30% (amount above 720, 000) plus T.sh. 120,000

Source: Hakielimu and Policy Forum (2008:53)

Gildenhuys (2010) holds that the instrument for redistribution of wealth emanates from the integration of the revenue side and the expenditure side of the budget. Musgrave (1986:12) argues that the revenue side plays a distributive role in a budget by: first instituting progressive taxation of higher income groups, second subsidizing lower income groups, and third lowering tax on quasi-collective services such as education and preventive health to benefit lower income groups.

Browne (in Gildenhuys 2010:400) mentions the economic regulation function. He argues that public financing by means of a public budget is an important stabilizing instrument that can be utilized to combat fluctuations within the economy. It is difficult to deliver quality services if the national economy is in a shambles. In order to stabilize it, economic regulation uses two types of stabilizer. One is the automatic fiscal stabilizer, which relate to tax on income. When the tax rates are not adjusted, taxation supplies more revenue when the incomes (tax base) increase. It supplies less revenue when the incomes decrease. The other is the discretionary fiscal stabilizer. It takes place when an authority deliberately adjusts its tax and expenditure policies in order to stimulate the economy. Therefore, a budget can be viewed as a stabilizing instrument for combating inflation within the economy. When private expenditure rises too high and causes inflation, the government cuts back on public expenditure (using the budget), and at the same time restricts money in circulation in the private sector by raising taxes. However, when private expenditure is too low, the government increases public expenditure and lowers taxes.

A Distinction between Public and Private Expenditure

The key distinction between the two types of expenditure is found in their defining features. To use the same terminology as Gildenhuys (2010) and Fozzard (2001), first, private (particular) services are apportionable. This means that their utilization can be assigned based on a quantifiable consumption unit and a price per unit consumed can be specified. Second, they are exclusive: people who cannot pay can be excluded from using these services. Third, they are exhaustible. Services disappear in the process of consumption. They must be replenished on a continuous basis. Fourth, they are usually financed by consumer tariffs. Consumers receive a direct "quid pro quo." Fifth, they are competitive. They can be provided by any entrepreneur as long as there is an absolutely free-market system where there are no monopolies.

In case of market failure the government intervenes by way of legislation and may decide to provide the services. When the government subsidizes particular services through taxes to be accessed by the public, they become quasi-collective services. They are provided to avoid the negative spill-over effect that would accrue should the citizens fail to access or afford them. Examples of such services include education and preventive health.

According to OECD (2010), Gildenhuys (2010), Fozzard (2001), Humphreys (1998) and Samuelson (1954), public (collective) services demonstrate numerous features. First, they are non-apportionable. They cannot be divided into consumption units, supplied per unit and sold at a price per unit. Second, they maintain their non-exclusiveness. Citizens cannot be excluded from utilizing them irrespective of whether they paid for them or not (e.g. street lighting). Third, they are inexhaustible (non-rivalry). They are not depleted in the process of utilization as long as they are maintained, for example, water. Fourth, they are financed by taxation only. It is usually difficult to charge a price per unit consumed, as in the case of street lighting. Here, there is no direct " quid pro quo." Consumers do not receive service of commensurate value with the value of the tax they pay. This is because the tax system and provision of services operate unconnectedly. Fifth, they are monopolistic in nature especially where there is no competition. For that reason most private organizations avoid incurring the cost of providing them. Consequently, the government is obliged to provide such services regardless of their tangibility or intangibility to the people.

Resource Allocation Principles and their Dynamics

It is not disputable that the government has to make sure that both tangible and intangible services are provided to the public. While not ignoring the role of the private sector, it is imperative to unearth the rationale for government intervention in the delivery of public services. Government intervention is guided by numerous principles that include: market forces of supply and demand; the principle of marginal utility; the principle of allocative efficiency; and the notion of bringing the government closer to the governed, which entails addressing citizens' preferences.

Market Forces of Supply and Demand

There are several reasons for allocating resources. One is to ensure that citizens get quality services. According to Fozzard (2001), in the perfect market an effective allocation of resources is based on the forces of supply and demand. The individual buys the products (goods and services) he or she needs. In this scenario government intervention is less important unless there is substantive market failure. Price is used as an instrument for resource allocation, this affects equal access to resources and increases social inequality. Pradhan (1996:4) suggests that "public expenditure should be concentrated first in goods and services that the private market will not provide or will provide too little, rather than mere substituting for or even marginally improving upon the private market outcomes." This implies that should the state neglect to provide such services, more negative repercussions are likely to emerge than accrued benefits from market operations. A good example is that if control of diseases is left to market forces and individuals, there is a likelihood that the country will lose a lot of citizens because they cannot afford health costs. And a state without people is nothing. So, safety is accorded first priority by any state. Second, the government cannot let its people go without education. In scenarios where citizens fail to access or afford it, the state has to intervene. It is very expensive to have a multitude of citizens illiterate.

Marginal Utility Principle

This principle provides the rationale for resource allocation. It holds that individuals will seek to equalize the marginal utility that they gain from each unit of spending across a range of goods and services they consume. Governments are called to allocate resources on the same basis (Fozzard 2001; Samuelson 1954). The diverse interests of government officials, politicians and citizens, each interest having its own benefits, puts Key's fundamental question back in the spotlight: "On what basis do governments decide to allocate x dollars to activity A instead of activity B." One of the challenges of public budgeting is how to apply the marginal utility principle in the provision of public services. Since each stakeholder has different objectives, each will have different priorities. And for that reason one stakeholder's interest is unlikely to have community marginal utility. It is unlikely to result in a service that accommodates the interest of every individual in the whole community. The stumbling block for this principle revolves around the lack of a common measure of utility that would allow comparison of the utility resulting from alternative uses of public funds (Key 1940). This probably explains why sometimes governments do not take into account public opinions or interests and rather address their own objectives.

Principle of Allocative Efficiency

This principle calls for maximization of social utility (welfare) function (OECD 2010). To make it operational, Fozzard (2001) makes two points. First, there is a need to have a mechanism (criterion) for reconciliation of individuals' relative utility differences across a combination of products (goods and services), so that a comprehensive social utility function can be described. Mikesell (1986:10) argues that "individual preferences and choices cannot easily be combined into a unique collective choice or community choice. A unique community choice is actually non-existent as is a unique community interest." Furthermore, individual preferences and choices demand full consensus, which in essence is unachievable. Fozzard's (2001) second point is, although a common denominator of utility as a basis for comparison of alternative uses of public funds is needed, it is difficult to measure their monetary outcomes and realize the net social benefit (utility) given by a particular intervention.

Gildenhuys (2010) argues that the quandary of diverse individuals' utility functions can be resolved by use of the normative principle of Pareto optimality. It states that a public intervention can be seen to express optimality, or allocative efficiency, if at least one individual is made better off and no one is made worse off. Fozzard (2001) criticizes this principle for being inclined toward the winners. He argues that it is impossible to identify all winners and losers. The problem is that the losers may have incentives to overstate their losses and this could result in the scope for public intervention being severely restricted. Kaldor in Gildenhuys (2010:70) gives a clearer picture. He holds that:

> A government policy or action improves the welfare of the community at large if those benefiting from the government policy or action, could, hypothetically, compensate in full those experiencing a relative loss from that policy or action and still have gain left over.

Fozzard (2001:13) maintains that: "an intervention is considered acceptable if the amount by which some individuals gain is greater than the amount that others lose, leading to a net benefit, so that, in principle, winners could compensate losers for their costs." Although, any decision to invest in public services ought to reflect this principle, investment decisions in developing countries, including Tanzania have been problematic. The marginalized have always been squeezed to the periphery. The eviction of citizens from arable land in Tanzania stands as a good example.

Citizens' Preferences Dynamics

In any democratic society, citizens' interests are at the forefront as a mechanism of bringing governments closer to the governed. The rationale for public resource allocation emanates from the government's desire to address collectively citizens' needs, preferences, or demands. According to Mikesell (1986:6), the logic of moving from individual choices (state-centric model) to choices made by society (collective action) as a whole is built on number of facets. First, individuals are the best judges of their own well-being and generally act to improve their well-being as they see it. So, superimposed decisions are discouraged. Second, the welfare of the community depends on the welfare of individuals in that community. This is because the community is an aggregate of individuals. Third, the impact of a social action can be judged on the welfare of the community by applying the Pareto optimality principle as supplemented by Kaldor. However, the puzzle of how to obtain community preferences remains.

According to Fozzard (2001), the commonly used method to obtain public preferences is consultation. Direct consultation reflects citizen preferences only when the number of beneficiaries is small, citizens' contributions tend to be relatively large, and the ultimate result is an increase in supply of a public good. In contrast, where the number of beneficiaries of a public good is large, the contributions from each individual tend to be minimal, and as a result there is little impact on supply. According to Kamugisha (2011), this scenario culminates in a common collective action problem called "free rider." So, individuals try to free-ride in order to benefit from a product without contributing to its cost.

Moreover, in the absence of a range of alternatives, direct consultation can provide only a partial view of individual preferences (Fozzard 2001). So, it is likely to be an ineffective strategy for revealing community preferences regarding broad expenditure allocation.

Musgrave (1986:77) suggests that "the problem of preference revelation through survey can best be resolved by constitutional and voting arrangements." Since resource allocation decisions can be reflected in the way citizens vote, they can reveal their true preferences. The problem normally lies in how to design the voting mechanism. Voting mechanisms, including the majority mechanism, are imperfect in the sense that they are unable to satisfy all reasonable conditions. According to Mueller (1979), a majority voting procedure may not generate Pareto optimal outcomes since the majority have incentives to approve policies that redistribute resources from the minority regardless of the allocative efficiency impact. According to Fozzard (2001), majority voting is tyrannical. It leads to inequitable and inefficient resource allocation more than to a desirable level of public expenditure on public services.

This problem can be addressed by a constitutional framework that protects individual rights. However, numerous countries' constitutions do not succeed in doing this because the elite class does not disclose relevant information, which is the most important basis for citizens to demand accountability. With this problem, budgeting has not effectively matched a desirable level of delivery of public services especially in developing countries, including Tanzania.

Budgeting Dynamics and Service Delivery in Tanzania

Budgeting is the cornerstone of quality service delivery. Available evidence across states indicates that a number of them undergo budgeting. The problems arise around how resources are solicited and allocated to finance public services. It has not been refuted that good revenue and expenditure plans are vital to realize effective and efficient service delivery. The challenge is how to execute them effectively. Henry (2007) has clearly articulated that for public services such as education, health, water, agriculture, among others, to be provided per community, a good amount of money (revenue) is needed to be efficiently located and expended across a range of community alternatives in order to improve the well-being of the people. This quest can be thoroughly and well achieved through budgeting. Tanzania is not an exception. Budgeting is accorded great attention in the hope of realizing the same.

The Interface between the Budgetary Process and Legal Framework

The budget process in Tanzania is a constitutional affair. Chapter 7, Article 135–144 of the Constitution of the United Republic of Tanzania of 1977 delineates provisions regarding the finances of the United Republic. It outlines who has the mandate to prepare the national budget, the institutions, revenue receipts, the accounts, and payment authorization. There are also numerous laws in Tanzania that support the budget system. The Public Finance Act of 2001 as amended in 2004 sets revenue, expenditure control, and accountability mechanisms. The annual Finance Act empowers the Minister for Finance and Economic Affairs to raise money by imposing taxes, levies, fees, and charges to mobilize funds to finance or meet budget objectives. The Local Governance Finance Act No. 9 of 1982 as amended by Miscellaneous Act No. 6 of 1999 provides the requirements and procedures that local government authorities (LGAs) should follow in preparation of annual estimates of revenue and expenditure. The annual Appropriation Act empowers the Minister for Finance and Economic Affairs to draw money from consolidated funds to be allocated to various votes. It also provides reallocation powers between votes with the aim of meeting budget objectives. The Public Procurement Act of 2004 and its corresponding regulations provide the legal framework for the procurement of goods and services using public funds. Other sources of legal authority include the Pay Master General's Circulars and Planning Commission Act of 1989, the Public Audit Act of 2008, and various Acts on revenue and expenditure. Provisions in parliament Standing Orders (Order Numbers 77–82) regulate the budget approval processes.

The legal framework regulates budget format, timing, procedures, formal powers allocation, and rights in the budget cycle or process. It also describes the roles and responsibilities of various actors in the budgetary process.

The Budgeting Process in Tanzania

The *de jure* budget process in Tanzania is prepared and executed on an annual basis. The budget in Tanzania runs according to the financial year, rather than the calendar year. The financial year runs from July 1–June 30 (for instance, July 1, 2014 to June 30, 2015). The Tanzanian budgetary process involves the following stages: formulation, approval, execution, evaluation, and stakeholders' consultation. The latter involves development partners (DPs) and local stakeholders such as company chief executive officers (CEOs), research institutions and the business sectors.

Budget Formulation Stage

The Tanzanian Constitution (1977) indicates that the process of budget formulation is an exclusive prerogative of the executive. REPOA (2009) indicate that the executive knows better the national resources and needs, and that they have the technical capacity to determine how much can be collected and spent. Although this is true the notion of capacity is very controversial. Many government institutions in Tanzania fail to collect non-taxable revenues. Capacity is at the heart of this predicament.

Article 137 (1) of the Tanzanian Constitution accords the president the power to initiate the Money Bill. It stipulates that "the president shall give directions to person concerned to prepare and submit to the National Assembly in each government financial year estimates of the revenue and expenditure of the government of the United Republic of Tanzania" (URT 1977). The formulation stage of the budget in Tanzania encompasses three substages: budget policy and resource projection, issuance of planning and budget guidelines, and revenue and expenditure estimates by ministries, departments, and agencies (MDAs), Regions and LGAs (Hakielimu and Policy Forum 2008).

The budget cycle in Tanzania begins in November with the formulation of budget policy objectives, priorities and resource projections, based on the findings and recommendations of the Public Expenditure Review (PER) and Macro-economic Performance Review (MPR). The reviews are carried out by the Budget Guideline Committee (BGC) every year. The BGC is charged with the responsibility for preparing annual budget guidelines, assessing the performance of previous budget objectives and targets, economic growth rate, inflation rate, government finance, and sectoral performance, especially those defined within the National Strategy for Growth and Reduction of Poverty (NSGRP). Members of BGC are officers from Ministry of Finance and Economic Affairs, President's Office–Public Service Management (POPSM), Presidents Office–Planning Commission (PO–PC), Prime Minister's Office–Regional Administration (PMO–RALG).

After the submission of the priorities of ministries, departments, and agencies (MDAs) and subsequent review by BGC, the Planning and Budget Guidelines (PBGs) are issued. PBGs are a set of instructions approved by cabinet every year to guide MDAs, regions and LGAs in preparing their annual plans, programs and budgets. PBGs[1] are submitted to the Inter-Ministerial Technical Committee (IMTC) and cabinet for discussion and approval.

After approval of the budget guidelines by cabinet in January every year, the Ministry of Finance prepares a consolidated budget overview and distributes the approved budget framework to MDAs. The MDAs' task is to revise their requested allocations based on the ceilings set in the budget guidelines in order for each body to produce a Medium-Term Expenditure Framework (MTEF) and a corresponding action plan. The Permanent Secretary of each Ministry in line with the budget committee for each MDA submits the MDA's budget to the Ministry of Finance (Treasury). The treasury then puts together the draft proposals of sector ministries for discussion and scrutiny by IMTC[2] before they are submitted to cabinet for approval. After approval the Minister of Finance prepares a draft cabinet budget paper and estimates covering the budget framework and financial demands of sector ministries. Then the Ministry of Finance makes recommendations for consideration by cabinet. Next the cabinet discusses and approves budget draft estimates, which become government budget proposals for the fiscal year to be submitted to the parliament.

Budget Approval Stage

Budget approval (authorization) in Tanzania is the responsibility of the parliament. Before the budget is presented in full to the parliament, the Ministry of Finance presents the budget estimates to the parliamentary Finance and Economic Affairs Committee for detailed examination and discussion. It also examines and discusses the sources of revenue and expenditure proposal (Msekwa 2006). The sectoral committees discuss estimate proposals for respective ministries. Then the Minister for Finance incorporates recommendations made by sectoral committees into the final budget before it is presented to the parliament. After the pre-budget scrutiny made by parliamentary committees, the budget is finally presented to the national assembly for debate and approval during the annual budget session. During annual debates on revenue and expenditure, two articles of the Constitution guide the parliament. First, Article 63 (3)(b) requires the assembly to debate the performance of each ministry during the annual debate session. Second, Article 99 outlines the procedures for legislation in financial matters. After the budget speech, the house votes to approve or reject the government budget. If parliament refuses to pass the government budget, the president of Tanzania is authorized by the constitution in Article 90 (2)(b) to dissolve the parliament. If government estimates are passed by the assembly as per Article 137(2), the parliament passes the Appropriation Act that authorizes the expenditures and assigns money for each item on the budget. After the approval about 45 days are used by the assembly to debate reports from various portfolio (sectoral) committees and consider expenditure estimates for each individual ministry. Throughout this process, the opposition spokesperson tables views on each ministry. According to Msekwa (2006), if the committee of the whole house passes the budget for a particular ministry, it is adopted by the house for execution.

Budget Implementation Stage

Budget execution means spending the money to meet public needs. In Tanzania spending begins each year on July 1 and ends on June 30 of the following year. Following the approval of the national budget by parliament by passing the Appropriation Act, the Ministry of Finance collects revenues through various MDAs and the Tanzania Revenues Authority (TRA). Most revenues from MDAs are non-tax and those from TRA are from tax. The ministry allocates such funds to the various accounting officers as stipulated by the Public Finance Act of 2001 that makes them receivers of revenues and accountable for expenditures. At this level MDAs are required to prepare detailed action plans, or work plans, which specify how they plan to implement their activities in the coming budget year. The action plan indicates the monthly disbursement or cash flow plan that describes the funding or disbursement of funds required by the institution. The action plan is also supported by a procurement plan that describes when procurement steps are expected to start and finish. Budget execution in Tanzania is based on a cash budget system. Under this system the government spends only the money it has. The main actors at this level include MDAs and donors. Ordinary citizens only participate as beneficiaries or consumers of services provided by government. Civil Society Organizations (CSOs) also participate in this stage as monitors of service delivery and share the information about the approved estimates to help the people follow up about their money and ensure it is spent as planned (Hakielimu and Policy Forum 2008).

Budget Evaluation

Evaluation (monitoring and control) of a budget is an ongoing process. It takes place alongside the other three stages of the budget process. A number of mechanisms are used for monitoring budget execution; first, the Ministry of Finance publishes quarterly budget execution reports in order to maintain transparency on actual use of public funds (taxpayers' money) based on budget estimates approved by the parliament. Second, the internal audit mechanisms require all accounting officers of all MDAs to report to the Controller and Accountant General (CAG) within three months of the close of the financial year. Third, the CAG determines and reports on whether the use of public funds by MDAs complies with the legal framework and regulations. He or she ensures that the expenditure of public monies has been properly authorized and applied for the intended purposes. He or she ensures that economy, efficiency and effectiveness have been achieved in the use of public resources. The CAG also produces an annual consolidated audit report within nine months of the end of the financial year and submits it to parliament after approval by the president. Fourth, the parliament oversight committees monitor and control the budget. The parliamentary standing committees include the Finance and Economic Affairs Committee, the Public Accounts Committee (PAC), the Local Government Accounts Committee, and the Public Corporations Accounts Committee. For accountability reasons, the PAC and Local Authorities Accounts Committee (LAAC) are chaired by members of the opposition. The PAC is responsible for reviewing CAG's external audit reports for MDAs and for holding relevant ministers and accounting officers accountable for their performance. PAC has power to make recommendations that are to be followed up by responsible MDAs. It also has powers to facilitate the establishment of a parliamentary select committee to probe deeper into queries raised by CAG. The LAAC has the responsibility for scrutinizing and responding to audit reports by the CAG on LGAs. The CSOs normally publicize findings of the budget execution and audit reports.

Stakeholders' Consultation

Stakeholders can be local or international. Local stakeholders include: company CEOs, research institutions, and the business sector. International stakeholders are known as development partners (DPs) or donors. The stakeholders' consultation echelon is where meaningful budget discussions regarding budget priorities and resource allocation negotiations take place and are approved before they are discussed and approved in the parliament. These are de-facto arrangements not embedded in the normal budget process.

DPs set macro-economic policy targets and get involved in the public expenditure review process and annual review of economic performance. They also support the development budget for projects and programs. However, finalization of the budget formulation includes scrutiny of estimates by government–DPs' consultation bodies after the estimates have been submitted to IMTC for approval. Government–DPs consultations facilitate the budget process whereby DPs confirm their financial commitments for the upcoming annual budget and MTEF period. DPs are very powerful in influencing public policies. This is because they play a major role in supporting the government budget. Most of their contributions go into the general fund. However, their support is not reliable. The experience of Tanzania is that sometimes donor funds come late or do not come at all. As a result government projects go unfunded and citizens continue to encounter failing services.

The local stakeholders' role is to air opinion on the budget. Hakika Catalyst (non-profit, non-political and non-religious organization committed to achieving social and economic justice) indicates that the role of stakeholders such as CSOs is to observe operational efficiency. This means the interface between inputs, outputs, and outcomes in order to get a level of efficiency. This role comes down to monitoring the various sectors on how they use their resources such as money and people, to accomplish their outputs and outcomes. This is possible if CSOs are integrated into the PER process. Sometimes they may not be consulted. Despite this they can ensure sector ministry accountability, increase the flow of information regarding budgets and sector plans, improve decision-making in the Ministry of Finance (since funds from DPs are included in PER). They can increase DPs' harmony (ibid.), among others.

Other stakeholders who are consulted by the Ministry of Finance include (CEOs) and business entrepreneurs. They air their views on the budget. Their contribution is important in economic development, so the state always seeks their opinion, and intends to satisfy them, because they pay taxes and render technical expertise.

Dynamics of Revenue Collection in Tanzania

The people in charge of the revenue collection regime in Tanzania have not yet realized the importance of pursuing a more inclusive, coordinated and integrated approach in order to achieve gains in tax administration, make more efficient use of public resources, and set up an appropriate fiscal policy. Gaps in revenue administration (revenue projection, collection and spending) have been experienced by almost all MDAs, something which affects their performance in delivering services (URT 2013, 2014). There is a mismatch between revenue projections and actual collection amounts, as well as collected revenues and public expenditure. In every financial year the government has not been able to achieve its intended objectives including increasing access and quality of social services because of inadequate finance.

The inadequacy of finance is largely a result of weakness in the revenue collection system (unintegrated, not inclusive), poor infrastructure, and antiquated businesses (URT 2012a). In tracking these challenges, the government through the TRA has demonstrated effectiveness in revenue administration by introducing the taxpayer's identification number (TIN), e-filing, diversifying modes of payment, and effecting reforms in tax administration. It has also introduced the electronic financial device (EFD) as an effective system of revenue collection and stock control. However, taxpayers have frequently rejected the use of EFD technology claiming that it is not user-friendly and collects more taxes than required.

Despite all these efforts, it has not been able to resolve key issues including strengthening of linkages between domestic taxes and customs databases and other major central databases such as the national Civil Registry and Social Security database, which would help improve tax registration and monitoring of medium and small taxpayers brewing up tax evasion and avoidance (ibid.). In addition the structures of levies and user fees as well as institutional capacities within MDAs, RSs and LGAs remain weak, which in turn undermines the effective, efficient and transparent collection of non-tax revenues, even though the government has instituted a Medium-Term Strategic Planning and Budgeting Manual (MTSPBM) that guides MDAs, RSs, and LGAs in planning, budgeting, monitoring, evaluation, and reporting (URT 2014/2015, p. 20).

Another strategy adopted by the government is the introduction of a cash management system in order to: increase efficiency and effective use of public finance; enhance the credibility and quality of cash flow plans for revenue and expenditures as well as reporting of public funds; and have the right amount of cash disbursed on time to the service delivery units (URT 2012a). Moreover, the government has also adopted an IT system, the Integrated Financial Management System (IFMS/EPICOR) with a view to processing financial transactions and providing input for preparation of financial statements. The IFMS/EPICOR simplifies and automates the financial recording and reporting system to enable the Ministry of Finance to control all the payments in a centralized manner. Although this system was intended to improve the quality of planning and budgeting controls within government institutions, this endeavor has proven not to be be the solution to tax and non-tax revenue collections. Planning and budgeting across MDAs are not yet reflecting the efforts made by the government to improve the financial management system in Tanzania.

In addition, a joint assistance program was also adopted as an extra quest with the same ambition, to improve financial management, in particular resource mobilization. The government and the DPs jointly developed the Joint Assistance Strategy for Tanzania (JAST) in 2006. The JAST, as a medium-term strategy has put in place a framework for dialog between the government and the DPs to help the government get requisite support. The Aid Management Platform (AMP) system was established to enhance transparency on issues relating to disbursing and reporting of foreign resources and improve projections in a more timely and regular manner and in accordance with the budget calendar. The budgetary support from donors (General Budget Support, GBS) is actually less than 10 percent of domestic revenue. Moreover, GBS constitutes 20–40 percent of foreign development assistance. For example, the 2012/2013 budget speech included the information that domestic revenue was TZS9,077 billion and GBS was less than 10 percent, TZS842.5 billion (URT 2013).

The trend indicates that GBS in Tanzania is decreasing as a proportion of aid funding. The trend in GBS funding signifies the relationship between the Government of Tanzania and the DPs and the growing importance of self-financing (ibid.). In addition, the disbursement of GBS funds depends on a number of conditionalities that vary according to the specific donors. Some provide GBS funding based on general conditions (progress on PFM and existence of a national development strategy) and others on specific policy actions. However, disbursement of foreign resources has been characterized by delay and sometimes approved resources are not disbursed at all. Table 12.2 below tells it all.

Table 12.2 reveals the extent to which tax revenue collection in Tanzania has been gradually decreasing. It has dropped from 84 percent (2011/2012) to 83 percent (2012/2013), to 75 percent (2013/2014), and to 72 percent (2014/2015). The same is reflected in the non-tax revenue, which has decreased from 83 percent (2011/2012) to 55.5 percent (2012/2013), although it then slightly rose to 57 percent (2013/2014) then 62 percent (2014/2015). Generally, revenue projections do not match with actual revenues collected. For instance, the budget speech of 2015/2016 indicates that "until April 2015, the actual budget support contributions received amounted to shillings 408 billion, which is equivalent to 44 percent of the annual projections of shillings 922.2" (URT 2015:17).

As regards to domestic borrowing, the trend shows that it has been going up. It rose from 61 percent (2011/2012) to 84 percent (2012/2013), to 106 percent (2013/2014), before it dropped to 60 percent (2014/2015). This implies that the government has placed a responsibility on internal institutions to address policy objectives. They must not use specific funds such as social security funds to address policy objectives. However, internal borrowing may decrease the fiscal capacity of internal institutions if the government does not reimburse the money, or does but charges interest. If the fiscal capacity of institutions becomes limited, they will fail to serve their clients and may also fail to fulfill their corporate social responsibilities.

General budget support (GBS) is another source of government income shown in Table 12.2. This type of income focuses on specific policy actions from development partners. It may also be paid based on certain conditions. The challenge is that sometimes GBS contributions are released late or not provided

Table 12.2 Government-approved Revenue Estimates and Actual Amounts Collected (T/Shillings)

S/N	*Sources of revenue*	*Financial year*							
		2011/2012		*2012/2013*		*2013/2014*		*2014/2015*	
	Domestic Revenue	*Approved*	*Actual collection*	*Estimate*	*Actual collection*	*Estimate*	*Actual collection*	*Estimate*	*Actual*
1	Tax Revenue	6,307.8	5,227.5 (84%)	8,080.1	6,717.2 (83%)	10,395.4	7,771.5 (75%)	11,318.2	8,106.5 (72%)
	Non-Tax Revenue	547.1	451.6 (83%)	644.6	357.8 (55.5%)	741.1	425.5 (57%)	859.8	534.4 (62%)
	LGAs' own source revenue	350.5	143 (40.8%)	362.2	177.4 (49%)	383.5	252.8 (66%)	458.5	296.7 (65%)
	Domestic borrowing	1,204.3	758 (61%)	1,632.0	1,364.7 (84%)	1,699.9	1,803.9 (106%)	2,955.0	1,767.9 (60%)
2	General Budget Support (GBS)	NIL	NIL	842.5	645.4 (77%)	1,163.1	2,302.6 (64%)	2,941.5	408 (14%)
3	Loans and Grants	3,923.6	–	2,314.2	–	2,692.1	–	2,019.4	–
4	External Market and Non-Concessional Borrowing terms	1,271.6	354.3 (28%)	1,254.1	1,006.2 (80%)	1,156.4	673.0 (58%)	1,320.0	514.0 (39%)
Grand Total		13,526.0	6,934.4 (51%)	15,120.0	10,268.70 (68%)	18,249.0	13,229.3 (72%)	19,853.0	11,627.5 (59%)

Source: Compiled from Government of Tanzania Budget Speeches, 2011/12–2014/15

at all. The unreliability of its provision impedes service delivery. For instance, in the fiscal year 2011/2012, it was not provided. In 2012/2013, the amount provided was 77 percent, in 2013/2014 64 percent and in 2014/2015 14 percent. The loan and grants are not well aligned. External market and non-concessional borrowing has been fluctuating. It has fluctuated from 28 percent (2011/2012) to 80 percent (2012/2013), to 58 percent (2013/2014), and to 39 percent (2014/2015).

The table also shows another source of revenue, local government's own revenues. The trend shows that local government's own revenue collections have burgeoned at a snail's pace. The figure has risen from 40.8 percent (2011/2012) to 49 percent (2012/2013), to 66 percent (2013/2014) and slightly dropped to 65 percent (2014/2015). However, over 92 percent of local government budget depends on central government transfers (see CAG reports 2011–2015).

The total general revenue collections have not been consistent. The trend in the table shows that it slightly rose from 51 percent (2011/2012) to 68 percent (2012/2013), to 72 percent (2013/2014) before it slightly fell to 59 percent. This implies that the government has been reluctant to meet or exceed its revenue projections. Despite a lot of effort that has been devoted to establishing institutional frameworks to enhance revenue collection from domestic sources and foreign aid, almost all the actual practices have remained unchanged. Therefore, it can be argued that the failure to collect revenues has been the stumbling block for sound allocation of resources to provide collective goods and services to the citizens.

Dynamics of Resources Allocation (Expenditure) in Tanzania

Tanzania uses MTEFs for allocation of resources to MDAs and LGAs. Although the system is operational, there are weak linkages between recurrent expenditure and development estimates and between administrative and executing units (URT 2012a). One of the limitations of the MTEFs relates to the recurrent budget format, which is not program based, and always fails to accommodate recurrent costs that arise from development expenditure. In addition, the expenditure plans have always remained unchanged as many of the funds are directed to finance recurrent expenditure, with the development expenditures being given scant attention, as shown in Table 12.3.

Table 12.3 indicates that there is a mismatch between approved budgets and actual disbursement of the total funds to meet recurrent and development expenditure. For example, up to the end April 2012 the government was able to distribute TZS10,007 billion against the approved expenditure budget of TZS13,526 billion; 26 percent of the money was not disbursed. The gap slightly fell to 24 percent in 2012/2013. It rose to 34 percent in 2013/2014 and slightly fell to 29 percent in 2014/2015. The trend shows the government has been constrained by its incapacity to solicit and accord full approved budget. The same trend was experienced in getting foreign resources. For instance in

Table 12.3 Planned Expenditure for the Same Periods in Billion Shillings

Budget allocation	*Financial year*							
	2011/2012		*2012/2013*		*2013/2014*		*2014/2015*	
	Approved	*Actual*	*Approved*	*Actual*	*Approved*	*Actual*	*Approved*	*Actual*
RECURRENT EXPENDITURE	8,600.0	7,349.8 (85.5%)	10,592.0	7,582.6 (71%)	12,575.0	8,928.25 (71%)	13,408.0	11,543.3 (86%)
(i) consolidated financial services	1,910.4		2,746.1		3,319.2		4,355.0	4,467.9
(ii) wages and salaries	3,270.3		3,781.0		4,763.2		5,317.6	4,349.1
(iii) other charges	3,420.0		4,066.0		4,493.0		3,736.0	2726.3
DEVELOPMENT EXPENDITURE	4,925.0	2,657.2 (54%)	4,528.0	3,956.3 (82%)	5,674.0	3,115 (55%)	6,445.0	2,578.1 (40%)
(i) Local finance	1,871.5	1,201.6 (64.2%)	2,214.0	2,277.2 (99.9%)	2,982.0	1,546 (52%)	4,426.0	1,998.9 (45%)
(ii) Foreign contribution	3,054.1	1,455.6 (48%)	2,314.0	1,679.1 (73%)	2,692.1	1,569 (58%)	2,019.4	579.2 (29%)
Total expenditure	13,526.0	10,007.0 (74%)	15,120.0	11,538.9 (76%)	18,249.0	12,043.25 (66%)	19,853.0	14,121.4 (71%)

Source: Compiled from Government of Tanzania Budget Speeches, 2011/12–2014/15

2014/2015, only 29 percent of the approved foreign resource was released to finance development expenditure. This trend negatively affects the development of priority sectors such as water, agriculture, education, health care, and infrastructure. Experience has shown that these sectors are receiving inadequate finances, which affects their performance in service delivery.

For instance, the Ministry of Finance and Economic Affairs indicates that the amount of money (capitation grants) going to local governments has been below 50 percent (URT 2012b). The government promised that for the development of primary and secondary education, it would ensure it confers 100 percent of capitation grant set at USD10 per enrolled pupil or student. It set USD4 (40 percent) for purchase of textbooks, teaching and learning materials and USD6 (60 percent) for development (URT 2012b). USD2 (20 percent) was for repair of school infrastructures, another USD2 (20 percent) was for materials, USD1 (10 percent) for school-based examinations, and another USD1 (10 percent) for purchase of chalks, pencils and pens (Mbelle 2008:16). Despite that promise, the fact is that the schools have been reciving below 50 percent of the required amount.

The problem is aggravated by the fact that capitation grants do not go directly to schools. The grants first go to local government authorities and then get distributed to schools. Experience shows that little money is further portioned out to cater for other local government activities. Almost 20 percent of the amount devolved to local governments for schools development is misappropriated (Kamugisha, 2015). This has affected the quality of school infrastructures, tools and equipment, and the rehabilitation of buildings. Clearly poor execution of a budget affects the delivery of social services.

Conclusion and the Way Forward

The chapter has shown that the observed trend of domestic revenues, including that from LGAs, has been going down. Despite the fact that the government has devised mechanisms to improve the collection of domestic (tax and non-tax) revenues, the amounts collected have always been below the projections. The government budgets from 2011–2015 attest to this. For instance, its budget (for 2015/2016 reveals that collections were below projections, which affected the disbursement of finances to effectively provide collective goods and services. From July 2014 to April 2015 TZS8.641 trillion, equivalent to 86 percent, were collected against the estimated revenues of 9.991 trillion. This trend is chiefly attributable to low collections of tax and non-tax revenue (partly due to lack of enthusiasm by some taxpayers to adopt the EFDs introduced by government to increase income), delays in the submission of collected revenue from LGAs, and reduced control of taxation on imports of products (goods and services).

Attempts to collect taxes did not meet with a positive response. Taxpayers, especially entrepreneurs, always demonstrate against new tax collection devices. The new devices cannot control cheating if the consumer does not request an electronic receipt for the transaction made. Experience has shown that some sale transactions are carried out without receipts, which affects revenue collection. The only area where the government gets actual revenues without problems is PAYE. This amount is directly deducted from employees' salaries by employers. As regards non-tax income, government projections through MDAs have always been unmet. This implies that the current policies are unworkable. Therefore, the government has to ensure that its policies are well designed and accorded requisite support to reflect the reality on ground. The fact that government projections are higher than the actual amounts collected by MDAs implies that such institutions lack the requisite capacity to undertake this function. Therefore, policies have to address among other things capacity issues among the planning and budgeting institutions. In addition the government has to align its expenditure policies with expected revenues; strengthen the control and management of public expenditure through preparation of budget acts, ensuring use of EFDs by all government institutions and agencies in procuring goods and services; ensure all MDAs and local government authorities submit their budget estimates to the Pay Master General for scrutiny and approval; continue with verification of arrears and claims; and ensure bulk procurement from producers instead of agents.

It is equally important for the government to enlarge its narrow tax base in order to improve revenue collection. This can be achieved by formalizing the informal sector and allowing it access to credit and other fiscal facilities in order to increase its capacity to generate wealth, leading to increased revenues. Therefore the empowering of the informal sector is imperative. It is also imperative to reduce tax evasion, curb tax exemptions, and rationalize the taxation system to ensure voluntary compliance. The government can increase its income if it accelerates economic growth though large-scale domestic and foreign investment in areas such as infrastructure and industry, with a view to creating jobs and raising the national income.

It is the role of the government to address all issues that impact revenue collection. Hakika Catalyst identifies such issues as: the cost of collecting revenue exceeding expectations, which diminishes net revenue; a burgeoning rate of inflation; external events such as fuel price increases and natural disasters; inability to meet predicted economic growth; over-dependency on donor funds that may not be received; unrealistic planning and budgeting; and inflated and unrealistic budget requests.

The chapter has shown that the government has been borrowing too much from internal institutions such as social security (specific funds), to finance recurrent expenditure. It has to implement a zero-borrowing policy from specific funds. In addition, MDAs and LGAs must operate in a quasi-commercial manner in order to be creative and innovative in revenue collection and uses.

The government must also continue to release funds based on the availability of resources and taking into account planned priorities. This can be achieved by improving tax administration, improving enterprise risk management, curbing tax evasion, improving information systems, and harmonizing various tax laws to remove duplication of effort in revenue collection by MDAs and LGAs.

Notes

1 Planning and budget guidelines inform respective institutions on key spending priorities, expenditure ceilings, and revenue targets for programs in the next year.
2 The inter-ministerial committee is composed of all permanent secretaries (accounting officers of ministries).

References

Cowden, J.W. (1969). *Holmes' Local Government Finance in South Africa.* 2nd ed. Durban: Butterworth.

Dye, T.R. (1981). *Understanding Public Policy*. Englewood Cliffs, NJ: Prentice-Hall.

Fozzard, A. (2001). The Basic Budgeting Problem: Approaches to Resource Allocation in the Public Sector and Their Implications For Pro-Poor Budgeting. *Working Paper 147*. London: Overseas Development Institute.

Gildenhuys, J.S.H. (2010). *Public Financial Management*. Pretoria, South Africa: J.L. Van Schaik.

Hakielimu and Policy Forum. (2008). *Understanding the Budget Process in Tanzania: A Civil Society Guide*. Dar es Salaam: Government of Tanzania.

Henry, N. (2007). *Public Administration and Public Affairs*. New Delhi, India: Prentice-Hall.

Humphreys, P.C. (1998). *Improving Public Service Delivery*. Dublin: Institute of Public Administration.

Kamugisha, D. (2011). Collective Action. In Josephat Itika, Ko de Ridder, & Albertjan Tollenaar (Eds.) *Theories and Stories in African Public Administration*. Leiden: African Studies Centre, pp. 11–24.

Kamugisha, D. (2015). *Decentralization and Service Delivery in Local Governments in Tanzania: The Case of Mvomero District and Moshi Municipal Councils*. (Unpublished Ph.D. dissertation).

Key, V.O. (1940). The lack of a budget theory. *American Political Science Review*, 34(6): 1137–1144.

Mbelle, A.V.Y. (2008). *The Impact of Reforms on the Quality of Primary Education in Tanzania*. Research Report No. 08.1. Dar es Salaam: REPOA.

Mikesell, J.L.(1986). *Financial Administration: Analysis and Application for the Public Sector*. Homewood, IL: Dorsey Press.

Msekwa, P. (2006). *Reflection on the First Decade of Multiparty Politics in Tanzania.* Dar es Salaam: DUP.

Mueller, D. C. (1979). *Public Choice*. Cambridge: Cambridge University Press.

Musgrave, R.A. (1986). Fiscal Functions: Order and Politics. In R.A. Musgrave (Ed.) *Public Finance in a Democratic Society*. Brighton, UK: Harvester Press, pp. 76–88.

Narayan, B.N. (2002). *Public Finance: A Dynamic Force in the Economic System*. New Delhi: Anmol Publications.

Organisation for Economic Co-operation and Development (OECD). (2010). *Strategies to Improve Rural Service Delivery*. Available at www.oecd.org/publishing/corrigenda.

Peters, B.G. (1988). *American Public Policy: Promise and Performance*, 2nd ed. New Delhi: Affiliated East-West Press

Pradhan, S. (1996). *Evaluating Public Spending: A Framework for Public Expenditure Reviews*. World Bank Discussion Paper 323. Washington, DC, World Bank.

REPOA. (2009). *Understanding the Patterns of Accountability in Tanzania: Analysis of Value, Incentives and Power Relations in the Budget Allocation Process*. Oxford; Bergen; Dar es Salaam: Chr. Michelson Institute.

Samuelson, P.A. (1954). The Pure Theory of Public Expenditure. *Review of Economics and Statistics*, 36(4): 387–389.

Thomson, W. (2005). *Managing the Public Sector*. New York: Thomson Learning Academic Center.

Thornhill, C. (1984). *Die Begroting in Die Openbare Finansiele Administrasie*.Pretoria: JL Van Schaik.

United Republic of Tanzania (URT). (1977). *Constitution of the United Republic of Tanzania*. Dar es Salaam: Government Printer.

United Republic of Tanzania (URT). (2012a). *National Budget Speech*. Dar es Salaam.

United Republic of Tanzania (URT). (2012b). *Public Financial Management Reform Programme Strategy Phase IV: 2012/13– 2016/17*. Dar es Salaam.

United Republic of Tanzania (URT). (2013). *National Budget Speech*. Dar es Salaam.

United Republic of Tanzania (URT). (2014). *National Budget Speech*. Dar es Salaam.

United Republic of Tanzania (URT). (2015). *National Budget Speech*. Dar es Salaam.

Vocino, T., & J. Rabin. (1981). *Contemporary Public Administration*. New York: Harcourt Brace Jovanovich.

13 Evaluating Public Budgeting and Fiscal Management in African Nations

Peter Fuseini Haruna and Shikha Vyas-Doorgapersad

Introduction

It is fair to say that budgeting and fiscal policy as a sub-field of public administration has been studied more intensely in developed than in developing societies. The Organisation for Economic Cooperation and Development (OECD) requires member nations to promote policies aimed at achieving "the highest economic growth and employment and the rising standard of living."[1] To that end, the *OECD Journal on Budgeting* has focused attention on publishing studies in budgeting and fiscal policy systems for the benefit of member and non-member nations (e.g., OECD 2002b). The OECD has also developed and refined a comprehensive instrument for systematically gathering, analyzing, and comparing budgeting and fiscal policy systems globally as a way of distiling international best and smart practices and norms (www.oecd.org/gov/budgeting/49042591.pdf). These focused studies have laid the foundation "for evidence-based analysis and recommendations" on issues such as fiscal sustainability, participatory and transparent budgeting, and fiscal management.

Unlike the OECD member nations, budgeting and fiscal policy in developing nations such as those in Africa are relatively under-researched and under-developed. To be fair, international research and donor institutions such as the World Bank and International Monetary Fund have provided valuable insights on budgeting and fiscal management systems in African nations. For example, the World Bank has illuminated Africa's budgeting, fiscal, and financial management systems and suggested insightful ways to improve them (e.g., www.worldbank.org/afr/wps/index.htm). As a result, there has accumulated much useful information on the implementation of continent-wide public financial management reforms. Nonetheless, Africa's home-led initiatives such as the Africa Parliamentary Strengthening Program (Draman, 2010) and Collaborative Africa Budget Reform Initiative (CABRI 2008), which are important trail-blazers, are only still at their nascent stages.[2] Moreover, most of the existing knowledge takes a rather practical and narrow perspective. However, as democratization deepens with interest in and focus on improving participatory, transparent, and accountable governance, more work is needed to expand the knowledge base. The central question is how to harness, allocate, and utilize resources to improve the quality of life.

As stated in the introductory chapter, the purpose of this book was to shed light on how African nations grapple with issues related to public budgeting and fiscal management and what the implications and consequences are for development. We build on the work of our chapter contributors in which they have provided valuable insights about their nations, covering issues related to the rationale, evolution, and change in budgeting and fiscal norms, approaches, methods, techniques, and practices. They also point out the faults and flaws of budgeting and fiscal management systems in specific countries while distilling lessons and proffering suggestions for increasing the efficacy of African governments.

This final chapter specifically provides a more focused evaluation of continent-wide public budgeting and fiscal management. First, we synthesize the models of public budgeting and fiscal management as depicted in the country studies before discussing the implications and consequences for sustainable development. Second, we argue the need for budgeting and fiscal management frameworks that support good governance and sustainable development. We contend that such frameworks must integrate the values of responsibility, accountability, and transparency in the interest of full and timely disclosure of fiscal and financial information. Finally, we highlight the lessons learned and argue that budgeting and fiscal management should be well aligned with good governance principles and practices needed to achieve inclusive economic growth, political stability, and social cohesion in Africa.

Models of Budgeting and Fiscal Management

As both a discipline of study and a professional sub-field, public budgeting and fiscal management is new even in the OECD nations. As Hyde (1992) notes in the case of the USA, budgeting was largely rudimentary before the twentieth century. He observes that before then budgeting was just a "little more than compilations of piecemeal appropriations" and that the passage of the Budget and Accounting Act (1921) laid the foundation for the federal budgeting system in the USA.[3] In the developing nations of Africa, budgeting and fiscal management as a deliberate government function is even newer. Subsumed under public administration at independence, budgeting and fiscal management meant nothing more than muddling through: Governments raised and spent money as they deemed fit. But the sub-field has evolved from its rudimentary origins through a bureaucratic stage to a performance management orientation as chapter authors have illustrated. Even so budgeting and fiscal management is still construed as a narrow and technically oriented field of practice.

Bureaucratic Budgeting and Fiscal Management

Much like the mother field of public administration, budgeting and fiscal management began as a narrowly conceptualized technical activity based in mathematical calculations and balancing accounting books. This restrictive or "nuts and bolts" approach emphasized objects of expenditure, as well as getting the figures right. In "Rethinking Public Administration," the United Nations (1998, p. 114) observed that historically, advanced countries approached budgeting in a narrow fashion. They raised revenues from limited sources and for specific purposes such as fighting wars (Lewis & Hildreth, 2013, pp. 85–86).[4] Following colonial rule Africa inherited institutional norms and practices that carried over to the post-colonial period. Unfortunately and as discussed in Chapter 1, a consequence of colonial rule was that Africa inherited little to no knowledge of economic or fiscal management. With a narrow knowledge base and a predominantly undeveloped institutional framework, governing and public administration depended on "muddling through" and budgeting focused narrowly on just the nuts and bolts. Even though the field has evolved, the nuts and bolts perspective has morphed into a bureaucratic approach that has focused mainly on the division of labor and specialization with implications and consequences for budgeting and fiscal management.

The conceptual framework based on which budgeting and fiscal management has developed both in advanced and developing societies is largely bureaucratic in nature. To be sure, governments now make efforts to connect taxing and spending decisions to their economies in a manner that they have never done before. In other words they now manage public resources with the explicit goal of achieving policy objectives such as economic growth and increased incomes, more so in advanced than developing nations. However, the bureaucratic conception has emphasized centralization, division of labor, and specialization in a way that views budgeting and fiscal management as separate, specialized institutional entities.

To take one example, the budget cycle is regarded as a useful tool, but it has broken up, rationalized, and assigned distinct budget and fiscal management functions to governing and public administration institutions: executive formulation, legislative review, executive implementation, and audit and evaluation. In this regard budgeting and fiscal management now entails a bureaucratic mindset, including multiple institutions, rules, procedures, processes, and strategies shaping resource mobilization and allocation. The complexity of the bureaucratic organizational process makes it "difficult to know for sure who is doing what, with whom, for what purpose, and at what cost" as Lewis and Hildreth (2013, p. 109) have noted.[5] This is particularly so in developing nations where there exists institutional and organizational capacity gaps and weaknesses, an issue that has been explored in greater detail elsewhere (e.g., Haruna & Vyas-Doorgapersad, 2015; Haruna & Kannae, 2013).

Almost universally, African nations have applied the bureaucratic approach to budgeting and fiscal management with considerable consistency since the attainment of independence as demonstrated in the respective country case studies. It is the approach that they have inherited from colonial rule and one that they have always known and are most familiar with. It is the dominant administrative culture, defining what is normal and acceptable in budgeting and fiscal management. Whether in Botswana, Cameroon, Ghana, Kenya, Malawi, South Africa, Rwanda, Uganda, or Zimbabwe, the bureaucratic approach with its complex processes and procedures is self-evident. In a study of seven African nations, Draman (2010, pp. 32–33) has synthesized ideas and common features of budgeting and fiscal management that clearly reflect the bureaucratic concepts of centralization, control, division of labor, and functional specialization. His study not only highlights the bureaucratic nature of budgeting and fiscal management, but also it embeds pitfalls and flaws that reinforce the analysis that our chapter authors have provided.

As Table 13.1 indicates, three governing institutional processes cover most if not all of the budgeting and fiscal management functions: executive preparation and presentation, legislative appropriation and authorization, and bureaucratic implementation (execution, monitoring, audit, and evaluation). The approach is a highly centralized, top-down process dominated by the executive in the formulation of macro-economic policy. Chapter 7 discusses Malawi's experience and argues that the executive dominated the budgeting and fiscal management process for three decades. The legislatures in Ghana, Kenya, and Uganda have no authority to increase the proposed executive spending items. Chapter 8 focuses on South Africa and explains that Parliament cannot amend or reject the executive budget proposals even though it has the "power to monitor and hold the executive to account for compliance with legal instruments and for their general performance." But because South Africa tends to score highly on the Open Budget Index it can be argued that public participation in and access to the budgeting and fiscal management process is considerable.[6] In contrast, while effort is made to seek public input through consultative processes, Draman (2010, p. 36) notes that such consultations as in Ghana and Uganda "tend to be a formality rather than an opportunity of fruitful discussion of inputs into the budget."

Likewise, the legislative appropriation processes are centralized and top-down with little or no public input in several African nations. Couched intechnical jargon and characterized by "high drama," legislative debates tend to be the preserve of sub-committees without assuring that the public's voice and priorities are reflected in the national core decision-making process. Budgeting and fiscal management implementation is just as centralized and top-down as executive preparation and legislative approval. The central budget and fiscal management office in African nations tends to be the Ministry of Finance, a super-agency that drafts macro-economic policies and budget guidelines and negotiates spending ceilings with other parastatal organizations (Draman, 2010). Although other ministries are considered to be key stakeholders in budgeting and fiscal management, they cannot initiate spending without the order or warrant of the Ministry of Finance. In fact, the norm is for Ministers of Finance to present budget and fiscal policies on behalf of the executive (www.mofep.gov.gh/sites/default/files/budget/budget-speech-2015.pdf).

As well public organizations with strong influence in the implementation of budgeting and fiscal policy such as national development planning, controller

Table 13. 1 Bureaucratic Approach to Budgeting and Fiscal Management in African Nations with a Focus on Centralization, Division of Labor, and Functional Specialization

Executive Preparation/ Presentation	*Legislative Appropriation/ Authorization*	*Bureaucratic Implementation/ Audit/Evaluation*	*Observations/ Comments/ Remarks*
Identifying, clarifying, and specifying fiscal policy objectives and fiscal targets Reviewing, synchronizing, and approving sector plans and estimates Presenting and justifying budgeting and fiscal management framework Agency supervision and executive oversight	Reviewing, analyzing, and debating fiscal policy objectives and fiscal targets Recommending, appropriating, and authorizing budgeting and fiscal management framework Reviewing, analyzing, debating, and recommending action on audit and evaluation report Supervision and legislative oversight	Preparing sector and agency plans and estimates Soliciting and synthesizing public views on needs and priorities Coordinating sector plans and negotiating budget ceilings Implementing plans and conducting audit and evaluation Monitoring, documenting, and reporting outcomes	The bureaucratic approach faces several serious challenges in Africa, including: poor institutional framework low level of education low level of expertise poor communication infrastructure low level of information flow inadequate and/or poor quality of data

and accountant-general, central bank, revenue authority, and auditor-general are equally highly centralized (Table 13.2). Not only are they centralized, but also they are reputed to be depositories of valuable education, expertise, and experience in budgeting and fiscal policy. They anchor public bureaucracies and civil service systems in African nations, providing "guardianship" and "technocracy" in budgeting and fiscal management. In playing these roles, they exercise considerable "discretionary authority" in managing the treasury systems and monitoring the execution of budgeting and fiscal policy. In Botswana, the Auditor-General has the authority to audit and keep the books of accounts in order (Chapter 2) while in Cameroon payment authorizing officers and accounting officers protect the integrity of the treasury system (Chapter 3). Together, they reinforce the bureaucratic approach in terms of hierarchy, control, and functional specialization in budgeting and fiscal policy management.

As the foregoing analysis shows, African nations have developed a hierarchical grid of national institutions and public organizations with the goal of achieving control of and compliance with budgeting and fiscal policy management. From day one, the political leaderships adopted predominantly state-led development budgeting and fiscal systems in which the national bureaucracy has played and continues to play a leading role. Although such bureaucratic structures and processes have served colonial rule well, most people agree that they have not been beneficial in the quest to achieve economic

Table 13.2 Bureaucratic Approach to Budgeting and Fiscal Management in African Nations with a Focus on Hierarchy, Chain of Command, Control, and Functional Specialization

No.	*Institution*	*Roles*	*Observation*
1.	Office of the Presidency	Executive preparation Executive conflict resolution Executive presentation Executive oversight	This is the highest ranking budgeting and fiscal policy authority reflecting executive dominance in African nations
2.	Parliament	Legislative consideration Legislative debate Legislative appropriation Legislative oversight	This is the second highest ranking budgeting and fiscal policy authority reflecting weak legislative oversight
3.	Ministry of Finance	Drafts budget guidelines Calls for estimates Seeks public input Drafts fiscal targets Negotiates spending ceilings Coordinates external funding Coordinates sector planning Monitors revenues Monitors expenditures	This is a super-agency/central budget office that serves as the nerve centre of all budgeting and fiscal policy including preparation, execution, monitoring, and evaluation of all planning
4.	Central Bank	Monitors money supply Monitors balance of trade Monitors public debt Monitors economic growth	This is the centre-piece of all monetary policy, including money supply and inflation, interest rates, international transfers, debt management, and economic growth
4.	National Development Planning Office	Coordinates sector planning Coordinates regional planning Consolidates national planning	This office focuses on aligning regional and sector planning to ensure prioritization and institutional alignment and coordination
5.	Controller & Accountant-General	Manages treasury system Monitors payments Monitors revenues	This office manages the general treasury system with a focus on authorized payments
6.	Auditor-General	Keeps book of accounts Conducts annual audits Monitors compliance	This office manages the general treasury system with a focus on proper accounting and compliance with financial rules and regulations
7.	National Revenue Authority	Monitors revenue receipts Enforces tax laws Imposes penalties and fines	This office focuses on the enforcement of tax laws and monitoring of revenue receipts to ensure that fiscal targets are met

prosperity and political progress (Haruna, 2008; Olowu & Wunsch, 2004). For one thing, the bureaucratic approach tends to have a short-term organizational focus, emphasizing compliance with organizational rules, regulations, processes, and procedures and de-emphasizing service delivery, results, and outcomes. For example, as a statutory requirement, the Auditor-General often assesses performance through annual financial reports to assure compliance with financial rules, a process centrally controlled, monitored, and managed without much society-wide input.

To be sure, measuring and assessing the performance of public organizations entails difficult-to-define political, social, and cultural dimensions, which lie at the core of much public management research and scholarship (e.g., Pollitt & Bouckaert, 2011). However, from a performance perspective, the bureaucratic approach makes it even more difficult to address big social and economic impact questions such as: "results for whom, defined by whom, against what criteria, and in pursuit of which objectives" as Pollitt and Bouckaert (2011, p. 126) have observed. Nonetheless, as the African experience makes clear, failing to assess and improve public performance has consequences, including mounting distrust of and diminishing support for development policies and programs. Moreover, without a credible and legitimate means of demonstrating the judicious use of public resources, public institutions and organizations tend to be perceived as mere symbols of corruption and their mission of promoting development regarded as neutralized. As a result, African nations have considered other budgeting and fiscal policy frameworks such as a more performance-oriented and results-oriented budgeting and fiscal policy approach.

Performance Budgeting and Fiscal Management

Having considered the key norms of budgeting and fiscal management derived from a bureaucratic viewpoint and its associated implications and consequences for development management, we now turn attention to performance-based and more results-oriented approaches, with which African nations have grappled over the past two decades. As currently conceptualized, performance budgeting and fiscal management reform is an off-shoot of a broader public management philosophy (new public management, NPM), the global movement that aims to replace state-led, bureaucratic development strategies with neo-liberal ideals, managerial principles, and market-oriented policies (OECD, 2005; Larbi, 1999). Against the backdrop of economic crisis and administrative failures, NPM created an opening for reform that infused the public sector with a more managerial, entrepreneurial, and technological orientation. Adjustment programs backed by the World Bank and International Monetary Fund set the tone in African nations by emphasizing democratization, economic liberalization, and de-bureaucratization policies. By the turn of the new millennium, Africa had implemented reforms inspired by the notion of governance (UNDP, 1997), anchored to the Millennium Development Goals (UN, 2000), and focused on performance budgeting and fiscal management (Shah & Shen, 2007).

At the core of performance budgeting and fiscal management is the respective national *Vision*, the organizing concept around which macro-economic policies have been derived and developed. As long-term strategic structural transformation plans, national *Visions* have enabled African nations to re-envision development, clarify policy goals and objectives, and specify the means to achieve them. In their discussions, chapter authors have highlighted several key components, including: short- to medium-term plans such as poverty reduction, growth and development, and medium-term expenditure frameworks. Botswana's *Vision 2016* embodies the national planning principles of economic growth and social justice (Chapter 2), while Rwanda's *Vision 2020* aims to achieve a middle-income status (Chapter 11). Likewise, Uganda's *Vision 2040* (Chapter 9) reflects the dream of transformation from a peasant to a prosperous society (http://npa.ug/wp-content/themes/npatheme/documents/vision2040.pdf).

Although long-term development planning is not new to Africa, contemporary national visions have sought to institutionalize budgeting and fiscal management in a manner that has not been done before. Unlike the centralized economic planning of the past that focused on the state as the engine of growth, the current national visions encompass all sectors in strategic partnership. The approach seeks to create a budgeting and fiscal management system with clear policy objectives, realistic fiscal targets, and objective benchmarks for assessing progress. Conceptualized as based in a framework of governance as "the manner in which power is exercised in the management of a country's economic and social resources for development" (World Bank, 1992, p. 1), national visions articulate efficiency, responsiveness, accountability, transparency, equity, and value for money, among others.

In addition to the broad national visions cited above, international development institutions and researchers have contributed conceptual frameworks, analytical tools, and techniques that can enhance the formulation and implementation of performance budgeting and fiscal management (Pollitt & Bouckaert, 2011; Andrews, 2010; Overseas Development Institute, 2009; Kaufmanet al., 2007). For example, the World Governance Assessment framework consists of a comprehensive package of indicators of governance performance from the perspectives of civil society, political society, government, bureaucracy, economic society, and the judiciary. Although designed to assess governance in the broad sense, it is useful for obtaining feedback and gauging how well budgeting and fiscal management can affect the quality of life in terms of participation, decency, fairness, accountability, transparency, efficiency, and effectiveness. Thus the framework can facilitate the assessment of political, economic, and corporate financial governance in a way that has not been done before.

Similarly, the World Bank's Worldwide Governance Indicators framework (WGI) captures political, economic, and institutional dimensions of governance that are both relevant to and useful for evaluating national performance budgeting and fiscal management. Comprising six aggregate indicators (voice and accountability, political stability and absence of violence, government effectiveness, regulatory quality, rule of law, and corruption control), the WGI framework broadens and extends budgeting and fiscal management beyond the traditionally circumscribed organizational focus. While the WGI framework has helped to assess governance and monitor changes in its quality especially in African nations, Kaufmann, Kraay and Mastruzzi (2007) recognize that indicators of this nature entail both "definitional ambiguities" and "measurement error." Nonetheless, used in combination with other credible assessment analytics, it can provide program- and policy-relevant information for improving performance. In the next section we focus more on financial management methods and techniques that African nations have applied and what the implications and consequences have been.

African nations have made efforts to transition to performance budgeting and fiscal management by adopting a variety of concepts, tools, methods, and techniques that our chapter authors have captured. Introduced as a part of public financial management reform (PFM), concepts such as integrated financial management information systems (IFMIS), public expenditure review (PER), and medium-term expenditure frameworks (MTEFs) have gained continental currency. Public financial management, which involves taxing, spending, and accounting rules, processes, and procedures, in African nations is regarded as non-transparent, inadequate, and outdated (Heidenhof et al., 2002).

On the revenue side, the tax base is narrow and governments have been unwilling to expand it for political reasons. In addition to external loans and grants, revenues include direct and indirect taxes, which account for about 75% and 63% of the total revenue of Cameroon and Botswana respectively. On the expenditure side, spending tends to be skewed toward national defense, internal security, and public debt-interest charges. In spite of debt-relief cancellation under the heavily indebted poor countries initiative, African nations remain at high risk of debt distress.[7] Moreover the vagaries of the weather, fluctuations in commodity prices, and unstable external aid complicate predictability in planning, resource allocation, and management.

Consistent with PFM reform, the use of MTEFs has sought to bridge the gap and strengthen the link between macro-economic, fiscal, and financial frameworks. The MTEF has almost become the standard public expenditure management tool and technique (www-wbweb.worldbank.org/prem/prmps/expenditure). As should be expected different nations have approached MTEF reform differently as either a comprehensive government-wide or a narrow priority-sector reform.[8] Also, as expected, MTEFs are at various degrees of implementation in African countries, but it is fair to say that the concept has garnered considerable political support and legitimacy. One of the earliest MTEFs was set up in Malawi (1996), where it has been considered "as the basis for a more strategic approach to public expenditure planning." In regard to Kenya it was introduced to "enhance fiscal discipline, expenditure prioritization, and operational efficiency" while the process in South Africa includes a review to assure coherence of budgetary requests and appropriations. From the viewpoint of Houerou and Taliercio (2002, p. 1), "the African experience with MTEFs has served as a catalyst for adopting similar reforms in other regions."

The questions of interest to the evaluation of budgeting and fiscal management is: how well do PFM and MTEF reforms work in African nations? What lessons do these reforms provide? On the positive side, such reforms have contributed in a large measure to the institutionalization and rationalization of the approach to budgeting and fiscal policy processes in the context of development management. In Ghana, Kenya, Rwanda, South Africa, and Uganda, MTEF has become an integral part of budgeting and fiscal management processes requiring executive approval. There has been a steady but visible shift toward achieving a fiscal balance between resource shortages and public demands for more and better public goods and services. Such a balance is critical to achieve macro-economic stability and sustainability in the long term. The accumulation of conceptual and experiential knowledge in central budget offices, sector ministries, and agencies bodes well for budgeting and fiscal management in the years ahead. In short, a budgeting and fiscal management culture change is emerging even if very slowly, emphasizing public and civil society involvement, open budgeting and transparency, and the need for monitoring and evaluating performance, and assessing outcomes toward the achievement of policy objectives.

One illustration of the potential of MTEF is the translation of policy objectives and strategies into concrete public expenditure programs within a coherent medium-term macro-economic and fiscal framework to meet the millennium development goals: poverty eradication, universal primary education, maternal and infant mortality reduction, gender equality, HIV/AIDS elimination, environmental sustainability, and global partnership. Poverty reduction and strategic policy priority sectors (education, health, and productive infrastructure) have gained varying spending increases. For example, in Cameroon, productive infrastructure expenditure has increased steadily since 2003. The education and health sectors in Botswana have witnessed increased spending since 2011. Likewise, the most recent evaluations of Ghana's medium-term plans indicate that poverty has reduced from 51.7 percent in 1991 to 28.5 percent in 2006. Of course, poverty continues to be a national concern, with high concentrations in the northern sector of the country.

However, beyond these positive signs and indicators of progress, there are several areas of concern, ranging from conceptual design flaws to implementation challenges and difficulties. As in many other fields, there is always a difference between the text and the translation of that text into actual practice. But it is a question of degree. In one of the earliest MTEF evaluative studies, Houerou and Taliercio (2002) exposed some weaknesses, including: insufficient attention to country conditions, inadequate political and institutional consideration; and variations between design and implementation. To address these weaknesses they made several recommendations, emphasizing the integration of MTEF into existing budgeting processes and serious consideration of the political and institutional environment. Houerou and Taliercio concluded that MTEF could be made more effective by grounding it in "a good macro-fiscal model and a solid budgetary management foundation." Although they point out that their findings were preliminary, they nonetheless offer useful insights for reconsidering and re-crafting more context and culture-sensitive MTEF reform.

Another evaluative study focusing more on PFM reform in 31 African nations provides interesting but strikingly similar findings and recommendations to the MTEF study summarized above. In his relatively recent PFM study, Andrews (2010) found that: budget formulation is stronger than implementation; process is different from actual practice; performance is stronger with actor concentration; and countries differ from each other in terms of PFM reform. In explaining these findings, he emphasizes the factors behind the differences: economic growth, stability, commitment, and colonial heritage. On the basis of these findings, Andrews makes a recommendation more generally that there should be: "less focus on technicalities, more on 'space,' less concentration and more coverage, and less similarity, but more context appropriateness" (p. 67).

Taken together, the studies raise critical questions and provide insights that go to the core of performance budgeting and fiscal management. Andrews suggests minimizing technicalities, expanding engagement, and substantially improving the "fit" with country-specific conditions. On their part, Houerou and Taliercio recommend "detailed diagnoses" of existing budget management systems and careful consideration of "political motivations and incentives" for adopting the MTEF model. Although each of these studies focuses on a specific reform initiative, both tease out information relating to the bigger picture about reform in African nations. In that regard, they follow a familiar path of development management inquiry, one that tends to be atheoretical, apolitical, and culturally neutral. Previous reform initiatives such as structural adjustment programs pursued this apolitical, technocratic, and cultural-neutral approach to no avail. To a large extent, contemporary good governance approaches are drifting along a similar or pragmatic path. The question, then, is on what basis should African nations ground budgeting and fiscal management? Before addressing this question, we offer a more in-depth critique of performance budgeting and fiscal management based on both the theory and practice of development management.

Critique of Performance Budgeting and Fiscal Management

While existing literature and critiques of Africa's reform have contributed useful insights, not enough attention has been targeted specifically at performance budgeting and the fiscal management framework in development management. For example, analysts of civil service performance improvement programs seem to take the context and culture for granted. In studying Ghana, researchers have attributed the program's failure to design and implementation weaknesses and unrealistic assumptions. Ohemeng (2009) blames the failure on a combination of factors, including institutional fragmentation, poor incentives, and inadequate political will and commitment. The current critique revolves around the nature of performance budgeting and fiscal management for development. In other words, what should authentic performance budgeting for development look like?

In general, Africa's experience shows that performance budgeting and fiscal management concepts, principles, practices, and processes, whether rooted in bureaucracy, managerialism, or governance have either European or North American origins. For example, the focus on materialism, the power of science and technology or technocracy, and the goals of efficiency, effectiveness, and economy are quintessentially Western in character (White & Adam, 1994). Such ideas have either been borrowed and transplanted in Africa or imposed as conditionalities for development assistance, loan, or grant facilities. Although the cross-cultural transfer of theories and concepts is fair game, it runs the risk of either overlooking cultural sensitivity or paying insufficient attention to cultural uniqueness. Africa's experience, as highlighted in greater detail in Chapter 1, shows that bureaucratic and performance budgeting and fiscal management models derive from outside; there has been no legitimately unique home-grown budgeting model, one that takes culture and the context of development into account (not merely paying lip-service to them as has been the case in several studies).

While the goals of achieving efficiency, effectiveness, and economy and of improving material welfare are obviously laudable, they often overlook the larger public interest issues even in developed nations: morality, ethics, equity, equality, social justice. As Africa's experience shows, both bureaucratic and performance budgeting and fiscal management perspectives not only fail to generate sustainable growth, but they also contribute to reinforce political, social, and economic inequalities and disparities. Successive Africa Progress Panel Reports (2013, 2014, and 2015) highlight inequalities and disparities in life chances among Africans. These models have largely been designed with misleading assumptions that they can be implemented in a political, social, and culturally neutral fashion, where an objective "invisible hand" ensures efficiency in resource allocation, rational decision-making, and thoughtfulness. The Africa Progress Panel Report of 2014 conveys the stark contrast between two Senegals: "Emergent Senegal" with "a multibillion-dollar strategy for transforming the country's infrastructure" and "the Senegal of Issa Fall," whose "livelihood is under threat."

With respect to managerialism, performance budgeting and fiscal management often translate to the reduction of the size of the public sector, as happened under structural adjustment programs, without first determining its appropriate size and role in a developing society such as Africa. Under structural adjustment programs, reform paralyzed the state in a manner that made it difficult to provide essential public goods and services to the needy and most vulnerable in African society. This is not to argue for uncontrolled state intervention in the economy, but to place public sector retrenchment in the proper context in which development management occurs. In short, performance budgeting and fiscal management reform has been skewed toward achieving the Western ideal of attaining the "good life" without much consideration for the historical, political, economic, and socio-cultural uniqueness and experience of Africa. Certainly such reforms are often easy to implement and solve immediate problems, but they fail to reflect sustainability and the underlying dimensions and meaning of development.

To be sure, the current performance budgeting and fiscal management approach has been conceptualized much more broadly and made more dynamic, thereby enhancing participation, ownership, and accountability on the part of public institutions, organizations, and citizens. This change demonstrates a clear shift from the traditional bureaucratic, narrow sense of budgeting and fiscal management to one that considers historical analysis and experience, institutional and organizational learning, and change. As summarized in Table 13.3, African nations have come a long way from the bureaucratic mind-set (Column 2) toward implementing performance budgeting and fiscal management (Column 3). The current approach reflects a sense of urgency and promotes performance budgeting and fiscal management as a holistic and collaborative endeavor involving multiple stakeholders: governments, civil society organizations, the private sector, the donor community, and citizens. But the core bureaucratic elements of state dominance, centralization, and top-down implementation techniques remain in varying degrees across the continent.

While performance budgeting and fiscal management has several strengths, it ignores important considerations for enhancing the depth and breadth of development management. It is a hybridized model that draws from both bureaucracy and managerialism along with their strengths and weaknesses. Like the bureaucratic approach, it does not give adequate reflective attention to cultural sensitivity and grounding in the domestic economic, social, political, and cultural uniqueness of Africa. Moreover, it makes the assumption that public institutions and organizations are ready to engage in intensive performance budgeting and fiscal management with all of its complexity: that they have adequate capacity (requisite resources, skills, abilities, and orientation), that political and administrative elites are responsive and supportive, and that the economic and political climate is stable.

Table 13.3 Comparing Bureaucratic and Performance Budgeting and Fiscal Management Approaches

Dimension	*Bureaucratic Approach*	*Managerial Approach*
Origin	Anglo-American/European	Anglo-American/European
Theory Base	Bureaucracy	Managerialism/Macroeconomics
Method	Descriptive	Descriptive/Analytical
Focus	Individual/Organizational	Individual/Organizational
Evaluation	Retrospective/Reactive	Retrospective/Prospective
Communication	Top-down/Hierarchy	Top-down/De-concentrated
Regularity	Annual/Short-term	Annual/Medium-term
Orientation	Internal/Domestic	Internal/External
Goal	Compliance/Control	Results/Outcomes

However, these assumptions are hardly borne out by observation of practice and experience continent-wide. Africa's policy and administration elites are not necessarily interested in improving budgeting and fiscal management, as that could limit their power and privileged access to rents and resources.[9] For this reason, the Collaborative Africa Budget Reform Initiative (CABRI), "a peer-learning and exchange network for senior budget officials working in African Ministries" has been created (http://cabri-sbo/org/). Likewise, the Africa parliamentary strengthening program (APSP) has been established to improve legislative oversight. Unfortunately, both APSP and CABRI might result in what Andrews (2010) cautions against: more financial management actor concentration. Performance budgeting and fiscal management specify a desirable goal (well-functioning, transparent, and accountable public-service institutions), but they do not yet clarify how to get there. Even in the best case scenario, the question of where and how to focus scarce public resources is elusive. In what follows, we turn attention on some building blocks for creating a more sustainable budgeting and fiscal management model in the context of development.

Toward Sustainable Budgeting and Fiscal Management

The argument thus far is that Africa has adopted and implemented bureaucratic and performance budgeting and fiscal management reforms with little impact. While considerable literature has accumulated, knowledge of how to harness, allocate, and judiciously manage public resources is somewhat vague and uncertain. Commitment to performance budgeting and fiscal management means that scarce public resources and public energies must be focused on achieving this worthy but very difficult goal, which is a good enough reason to be careful about how reform is framed to assure a reasonable chance of success. Because budgeting for development has taken on a strong normative content, the complexity and nuances it entails are often glossed over. But experience elsewhere and the development literature caution against quick fixes and suggest ways for moving forward. In the following section, we argue that legitimate budgeting and fiscal management for development should pass the test of sustainability, i.e., it should be contextualized, bottom-up, and long-term with the goal of connecting public-service institutions to individuals, local communities, and the international community. It should then develop appropriate measures, metrics, targets, and indicators to reliably and validly track the progress of citizen and community improvement. We begin with the rationale for a sustainability approach to budgeting and fiscal management.

Sustainable Development

Re-conceptualizing budgeting and fiscal management reform must begin with a clear understanding of the global development agenda that the United Nations High Level Panel (2013) and Africa Progress Panel (2013) have framed.[10] The United Nations High Level Panel advocates sustainability, partnership, inclusion, transparency, and accountability (pp. 7–9), while the Africa Progress Panel calls for the investment of natural resources revenue in people (p. 4). Both panels emphasize providing opportunity, empowering people, and improving lives. Thus development and its theoretical underpinning should address and be grounded in the concrete, material, and lived experiences of the people. For it to be sustainable, development should seek to transform society "from traditional relations, traditional ways of thinking, traditional ways of dealing with health and education, traditional methods of production, to more 'modern' ways" (Stiglitz, 1998, p. 3). Transforming African society requires understanding its socio-cultural, economic, and political structure, as well as developing partnerships among citizens, public officials, and development partners. Because citizens are and should be considered as active partners in development, they must interact with public-service institutions and be more engaged in budgeting and fiscal management in a way similar to Douthwaite's (2002) "bazaar approach" to innovation and social change.

Conceptualized as based in sustainable innovation, the bazaar approach describes interactions, linkages, and free information flow among customers, users, manufacturers, and researchers as partners and co-producers (Biggs & Matsaert, 2004, pp. 1–2). This approach is appropriate to the unique context of Africa, especially as it seeks to create "space" and expand "coverage," as Andrews (2010) argues, for under-represented and under-served people in a sustainable budgeting and fiscal management approach. For example, the 2010 Population and Housing Census indicates that Ghana is rural, multi-ethnic, and illiterate (http://statsghana.gov.gh/docfiles/2010phc/Census2010_Summary_report_of_final_results.pdf). But beyond this broad demographic characterization lies the stark reality that "poverty is synonymous with rural life in Ghana" (Haruna & Kannae, 2013, pp. 142–144). Large rural communities are physically isolated and inaccessible due to poorly developed education, transportation, and communication infrastructure. Urban settlements also include "zongo" communities, unplanned, under-serviced, and poverty-stricken low-income enclaves, which should be the focus of the envisioned "transformative shifts" in African society.[11]

As chapter authors have argued, meaningful development is not only about extending programs designed to reduce hard-core poverty in disproportionately low-income and rural communities, worthy as that may be. Nor is it just about token citizen involvement in participatory budgeting and fiscal management processes. In the sense in which it is used here, development must mean total community immersion in macro-economic and fiscal policy formulation, implementation, monitoring, and evaluation. Involving communities in public decision-making about how policies are made, executed, monitored, evaluated, and reformed makes such policies meaningful and likely to succeed. Although community and public involvement is hardly new, there is steady resurgence in the public administration and policy literature, promoting dialogue on how to develop linkages and connections between theory and practice. The steady shift from bureaucracy to good governance and sustainable development offers Africa the opportunity to tap into the idea that pursuing public ends can occur through networks and collaboration between private, public, and non-profit sectors (e.g. Osborne, 2010; Stivers, 2008; Bingham et al., 2005).

Because the idea of governance as an open, delegated, shared, and collaborative effort is taking root in developing nations, there is sustained emphasis on the co-production of essential services such as crime prevention and public school education. Recent theoretical perspectives emphasize public involvement as "citizen, customer, and partner" as well as "voter and taxpayer" (Eichenthal, 2013, pp. 797–798; Thomas, 2013, pp. 786–788). To this list one must add the citizen as a budgeting and fiscal manager. As Eichenthal points out in the case of the USA, participatory budgeting and fiscal management as a form of direct public involvement "leads to direct and meaningful results." Unfortunately, this is not the case in much of Africa where implementation of budgeting reform is sketchy and scattered in spite of considerable donor support and domestic policy changes (Haruna & Kannae, 2013). As Africa refocuses on and pursues sustainable development, communities should be active partners in the co-production, delivery, and evaluation of budgeting and fiscal management.

This is not to underestimate the complexity and challenge of development management. Politically, inclusive development for all people, worthy as it may seem, is contestable and often contested by those benefiting from the status quo. It is also contestable based on ideology, especially in regard to what the role of government is or ought to be in pursuing pro-poor policies and bringing development about. Economically, the underlying presumption of equitable growth is questionable. As Africa's experience attests, recent economic and fiscal performance is sobering: South Africa's budget deficit has ranged from 6.6 percent to 3.8 percent of GDP since 2010, while Ghana's has increased from 4 percent to nearly 12 percent. In fact, inflation has been accelerating in Ghana, Kenya, and Uganda (www.moneyweb.co.za/news/africa.af). Moreover, UNECA (2014) has observed that Africa's total external debt has averaged an 11 percent increase (2006–2011), while seven nations are at high risk of debt distress. Despite the projected growth of the estimated GDP of 5.2 percent, Africa faces challenges, but by focusing on sustainable development rather than on technicalities and control of resources, it stands a chance of making a solid start.

The Building Blocks of Sustainable Budgeting and Fiscal Management

Setting out *what* the goal of sustainable budgeting and fiscal management ought to be is important but it is not nearly enough. It remains to be clarified *how* to get there, i.e., *what policies have to change* (or not change) so that Africa can make a solid start. While the question of how to get there by aligning means-ends calculation and assuring that the goal of achieving sustainable development has a good fit in the context of development is becoming clearer, it often gets mired in domestic partisan politics and donor conditionalities or technicalities.

In this section, we outline and discuss some elements of sustainable budgeting and fiscal management that align well with Africa's unique historicity and social, economic, and political circumstances (Figure 13.1). We draw mostly from contemporary public administration and policy thought, international development perspectives, and Africa's accumulated experience with reform, to argue that a sustainable budgeting and fiscal management model should consider context, culture, collaboration, coverage and have a bottom-up character (Savage, 2013; Andrews, 2008; Aerni, 2006).

As conceptualized in this chapter, sustainable budgeting and fiscal management must shift from being process-oriented and focus on development, i.e., must be concerned with improving the quality of life of citizens. Almost all international development assistance now requires improving human capacities and development performance measurement by focusing on achieving results, outcomes, and accounting to clients (United Nations High Level Panel, 2013; Pollitt & Bouckaert, 2011; Overseas Development Institute, 2009; Organization for Economic Cooperation and Development, 2009). The United Nations High Level Panel is specific in setting out 12 "illustrative" goals broken down into fifty-four "illustrative" targets. Also, the worldwide governance assessment tool facilitates the assessment of the relative strengths and weaknesses of good economic and fiscal governance, which helps in informing the structuring of

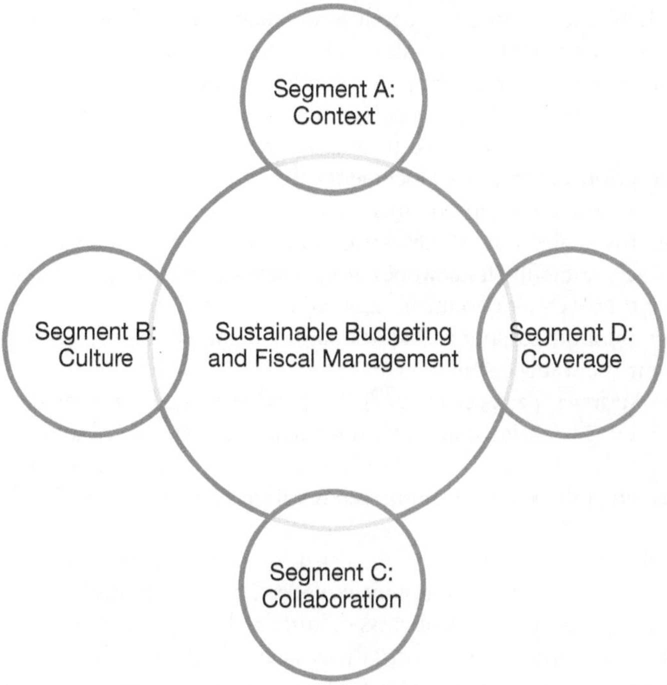

Figure 13.1 Conceptual scheme of sustainable budgeting and fiscal management

budgeting and fiscal management. To that extent, sustainable budgeting and fiscal management must emphasize policy objectives, fiscal targets, outcomes, and accountability. Statistical targets provide verifiable development impact, but one should be careful that the targets do not become ends in themselves.

In contrast to previous approaches, sustainable budgeting and fiscal management must be customized, focused on, and tailored to the material conditions lived. In their recent study of public management reform in Europe and North America, Pollitt and Bouckaert (2011) emphasized the significance of context, culture, and governing traditions in framing how governance reform has been approached (Figure 13.1 segments A and B). They argue that national context does make a difference "to the effects yielded by a particular model or tool of management change" (p. 44). Their analysis indicates that while governmental structure influences reform, it is shaped by culture. In that regard, cultures and socio-economic conditions are important in considering budgeting and fiscal management reform.

Africa's context indicates that the costs of utilities such as water and electricity have devalued wages in African nations. UNECA (2014) notes that by 2012 only 69 percent of Africans "used an improved water source" while performance on sanitation remains substandard. Also, UNECA has estimated that the proportion of people living on less than USD1.25 a day decreased only modestly from 56.5 percent in 1990 to 48.5 percent in 2014. But the question is not the quantum decrease but whether and how the decrease can be sustained. Under these socio-economic conditions, budgeting and fiscal management reform that over-emphasizes rules and processes takes away much valuable attention and scarce resources. As Andrews (2008) found out, the implementation of the World Bank's public financial management reforms in developing countries has contributed little to improve transparency, accountability, and corruption control. He documents that 145 developing countries have experienced reductions in administrative effectiveness over a 10-year period. Likewise, his analysis of 10 African nations using the public expenditure and financial accountability framework revealed disappointing results. Thus Andrews theorized that recipient countries have often adopted such reforms as a way of persuading donors to approve additional financial assistance, while failing to implement them successfully.

From Andrews' perspective, budgeting and fiscal management should focus more on lived realities and work toward improving lives. He suggests that donors should strive to avoid standardized, one size fits all "solution-driven methods" and follow a "problem-driven iterative adaptation" strategy. He argues that such a strategy considers the concerns at hand, takes domestic capacity and capability into account, and respects the unique local political, social, and cultural context. Sure, being contextualized does not preclude borrowing, learning, and adapting relevant cross-cultural and comparative experiences. But contextualizing intervention initiatives faces challenges. It requires deeper knowledge of and information about African societies, which takes time and in post-conflict societies is difficult. While a pragmatic problem-driven strategy is helpful, it needs to address the challenge of "governmental and patron demands for stricter accountability of donor funds, detailed planning, and for use of metrics reflecting international best practices" (Savage, 2013, p. 894). As well, it must address issues related to organizational and inter-jurisdictional coordination arising from different donors pursuing different development agendas.

In addition, sustainable budgeting and fiscal management must be a collaborative effort with "less actor concentration" (Andrews, 2008) and more coverage from the bottom-up (Figure 13.1 segments C and D). This involves sustained multi-actor engagement across agencies, organizations, institutions, and sectors. Informed by insights from collaboration literature within the broader framework of good governance reform, this perspective considers the influence of non-state actors, the hollowing-out of institutional capacity, and increasing demands for transparency and accountability (Grudinschi et al., 2013; Hartley et al., 2013). In documenting the globalization of politics and economics, and blurring of jurisdictional boundaries, this strand of literature rationalizes the need for rethinking economic, fiscal, and financial governance. As a result, there is increasing inter-sector, inter-organizational, and inter-institutional mutual dependence for addressing common issues and problems. While public institutions continue to bear primary responsibility for steering the economy and society, they need to do so collaboratively with non-state actors. Moreover, network governance theories emphasize the role of collaborative networks in finding innovative solutions to public problems. Grudinschi and associates argue that collaboration leads to innovations in governance that "creates social value."

Collaboration in the sense of a process in which multiple actors engage constructively in managing differences to define common problems and develop joint solutions is particularly applicable to sustainable budgeting and fiscal management in Africa. For example the African Capacity-Building Foundation initiative includes programs to strengthen inter-sector interfaces under the African regional partnership for capacity building. Sako (2002, pp. 76–81) argues that the public–private interface, which involves identifying and assessing needs, as well as "developing and implementing programs to address these needs" is required for sustainable development. Similarly, several collaborative initiatives at nascent stages involve negotiations between governmental and non-governmental organizations to develop policies for strategic partnerships that will pave the way for collaboration.

These developments across the continent hold out good prospects for strengthening government–civil society collaboration toward achieving sustainable fiscal and financial governance reform. For example, women's initiatives for self-empowerment collaborate with police to provide counseling for domestic violence victims, while federations of women lawyers provide pro-bono legal advice. Furthermore, integrity initiatives continue to conduct periodic corruption perception surveys as a part of the fight against corrupt practices in public financial management. From the foregoing, an enabling environment seems to be emerging steadily in favor of collaboration in budgeting and fiscal management, but some challenges remain to be addressed. As Hartley and associates argue, such issues border mainly on how to identify and formulate the appropriate respective roles and responsibilities of public, private, and civic society actors in budgeting and fiscal management processes and procedures.

The significance of budgeting and fiscal management reform hinges on demonstrating the judicious use of public resources and gaining thereby stakeholders' trust and support. In that sense the link between government fiscal performance and public trust is crucial for strengthening the legitimacy of government action. To this end budgeting and fiscal management must "measure what citizens really care about, be systematic and integrated across all agencies, include other governing entities, and become an ongoing participatory process in which governments and citizens are transformed" (Yang & Holzer, 2006, p. 114). It is argued that such a process must aim to generate and connect valid and reliable information toward enhancing decision-making and improving public performance.

As the bread and butter of budgeting, measures, metrics, and targets must be relevant and meaningful. Most authorities on the subject of performance measurement agree that this is the purpose and basic characteristic of the US Government Performance and Results Modernization Act (2010). The empirical literature suggests to some extent that "engaging more proactively in what have become conventional performance management practices is indeed associated with gains in outcomes" (Poister et al., 2013, p. 632). To be relevant and meaningful in Africa, sustainable budgeting and fiscal management measures, metrics, and targets must reflect and generate information for gauging improvements in the overall quality of life. As well, they must motivate continuous learning and experimentation in the context of development. Above all, they must result in the improvement of the abilities of individuals, organizations, and institutions to create and own the culture of budgeting and fiscal management. Ultimately, this kind of reform process is essentially about motivating and facilitating changes in individual attitudes, institutional standards, and socio-cultural norms as a way of building sustainable bottom-up capacity.

Africa's experience thus far shows that there is a good chance for sustainable budgeting and fiscal management reform to succeed. The Millennium Development Goals specifically target poverty reduction among others, while commitment to the New Partnership for Africa's Development emphasizes efforts at socio-economic development. Also, Africa has already implemented variants of sustainable budgeting under medium-term plans such as Ghana's Growth and Poverty Reduction plan and Zimbabwe's Three-Year Medium-Term Development plan, which seek to track progress, outputs, and outcomes. Both of these plans have helped to streamline institutional relationships, roles, and responsibilities, establish targets and indicators, and institute measures for sharing information. They have also contributed to creating progress report mechanisms and social impact analyses as measuring, monitoring, and evaluation tools for determining policy impacts on targeted populations.

It is true that Africa has systematically and authoritatively pulled together continent-wide experiential budgeting and fiscal management knowledge and understanding through the medium-term planning processes. Our overall assessment is that Africa has made progress in most key thematic areas, particularly with respect to political, economic, and fiscal good governance, targeting basic education, healthcare and the provision of safe drinking water. But at the same time questions and concerns have remained. A key question is whether as unitary systems African nations have the political will to adopt a bottom-up, decentralized, and sustainable budgeting and fiscal management reform with minimal centralized direction.

The above question is not entirely baseless because even with the ongoing devolution-oriented reforms, African nations have over-emphasized centralized direction and information extraction from sub-national jurisdictions. In South Africa, which is somewhat fiscally federalized, centralization is self-evident. The existing medium-term planning frameworks tend to be top-heavy and unbalanced. Institutional roles and responsibilities have reflected and reinforced the bureaucratic mind-set of budgeting and fiscal management control. But as Andrews has noted, financial management tends to be weaker "downstream" in the thirty-one countries that he has studied. Thus there is a potential risk of a value conflict entailed in implementing a sustainable bottom-up budgeting and fiscal management reform with a bureaucratic mind-set and technique. In sum, Africa still has a long way to go in implementing more inclusive and participatory budgeting and fiscal management. But a window of opportunity exists based on the momentum that the donor community and regional institutions have generated for economic and fiscal good governance reform.

Summary and Conclusion

The focus of this chapter is the evaluation of budgeting and fiscal management systems in African nations with the goal of suggesting a reform culture tailored to the context and appropriate for implementing development policies, programs, and projects. The argument is that budgeting and fiscal management reform is much needed but that it should begin with fundamental reconceptualization based on the notion of sustainability with a focus on the substance of development. Past and current budgeting and fiscal management approaches that focus on organizational goals, functions, and processes are not nearly enough to sustain budgeting and fiscal reform and thereby create the needed transformative public-service mind-set. Specifically, the bureaucratic budgeting and fiscal management model that offers a narrow set of top-down directions on policy planning has been incapable of creating the space and coverage required to achieve inclusive growth and development. While performance budgeting and fiscal management has introduced more useful frameworks, there is still considerable financial management "actor concentration" and inadequate space for creating a culture of participatory budgeting and fiscal management. The weaknesses and failures associated with such reform approaches are reflected in but not necessarily limited to concerns about systemic and systematic corruption and the downward spiral of public integrity.[12]

The perspective taken in this chapter calls for a broader reconceptualization of budgeting and fiscal management framework, one that responds to the needs and pressures of contemporary economic and fiscal good governance reform by emphasizing a blend of theoretical, experiential, and contextual knowledge. The proposed building blocks for implementing sustainable budgeting and fiscal management reform offers policy-makers, public managers, development practitioners, and citizens a glimpse of a strategy and tool for transforming and orienting the public service toward sustainable development. One underlying assumption is that budgeting and fiscal management reform can hardly occur in a weak and disconnected institutional framework. Nor can policy planning, revenue mobilization, and financial management succeed in a weak institutional context. Taken together, the proposed building blocks aim to:

a) motivate interactions and encourage relationships among public managers, development partners, and the public in a collaborative and cooperative fashion;
b) connect theories and concepts of budgeting and fiscal management to lived experience in Africa's context and culture;
c) break down barriers/bureaucratic hoops and create the needed space for sharing experience and accumulated knowledge both horizontally and vertically; foster a dynamic inter-jurisdictional and multi-dimensional information flow and dialog; and
d) reinforce decentralized budgeting and fiscal management by giving communities and civil society organizations a meaningful say in development planning and management.

The suggested building blocks for developing a robust budgeting and fiscal management model are grounded in and supported by Africa's own experience, development literature, and public administration and policy research and scholarship (e.g., Picard et al., 2015). Africa's experience is that budgeting and fiscal management reforms have been largely conceptualized and implemented as apolitical and atheoretical. While this is widespread across the continent, pioneering scholarship from Anglo-American society has severely questioned and criticized it (e.g., Rubin, 2015; Wildavsky, 1961; Key, 1940). To paraphrase Wildavsky, it is not sensible to consider reforming budgeting and fiscal management, the core of public decision-making, without also changing the political power structure and influence. In short, sustainable budgeting and fiscal management reform in Africa must also involve political, economic, and administrative restructuring in a bottom-up manner. That effort, as difficult as it is because of the unitary systems of African nations, anchors our argument for more and better budgeting and fiscal management reform.

Alongside most of the international development literature now approaches development as a complex system and has done so for some time: one that requires changes toward collaboration, partnership, and sustainability. The Common African Position (CAP) on the post-2015 development agenda emphasizing inclusive growth, productive capacity, and poverty eradication among others is correct. The CAP's six pillars (structural economic transformation and inclusive growth; science, technology and innovation; people-centered development; environmental sustainability, natural resource management and disaster risk management; peace and security; and finance and partnership) require a broad-based and robust budgeting and fiscal management framework as this chapter has suggested. But it will also require bottom-up, decentralized restructuring of political and administrative power.

Notes

1 The Organization for Economic Cooperation and Development (OECD) brings European and North American countries into a union for economic purposes. Its convention was signed in Paris on December 14, 1960. Some of the most recent member nations are: Czech Republic (1995), Hungary (1996), Poland (1996), Korea (1996), and Slovak Republic (2000).

2 With the support of the OECD, the Collaborative Africa Budget Reform Initiative (CABRI) brings senior budget professionals together at conferences to share knowledge and experiences about how to plan for and manage budget reforms across the continent (see: http://cabri-sbo.org).

3 Albert Hyde has provided a concise and illuminating account of the evolution and change of budgeting and fiscal management in the USA that basically sums up the experience of most if not all OECD member nations. The highlight of this account is the practical orientation of budgeting and fiscal management, which subsequently became the central concern of V.O. Key's seminal piece, "The Lack of Budgetary Theory" (1940).

4 In the case of the USA, Lewis and Hildreth (2013) point out that federal budgeting began in a rather rudimentary fashion with only four annual appropriations acts (treasury, department of war, civil list, and other expenditure categories). In fact, Congress passed the first appropriations act in 1989 for a total of USD 639,000.

5 This critical observation refers specifically to the federal budgeting system in the USA but it equally well applies to African nations whose models have derived mainly from European colonial rule.

6 Developed through the Open Budget Survey, the Open Budget Index is a quantitative score that assesses the extent of public participation in the budget process, as well as the extent to which budget and fiscal management-related information is accessible to the public. South Africa was ranked at the very top internationally in 2010 (Chapter 8, p. 187).

7 In 2006 African nations benefited from the cancellation of debt under the heavily indebted poor countries (HIPC) debt-relief initiative. However, several African nations are still at risk of crossing the 70 percent debt-to-GDP ratio threshold based on which they can fall back to and be classified in the infamous HIPC status.

8 A comprehensive MTEF approach raises capacity questions while the narrow priority-sector approach raises aggregate spending questions. Nonetheless, country and context-specific circumstances should determine the most appropriate MTEF approach. As discussed in Chapter 1, context should be the overriding factor in considering reform proposals.

9 As used here, rent is considered as a form of corruption in which government officials access and control opportunities for private gain. Because African public service systems do not always reward officials for honesty and competence, they often turn toward rent-seeking opportunities through family members, close allies, co-workers, professional colleagues, etc.

10 The Africa Progress Panel (APP) consists of 10 distinguished individuals who advocate for shared responsibility between African leaders and international partners to promote equitable and sustainable development in African nations. The United Nations Secretary-General appointed a 26-member panel of distinguished individuals to frame a vision for the post-2015 development agenda in July 2012 with a focus on sustainability.

11 Africa's urban settlements are not only highly densely populated, but also notoriously segregated along class, religion, and ethnic lines. "Zongo" (Ghana), Agege (Nigeria), and Soweto (South Africa) are a few of the unplanned, under-serviced, poverty-stricken low-income settlements often inhabited by ethnic minorities.

12 Transparency International's corruption perception indices consistently indicate that Africa has some of the most corrupt countries in the world. The two main corruption categories are systemic (government by corruption) and systematic (organizational corruption). Ironically, African nations have ratified the 2005 United Nation's convention against corruption and other initiatives including the OECD Anti-Bribery Convention.

References

Aerni, P. 2006. The Principal-Agent Problem in International Development Assistance and its Impact on Local Entrepreneurship in Africa: Time for New Approaches. *ATDF Journal*, 3(2): 27–33.

Africa Progress Panel. 2013. *Equity in Extractives: Stewarding Africa's Natural Resources for All.* Retrieved from www.africaprogresspanel.org.

Africa Progress Panel. 2014. *Building on a Decade of Growth.* Retrieved from www.africaprogresspanel.org/publications/policy-papers/2014.

Africa Progress Panel. 2015. *Why Climate Challenges are an Opportunity for Africa.* Retrieved from www.africaprogresspanel.org/why-climate-challenges-are-an-opportunity-for-africa.

Andrews, M. 2008. PFM in Africa. *Where Are We, How Did We Get There, Where Should We Go? Lessons From Recent PEFA Data and World Bank Public Financial Management Performance Reports. Research Study Prepared for the Brookings Institution and the World Bank.* Retrieved from www.resultsfordevelopment.org/sites/resultsfordevelopment.org/files/resources/PFM-in-Africa-pdf.

Andrews, M. 2010. *How Far Have Public Financial Management Reforms Come in Africa?* Harvard: Harvard Kennedy School. Retrieved from http://nrs.harvard.edu/urn-3:HUL.InstRepos:4448885.

Biggs, S., & Matsaert, H. 2004. Strengthening poverty reduction programs using an actor-oriented approach: Examples from natural resources innovation systems, *AgREN Network paper No. 134.*

Bingham, L.B., Nabatchi, T., & O'Leary, R. 2005. The New Governance: Practices and Processes for Stakeholder and Citizen Participation in the Work of Government. *Public Administration Review*, 65(5): 547–558.

Collaborative Africa Budget Reform Initiative (CABRI). 2008. *Budget Practices and Procedures in Africa.* Retrieved from: www.afdb.org/fileadmin/uploads/afdb/Documents/Publications/CABRI%20AfDB%20ENG.pdf.

Collaborative Africa Budget Reform Initiative (CABRI). 2015. Retrieved from www.cabri-sbo/org.

Douthwaite, B. 2002. *Enabling Innovation: A Practical Guide to Understanding and Fostering Technological Change*. New York: Zed Books.

Draman, R. 2010. *The Budget Process in Africa: A Comparative Study of Seven Countries*. Retrieved from: www.agora-parl.org/sites/default/files/the_budget_process_in_africa_2010_en.pdf.

Eichenthal, D.R. 2013. What about the Public as Voter and Taxpayer? *Public Administration Review*, 73(6): 797–798.

Grundinschi, D., Kaljunen, L., Hokkanen, T., Hallikas, J., Sintonen, S., & Puustinen, A. 2013. Management Challenges in Cross-Sector Collaboration: Elderly Care Case Study. *The Public Sector Innovation Journal*, 18(2): 1–22.

Hartley, J., Sorensen, E., & Torfing, J. 2013. Collaborative Innovation: A Viable Alternative to Market Competition and Organization Entrepreneurship. *Public Administration Review*, 73(6): 821–830.

Haruna, P. F. 2008. Recovering Integrity in Ghana's Governance: A Transcultural Study in Public Service Ethics. *Public Integrity*, 10(2): 113–132.

Haruna, P. F., & Kannae, L.A. 2013. Implementing Good Governance Reform in Ghana: Issues and Experiences with Local Governance. In S. Vyas-Doorgapersad, L.M. Tsombe, & E.P. Ababio (Eds.), *Public Administration in Africa: Performance and Challenges*. Boca Raton, FL: Taylor & Francis, 135–151.

Haruna, P. F., & Vyas-Doorgapersad, S. 2015. *Public Administration Training in Africa: Competencies in Development Management*. Boca Raton, FL: Taylor & Francis.

Heidenhof, G., Grandvoinnet, H., Kianpour, D., & Rezaian, B. 2002. *Design and Implementation of Financial Management Systems: An African Perspective*. Retrieved from www.worldbank.org/afr/wps/index.htm.

Houerou, P. L., & Taliercio, R. 2002. *Medium Term Expenditure Frameworks: From Concept to Practice*. Retrieved from www.worldbank.org.afr/wps/index.htm.

Hyde, A.C. 1992. *Government Budgeting: Theory, Process, and Politics*. Belmont, CA: Wadsworth.

Kaufmann, D., Kraay, A., & Mastruzzi, M. 2007. A *Decade of Measuring the Quality of Governance*. Washington, DC: World Bank.

Key, V.O. 1940. The Lack of a Budgetary Theory. *American Political Science Review*, 34(December): 1137–1140.

Larbi, G.A. 1999. The New Public Management Approach and Crisis States. *The United Nation's Research Institute on Social Development Discussion Paper No. 112*.

Lewis, C.W., & Hildreth, W.B. 2013. *Budgeting: Politics & Power*. New York: Oxford University Press.

Ohemeng, F. K. 2009. Constraints in the Implementation of Performance Management Systems in the Developing Country: The Ghanaian Case. *International Journal of Cross Cultural Management*, 9(1): 109–132.

Olowu, D., & Wunsch, J. 2004. Introduction: Local Governance, and Democratic Decentralization in Africa. In Dele Olowu & James Wunsch (Eds.), *Local Governance in Africa: The Challenges of Democratic Decentralization*. Boulder, CO: Lynne Rienner, pp. 1–27.

Organization for Economic Cooperation and Development (OECD). 2002a. *Models of Public Budgeting and Accounting Reform*. Paris: OECD. Retrieved from www.oecd.org/gov/budgeting/49042591.pdf

Organization for Economic Cooperation and Development (OECD). 2002b. *OECD Journal on Budgeting*. Paris: OECD.

Organisation for Economic Cooperation and Development (OECD). 2005. *Modernizing Government: The Way Forward*. Paris, France: OECD.

Organization for Economic Cooperation and Development (OECD). 2006. *OECD Journal of Budgeting (Collaborative Africa Budget Reform Initiative)*, 6(2): 9–153.

Organization for Economic Cooperation and Development (OECD). 2009. *OECD Journal*, 9(1): 1–11.

Osborne, S.P. 2010. The (New) Public Governance: a suitable case for treatment? In S. P. Osborne (Ed.), *The New Public Governance? Emerging perspectives on the theory and practice of public governance*. London: Routledge, pp. 1–8.

Overseas Development Institute. 2009. *Mapping Political Context: World Governance Assessment*. Retrieved from www.odi.org.uk/publications/5331-world-governance-assessment.

Picard, L.A., & Lelei, M.C. 2015. Achieving Sustainable Development in Africa: A Governance Perspective. In Louis Picard, Terry Buss, Taylor Seybolt, & Macrina Lelei (Eds.), *Sustainable Development and Human Security in Africa: Governance as the Missing Link*. Boca Raton, FL: Taylor & Francis, pp. 3–19.

Picard, L.A., Buss, T.F., Seybolt, T.B., & Lelei, M.C. 2015. *Sustainable Development and Human Security in Africa: Governance as the Missing Link*. Boca Raton: Taylor & Francis Group.

Poister, T.H., Pasha, O.Q., & Edwards, L.H. 2013. Does Performance Management Lead to Better Outcomes? Evidence from the U.S. Public Transit Industry. *Public Administration Review*, 73(4): 625–636.

Pollitt, C., & Bouckaert, G. 2011. *Public Management Reform*. Oxford: Oxford University Press.

Rubin, I. 2015. Past and Future Budget Classics: A Research Agenda. *Public Administration Review*, 75(1): 25–35.

Sako, S. 2002. The Public-Private Sector Interface: The ACBF Perspective. In D. Olowu & S. Sako (Eds.), *Better Governance and Public Policy: Capacity Building and Democratic Renewal in Africa*. Bloomfield CT: Kumarian Press, pp. 75–83.

Savage, J.D. 2013. The Development Dilemma: What's Going Wrong and What Can Be Fixed. *Public Administration Review*, 73(6): 893–895.

Shah, A., & Shen, C. 2007. A Primer on Performance Budgeting. In A. Shah (Ed.), *Budgeting and Budgetary Institutions*. Washington, DC: The World Bank.

Stiglitz, J. E. 1998. *Towards a New Paradigm for Development: Strategies, Policies, and Processes*. Prebisch Lecture at UNCTAD, Geneva.

Stivers, C. 2008. *Governance in Dark Times: Practical Philosophy for Public Service*. Washington, DC: Georgetown University Press.

Thomas, J.C. 2013. Citizen, Customer, Partner: Rethinking the Place of the Public in Public Management. *Public Administration Review*, 73(6): 786–796.

United Nations. 1998. *Rethinking Public Administration: An Overview*. New York: United Nations.

United Nations. 2000. *About MDGs*. Retrieved from www.unmillenniumproject.org/goals.

United Nations Development Program (UNDP). 1997. *Governance for Sustainable Human Development*. New York: United Nations.

United Nations Economic Commission for Africa (UNECA). 2014. *MDG 2014 Report*. Retrieved from www.afdb.org/fileadmin/uploads/afdb/Documents/Publications/MDG_Report_2014_11_2014.pdf.

United Nations High Level Panel. 2013. *A New Global Partnership: Eradicate Poverty and Transform Economies Through Sustainable Development*. New York: United Nations.

White, J., & Adam, G. 1994. *Research in Public Administration: Reflections on Theory and Practice*. Thousand Oaks CA: Sage Publications.

Wildavsky, A. 1961. Political Implications of Budgetary Reform. *Public Administration Review* (21): 183–190.

World Bank. 1992. *Governance and Development*. Washington, DC: World Bank.

Yang, K., & Holzer, M. 2006. The Performance-Trust Link: Implications for Performance Measurement. *Public Administration Review*, 66(1): 114–126.

Index

Italic page numbers indicate tables; bold indicate figures.